D1502238

BARRON'S

Encyclopedia of Cat Breeds

BARRON'S

Encyclopedia of Cat Breeds

A Complete Guide to the Domestic Cats of North America

2ND EDITION

J. Anne Helgren

Illustrations by Michele Earle-Bridges

AURORA PUBLIC LIBRARY

© Copyright 2013, 1997 by Barron's Educational Series, Inc.

All rights reserved.
No part of this book may be reproduced or distributed in any form or by any means without the written permission of the copyright owner.

All inquiries should be addressed to:
Barron's Educational Series, Inc.
250 Wireless Boulevard
Hauppauge, NY 11788
www.barronseduc.com

International Standard Book No. 978-0-7641-6580-1

Library of Congress Catalog Card No.: 2012037188

Library of Congress Cataloging-in-Publication Data
Helgren, J. Anne.
    Barron's encyclopedia of cat breeds : a complete guide to the domestic cats of North America / J. Anne Helgren ; with photographs by Bob Schwartz ; illustrations by Michele Earle-Bridges. — 2nd edition.
        pages cm
    Includes bibliographical references and index.
    ISBN 978-0-7641-6580-1
1. Cat breeds—Encyclopedias. 2. Cats—Encyclopedias.
3. Cat breeds—North America—Encyclopedias.
4. Cats—North America—Encyclopedias. I. Title.
II. Title: Encyclopedia of cat breeds.
    SF442.2.H448 2013
    636.8003—dc23   2012037188

About the Author:
J. Anne Helgren has written six books for Barron's Educational Series, Inc.: *Abyssinian Cats, A Complete Pet Owner's Manual; Himalayan Cats: A Complete Pet Owner's Manual; Barron's Encyclopedia of Cat Breeds; It's Showtime* (co-authored); *Communicating with Your Cat;* and *Rex Cats: A Complete Pet Owner's Manual. Himalayan Cats* and *Barron's Encyclopedia of Cat Breeds* received Certificates of Excellence from the Cat Writers' Association, and *Communicating with Your Cat* and *Rex Cats* won CWA's top award, the Muse Medallion. A revised edition of *Himalayan Cats: A Complete Pet Owner's Manual* was released in fall of 2006.

Ms. Helgren has been published in national and regional magazines including *Cat Fancy, Purina ProCare,* and *I Love Cats.* A contributing writer for *Cats Magazine* from June 1992 until August 2001, Ms. Helgren wrote a monthly cat breed profile for which she was awarded CWA Certificates of Excellence in 1994, 1996, 1997, and 1999, and Muse Medallions in 1997 and 1999. In 2005, she received a CWA Muse Medallion for the breed profile in the May 2005 issue of *Cat Fancy.* In addition, she's written more than forty articles for PetPlace.com and fifty breed profiles and supporting text for Telemark Productions, Inc. (*www.iams.com/pet-health/cat-breeds*), for which she was awarded the Purina ProPlan Pedigreed Cats Award in November 2007. While specializing in companion animal content in general and cats in particular, Ms. Helgren has also written articles and stories on many other topics for national and regional magazines, newspapers, and websites. Ms. Helgren has been a professional member of the Cat Writers' Association since 1993. In addition to her writing career, Ms. Helgren was a writing instructor for the Long Ridge Writers' Group for more than ten years.

Born in Southern California, Ms. Helgren earned a Bachelor of Arts degree from San Jose State University. She now lives in Northern California with her husband, Bill, and a family of random-bred domestic cats.

Contents

DEDICATION

To Bill, Libby, Rose, and all my cat companions,
with love always. In memory of Bitty and Squeak.

—J. Anne Helgren

ACKNOWLEDGMENTS

The author would like to thank Anna E. Damaskos, Senior Editor and project editor, for all her invaluable help, hard work, and guidance; Wayne Barr, Barron's Acquisitions Editor, Amy Shojai, and the members of the Cat Writers' Association; the American Association of Cat Enthusiasts, American Cat Association, Canadian Cat Association, American Cat Fanciers Association, Cat Fanciers' Association, Cat Fanciers Federation, The International Cat Association, and the United Feline Organization. The author would also like to thank Bill Helgren for his support and advice, Libby Basore, and Rose Basore for their love and encouragement, Darlene Arden for her assistance and friendship, and last but certainly not least Clancy, Frodo, Bear, Tripod, Sherbert, Sheriff, Prancer, and Skittles for the love, companionship, and the cat hairs on my keyboard.

IMPORTANT NOTE

When you handle cats, you may sometimes get scratched or bitten. If this happens, have a doctor treat the injuries immediately. Make sure your cat receives all the necessary shots and dewormings; otherwise serious danger to the animal and to human health may arise. A few diseases and parasites can be communicated to humans. If your cat shows any signs of illness, you should consult a veterinarian. If you are worried about your own health, see your doctor, and tell him or her that you have cats.

Some people have allergic reactions to cats. If you think you might be allergic, see your doctor before you get a cat.

It is possible for a cat to cause damage to someone else's property and even to cause accidents. For your own protection you should make sure your insurance covers such eventualities, and you should definitely have liability insurance.

Preface

"It is difficult to obtain the friendship of a cat. It is a philosophic animal . . . one that does not place its affections thoughtlessly." —Theophile Gautier (1811–1872)

To us cat lovers nothing is more natural than loving our feline friends for their grace, beauty, independent personalities, and myriad other attractive qualities. The fascination of cats is hard to define—if you are a cat lover, you understand; if you are not, no amount of mere words could persuade you. Since you are reading this, I assume that you are acquainted with the charm and joy of having a feline companion.

In the more than 20 years that I've been researching and profiling pedigreed breeds, I've developed a real love for these beautiful and intriguing cats. Exploring their histories, personalities, and myriad colors, patterns, and fur types have been a personal journey into the mystery and magic of the feline. In this book I'll try to share that journey with you.

The fascination with pedigreed cats is easy to understand since these beautifully colored and coated examples of the species seem to legitimize our feelings about felines. It's natural to want others to look at our beloved kitties with as much admiration as we do ourselves. These cats, with their colorful coats, histories, and temperaments, fascinate the novice and experienced cat fancier alike. Still, the cat fancy— the common term used to describe the

people involved with showing or breeding cats—has become so much more than that. For many of those involved, it's a way of life, a community of people dedicated to breeding, showing, and loving cats.

Keep in mind, however, that pedigreed cats comprise less than five percent of the total cat population in the United States today, and cat lovers are of two minds when it comes to pedigreed cats. On one side, cat lovers wish to retain the right to breed the cats they have worked so hard to protect, promote, and perfect. On the other, cat lovers watch as an endless tide of equally beautiful and worthy cats are euthanized because there aren't enough homes for them all. Do pedigreed breeds contribute to the overpopulation problem? Yes. Would the overpopulation problem end if all pedigreed breeding stopped tomorrow? No. Pedigreed cats make up too small a percentage. It will take an effort on the part of all of us cat owners to put an end to what is certainly a national tragedy. I offer this book as a modest tribute to the lovely pedigreed and random-bred members of the species *Felis silvestris catus*, and urge that you think long and hard before you decide to breed cats—pedigreed or random-bred.

CHAPTER ONE

FELINE HISTORY

"If a cat does something, we call it instinct; if we do the same thing, for the same reason, we call it intelligence."
—Will Cuppy

EVOLUTION

The official connection between the domestic cat and us mere humans started at least 9,500 years ago, but in actuality, the cat's journey to its present form began about 54 million years ago, give or take a year. Around the time Australia split from Antarctica and moved northward, ecological niches not previously available to mammals opened up by the passing of the dinosaurs. The mammals (warm-blooded vertebrates that suckle their young) then came into their own and flourished, diverged, and evolved in an intricate, complex dance of life.

After the dinosaurs became extinct, mammals became the dominant life forms, and they still reign today. A group of forest-dwelling mammals called the miacids developed around 54 million years ago; these animals evolved into subgroups that include the ancestors of our modern species of cats, bears, beavers, raccoons, weasels, hyenas, and dogs. In fact, all carnivorous mammals developed from the miacids. We would not have recognized our feline companions then, of course. Short-legged, long-bodied, and pea-brained, the miacids looked more like modern weasels than they did our feline

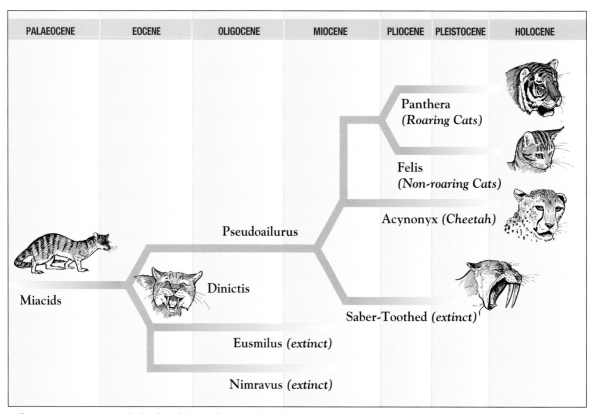

| PALAEOCENE | EOCENE | OLIGOCENE | MIOCENE | PLIOCENE | PLEISTOCENE | HOLOCENE |

Miacids

Dinictis

Pseudoailurus

Panthera (*Roaring Cats*)

Felis (*Non-roaring Cats*)

Acynonyx (*Cheetah*)

Saber-Toothed (*extinct*)

Eusmilus (*extinct*)

Nimravus (*extinct*)

All carnivorous mammals developed from the miacids. The first ancestor of the modern-day cat, the Dinictis, *dates from the Eocene Epoch, approximately 56 to 34 million years ago.*

Saber-toothed cats developed around 40 million years ago. Extinct now, some saber-toothed cats were still alive as recently as 13,000 years ago.

friends. However, without the miacids we wouldn't have the felids we know and love today.

From the miacids developed *Dinictis*, a lynx-sized animal with catlike teeth for stabbing prey. *Dinictis* was the first modern day cat look-alike, and was an important ancestor in the felid evolutionary line. The *Dinictis'* brain was much smaller than today's intelligent feline's. To compensate, its teeth were bigger.

From the *Dinictis*, felid evolution diverged. In one branch were the saber-toothed cats, in which the canine teeth became true stabbing weapons. These cats were found worldwide from the mid-Eocene Epoch (around 42 million years ago) to the end of the Pleis-

tocene Epoch (about 11,000 years ago, when the last of the subspecies became extinct). The other branch, in which the upper canine teeth became smaller and the brain larger, developed later, around 15 million years ago. The smaller-toothed cats, quicker and smarter than the saber-toothed cats, continued to adapt and thrive into the 36 recognized felid species that exist in the world today—all descended from the same ancestor.

DIVERGENCE

When animals first began to evolve into identifiable mammals, the enormous supercontinent called Pan-

Panthera leo, *the lion.*

gaea was moving apart in a process known as continental drift, eventually becoming the continents of the world we know today. Of course, the continents are still drifting. What the planet will look like in the expanse of time is still being debated.

When the continents began drifting apart, the plants and animals that existed at that time drifted as well. That's why the species of cats are located as they are. No indigenous cats can be found in Antarctica or Australia, and cats have only arrived in South America in the last two million years. The southern continents split away from Pangaea around 180 million years ago, before any modern-type mammals evolved.

Marsupials (mammals whose young are born at an early stage and continue their development in a pouch) evolved in Australia where they developed into the most advanced mammals in the area. They then spread into modern North America, which was still attached to Eurasia at that time. They then spread to South America, which was still connected to North America until around 65 million years ago.

Because no true cats made it to Australia, marsupials evolved to inhabit the same ecological niches as do cats in other parts of the world. Thus, the marsupial cats, while not true members of the felid family, evolved similar characteristics. For example, the Miocene marsupial lion *Thylacoleo* was the size of a leopard and even had teeth similar to the saber-toothed cats of North America. These marsupials lived in Australia from about two million to 46,000 years ago, when they became extinct.

South America had no felines until the Isthmus of Panama formed to connect Central America and South America, and cats migrated down from North America. With the forming of this land bridge about three million years ago, many kinds of animals (including cats) traveled down into South America, and many marsupials (and other animals) subsequently became extinct, likely because of competition for the available ecological niches.

THE CAT FAMILY

All of the nonroaring cats are members of the genus *Felis*. For example, *Felis silvestris catus* is the name for the domestic cat, the mountain lion (also called the cougar) is *Felis concolor*, and the bobcat is *Felis rufus*. The roaring cats are members of the genus *Panthera*, which includes, among others, the lion *Panthera leo*, the leopard *Panthera pardus*, and the tiger *Panthera tigris*. A third genus of cat, called *Acinonyx*, has just one existing member—*Acinonyx jubatus*, the cheetah. It warrants a genus of its

Acinonyx Jubatus, the cheetah. Current DNA studies show that cheetahs are closely related to pumas.

own because, among other differences, its claws are not fully retractable like other members of the cat family. The genuses *Felis* and *Panthera* are divided not because of size, but because of the differences in construction of the vocal apparatus. The hyoid bone at the base of the tongue is partially made of cartilage in the great cats, which gives the vocal apparatus the mobility necessary to produce roaring sounds.

The classification of cat species is not easy, and not all experts agree on the number or placement of each. For example, some authorities place the clouded leopard in a genus of its own, *Neofelis*, because of its very long upper canine teeth, among other differences. Some experts divide lynxes, ocelots, and Geoffroy's cat into genuses of their own. Despite these disagreements, most experts agree on the basic classifications.

Our domestic cats most likely descended from the African wildcat *Felis silvestris lybica*. A 2007 genetic study indicated that all domestic cats descended from as few as five female African wildcats in the Mid-East around 8000 B.C.E. (10,000 years ago). Native to Africa, western Asia, Scotland, and southern Europe, the African wildcat has the same structure and number of chromosomes as the domestic cat. If you put one beside the other, you might have a difficult time distinguishing the African wildcat from its domestic buddy. *Felis silvestris lybica* is lithe, tabby striped, tan in color, and bears ticking similar to the Abyssinian. *F. lybica* interbreeds easily with domestics, so much so that it is teetering on the brink of extinction as a pure spe-

cies. Unlike other wildcats, *F. lybica* is fairly easily domesticated and often lives near humans to prey on the small animals that live on human stores of foods. Many of the cat remains mummified by the cat cult that existed some 4,000 years ago in Egypt are *F. lybica*.

It's possible that later on the European wildcat *Felis silvestris* and the jungle cat *Felis chaus* played some role in the development of the domestic. *F. silvestris* has well-defined mackerel tabby markings and could have introduced this pattern into the species—a pattern that provided better camouflage in wooded areas, and that all modern domestic cats possess (see Chapter Four). A certain amount of crossbreeding likely occurred, and it is thought that the more stocky breeds such as the Persian and British Shorthair were influenced by the stocky body types of the European wildcats, while the slimmer foreign and Oriental breeds show more of the *F. lybica* influence.

DOMESTICATION

Cats were one of the last animals to be domesticated. Before humans settled down to an agrarian culture, humans domesticated animals, such as goats, pigs, and sheep so they could transport with them a ready supply of food. Dogs (*Canis lupus familiaris*), too, became allies in hunting and in defending the herds from predators. Being pack animals, dogs were (and still are) more easily trained than cats when raised among humans. Estimates vary, but archaeologists have found that the earliest known domestication of the gray wolf (*Canis lupus*, from which

African wildcat Felis silvestris libyca.

domestic dogs developed), occurred approximately 30,000 B.C.E. The present bloodlines of *Canis lupus familiaris* arose about 16,000 years ago. Cats, on the other hand, have been "tamed" for about 9,500 years (that we know of) and have always accepted domestication with reservations.

Domestication is somewhat of a mysterious process that is not yet fully understood. That this process has a genetic basis seems clear, since the docile behavior and dependency of domestic animals develop after years of selective breeding. One likely theory is that cat domestication occurred gradually, since the cats that tended to hang around humans would interbreed and pass along their "docile" genes, while the less docile specimens would leave for less inhabited regions.

Domestic cats have smaller brains than their wild cousins, and this may be a factor in the domestication process (in other words, the smaller your brain, the more likely you are to trust humans). However, other experts believe the reason for the smaller brain size is due to the lack of the need of certain parts of the brain relating to vigilance and sensorial processing, which are needed for survival in the wild.

At any rate, cats cannot be defined as truly domesticated animals since they could still return to the wild and survive, as a species if not as individuals.

Most cat lovers would agree that it's the feline's independent spirit and devotion to its human companions despite its inclinations otherwise that make it so worthy of our love.

With that said, some experts believe that cats domesticated humankind, rather than the other way around. At times it certainly seems that way, since cats manage to get what they want from us humans without undue effort on their part. When humans evolved from hunter-gatherers to an agricultural existence, cats may have learned that humans provided a reliable food source in the vermin attracted to stored grain. In effect, these cats filled a newly developed ecological niche. Humans soon learned that felines were invaluable in controlling the rodent populations that destroyed their crops and ate their stored food. Somewhere along the way, humans also discovered that it was pleasant to sit by the fire with a lapful of warm cat.

THE SPREAD OF THE FELINE

Since *Felis silvestris lybica* originally came from Africa, the Mid-East, and southern Europe, it's logical to assume that domestication first occurred there. Evidence exists that cats were kept as pets at least 9,500 years ago; on the Island of Cypress in the Mediterranean Sea, a kitten was unearthed in a young girl's grave. Radiocarbon dating determined the kitten was 9,500 years old. Since Cyprus has no indigenous wild cats, including African Wildcats, this indicates cats were domesticated thou-

sands of years before the Egyptian cat cult left written records of their alliance with cats.

Cats became household companions to the Egyptians between 4,000 and 6,000 years ago, as evidenced by the period's writings and the depictions of cats on ornaments, statues, bas-reliefs, and paintings. Although presumably at first they were welcomed for their rodent-catching abilities, later they became much more than that. They were treated as beloved household companions, much as they are today. Plutarch, the Greek philosopher and biographer (46–120 C.E.), commented that the Egyptians were noted for breeding their cats for comparable traits. If true, the Egyptians were the first known cat fanciers to breed domestic cats for specific characteristics.

At one point, cats were also worshipped as the physical manifestations of the gods. In Egyptian theology, the cat was identified with the goddess Bast (also known as Ubastet, Bastet, and Pasht), who was often depicted as a woman with the head of a cat. The loved companion of the great sun god Ra, Bast symbolized the sun's gentle, life-giving warmth, and also was associated with fertility and the Moon. The way cats' eyes reflect light was compared with the way the moon reflects the sun's light. Cats were therefore believed to have power over darkness. "Mau" is the Egyptian word for "cat" and also meant "to see."

For a time, felines were so revered as Bast's physical symbol by the people of Lower Egypt that the Egyptians would go into deep mourning upon the death of a cat, shaving their eyebrows as a sign of their grief. The penalty for killing a cat was severe. A Sicilian historian tells of a Roman soldier who killed a cat by running it down with his chariot. Some accounts say it was an accident. Despite King Ptolemy's pleas for clemency (he didn't want to antagonize the powerful Roman Empire), the soldier was killed by the outraged mob.

Like humans, cats were often mummified so they could rejoin their human companions after death. Archaeologists found thousands of such cats buried with mummified mice and shrews preserved to sustain the cats on their journey to the afterlife.

However, researchers who have X-rayed mummified cat remains have found that a great many of the mummified cats were under two years old and had their necks broken, indicating that in some areas of Egypt people sacrificed felines to the cat goddess. These mummies date from 330 to 30 B.C.E. No evidence of animal sacrifice has been found before or after that time.

Morrison Scott of the British Museum examined mummified cats and came to the conclusion that these spotted cats were *Felis lybica ocreata*, a subspecies of the African wildcat originally from the Ethiopian highlands.

The Egyptians were fiercely protective of their cats, but eventually Phoenician traders transported domesticated felines to Europe and the British Isles, where the cats were used to control rodent populations. Romans smuggled cats out of Egypt and brought them into conquered regions, such as France, Germany, Holland, England, and Spain. Monks transported cats to the Orient. Slowly, domestic cats spread. The development of specific breeds within the domestic cat species was still hundreds of years away, but because of geographical location, climatic conditions, human intervention, and other factors, specific traits and breeds slowly began to develop (see the breed profiles in Chapter Six).

An ancient Egyptian statue representing the goddess Bast.

11

An Egyptian mummy of a ram. The Egyptians mummified various animals, including many cats.

By the birth of Christ, many cultures, such as those of the Japanese, Siamese, East Indians, and Chinese, had come to appreciate felines for their beauty, wisdom, and usefulness. For a long time in the Hindu religion, for example, believers were required to feed and shelter at least one cat.

Not all cultures appreciated cats, however. Religious sects in Europe, beginning around the middle of the thirteenth century, persecuted and killed cats for a supposed link with the devil. The reason for this may have been genuine, if misguided, religious fervor, but the coincidental timing suggests political reasons as well. The Middle Ages was a time when the Christian church had strong motivation to discourage the practice of the

pagan religions, particularly those that worshiped deities, such as the Egyptian goddess Bast and the Norse goddess Freyia who rode about the skies in a cat-drawn chariot. Therefore, pagan deities were often cast as devils or servants of Satan. Cats and other animals previously worshipped were tortured and killed in the most terrible ways. Mass "purges" required that cats be rounded up and destroyed, and ritualistic ceremonies were held to symbolize casting out evil by the killing of cats. For example, as late as 1757, an annual celebration in Provence, France, required that a live tomcat be thrown into a blazing bonfire built in the city square. This ritual apparently had the full support of the church, since church officials sang anthems in honor of the ritual during the performance. These were bad times for cats and humans alike because, of course, the animals were not alone in the persecution. People suspected of witchcraft (sometimes the owners of cats) were also persecuted, tortured, and killed.

It has been theorized that the reduced cat population in Europe contributed to the spread of the bubonic plague. Rodents and their fleas flourished at this time and with them so did the Black Death, which from 1347 to 1351 C.E. killed approximately one third to one half of the population of Europe. Even after the great plague ended, outbreaks continued even into the 1900s; however, domestic cats later played a role in reducing outbreaks by ridding towns and villages of disease-bearing rodents. Even though the people of the time didn't know of the connection between plague and rats, the ability to eliminate vermin helped increase cats' popularity and eventually end the persecution.

With the advent of sailing ships, domestic cats spread. In addition to (and maybe because of) their usefulness in catching rodents, it was thought that having cats aboard ship brought good luck, and thus cats spread across the globe and eventually came to the New World (see Chapter Eight for the history of their arrival).

IN THE FUTURE

Where will cat evolution go from here? Of course, no one really knows. Cats, great and small, are among the world's most efficient predators, and that is why they have thrived for so many millions of years on so many of the world's continents. However, humankind's predation and encroachment upon habitat has severely limited the populations of many wild cat species. Without our help many will become extinct.

In *After Man: A Zoology of the Future*, a fanciful but scientifically based book by Dougal Dixon (St. Martin's Griffin),

the author predicts that in 50 million years the only remaining descendant of the true cats will be the striger, a tiger-striped creature with opposable claws and a prehensile tail that allows the animal to swing through the trees in search of prey. But humankind, Dixon predicts, will have gone the way of the dodo long before that time. Who knows? Perhaps we will.

As far as our cat companions are concerned, humankind will have a profound influence on the future of *Felis silvestris catus*. Just as dog breeds have evolved, diversified, and changed, so will cat breeds. It is possible that hundreds or thousands of years from now we will have Great Dane cats, Toy Poodle cats, cats with Basset Hound ears, perhaps even cats with opposable claws (and you think the couch gets shredded now). Minor differences may become more extreme as selective breeding separates the pedigreed breeds. Is this a good thing? Not necessarily. As we've seen in the dog fancy, breeds can be virtually ruined by unwise breeding goals. Breeds can also be improved by responsible breeding practices. It will depend on the cat fancy and the responsibility and objectives of the breeders and exhibitors. Mother Nature is a few billion years ahead of us when it comes to selective breeding, and it stands to reason that she is rather better at shaping her creations than we are.

CHAPTER TWO

WHAT IS A PUREBRED?

"A god among creatures! Yet also a stray like me."
—Tony Ross

DEFINING A PUREBRED

What makes a purebred different from a rough-and-tumble alley cat? The term purebred is misleading, because purebreds are really no more "pure" than household pets, from a certain point of view. This is why most cat fanciers prefer the term "pedigreed" rather than "purebred."

On the most basic level, a purebred is a feline with a pedigree—the cat's ancestry can be traced back a certain number of generations (usually four or five). Because of this pedigree, and because the cat is a member of a recognized breed, the cat can be registered with any of the cat associations that recognize the breed. Of course, it's not as simple as that, and it would be misleading to imply that having a piece of paper stating a particular cat is a member of a specific breed is the only method of determination.

Usually, a major determining factor is whether or not the cat can breed true—meaning that it produces uniform offspring. However, accepted breeds exist that do not. The Manx doesn't breed true, and no one would deny that it's considered an accepted breed.

If you choose to look at it another way, what constitutes a breed of cat (or any breed of domestic animal) is largely a human perception, particularly when you are referring to breeds that have been created by selective breeding. With this thinking, a cat breed is a group of felines recognized as such by an organized group of like-minded humans. But of course that doesn't tell the whole story, either.

In the dog fancy, the original system of defining separate breeds was based on function, so the lines drawn between breeds were more clear-cut. For the most part (with the exception of show cats), all cat breeds have the same function in human society—they provide companionship and kill vermin. Also, since dogs were first domesticated an estimated 31,000 years ago, dog breeds have had more time to evolve, change, and be selectively bred for the function for which they were needed. The differences in size, conformation, ability, coat type, color, and personality are more obvious and extreme.

In the cat fancy, cat breeds are not separated by function

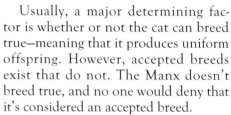

Siamese queen with her kittens. Pedigreeds generally breed true— their offspring will look like them.

and fewer conformation types exist; there aren't as many sizes and shapes to help distinguish the breeds. Therefore, the term "breed" is used in a more flexible manner. Other features are used to define the differences between breeds, such as color, pattern, hair length and texture, and body type, including head shape, ear type, the set of the eyes and ears, and the length and type of the tail. The breeds also differ by personality and activity level.

A pedigreed breed's "standard of perfection," written (usually) by one or more breeders, is a guideline describing the characteristics that make an ideal example of the breed. A breed group or committee updates the standard as necessary. The standard is an ideal for which to strive rather than a description of each member of the breed. In the standard, each characteristic is assigned a specific number of points, depending upon the importance of the trait, equaling a total of 100 points. Undesirable characteristics (called objections, faults, or penalties depending upon the association) reduce the chances that the judge will award that cat a ribbon.

Keep in mind, however, that judges do not mentally add or subtract the standard's points when judging a particular cat. The points simply tell the judge which attributes are most important for that breed. For example, if the coat is assigned 30 points and the eyes are assigned five points, the judge will focus his or her attention far more on the coat than the eyes. In other words, a cat could have the most magnificent eyes the judge has ever seen, but if the coat is lacking, no ribbon will be forthcoming.

The Cymric (bottom) is a longhaired version of the Manx (top).

Another factor complicating the issue is that the registries sometimes have different breed standards and policies concerning the breeds. For example, in the Cat Fanciers' Association (CFA), the Colorpoint Shorthair is defined as a breed that possesses the svelte body type and pointed pattern of the Siamese but that is dressed in colors that don't conform to the four original Siamese colors the CFA recognizes. However, The International Cat Association (TICA) and some of the other associations consider these cats to be part of the Siamese breed group, since the conformation, hair length, and temperament are the same. These associations merely extended the color parameters of the breed to accommodate the new colors.

So how can we define a pedigreed breed? As an overall guideline, a breed is a group of related felines that share a unique conformation, pattern, coat length and type, color parameters, and temperament, and often come from a particular geographic region. The members of a pedigreed breed generally produce uniform offspring—you can count on certain characteristics to be passed from generation to generation. In some cases, one particular defining characteristic sets the breed apart from other

cats, as in the case of the unique ears of the Scottish Fold and the American Curl. In other cases, the determining characteristics are more subtle, as in the Burmese breed with its particular color scheme and body type. To be considered a breed by the cat associations, the cats must be in some significant way different from other existing breeds, or be a distinct variant of an existing breed. Since all modern breeds arose from several original types, and interest in cat breeds didn't really get started until the nineteenth century, the twentieth century has seen an explosion of new cat breeds accepted by the cat associations.

WHY PEDIGREEDS?

Who knows what cats think about the cat fancy? They possibly consider it another of those incomprehensible things humans do with their time. Cat fanciers, however, find the preservation of pedigreed characteristics more than a passing whim. One of the goals of the cat fancy is to preserve and promote feline characteristics fanciers find attractive or unique, because otherwise many of these traits would disappear from the feline gene pool. Some of these traits are aesthetically pleasing, some

The American Curl (left) and the Scottish Fold (right), two breeds defined by their unusual aural arrangements.

18

Spotted Ocicat. The Ocicat was developed by crossing Abyssinians, Siamese, and American Shorthairs.

give us a clearer picture of feline evolution and the history of cats, and some enhance our understanding of the feline species in general. Therefore, these characteristics are valuable to people who love, own, breed, show, and study cats. Fanciers are dedicated to preserving the infinite variety of their feline "children" for subsequent generations to enjoy.

Also, knowing a breed's characteristics allows fanciers to determine which breed is right for them. It is helpful to know a cat's general temperament, conformation, grooming needs, and health concerns before investing time and money. While the characteristics of dog breeds vary more widely than cat breeds, it's still possible to get a pretty good idea what a given member of a cat breed will be like by examining its forebears.

NEW BREEDS

Several methods exist for arriving at new breed varieties. The most common method is mutation. Mutations occur spontaneously within the feline gene pool—that's the way evolution works its magic. Oftentimes, the mutation is not apparent to the eye and frequently dies out without anyone noticing. Other times, the mutation is obvious, as in the American Curl's ears or the Munchkin's short legs. In wild cats, many mutations cease to exist because they aren't beneficial or suited to the cat's environment; a new variation that decreases the cat's effectiveness at, say, pouncing on a rodent or surviving the area's extremes in temperature won't survive long enough to become a unique breed. That's the criteria Mother Nature uses to gauge mutations: Is the animal more or less likely to survive than it was before?

Sometimes, however, because of geographic conditions, serendipity, or human intervention, a mutation that's not necessarily beneficial or that doesn't increase survival odds thrives anyway. The Manx is a good example. Even though the mutation that causes its taillessness is potentially damaging because it can cause foreshortening of the spine, the protected and confining nature of the Isle of Man allowed it to develop and flourish.

Combining established breeds is another method used to create new breeds. Typically, this is done with some goal in mind, but sometimes the crosses happen accidentally or yield unexpected results. This method is most often used by breeders to establish new colors or intensify existing color variations, but can also be used to develop new breeds. For example, the Himalayan, originally a cross between the Persian and the Siamese, is considered by many associations to be a breed in its own right. In CFA, however, the Himalayan is considered a color division of the Persian breed, and in TICA the Himalayan is part of the Persian breed group. Other examples of breeds created by combining established breeds are the Tonkinese, Exotic Shorthair, Ocicat, and Oriental Shorthair, among others.

A third method of creating new breeds is by the deliberate modifying and shaping of "polygenes" that control particular characteristics to create new forms (see the discussion of colors in Chapter Three). This is not done through science fiction DNA tinkering

as theorized in Jurassic Park (although that technology is becoming a reality), but rather through old-fashioned selective breeding. A common practice, this method is often used to refine color or conformation in existing breeds, and as such can create detrimental effects. For example, the selective breeding that has modified the Persian's facial structure has created breathing problems and perpetual runny eyes in some cats. Numerous fanciers are concerned with this trend and doubt the value of breeding for traits that can be detrimental.

Many new breeds created by crossbreeding and other methods appear to be variations of existing breeds. This is true of a number of shorthaired breeds that have longhaired counterparts. The ways these variations are handled depend a great deal on how enthusiastic the proponents of the new breed are and the methods used in the breed's creation. For example, the Abyssinian is a well-established shorthaired breed. When breed proponents selectively bred and promoted the longhairs that occasionally cropped up in Abyssinian litters, the longhaired variety became a new breed called the Somali. The Somali is considered a separate breed, even though it originated from the Abyssinian. Another example of this includes the Siamese and the Balinese.

Breeds are not always separated by hair length. For example, the Japanese Bobtail has long- and shorthaired varieties, but they are considered divisions of the same breed in many associations, including CFA and TICA, the two largest cat organizations. The American Curl, Scottish Fold, and the Manx are other examples of breeds that possess long- and shorthairs within the same breed category, depending upon the association. In the case of the Manx, the shorthaired and longhaired versions used to be considered separate breeds in the CFA (the longhaired version is still called the Cymric in many associations), but in CFA and TICA are now considered divisions of the same breed. Other associations, such as the American Cat Fanciers Association (ACFA) and the Canadian Cat Association (CCA), still consider the Cymric a separate breed. The Cat Fanciers' Federation (CFF) is the only North American cat organization that doesn't accept the longhaired Manx.

Breeders have good reason to campaign for combining long- and shorthaired varieties of breeds. When longhaired and shorthaired varieties are considered to be divisions within a single breed, they can be bred together and the offspring registered either as longhairs or shorthairs of the breed, depending upon the fur length. However, this is not always true when longhairs and shorthairs are considered separate breeds. For example, if an Abyssinian queen bears a litter that contains a longhair kitten, that kitten cannot then be shown as a Somali. The only current exception is in TICA, which considers the Somali a member of the Abyssinian Breed Group.

ESTABLISHING NEW BREEDS

At the best of times, establishing a new breed of cat is difficult, frustrating, expensive, and time-consuming. The new breed's proponents must write a breed standard describing the ideal example of the breed, promote the breed by exhibiting whenever and wherever possible, breed conscientiously and work to attract other breeders, win the support and acceptance of fanciers, and work to earn association acceptance and awards. The breed's proponents must also win over (or outlive) fanciers who wish to thwart their efforts. It's usually an uphill battle, particularly if the breed bears some trait that other fanciers don't consider beneficial to the cat fancy.

For example, one of the battles being fought in the cat fancy today is over a spontaneously mutated breed called the Munchkin, named so because it has very short, Dachshund-like legs (see profile, page 300). Opponents call it an abomination that will likely develop serious spinal problems; proponents call it the "sports car" of felines and discount the concerns of health difficulties.

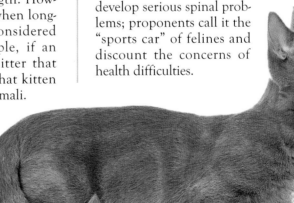

The Munchkin's short legs are due to a spontaneous mutation.

CHAPTER THREE

FELINE GENETICS

*"If man could be crossed with the cat, it would
improve man but deteriorate the cat."*
—Mark Twain

FELINE GENETICS

BASIC GENETICS

How can a shorthaired Abyssinian breeding pair produce a litter that contains a longhaired Somali kitten? Why is it that a cross between a black Persian and a seal point Siamese produce only black kittens in the first generation? The answers can be found in genetics.

Traits are passed from one generation to another by a system of genetic inheritance. The basis of this system was discovered by Austrian scientist and Augustinian friar Gregor Mendel (1822–1884), the first person to develop an understanding of how traits are inherited. He did his experiments on pea plants, not felines, but his basic conclusions were sound, and his laws of inheritance still hold true today, although a great deal more has been discovered about genetics. Ironically, it wasn't until the early 1900s, years after his death, that the importance of his work was recognized and Mendel's hypotheses were seriously considered.

Mendel isolated units of heredity he called factors but that we now know as genes. Genes are the building blocks of life and basically provide a blueprint for putting together an animal. Each gene provides the genetic instructions necessary to produce a single protein, and each protein influences the structure, function, metabolism, and embryonic differentiation of the body's cells. Genes are responsible for the determination and transmission of all the hereditary characteristics, such as eye color, hair length, and hair color. The study of genetics helps predict what results will be produced from any given mating.

Chromosomes are made up of thousands of genes. The easiest way to visualize chromosomes is to imagine two long spiraling strings called a double helix. Along these two strings are a series of beads—the genes. Each gene occupies a particular location on the chromosome called a locus, and because each cat has two of each chromosome, it also has two copies of each gene for each trait. The thousands of genes in combination with their corresponding genes on the affiliated chromosomes determine the genetic makeup of the cat, called the genotype (the genetic makeup).

Felines have 19 pairs of chromosomes (38 total), which exist inside each cell nucleus. Cats inherit nineteen chromosomes from each parent—one strand of nineteen chromosomes from the mother's egg cell and one strand of nineteen from the father's sperm cell.

The sex cells are constructed differently from the rest of the body's cells. These cells, called eggs in the female and sperm in the male, contain nine-

The double helix.

24

teen unpaired chromosomes. The female sex chromosome is known as X, and the male is known as Y. When sperm fertilizes an egg, the resulting progeny cell then acquires nineteen chromosomes from each parent cell, resulting in a total of thirty-eight chromosomes arranged in pairs. In this manner the offspring acquires characteristics from both parents, and this is the way nature maintains genetic diversity in animals that reproduce sexually.

The sex chromosomes determine the gender of the cat. The female has two X sex chromosomes, and the male has one X and one Y sex chromosome (XX = female, XY = male). If a kitten inherits an X chromosome from its mother and an X from its father, the kitten will be female. If, however, it inherits the Y chromosome from the father, the kitten will be male. The male determines the gender of the kittens; roughly half of a male's sperm cells are X, and roughly half are Y. Genes that are carried on the X or Y chromosomes are called sex-linked genes. The X gene is large and carries about as many genes as would an ordinary chromosome its size. The Y chromosome is much smaller and carries fewer genes.

An alternative form of gene that occupies the same locus on its corresponding chromosome and controls the same characteristic as its comparable gene is known as an *allele*. When both copies of a particular gene are identical (in other words, when the cat receives the same gene for a particular trait from both parents), we say that the cat is homozygous for the trait governed by that gene. That

trait, of course, will be expressed in the cat's phenotype (physical appearance). If the cat has two different genes for a particular trait, the cat is said to be heterozygous for that trait. Heterozygous traits can express in a variety of ways, depending on the kind of protein produced by the genes and the type of resulting change.

Sometimes, both genes can express themselves and this is called nondominance or codominance. In these cases, both genes would affect the phenotype. Usually, however, dominant genes determine the animal's physical appearance; dominant genes mask the effect of recessive genes and will be expressed in the phenotype of the cat, while the recessive gene will be present only in the cat's genotype. The recessive gene will not be expressed in the physical appearance but can be (and often is) passed onto the cat's offspring.

For example, the color black is dominant over the color blue. If a cat carries the gene for black it will be expressed. Put another way, if the cat is not black, it cannot have the gene for black.

The color blue (also known as gray) is a dilution of black and is therefore recessive (the governing gene causes the color to possess less pigmentation). The gene for blue can be present but unexpressed because it is masked by the black gene. Only if a cat has received the recessive blue gene from both parents will the cat be blue.

So, theoretically, if you breed together a homozygous black cat (DD) and a homozygous blue cat (dd), all the first-generation offspring will be

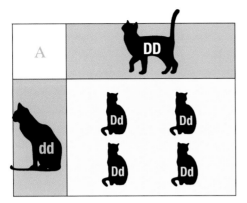

black. All, however, will be heterozygous and carry the gene for blue (Dd) (see the Punnett square example A, above; dominant genes are represented by capital letters while recessive genes are represented by lowercase letters).

If you breed together two of the heterozygous kittens (Dd) from the first litter, the characteristics of both their grandparents will show up again in pure (homozygous) form. These second-generation kittens will not all look alike and will have different combinations of genes. Theoretically, they will exhibit three different gene combinations in a ratio of 1:2:1— one homozygous black (DD), two heterozygous black masking blue (Dd), and one homozygous blue (dd), which, of

all the kittens, is the only one that actually exhibits blue coloration (see example B, below, left).

In the third generation, if you backcross one of the heterozygous black cats (Dd) to the homozygous blue (dd), you'll get a theoretical 1:1 ratio of heterozygous black cats (Dd) and homozygous blue cats (dd) (see example C, below).

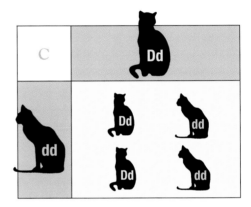

It's important to keep in mind that these Punnett squares are diagrams that are used to predict the possible outcomes of particular crosses or matings. Just because the Punnett square predicts a certain outcome, that doesn't mean a litter will produce that exact genetic conformation. It's simply a helpful tool to determine the probability of offspring having a particular phenotype or genotype, not a hard and fast predictor of the actual results.

MUTATION

This leads to the next point: how changes occur within the genetic structure. A gene at a particular locus on the chromosome may have more than one form because genes can mutate into alternate forms. The existence of these alternate forms allows for the immense variety of variation in color, body conformation, and coat in our feline friends. These changes sometimes can be passed along to future generations.

Some mutations have positive effects. For example, the mutation that created the agouti (ticked tabby) protective camouflaging (see Chapter Four) benefited the species because the coloration helped the cat blend in with its environment, and thus evade predators. Other mutations have negative effects, such as the Scottish Fold gene, which can cause crippling bone disorders.

If a particular mutation is harmful enough that the offspring doesn't survive long enough to reproduce, the mutation dies out and doesn't influence the cat gene pool. However, some mutations become part of the gene pool because, while they are not particularly helpful, they do not significantly reduce the cat's chances of survival. Some detrimental genes are passed onto subsequent generations because they are recessive. It takes two copies of the gene for the trait to express itself, and therefore the gene can be carried for many generations without any effect (and without anyone knowing it's there) until paired with a second copy of the gene. At that point it will be expressed in the cat's phenotype, unless it's harmful enough to cause the death of the kittens. This is one factor that makes breeding cats (or anything else) challenging.

Black kitten (right) and blue kitten (left). Blue is a dilution of black.

GENETIC SYMBOLS

In order to make it easier to keep track of all this, a system of internationally recognized symbols has been established. The table on page 28 shows a few of the symbols assigned to particular genes. In this system, capital letters indicate dominant genes while lowercase letters represent recessive genes. The list on the left shows the original gene forms, and the list on the right shows the mutated forms. You'll notice that most of the original genes are dominant, but that exceptions exist.

Of course, if a gene can mutate once, it can do so again, as can be seen in the mackerel, agouti (also called ticked), and blotched (also known as classic) tabby genes. Since mackerel is the original dominant form, it is represented as T. However, the agouti gene is dominant, and so is represented as T^a with the superscript to indicate that it is an allele. The blotched tabby gene, recessive to both the mackerel and the ticked tabby genes, is therefore represented as t^b.

POLYGENES

Most of the genes we've discussed have major effects upon the cat's appearance, but many genes exert a minor, rather than major, influence upon the phenotype. These are called polygenes or modifiers. Polygenes by themselves have little effect on the cat's phenotype but can act together with other genes to yield noticeable variations. Breeders can use polygenes to influence the intensity of colors, as well as many other traits. Polygenes are difficult to control, but breeders rely on their influence in selective breeding programs. The influence of these genes can be increased gradually over many generations by choosing studs and queens with desirable characteristics.

Original genes		Mutant genes	
Symbol	Designation	Symbol	Designation
A	Agouti tabby pattern	a	Non-agouti
T	Mackerel tabby pattern	T^a	Abyssinian tabby pattern
		t^b	Blotched tabby pattern
B	Black	b	Blue
		b^l	Light brown
C	Full color	c	Albino
		c^s	Siamese
		c^b	Burmese
		c^a	Blue-eyed albino
D	Dense color	d	Dilute
w	Normal color	W	Dominant white
o	Normal color	O	Orange
s	Normal color	S	Piebald white spotting
i	Normal pigmentation	I	Inhibitor
R	Normal coat	r	Cornish Rex
Re	Normal coat	re	Devon Rex
wh	Normal coat	Wh	Wirehair
Hr	Normal coat	hr	Hairlessness
fd	Normal ears	Fd	Folded ears
		Cu	Curled ears
m	Normal tail	M	Manx tail
L	Short hair	l	Long hair

BREEDING METHODS

Four major breeding methods are used to develop and change a breed's bloodlines: inbreeding, linebreeding, linecrossing (also called outcrossing), and crossbreeding.

- **Inbreeding** involves mating closely related cats to one another, for example, father to daughter, mother to son, brother to sister, and first cousin to first cousin. In humans we call that incest; in cats, it's inbreeding. Inbreeding is used to "set" desired traits into the bloodline of a breed to make the cats more uniform by creating more homozygous gene pairs.

  This sounds good in theory; however, detrimental traits can also become established in the lines by the use of this method, and can cause medical problems, deformities, and more. To avoid setting detrimental genes in the breed's bloodlines as well, responsible breeders start with the widest gene pool possible.

- **Linebreeding** is a form of inbreeding and involves breeding cats that share the same bloodline but are not as closely related. For example, mating a cat to a great-grandparent, second or third cousin, or great-aunt or -uncle is considered linebreeding. The common ancestors are farther apart, but the pedigree of a linebred cat will show the same related cats several times in its ancestry. This method is used to concentrate the good qualities of outstanding feline examples without direct inbreeding. However, over time linebreeding is likely to reduce the genetic diversity

of the cat breed in which it's used and cause genetic problems due to a smaller than desirable gene pool, which is likely to cause an increase in genetic disorders.

- **Linecrossing** or **outcrossing** involves mating two good examples of the same breed that do not share a bloodline in order to profit from the good qualities of both lines. Linecrossing is also used to rid a bloodline of negative traits. Ideally, the bloodlines used should not have the same strengths and weaknesses. For example, if you were to breed a cat from a bloodline known for its outstanding eye color together with a cat from a bloodline known for its outstanding head shape, a small percentage of the offspring produced would have both outstanding eye color and head shape. However, outcrossing can cause harmful recessive traits to spread across a breed, actually increasing the number of cats carrying genetic diseases. These harmful genes will then appear in the phenotype when two cats carrying the gene are bred together. Fortunately, researchers have given breeders tests for some of these widespread genetic diseases.

- **Crossbreeding** involves mating cats of different breeds. In some cases, it's used to bring genetic diversity to established breeds, and to create new breeds of cats. For example, the Himalayan was the product of an original cross between a Persian and a Siamese. In most breeds, however, crossbreeding is not allowed. Crossbreeding is unnecessary in breeds with enough genetic diversity.

4
CHAPTER FOUR

CONFORMATION, COLOR, AND COAT

"The smallest feline is a masterpiece."
—Leonardo Da Vinci

CONFORMATION

Conformation, also called "type," refers to the physical appearance of the cat. What is appropriate for a particular breed is determined by the standards accepted by the cat associations (see in Chapter Six). The standards define the ideal characteristics for the breed: the proper body type, color or colors, pattern, eye and ear shape and set, head type, and other more subtle differences.

Seven different conformation types exist, but most championship breeds fall within three general conformation types: cobby, such as the Persian, svelte, such as the Siamese, and moderate, such as the Havana Brown. The cobby body design is short and compact, deep-chested, and broad across the shoulders and rump. The head is also large and round, and the tail is often shorter and blunt at the tip. In contrast, the svelte type is very slim and lithe with long, tapering lines. The head is narrow and forms a wedge shape, and the tail is usually long, slender, and pointed at the tip.

The moderate lies between the two and is neither cobby nor svelte; a number of breeds are moderate in conformation. The American Curl, Burmese, and Havana Brown breeds are examples of moderate body types.

Groups of polygenes are responsible for most conformation changes, except a few major mutations such as the folded-ear gene of the Scottish Fold and the taillessness of the Manx. Selective breeding, using the breeding methods discussed in the previous chapter, manipulates these polygenes and creates the breeds we know today.

What is desirable in a particular breed depends upon many factors, including, and perhaps particularly, human sensibilities and goals. Many of our breeds began with a particular characteristic or determining gene, such as the Siamese with its pointed pattern and the Manx with its lack of tail. Over time, however, other char-

Three conformation types: cobby Exotic Shorthair (top left), svelte Siamese (bottom middle), and moderate Russian Blue (right).

32

Svelte Siamese, also called the Extreme (right) and sealpoint Old-Style Siamese, also known as the Thai (left). Notice the differences in conformation.

acteristics become associated with the breeds, because selective breeding causes the cats of particular breeds to develop similar traits. As time passes, these characteristics become part of the breed standard. For example, when the Scottish Fold was discovered in 1961 in Scotland, its primary characteristic was its folded ears. Now, however, its body type, its accepted colors and patterns, and even its temperament are well-defined and established in its members.

Breeds also can change over time by selective breeding. For example, when the Siamese was first introduced in England, its conformation was more moderate than is seen in the show halls today; today's breed is much more extreme than the type originally imported from Siam (now Thailand). The Persian's muzzle has undergone considerable changes within the last 100 years, becoming increasingly fore-shortened to the point where today some members of the breed have difficulty breathing and have eyes that constantly tear. Also, the down hairs have become much longer, making daily grooming a must to keep them from becoming matted.

COLOR AND PATTERN

The African wildcat, thought to be the main predecessor of our modern domestics, is decorated with the agouti tabby pattern (also called ticked tabby) with mackerel tabby striping on the legs, tail, and face, with a distinctive "M" on the forehead. Their coats are usually a sandy brown. The agouti pattern occurs in many species, including the agouti for which the pattern is named (a rabbit-sized rodent native to Central and South America). This pattern acts as camouflage to protect animals from their predators in the wild. Why then, if domestic cats are descendants of the African wildcat, does the domestic cat come in so many colors, patterns, conformations, and coat varieties? As we've discussed in the previous chapter, the answer lies in genetic mutation. No matter what color or pattern they appear to be, all domestic cats are genetically tabbies like their African ancestors. All domestic varieties possess one or more of four tabby genes: classic (also called blotched), agouti (sometimes called Abyssinian), mackerel, and spotted. Classic tabbies have wider stripes and often have swirls or "bullseyes" on their sides. Mackerel tabbies have thinner stripes that extend down the cat's sides from the spine like the bones of a fish, hence the name. Cats possessing the agouti pattern usually have only striping on the face, legs, and tail; the shafts of the individual hairs are decorated with alternating dark- and light-colored bands, ending in a dark tip, with the lighter band lying closest to the skin.

Blotched (classic) tabbies.

Spotted tabbies have, understandably, spots, and usually have tabby striping on the face, legs, and tail. Although these four are quite different in appearance, they are all variations of the same tabby gene—the mackerel gene from which the others arose.

Other mutations produced the plethora of pattern and color combinations that we see in domestic cats today. A cat's markings depend upon the particular combination of genes inherited from its parents. Since each parent passes on a gene that influences pattern, the outcome can vary greatly.

One important mutation is the recessive non-agouti gene (symbolized "a"), which masks the light and dark bands of color that give the Abyssinian breed its distinctive ticked look. If a cat inherits two copies of the non-agouti gene, the

Agouti (ticked) tabbies.

Mackerel tabbies.

cat will appear solid in color (also called "self-colored"), although genetically it's still a tabby. Self-colored cats can be found in many breeds. In some breeds, breeders have worked very hard to eliminate residual tabby striping and make the coat a consistent shade.

A cat's color depends upon the presence of pigmentation—melanin—in the epidermis. In cats, the two most common forms of melanin are *eumelanin*, which produces black and brown pigmentation, and *phenomelanin*, which produces red and yellow pigmentation. Both are produced in cells called melanocytes in the basal layer of the epidermis controlled by melanocyte-stimulating hormones. The distribution and number of these cells are genetically determined. These cells pass the pigment onto the cat's skin and hair, and create the pattern and color. The possible variations are numerous.

BLACK AND ITS DILUTES

Just as all cats are tabbies, all cats are either black or orange (or in female cats, a combination of the two). The many variations in color and tone are created by alleles of the original genes. Self-black cats can be found in many breeds, such as the Persian, Oriental Shorthair, and the Bombay.

Spotted tabbies.

In order for a cat to appear black, the cat must possess three genes: B for black pigmentation, D for dense coloration, and C for full color or maximum pigmentation (see Chapter Three). These are all dominant traits; however, these genes have corresponding alleles that can affect the appearance of the color. These alleles can produce lighter color tones.

Black Persian.

Mutations of the dense gene D affect the amount of the pigmentation in a cat's hair. The hair will then reflect white light, giving the hair a lighter appearance. If the cat possesses two copies of the recessive dilute color gene d instead of the dense gene D, black will appear gray, a color known to fanciers as blue. Self-blue cats can be seen in many breeds, such as the Russian Blue, Korat, Chartreux, and British Shorthair.

If a cat possesses two copies of the recessive brown allele b rather than the black gene B, the cat's coat will appear brown or chocolate, as in the Havana Brown, known for its rich and even shade of brown. If a brown cat inherits two copies of the dilute d gene, the brown becomes

Cream Persian.

36

a soft gray known as lavender. Red becomes cream with the addition of the d gene. A second recessive mutation of the black gene, b1, produces a lighter brown or cinnamon color, which can be seen in red Abyssinians. (Abyssinian red is not the sex-linked red seen in other breeds but rather a light brown that appears red.)

The full color gene C gave rise to four recessive gene mutations called the albino series of alleles. The albino series causes solid black to appear lighter by reducing the pigment in the hair and eyes. One mutation (c) creates a true albino, in which there is no pigmentation in the coat or eyes (the eyes appear pink because of the blood vessels they contain). The second (ca) produces pale blue eyes and a white coat. A third (cb), the Burmese gene, creates dark sepia-brown coloration. The fourth (cs) is the pointed allele and creates the Siamese coat pattern (also known as the Himalayan).

THE POINTED PATTERN

In the Siamese color pattern, the hair contains little pigment, but the "points" of the body (face, tail, feet, and ears) contain more and therefore appear darker. Even at the darkest points of the body, however, the pigmentation is diminished, so that, for example, black appears dark brown, or what is known as "seal." The amount of pigment distributed in the hairs depends on temperature—the cooler the temperature, the more pigment is produced. The skin temperature of the body's extremities is a few degrees lower than the rest of the body and therefore attracts more pigmentation.

Sealpoint Siamese. Notice the concentration of color at the points.

Lavender Oriental Shorthair.

SEX-LINKED ORANGE

Orange coloration (also called red) in cats is more complicated, because the gene is located on one of the sex chromosomes, which is why it's called "sex-linked orange" or "sex-linked red." Female cats have two X chromosomes; males have one X chromosome and one Y chromosome (see Chapter Three). The gene for orange is carried on the X chromosome. Since the X chromosome is much longer than the Y, no locus for the orange gene (O) exists on the Y chromosome. Therefore, male cats with their one X chromosome express whatever color gene is present on that chromosome. If the gene is O, he will be an orange tabby. (He will always be a tabby because the non-agouti gene cannot act upon orange coloration.) If he receives the non-orange ("normal") gene (o), he will be black or one of its variations, depending upon his genotype.

Female cats can have two orange genes, since they have two X sex-linked chromosomes. If, however, she inherits the orange gene and the non-orange gene, she can possess a colorful patchwork pattern known as tortoiseshell, a combination of orange and black or their dilute colors. The only way a male cat can be tortoiseshell or calico is if he is born with three sex chromosomes, making it possible for him to possess two Xs and therefore have both the sex-linked orange gene and non-orange ("normal") gene (o). They are often sterile and live their lives without producing offspring. They also can exhibit female behavior, such as nurturing kittens. Tortoiseshell and calico males, by the way, are not extremely valuable as is sometimes thought, although some people may try to convince you otherwise if they have one for sale.

WHITE SPOTTING FACTOR

Calico cats have one major difference from tortoiseshell cats—they possess the white spotting factor that gives such cats patches of white along with their spots of orange and black. This piebald gene (S) is dominant to its corresponding normal coloration gene (s), and if one copy of the gene is present it will cause the cat to have spots of white. The white spotting factor is difficult to control, and the distribution and amount of white vary greatly from cat to cat. Geneticists think that this gene is incompletely dominant to the normal color (s) form of the gene, and therefore can impact the results. Polygenes may also play a role. A cat with this factor may have just a few small spots of white, or it can be predominantly white with only a few spots of color.

DOMINANT WHITE

Another gene that causes white coloration is the dominant white gene (W). The white gene masks the expression of other color genes, meaning a totally white cat could possess the genes for nearly any pattern or color. Mating two white cats together can produce offspring of virtually any pattern or color, depending on the underlying genotype of the parents. This presents many problems for breeders, since it's difficult to tell what color combinations are present. Most white cats possess eyes colored either copper or blue, and they may have one of each color (these cats are called "odd-eyed"). This gene also causes a higher incidence of a form of degenerative deafness. White blue-eyed cats

Tortoiseshell cat.

39

are particularly susceptible. With odd-eyed cats, the cat may be only deaf on the side with the blue eye.

CHINCHILLA, SHADED, AND SMOKE

Tipped, shaded, and smoke colors (also called the "silver" group) all possess darker colored hair tips overlying a paler undercolor (also called ground color), giving the coat a contrasting or shimmering appearance, depending upon the amount of pigment. This effect is created by the dominant inhibitor gene (I), which inhibits the pigmentation in the hair. The amount of pigment depends upon the modifying polygenes. Chinchilla coloration has the least amount of tipping pigment. Only the ends of the hairs are heavily pigmented and this gives the coat a characteristic sparkling or silvery appearance, especially when the cat moves. This is particularly dramatic on longhaired breeds

Chinchilla, shaded, and smoke hair types.

such as the Persian. In the shaded varieties, more of the hair shaft is heavily tipped with color, but still has a distinctive and apparent undercolor. In the smoke varieties, most of the hair shaft is heavily tipped with color and is sometimes difficult to tell from a self-colored cat, because the undercolor is minimal. However, when the cat moves, the fur usually parts so the ground color can be seen, particularly with longhairs. The face, back, and feet are usually more heavily tipped.

These colors may also have tabby patterns. With the chinchilla color, the pattern usually is not noticeable since the fur is so lightly pigmented; however, if the inhibitor gene's effect is limited, the result can be, for example, the striking silver tabby, with an intensely black tabby pattern and an almost white ground-color.

Since it's possible to combine the inhibitor gene with other color genes such as black, orange, brown, or their dilutes, virtually any color or combination of colors is possible. However, when the inhibitor gene is combined with the sex-linked orange gene, "cameos" may be produced. These cats possess varying shades of orange and its dilute cream. In orange, the color can vary from pale shell to deep red; in cream, the color can vary from creamy-white to rich warm cream.

GOLDEN COLOR

The golden group is similar in appearance to the above colors, except that the effect is not created by the inhibitor gene. The ground color is a rich cream rather than white; this

Some breeds, such as the Maine Coon (above) go through seasonal variations in coat thickness and length.

wildcat. The gene for long hair appears to have originated in southern Russia, where it spread to Turkey and Iran and eventually developed into the breeds we know as the Persian and Angora. To have long hair, a cat must possess two copies of the recessive longhair gene (l). This gene appears to increase the period of hair growth so that the fur reaches a longer length before the dormant phase begins.

Whatever the length of the coat, all cats, except for certain Rex breeds and the Sphynx, have three kinds of hairs: guard, awn, and down. The guard hairs, which are the least numerous of the three types, are long and stiff and cover the top layer of the cat's coat. The guard hairs help keep the cat dry by protecting the downy underlying hairs. These hairs also have attached *arrector pili* muscles that contract when the cat is cold, allowing the hairs to fuzz out and provide more insulation. These same muscles make the fur stand up when the cat is frightened or angry to give the cat the illusion of size.

The down and awn hairs are also called the secondary hairs or the undercoat and are more numerous than the protective guard hairs. The

effect is created by a group of polygenes that increases the yellow pigmentation in agouti hairs. It can be seen in the Persian breed, where the long fur gives this color a particularly spectacular look.

COAT

Here cats can be divided into two general classifications: longhairs and shorthairs. However, domestic cats evolved from the shorthaired African

41

Sphynx cats are not truly hairless. A fine down covers most of their skin.

awn hairs are thin and usually have stiff pointed ends, and the baby-fine down hairs have a soft, wavy texture. The down is the most numerous of the hairs, and it also mats the easiest.

The thickness and length of the coat changes from season to season, typically reaching its heaviest and longest length in the winter. In the fall, the summer coat is shed, and the awn and down hairs become more numerous to provide warmth and insulation in preparation for the cold winter months. In the spring, the thicker undercoat is shed to prepare for the warm season. The cat's hair growth and shedding cycle respond to the photoperiod (the length of daylight to which the cat is exposed). The photoperiod affects outdoor cats to a greater extent than indoor cats, whose cycles are affected by the indoor lights. Indoor cats shed more hair all year round because of this, although they do go through the two major shedding cycles as well.

Polygenes influence the length and texture of the hair and are responsible for the considerable variation in coat type. A pedigreed cat's coat is usually substantially different from a mixed-breed's coat since selective breeding and polygenes have changed the texture, length, number of hair fibers, and other properties of the fur. For example, the Persian's coat has been refined so that the down hairs are almost as long as the guard hairs, giving the coat a particularly soft, silky texture. The fur can be as much as 8 inches (20 cm) long. The coat is beautiful to look at; however it's impossible for the cat to groom such long hair without help from its human companions. Other breeds, such as the Angora and Balinese, although considered long-hairs, have silky coats largely lacking the easily matted downy undercoat, and the length is much shorter than the Persian's.

Genetic mutation can alter the coat's properties. Spontaneous mutations occur now and then within the cat gene pool, and sometimes they survive long enough for the cats to become distinct breeds. The Cornish Rex, Devon Rex, Selkirk Rex, American Wirehair, and Sphynx are the five most prominent breeds with uniquely mutated coats. Rex breeds (see the breed profiles for specifics) have short curly or wavy coats. Both the Cornish and the Devon mutations are governed by recessive genes—Rex genes (r) and (re), respectively. Both create similar changes in the coat. The Cornish Rex completely lacks guard hairs. The soft awn and down hairs make up the Cornish coat, and form a tight, uniform wave that lies close to the body. The Devon's coat contains all three hair types, but the guard hairs are typically fragile and stunted and the whisker hairs are often missing altogether. The genes seem to affect the body type as well, since Rex kittens also have different conformation types.

The Selkirk Rex's coat is produced by a dominant gene and affects the guard, down, and awn hairs, giving the cat a distinctly curly coat. Unlike the Cornish and Devon Rex, the Selkirk comes in both longhair and shorthair varieties. Rex mutations have been seen in many species, including rabbits, mice, and horses.

The American Wirehair's hairs are crimped, curled, hooked, or bent, resulting in a dense, resilient coat that leads to a ringlet formation rather than waves. Like the Selkirk Rex, the Wirehair gene is dominant.

Perhaps the most dramatic coat mutation is hairlessness, as can be seen in the Sphynx. The Sphynx, however, is not the first instance of hairlessness. This mutation has been seen in various locations around the world since at least the early 1900s, and at least three distinct mutations have been noted. The first real attempt to develop this mutation into a distinct breed began in Canada, where it was also called the Canadian Hairless. Hairless cats are not completely hairless; their skin, or parts of it, is covered with a vestigial covering of fine down. The gene that governs the Sphynx's hairlessness is a recessive gene (hr) and can be considered a genetic disorder since the cat is more susceptible to heat, cold, and sunburn.

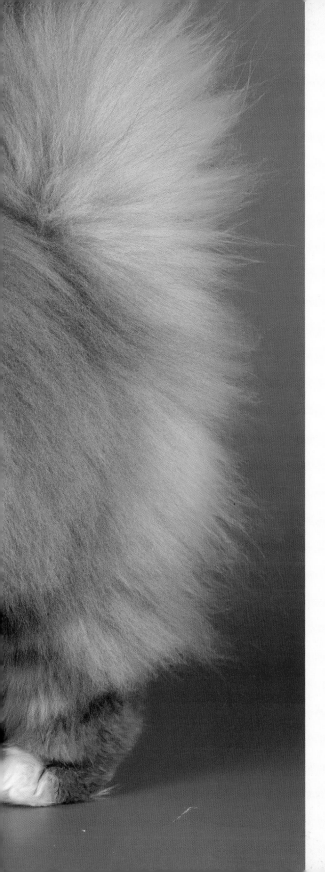

CHAPTER FIVE

THE CAT FANCY

"Who can believe that there is no soul behind those luminous eyes!"
—Theophile Gautier

THE CAT FANCY

HISTORY OF THE CAT FANCY

The term "cat fancy" has become the common term used to describe the group of people interested in and involved with showing or breeding cats. It can also be used in a broader way—to describe those who fancy their feline friends. At any rate, the habit of showing cats and entering them into competition is a very recent development, in the greater scheme of things. While the earliest recorded cat show was held in England at the St. Giles Fair, Winchester, in 1598, it was not until the mid-1800s that people began taking a serious interest in showing their cats. The first cat show as we know them today was held in 1871 at the Crystal Palace in

Sydenham, London. The show was staged by Harrison Weir, a noted cat enthusiast whom many regard as the father of the cat fancy. The show featured British Shorthairs, Persians, and Angoras, as well as Siamese; 170 cats in all were present. The show was such a success that exhibiting pedigreed cats suddenly became all the rage among the upper classes in the United Kingdom. In Britain in 1887 Weir helped form the National Cat Club. The club instituted a system of recording the ancestry of purebred cats and set up a purebred cat registration system. In 1910 the Governing Council of the Cat Fancy (GCCF) was formed to keep the registers of the breeds, to license and control cat shows, to insure that the rules of the organiza-

Exhibitors at cat show.

tion were not broken, and to protect and promote pedigreed cats.

Another prominent European association is the Fédération Internationale Féline (FIFe), which refers to itself as "the United Nations of Cat Federations." Officially founded in 1950 in Ghent, Belgium, at the time of this writing it has member organizations in 40 countries around the world. The member organizations follow the same rules and uphold the same values regarding breed standards, shows, and judges.

In the late 1800s cat shows in New England featured mostly Maine Coons, an all-American breed. At that time, American cat lovers caught the cat fancy fever as well and, emulating European cat shows, began breeding and showing European breeds. Persians and Angoras began appearing on the American scene and in short order became more popular than American breeds. The first American all-breed cat show was held in 1895 in New York's Madison Square Garden. Since then, more and more fanciers have caught the fever and the cat fancy has grown and flourished into the thriving phenomenon it is today.

CAT ASSOCIATIONS

When the cat fancy began, no North American cat registries existed, and stud books were kept for a time by a branch of the government. Soon after, however, cat organizations and governing bodies formed to keep records of offspring produced by pedigreed cats. The first North American association, the American Cat Association (ACA), was incorporated in 1904, although shows were held for some years before that time. Today, many cat associations and organizations exist, and many differences between the associations, but they all share the same basic goals— the improvement and preservation of recognized cat breeds and the promotion and welfare of all domestic cats. The associations keep stud books and records, register pedigreed cats that are accepted members of recognized breeds, sanction shows, track points and grant titles, provide information for breeders and training for judges, communicate with cat associations in other countries, maintain websites for their members and the general public, educate cat owners, and further cat welfare and causes. Some produce publications for their members. All associations have codes of ethics or policies to help maintain humane standards.

One of the most important functions of the associations is to keep records, which is why such organizations are called "registries." The purpose of registering pedigreed cats is to give breeders a recorded history of their breed and of their individual bloodlines, and thereby ensure the show-quality offspring can be registered and shown.

The American Cat Association (ACA) is the oldest existing North American association and registry. The ACA was originally associated with the Beresford Cat Club of Chicago, which formed in 1897 and sponsored one of the first cat shows held

Cat show judge evaluates a white Persian.

in the United States in 1899. The Beresford Cat Club also started the first North American cat stud book, and established the first show rules. In 1904 some members of the Beresford Cat Club split away and incorporated the American Cat Association. Their original goal was to connect with other cat clubs in North America and develop ties so all could share their stud book registry. Although now a small association, the ACA is the longest standing association in North America and has an active following of fanciers.

The Cat Fanciers' Association (CFA) was founded in 1906, and licensed its first two cat shows the same year. CFA held its first annual meeting in 1907 at Madison Square Garden, New York. In 1909, CFA published the first volume of its stud book in book form, and also published its stud book and register in the *Cat Journal Magazine*. It incorporated in 1919 in New York State. Since then, CFA has grown steadily to become the largest association in North America, and has member clubs and sanctioned cat shows all around the world, including Brazil, Bulgaria, Canada, China, France, Germany, Hong Kong, Indonesia, Italy, Japan, Malaysia, Russia, South Korea, Spain, Sweden, Taiwan, and Thailand, among many others. CFA's main objectives are improving and advancing the breeds CFA accepts (and those they may accept in the future); maintaining high quality registration records and breed standards by carefully registering or recording the names and/or pedigrees of the cats and kittens the association recognizes; licensing cat clubs that hold the cat shows and conveying the official CFA rules to such clubs; promoting breeder and exhibitor concerns and interests; and preserving high qualification criteria for CFA's judges, who must complete an exhaustive training program so they are well qualified to assess the association's pedigreed and household pet cats. CFA also has high standards for its clerking program. Also, CFA has a long history supporting feline health research, and breeder, exhibitor, and cat owner education, and the association cares about the welfare of all cats, pedigreed and otherwise. For example, in 1968 CFA founded the Winn Feline Foundation to fund medical research, improve cat health, and award grants for studies on a variety of cat health issues, which helps find solutions to cat illnesses and diseases. Unlike many of the other associations, CFA doesn't recognize any breed that was originated from a hybrid of a wild cat and a domestic cat; that's the reason the very popular Bengal (among other breeds) is not accepted in CFA.

The Cat Fanciers' Federation (CFF) formed in 1919 in Rhode Island, making it one of the oldest cat associations. Its judges and clubs are in northeastern portions of the United States, and therefore its shows are held in those areas. The member clubs hold the shows and, in the past, fanciers would join the clubs rather than the association. Now, however, cat fanciers can become individual members of the association itself, or join a local member club, or both. One of CFF's main focuses, besides upholding high cat fancy standards, is to be known as "The Friendly Cat Club," enjoying the company and friendship of other members and their cats, and encouraging friendly competition. This association strives to bring all members together into one big family, while still taking the welfare of pedigree cats, the cat fancy, and domestic cats in general very seriously. CFF holds most of its shows in the Northeast.

The American Cat Fanciers Association (ACFA) formed in 1955 in the Dallas and Fort Worth area. The association's originators wanted to establish a democratic form of management in which the members approve changes in show or registration rules. They wanted the members to dictate ACFA's future, rather than the board of directors, the clubs, or the commit-

Cat shows can be lavish affairs with hundreds of cats, exhibitors, and spectators.

tees. In addition, ACFA was the first association to accept altered cats for championship competition and the first to require judges to pass written exams before becoming licensed. Their overall mission is to provide friendly, accurate, professional services to their customers and members; they consider the members their most valuable asset. Member elections are held to select representatives for the board of directors, and the members propose and approve amendments to the association rules. In addition, the member breeders and exhibitors vote on their breed committees and on any potential changes to their specific breed's standards. Similar to CFF, they call themselves "The Friendly Association," with the objective of being the fairest, friendliest, and most fun feline association. Their main goal is promoting the welfare of all domesticated, pedigreed and non-pedigreed cats, and to support and educate breeders, owners, cat exhibitors, and the cat-loving public. Their shows are generally held in Midwest and Northeast states, with some shows in Maryland and Florida, and some areas of Canada.

The Canadian Cat Association (CCA) formed in 1961 and is the only Canadian cat association and registry. In 1960, a small group of Canadian cat fanciers got together and began creating the CCA, so Canadian cat shows could have their own rules and be registered in Canada. Before CCA-affiliated clubs were formed and official show rules were published in 1961, all pedigree Canadian cats were registered in the United States or Europe, and all Canadian cat shows were governed by the American cat association rules. The founding fanciers formed the CCA to promote the welfare of all Canadian cats, maintain a pedigreed cat registry, and improve all breeds of cats in Canada. Originally the association held most of its shows in Ontario and Quebec, but at the time of this writing the CCA has affiliated cat clubs across Canada. Since 1960, the CCA has grown in size and quality, and the association plans to continue to follow its founders' dreams to provide the Canadian cat fancy with an association that is governed by its members and is committed to the well-being of all cats, both pedigree and household pets.

The International Cat Association (TICA) was formed in 1979 by a handful of cat lovers whose dream was to build the most progressive, innovative, and flexible cat registry in the world—an association that would be run by and for its members. TICA broke new ground in the way cats were shown and registered, largely because it was organized after feline genetics was better understood. TICA registers its cats according to their genetic makeup (genotype), but shows its cats according to their physical appearance (phenotype). In other words, if a Himalayan cat has Persian in its ancestry, it is shown as a Himalayan, but is part of the Persian breed group (which includes Persians, Himalayans, and Exotic Shorthairs), and the Himalayan's registration number would reveal the Persian ancestry. Since 1979, TICA has grown and matured; TICA is the second-largest association in North America. The association

The Extreme Siamese (left) and the Old-Style Siamese (right). The Extreme is favored in the show halls, but the Old-Style has made strides in gaining acceptance in the mainstream cat fancy.

not only is represented by TICA members and chartered clubs in all 50 U.S. states, but also has clubs and members in countries around the world, including Argentina, Austria, Belarus, Belgium, Brazil, Canada, Colombia, Denmark, Estonia, Finland, France, Germany, Japan, Poland, Russia, United Kingdom, and Uruguay, among many others. Breeders, exhibitors, and cat fanciers join TICA rather than the chartered clubs; the clubs do not vote on association matters or in the elections. Rather, the members vote on these issues. TICA judges must complete extensive apprenticeships and examinations before being qualified to judge TICA cat shows. TICA also prides itself on being the world's largest registry of random-bred cats and

kittens. Household pets, even if (especially if) adopted from shelters or rescued from abandonment, can and do compete for titles and awards, just like the pedigreed cats. In addition, TICA encourages altering all cats not being used in breeding programs to cut down on the domestic cat overpopulation problem. TICA's mission is to encourage members to be responsible owners and breeders and to promote alter awareness; to preserve the pedigreed cat breeds; to maintain the most accurate, comprehensive registry in the world; to provide professional sanctioned cat shows that promote pedigreed and random-bred cats; to foster responsible cat health and welfare legislation; and to distribute information to breeders, exhibitors, cat owners, and

Cat breed judge evaluating an Exotic Shorthair show cat.

the general public regarding breeding, exhibition, and the care and welfare of random-bred cats.

The American Association of Cat Enthusiasts, Inc. (AACE), founded in New Jersey in 1993, is the second newest North American cat organization. One of the smaller associations, AACE usually licenses shows in the Mid-Atlantic U.S. states of New York, New Jersey, and Pennsylvania. The founding fanciers' main goals in creating AACE were to make sure exhibitors get fair appraisals of their cats while providing a rewarding and fun show experience in the process, something members claim is missing in some other associations. While AACE strives to have one of the friendliest groups of exhibitors and judges around, willing to

take time to talk to visitors and advise new or aspiring breeders and exhibitors, they also they take their commitment to the association and the advancement of the pedigreed breeds seriously. They strive to ensure judges are treated fairly and not pressured by political factions within the association and the cat fancy in general. Unlike some of the other associations, breeders and exhibitors pay a yearly fee to become members of the association itself, rather than join the cat clubs licensed by AACE. The members vote on additions or changes to AACE's by-laws, giving each member a say in how the association is governed. The licensed show clubs vote on the show rules, however, with the understanding that no new rules will place a burden on the clubs or add fees that will be passed onto the membership. Breed clubs, made up of members who have registered at least one cat of that breed, vote on breed standard changes.

The United Feline Organization (UFO), founded and incorporated in Washington State in 1994, is the newest North American cat registry. Their first show was held in 1995. A relatively small association, the founding members originally formed UFO to provide a professional association in which breeders and exhibitors can have fun while pursuing their passion for exhibiting and breeding pedigreed and household pet cats. UFO strives to provide an alternative to cat lovers who were tired of the sometimes adversarial competition members found in some associations. This close-knit fellowship of fanciers considers their members one large, cat-loving family, offering support, friendship, fair evaluations of the exhibitors' cats, and mutual respect for members and judges. Fanciers can join the association itself for a small yearly fee; after two years of consecutive membership members can vote on the board of directors, the officers, and the bylaws. The board of directors is responsible for UFO's business operations, which includes chartering cat clubs. Member cat clubs are responsible for holding shows, and for sending one representative to the annual meeting to propose, alter, or terminate show rules or the bylaws. Breed committees, composed of member breeders/exhibitors, are responsible for creating and maintaining the breed standard for their breed and the registration rules, within UFO's guidelines. At the time of this writing, shows are sponsored by cat clubs in Washington State and Florida. UFO accepts any color genetically possible for the breeds they recognize for exhibition.

WHY SO MANY CAT REGISTRIES?

Why do we have so many registries for cats? In the dog fancy, three main registries exist in North America: the American Kennel Club (AKC), the United Kennel Club (UKC), and the Canadian Kennel Club (CKC). For cats, the eight previously mentioned registries exist, but some are larger, older, better known, and are found in more locations; they sponsor more shows and are generally better organized than the smaller asso-

ciations. Many of these associations were formed because of differences of opinions about how the associations should be run or which pedigreed breeds should be accepted. For example, in 1906 a group of ACA members broke away and formed CFA for such reasons. In 1919 a group of CFA members separated from that association and formed CFF. The ACFA formed in 1955, and a group of members broke away in 1979 to form TICA. That's the main reason so many exist today; virtually all of the associations were formed to offer something the founding members thought was lacking in the other associations of the cat fancy.

It's not surprising, therefore, that each association has its own set of rules and regulations governing the showing and registering of pedigreed and household pet (HHP) cats. A copy of the breed standards, show rules, bylaws, and other information can be obtained from most of the associations' Web sites (see Additional Information, page 374). Differences of opinion are not unique to the cat fancy, but are inherent in the dog fancy as well, and in fact any group of humans who feel passionately about a given topic.

CAT SHOWS

From its humble beginnings in London in 1871, the cat fancy has grown in size, scope, and popularity, and has spread to every continent in the world except Antarctica. Cat shows are held in North America, Canada, South America, Africa, Australia, New Zealand, Russia, most European countries, and many Asian

A typical cage in a cat show benching area, decorated and furnished for safety, eye appeal, and comfort.

countries, such as China and Japan. Hundreds of cat shows take place every weekend of the year; almost every weekend a cat show will be taking place somewhere in North America. Even if you don't plan to show, go to at least one for the experience. Cat shows are great places to meet like-minded people, see quality examples of the breeds, and gather valuable information about pedigreed cats and cats in general. If you are looking for a particular breed, cat shows are also excellent places to see show-quality examples of the breeds and to find breeders. This is particularly important if you plan to show your cat. The best way to obtain a show-quality pedigreed cat or kitten is by doing your homework (reading the breed profile and standard, and gathering as much information as you can about your breed),

and then going to shows and getting to know the breeders, judges, and exhibitors (see Chapter Ten). You will become more knowledgeable about the breeds, and understand more about the standards by which they are judged, by talking with show participants.

Also, the experience you gain from being around breeders and exhibitors is invaluable. Most fanciers, if approached politely when they aren't scrambling to get their cats to the show ring, are happy to answer questions and talk about their cats. Cat judges are also good sources of information; they receive a great deal of training and practical experience before they begin their judging careers, and are often breeders of long experience as well. If you are courteous and they have time, they'll be willing to answer your questions.

HOW A SHOW WORKS

A cat show is an event where exhibitors enter their cats in judged competition to compete for wins, ribbons, and titles. Generally, two types of cat shows exist: specialty, in which either longhaired or shorthaired breeds are exhibited and judged, and all-breed, shows in which all breeds that are accepted by the sponsoring association can be exhibited and judged. Some shows also have experimental classes, where new cat breeds (or new colors not yet accepted within established breeds) can gain exposure and be presented to exhibitors and judges without being required to compete.

To compete in a show, a pedigreed cat must be registered with the association sponsoring the show, be vaccinated and free of parasites, and must not be declawed (except in AACE, ACFA, and TICA). The claws must be clipped before the show for the safety of the judges. No pregnant or lactating cats are allowed, and if entered will be disqualified. Because cat and cattery owners are protective of their cats and concerned about their continued good health, all cats entered in the show must be healthy. No cats or kittens can be entered in any show if their cattery or home has had any infectious or contagious illnesses or diseases within four weeks of the first day of the show. Any cat showing signs of illness can be disqualified and removed from the show hall. The threat of contagion is very real; some diseases can be passed from hand contact with a contagious cat—that's why most exhibitors will not let you touch or handle their cats.

Cats are registered in one of three show classes: non-championship, championship, and alter (known as premiership in CFA). The championship class is divided into two divisions: championship (unaltered cats of either gender), and alter or premier (altered cats of either gender). Alter or premier classes are for spayed and neutered cats that would, as whole (unaltered) cats, be eligible for championship status. The alter classes have the same eligibility requirements as the championship classes.

In the championship class, three classes exist: open class, for whole or altered cats eight months or older that have not met the requirements for championship; champion class, for whole or altered cats that have met the requirements for championship but haven't met the requirements for the title of grand champion; and grand champion class, for whole or altered cats that have met the requirements for, or that have achieved, one or more grand championships.

The non-championship classes are usually separated into five divisions: kitten class (cats between four and eight months old at the time of the show); any other variety (AOV) class (any registered pedigreed cat or kitten that qualifies for championship or alter competition but does not conform to the standard in color or coat); provisional or new breed or color (NBC) class (breeds not currently accepted for championship or alter status but that have a preliminary breed standard approved); miscellaneous or non-competitive class (breeds not accepted for provisional or NBC breed competition); and the household pet (HHP) class.

Each breed is judged according to the breed standard of the association that sponsored the show. The breed standard is an ideal for which to strive; very few cats meet it precisely. The cat that is judged to be closest to the ideal—the best specimen of the breed entered in each ring—is awarded a win, and points are awarded based on the number of cats entered in the ring. Although the breed's attributes are given a certain number of points in the standard, keep in mind that judges do not think in terms of the points when judging; they don't mentally add or subtract points for perfections or faults. The purpose of the points in a standard is to emphasize the features breeders regard as essential to the breed's appearance. Points are a tool judges use to determine the importance of each attribute in each particular breed.

Since breed standards can differ from association to association, sometimes greatly when it comes to the accepted colors, most exhibitors show with only one or two associations. Exhibitors must be familiar with all registration requirements, show rules, and association bylaws, in order to comply with the necessary regulations.

Usually, both qualified pedigreed (champion and alter class) and household pet (HHP) cats are admissible, although the rules regarding HHPs vary by association; some associations are more HHP-friendly than others. A non-pedigreed cat, a part-purebred kitten or cat, or a pedigreed cat that is not show quality can be shown in the Household Pet (HHP) category (see Chapter Eight).

The first thing you'll notice upon entering a cat show is rows and rows of cages, all containing beautiful examples of the breeds. The area in which these cages are located is called the benching area. This is where the cats stay between judgings. The sponsoring cat club provides all of the cages and tables and (usually) the litter boxes and the food for the cats. Most exhibitors, however, dress up their cages with pillows, curtains, beds, and other goodies to keep the cats comfortable and visually isolated from the other felines.

The ring area, usually along the sides, in the middle, or at the ends of the room, is where the cats are taken to be judged. When the cat's number is called, the exhibitor takes the cat to the appropriate show ring and puts it into one of the cages behind the judging table. The numbers placed on the top of the cages correspond to the cats' entry numbers listed in the show catalog. The cages are sanitized before a new cat is placed inside to prevent the spread of disease.

The cats are taken out of the cages and judged by a select group of experienced judges.

The qualifications necessary to become a judge vary by association, but in general it takes many years to become a judge. Not only does a judge have to have bred, shown, and championed pedigreed cats, in many associations he or she must have to have served as an entry clerk, show manager, master clerk, and judge trainee. Some associations require judges to pass written exams. By the time a person is experienced enough to serve as a judge, he or she is extremely knowledgeable about the breeds, the association, and the cat fancy. Judges are designated either "allbreed" or "specialty." An allbreed judge is qualified to judge all breeds against each other; specialty judges handle either longhair cats or shorthairs.

Each cat is first judged according to its own breed standard, and then is judged against all the cats in the ring. After all the cats have been judged, the judge hangs ribbons on the cages of the cats who earned awards, and the cats are removed to their benching cages. When all the cats in the color, breed, and division are judged, the "finals" begin, where the judge chooses the ten best cats in order of quality, as long as enough cats were entered. This number varies by association; if not enough cats were entered, the number of best

cats is reduced accordingly. The winning cats are called back into the ring so that their rosettes can be awarded. Specialty judges give out two sets of finals for each category, one for each hair length, while allbreed judges present only one set of finals per breed or division. Generally, wins made in the championship classes are not transferable to the alter classes. If a Champion cat is later altered, however, he retains his previously won titles.

The associations total the wins so at the end of each show season, the cats with the most points for that season are given end-of-year awards; in CFA this is called the National Winner award; other associations have similar end of season awards. Awards are also given regionally in the associations large enough to have regional districts.

Children asking a breeder questions at a cat show.

CHAPTER SIX

THE RECOGNIZED BREEDS

"Cats are a mysterious kind of folk. There is more passing in their minds than we are aware of."
—Sir Walter Scott

THE RECOGNIZED BREEDS

INTRODUCTION

The following is an exploration of the current accepted championship cat breeds of North America. Three areas are covered in each profile: history, personality, and conformation. Also provided is a chart in which various characteristics are rated on a scale of 1 to 10 (1 means the breed exhibits the least amount of this characteristic; 10 means the breed exhibits the most of this characteristic). These characteristics can vary from cat to cat and from breeder to breeder, but the ratings serve as a guide to help you get an overall picture of the breeds to help you determine which breed is right for you. Keep in mind that these are general ratings and that individual members of any breed may not follow true to form. Bloodlines may differ, environmental conditions can play a role, and geographical regions also can play a part in the overall characteristics.

In the chart, "activity level" relates to the amount of hustle and bustle to which the cat is prone. A breed with a rating of 10 is likely to be animated, busy, and forever underfoot, whereas a breed with a rating of 1 tends to be relaxed and sedentary. "Playfulness" relates to the cat's desire to play with its human companions and with other animals. Most cats exhibit some playfulness, but some breeds have a greater need for this kind of contact with their owners. A breed with a high rating needs more playtime than a breed with a low rating. "Need for attention" describes the breed's overall demand for human interaction. Some breeds seem to get by quite well if left alone for periods of time and rate low in this charac-teristic, whereas others can pine or even become depressed if left alone too much, earning a high rating. The rating in the "affection toward its owners" category tells you if this breed tends to be loving and devoted or reserved and remote. A high rating indicates a highly affectionate breed. "Vocality" indicates the amount of vocalizing the breed is likely to do. Some breeds, such as the Siamese, tend to keep up a running dialogue with their owners, earning a high rating, whereas others, such as the Chartreux, vocalize very little, earning a low rating for this characteristic. "Docility" indicates how amenable the breed is to handling. A high rating indicates a breed that tends not to object to handling and routine care. Keep in mind, however, that any cat will defend itself if it feels threatened. Don't count on a high rating to protect you if you handle a cat roughly. "Intelligence" relates to, of course, the general amount of mental capacity the breed tends to exhibit, and a high rating indicates high intelligence. "Independence" relates to the breed's desire for human contact. A breed with a high rating will be less dependent upon humans; a breed with a low rating desires a strong connection with its human. "Healthiness and hardiness" indicates the breed's overall vigor, strength, and vitality. A high rating indicates a breed with few inherent weaknesses. "Need for grooming" is self-explanatory; a high rating means that you'll spend a lot of quality time grooming your feline buddy. "Compatibility with children" indicates how well the breed tolerates children's sometimes rambunctious antics; a high rating means that this breed would be a good choice for a household with children. Likewise, "Compatibility with other pets" indicates how well the breed gets along with other animals. A high rating means that the breed should integrate well into a household with existing pets, although this also depends on the compatibility of the existing pets.

Keep in mind that cats require effort to become the best companions they can be. For example, just because a cat breed has an affection rating of 9 doesn't mean that a member of the breed will give you its devotion if you ignore or mistreat it. Cats will meet you halfway if you give them a chance, but you must earn their trust and loyalty in order to have the closest relationship possible.

Not all cat breeds are accepted in all associations because of differing policies or lack of breeder involvement; breeders and fanciers must actively promote their breeds in each association and satisfy the requirements in order for acceptance to be granted. For example, the popular Bengal, first developed from a leopard cat and domestic cat union, is not and may never be recognized in CFA because of concerns about breeding domestic cats with wild cats. Other associations accept domestic and wild hybrids, with differing rules on how many generations away from any wild blood show cats must be. Because of these differences in recognition, each profile notes which associations recognize the breed at the time of this writing.

The conformation standards provide aesthetic guidelines that define an ideal specimen of the breed. They are goals for which to strive rather than descriptions of all cats of that breed. Overall balance, artistic harmony, and proportion can be as important as the proper ear set and head shape. The standards not only provide general guidelines that define an ideal specimen, they also define characteristics that penalize or disqualify cats from show competition. Although not always noted in the standards, in general the following characteristics are grounds for penalty or disqualification in most breeds: kinked or abnormal tail (except in breeds known for their abnormal tail types), incorrect number of toes, crossed eyes, any evidence of illness or poor health, flabbiness or emaciation, signs of weakness in hindquarters, and defects, such as malocclusions, breathing difficulties, and deformity of the skull. Declawed cats are disqualified except in AACE, ACFA, and TICA. Allowances are usually made for jowls and larger physical size in male cats.

The associations vary in the number of breeds they recognize. This depends on the number of breeds accepted, but also upon the way longhairs and shorthairs are counted. For example, all associations accept the Abyssinian and the Somali as separate breeds, since the longhaired Somali was developed from shorthaired Abyssinian lines many years after the Aby was accepted for championship. Other breeds, such as the Scottish Fold and the Highland Fold, are grouped in the same breed division by some associations, while others count them as separate breeds. When a longhaired or shorthaired version of a breed has a different history and/or different body conformation than its counterpart, it is generally profiled separately in this book. The CFA standards have been used for the conformation section unless otherwise noted. Many of the conformation terms are defined in the glossary.

HISTORY

The Abyssinian is unquestionably one of the oldest known breeds, but no one knows positively when or where it originated. Some fanciers think the Aby's ancestors came from Abyssinia (now Ethiopia), and was named for that country. Other fanciers think the breed originated on the coast of the Indian Ocean and in parts of Southeast Asia; recent genetic studies indicate today's Abyssinian may have descended from a type of cat found in those areas.

The best known tale is that today's Aby is a descendant of the sacred cats worshiped as the physical manifestations of the gods in the temples and palaces of the ancient Egyptians some 4,000 to 6,000 years ago. Abyssinians do look like the cats depicted in Egyptian murals and sculptures, but so does the African wildcat (*Felis silvestris lybica*), the species known to have been mummified by the ancient Egyptians and from which feline experts believe all domestic cats arose.

Blue Abyssinian. Abyssinians are known for their lively temperaments.

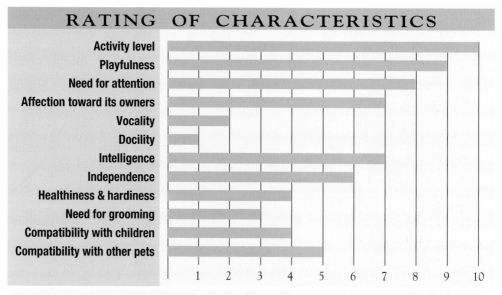

RATING OF CHARACTERISTICS

Characteristic	Rating (1–10)
Activity level	10
Playfulness	9
Need for attention	8
Affection toward its owners	7
Vocality	2
Docility	1
Intelligence	7
Independence	6
Healthiness & hardiness	4
Need for grooming	3
Compatibility with children	4
Compatibility with other pets	5

1—breed exhibits the least amount of this characteristic, 10—breed exhibits the most of this characteristic

❋ **Championship status in all associations**

A cat named Zula owned by Mrs. Captain Barrett-Lennard was transported from Abyssinia to England at the end of the Abyssinian War in 1868, according to Dr. William Gordon Staples in his 1874 book, *Cats: Their Points and Characteristics, with Curiosities of Cat Life*, but whether Zula was an Abyssinian is subject to debate. The illustration of Zula shows a cat with very small ears and a head type unlike the Aby's. Since there's no written evidence linking Zula with today's breed, some breeders maintain that the original lines died out, and the Abyssinian was recreated by British breeders from existing British Bunny cats that have Abyssinian-like ticking. Without question, the breed was promoted and refined by early British fanciers until World War II decimated the breed, forcing British breeders to start over from scratch.

Wherever the breed came from originally, the Abyssinian was exhibited in the first modern-day cat show held in 1971 at London's Crystal Palace. The show was staged by Harrison Weir, a cat lover whom many regard as the father of the cat fancy. An Abyssinian placed third out of the approximately 160 entries, showing that even at the cat fan-

cy's infancy the Aby was appreciated for its beauty and grace. In Harrison Weir's 1889 book, *Our Cats and All About Them*, he writes that the cats imported from Abyssinia were of stouter build than the English variety, with fewer markings.

Two Abyssinians arrived in America from England in the early 1900s and were first exhibited in 1909. However, the Abyssinians who became the foundation stock for today's North American breed were imported from Britain in the 1930s. At that time active breeding of Abyssinians began, and breeders made up for lost time. The breed gained popularity as cat lovers discovered the Aby's beauty and acrobatic antics. Today, the Abyssinian one of the most popular shorthairs.

PERSONALITY

Abyssinians aren't for those who want decorative cats to match the rust-colored carpet, or for those who want cats that enjoy being picked up and cuddled. Courageous, curious, and high-spirited, when restrained Abys tend to become struggling bundles of fur with more than the usual number of elbows. However, that's not to say Abyssinians are aloof or standoffish; they're affection-

Ruddy Abyssinian.

ate, devoted, and loving companions. They just aren't lap cats, and prefer to sit next to you rather than on you. Nevertheless, they'll follow you from room to room to keep an eye on what you're doing. While Abyssinians will cheerfully entertain themselves, they are most happy when involved in every aspect of your life. They are particularly involved at dinnertime. In fact, you'll know it's dinnertime when small, furry, food-seeking missiles attach themselves to your legs.

Abyssinians regularly perform antics for your—and their—amusement, earning them the reputation of the clowns of the cat kingdom. They perch on shoulders, crawl under covers, and sit beside you purring madly before racing off to bat imaginary butterflies and make flying leaps at the tallest bookcases. Natural athletes, no closed room or cupboard is safe from their agile paws and inquiring minds. Vocally they tend to be quiet, or they might be too intense as companions with their warp-speed activity levels. They purr with great enthusiasm, however, particularly around dinner

time. If you'll be away all day earning the cat food, provide a cat companion to keep your Aby entertained or she will become bored and may get into things you'd rather she didn't. If you work all day and have an active social life at night, a more sedate breed would be a better choice.

CONFORMATION

The Abyssinian is a ticked or agouti breed. The distinctive coat appearance comes from the combination of colors on each hair shaft (see Chapter Four, page 32). The lighter or ground color lies closest to the skin, and each hair shaft has dark-colored bands that are contrasted with lighter-colored bands. The hair shaft ends with a dark tip.

Abyssinians have few genetic defects but, like their longhaired cousin the Somali, are prone to plaque, tartar buildup, and gingivitis. Untreated, gingivitis can lead to the dental disease periodontitis that can lead to tooth, tissue, and bone loss, which can undermine an Aby's overall health. Renal amyloidosis, a hereditary disease that can lead to kidney failure, and PK deficiency have been found in some Aby lines. Some breeders screen for PK deficiency; be sure to ask, and get a written health guarantee from your breeder.

Red Abyssinian. Abyssinians are known as the clowns of the cat fancy.

GENERAL	The ideal Abyssinian is a colorful cat with a distinctly ticked coat, medium in size and regal in appearance; lithe, hard and muscular, showing eager activity and lively interest in surroundings. Well balanced temperamentally and physically.
BODY	Medium long, lithe, and graceful, showing well developed muscular strength without coarseness; conformation strikes a medium between extremes of cobby and svelte lengthy type. Proportion and general balance more desired than size.
HEAD	Modified, slightly rounded wedge without flat planes; brow, cheek, and profile lines all showing gentle contour. Slight rise from bridge of nose to forehead, of good size, with width between ears and flowing into arched neck without a break. Muzzle not sharply pointed or square; chin neither receding nor protruding.
EARS	Alert, large, and moderately pointed; broad and cupped at base, set as though listening. Hair on ears very short and close lying.
EYES	Almond-shaped, large, brilliant, and expressive. Neither round nor Oriental. Eyes accentuated by fine dark line, encircled by light colored area. Eye color gold or green, the more richness and depth of color the better.
LEGS AND PAWS	Legs and feet proportionately slim, fine boned; stands well off the ground giving impression of being on tip toe. Paws small, oval, and compact. Toes five in front and four behind.
TAIL	Thick at base, fairly long and tapering.
COAT	Soft, silky, fine in texture, dense and resilient to the touch with lustrous sheen; medium in length but long enough to accommodate two or three dark bands of ticking.
COLOR	Ruddy, red (cinnamon gene; also called sorrel), blue, and fawn. In England, Australia, and New Zealand, a fifth color, silver, has been accepted.
DISQUALIFY	White anywhere other than nostril, chin, and upper throat; kinked or abnormal tail; dark unbroken necklace. Gray undercoat close to skin extending through a major portion of body; black hair on red Abyssinian; incorrect number of toes; any color other than the four accepted colors.
ALLOWABLE OUTCROSSES	None.

HISTORY

Until quite recently the American Bobtail received little attention from the cat associations, so many people are surprised to learn that this breed has been catting around North America since the 1960s. Because of its haphazard debut, however, the American Bobtail is just now beginning to come into its own and be recognized by the cat fancy.

The American Bobtail began its long road to acceptance in the early 1960s. The original Bobtail was a short-tailed brown tabby male named Yodie, found at an Arizona motel, supposedly dropped off by a child from the nearby Native American reservation. John and Brenda Sanders of Clinton Country, Iowa found Yodie while they were vacationing at the motel. Yodie's parents and ancestry were unknown, but rumor had it he was a bobcat/domestic cat hybrid because of his feral appearance

Shorthaired American Bobtail.

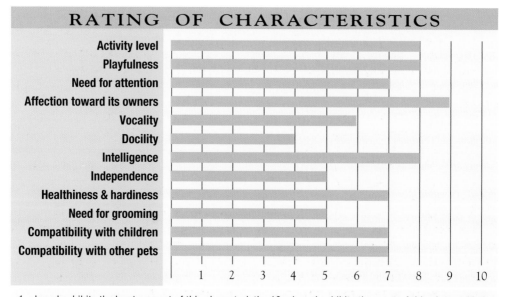

RATING OF CHARACTERISTICS										
	1	2	3	4	5	6	7	8	9	10
Activity level								8		
Playfulness								8		
Need for attention								8		
Affection toward its owners									9	
Vocality						6				
Docility				5						
Intelligence								8		
Independence					5					
Healthiness & hardiness								8		
Need for grooming					5					
Compatibility with children							7			
Compatibility with other pets							7			

1—breed exhibits the least amount of this characteristic, 10—breed exhibits the most of this characteristic

❋ **Championship status in ACFA, CFA, and TICA in both long and short hair lengths; New Breed or Color status in UFO in both long and short hair**

and short, bobcat-like tail. While it's possible for domestic cats to mate with bobcats (*Felis rufus*, an indigenous North American spotted cat closely related to the lynx), such hybrids, particularly the first generation males, would almost certainly be sterile. It's more likely that Yodie's short tail occurred as a spontaneous mutation within the domestic cat population.

Charmed by Yodie's friendly personality and short stub of a tail, John and Brenda Sanders returned home with their unique souvenir. Back in Iowa, Yodie impregnated the Sanders' sealpoint Siamese (proving himself fertile and not half bobcat). This first litter contained some normal-tailed and some bobtailed kittens, suggesting the gene governing Yodie's bobbed tail was dominant, since their Siamese had no history of short-tailed ancestors. Only one copy of a dominant gene was needed for the trait to appear in offspring.

They chose the name American Bobtail for the breed. Mindy Cave, a friend of John and Brenda Sanders and one of the first Bobtail breeders, wrote the first provisional standard in the early 1970s. This standard called for a pointed pattern cat with white mittens, a white facial blaze, blue eyes, long hair, and a bobbed tail. More breeders joined the Bobtail fan club, and Birman, Himalayan, and Himalayan/Siamese crosses were added to the bloodline. However, at that time the breed exper-

ienced setbacks due to the usual obstacles; developing and promoting a new breed of cat is an endeavor that requires the patience of Job, the wealth of Midas, the wisdom of Solomon, and the tenacity of the Terminator.

In addition, early breeders became increasingly frustrated by the complicated combination of genes required to produce cats resembling the standard—pointed pattern, white mittens, facial blaze, blue eyes, long hair, and short tail. Some breeders gave up in disgust. The original lines from Yodie and his descendants became inbred and unhealthy.

In the mid-1980s a group of Bobtail breeders broke away from the breed's blueprint, and took on the task of creating a breed that looked like Yodie: a large, feral-looking tabby with long hair and a bobbed tail. Their goal was to create a breed that resembled the bobcat but came from entirely domestic stock. These breeders chose short-tailed random-bred domestic cats to refurbish the breed. They included no Manx, Japanese Bobtails, or any other pedigreed breeds, nor did they use any short-tailed wildcat species. The new standard called for a slightly rounded brow from forehead to eye ridge; this fleshy brow border creates the prized "hunting gaze" that enhances the breed's feral look. The new conformation was much more successful, not to mention easier to breed. The American Bobtail has been accepted by four North American associations.

GENERAL	American Bobtail is medium to large, naturally occurring, bobtailed cat; athletic animal, well-muscled, with look and feel of power. It possesses a natural hunting gaze that combines with breed's body type and bobtail to give American Bobtail a distinctive wild appearance.
BODY	Moderately long and substantial with a rectangular stance. Chest full and broad. Slightly higher in hips with prominent shoulder blades. Hips substantial almost as wide as chest. Deep flank. Muscular and athletic in appearance. Allowance should be made for slow maturation.
HEAD	Broad modified wedge without noticeable flat planes or doming, in proportion to the body. Cheekbones are apparent. In profile slightly concave curve between nose and brow with good length between brow and ears. Widening of the head and stud jowls apparent in adult males. Brow distinctive, evidenced by a slightly rounded forehead to eye ridge.
EARS	Medium; wide at base with slightly rounded tips, wide-set, upright with a slight outward tilt. Ear tipping and furnishings highly desirable. Lighter colored thumbprints on the back of the ears desirable on all tabbies including lynx points.
EYES	Large, almost almond in shape; deep set; outside corner angled slightly upward towards the ears. Medium-wide apart. Distinctive brow above the eye creates a top line to the eye and produces the breed's natural hunting gaze. All eye colors acceptable; eye color can be copper, gold, yellow, or green; blue in bi-color/van, colorpoint, lynxpoint, or odd-eyed white cats.
LEGS AND PAWS	In proportion to the body, of good length and substantial boning. Paws large and round. Toe tufts desirable in longhaired varieties. Five toes in front, four in back.
TAIL	Tail short, flexible and expressive; may be straight, slightly curved or kinked, or have bumps along length. Set in line with top line of hip. Broad at base, strong and substantial. Straighter tails exhibit fat pad at end of tail. Must be long enough to be clearly visible above back when alert, not to extend past stretched hind hock; no one length preferred.
COAT SHORTHAIR	Length medium, semi-dense; texture non-matting, resilient with slight loft; density-double coat, hard topcoat with a soft, downy undercoat; miscellaneous-seasonal variations of coat should be recognized. Coat may be softer in texture in dilute colors, lynx points and silvers.
COAT LONGHAIR	Length medium-longhair, slightly shaggy; tapering to slightly longer hair on ruff, britches, belly and tail; ruff slight, mutton chops desirable. Texture is non-matting, resilient; density-double coat. Undercoat present, not extremely dense; seasonal variations of coat should be recognized.

COLOR	Any genetically possible color or combination of colors is allowed. Preference shall be given to colors and patterns that enhance the natural wild appearance of the breed.
DISQUALIFY	Total lack of tail or full-length tail. Delicate bone structure. Incorrect number of toes.
ALLOWABLE OUTCROSSES	Domestic longhairs and shorthairs; no tailless cats, recognized breeds, or wild blood permitted.

The three largest North American associations, ACFA, CFA, and TICA, have granted championship status.

The new and improved American Bobtail comes in all colors, categories, and divisions. Breeders now aim for a sweet, domestic cat that has the feral look of the bobcat. Originally recognized only as a longhair, a shorthair version has been accepted for championship in the three associations to grant championship status. Outcrossing the Bobtail to domestic stock is still allowable in some associations. The goal is to keep the gene pool healthy since it is still fairly small.

PERSONALITY

The American Bobtail has a wild look, not a wild temperament, say fanciers. This breed's devoted, loving, and intelligent personality has kept breeders working on the breed throughout the long years of frustration and difficulty. These confident, friendly cats bond emotionally with their human families and become extremely devoted companions that adapt quickly to most home environments. Not as vocal as breeds like the Siamese, Bobtails nevertheless are not shy about making their feelings known.

Bobtails are playful, energetic, and friendly, and possess an uncanny intelligence for Houdini-type escapes from closed rooms and fastened cages. Very people-oriented, they are not above demanding human attention by meowing or commandeering available laps. On the cat activity scale, the Bobtail rates an 8—fun-loving and frisky but not overactive.

American Bobtails usually get along well with other cats and cat-friendly dogs if properly introduced. Instead of hiding under the bed, they are curious and outgoing when unfamiliar humans come to call. If trained from an early age, they tend to be good travelers, which is an advantage for cats that will be shown.

CONFORMATION

Bobtails are slow to develop, reaching maturity somewhere between two and three years. Like the bobcat's, the Bobtail's hind legs are slightly longer than the front legs, and the feet are large and round and may have toe tufts.

The Bobtail's most noted feature—its succinct tail—is one-third to one-half the length of an ordinary cat's, and should not extend below the hock. Like the Manx, the Bobtail's tail appears to be governed by a dominant gene. The tail is straight and articulate but may curve, have bumps or be slightly knotted. Bobtails with no tails are disqualified in the show ring because of the health problems associated with the foreshortened spine. To widen the gene pool and keep the breed healthy, outcrossing is still allowed with domestic longhair and shorthair cats that are not members of recognized breeds. Therefore, the color, pattern, hair length, coat type, and body and head conformation may vary somewhat until the gene pool is closed to new swimmers. In CFA, the registration of domestic shorthair or longhair cats with a natural bobtail is allowed with written approval of the American Bobtail Breed Council Secretary, CFA Breeds and Standards Chairperson, and one CFA Allbreed judge, for cats and kittens born between January 1, 2002 and January 1, 2020. In TICA, however, domestic longhairs and shorthairs that are not members of recognized breeds are allowable outcrosses; no written approval is required. No tailless cats, any recognized breeds, or wild blood can be used in any American Bobtail breeding program.

American Bobtail. The succinct tail is well covered with fur on this semi-longhair.

HISTORY

The American Curl originated as a spontaneous genetic mutation.

While some new cat breeds have had to bang their furry little heads against the cat fancy walls for decades to gain acceptance, the American Curl purred its way into the hearts of judges and cat fanciers in an amazingly short time. The breed originated in June 1981 as a spontaneous genetic mutation in the domestic cat population. A breeding program started in 1983, and by 1986 it was recognized by CFA and CFF, and accepted for championship by TICA, one of the largest North American cat registries.

In June 1981 two cats with ears that curled backwards arrived on the doorstep of cat lovers Grace and Joe Ruga of Lakewood, California. One died shortly afterward in an unfortunate accident, but the other, a friendly longhaired female, stayed on for the free food and lodging the Rugas were happy to provide. Grace Ruga named the graceful black-haired cat Shulamith,

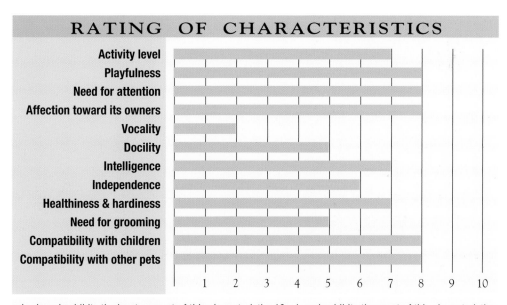

RATING OF CHARACTERISTICS

	1	2	3	4	5	6	7	8	9	10
Activity level										
Playfulness										
Need for attention										
Affection toward its owners										
Vocality										
Docility										
Intelligence										
Independence										
Healthiness & hardiness										
Need for grooming										
Compatibility with children										
Compatibility with other pets										

1—breed exhibits the least amount of this characteristic, 10—breed exhibits the most of this characteristic

✳ **Championship status in AACE, ACFA, CCA, CFA, CCF, TICA, and UFO for American Curl Longhair; Championship status in ACFA, CCA, CFA, TICA, and UFO for American Curl Shorthair; and AACE and CCF under the name Shorthair Curl**

a variation of a Hebrew term that means "black but comely." At first, the Rugas paid little attention to Shulamith's unique curled ears; they were more taken with their new feline friend's devotion and sweet trusting temperament. They assumed Shulamith was one of many curly-eared cats, even after visits to local libraries and book stores provided no mention of Shulamith's supposed kin. In December 1981 Shulamith gave birth to a litter of four; two of the kittens had the same curled-back ears.

The father, a local longhaired tom named Mr. Grey, did not have curly ears or, it soon became apparent, the gene for them. Although the Rugas didn't understand cat genetics at the time, the gene governing the curled ears is dominant, and therefore only one parent needs to have the gene to pass on curled ears to at least some of the offspring. Likewise, if a cat doesn't have curled ears, it cannot possess the gene for them; a dominant gene will always appear in a cat's physical appearance.

Shulamith continued to have litters by the local toms, adding to the local Curl population. Both long and short hairs appeared in early litters, and many colors and patterns, including the pointed pattern. Grace and Joe

Longhaired Lynxpoint American Curl.

Ruga gave kittens to friends and family, including Grace's sister, Esther Brimlow, who was given two of Shulamith's kittens. Nancy Kiester, a former breeder of Australian Shepherds, saw Brimlow's two Curl kittens while at her house and fell in love with their unique ears and gentle temperament. She obtained the two kittens from Brimlow.

After reading an article on the Scottish Fold, another breed celebrated for its distinctive ears, it occurred to Kiester that this might be an entirely new breed. Kiester showed her Curls to cat judge and Scottish Fold breeder Jean Grimm. Grimm told Kiester that Curls were unknown to the cat fancy.

Nancy Kiester contacted the Rugas, relayed the exciting news, and offered her support and breeding knowledge to help bring the Curl into the cat fancy limelight. Grace Ruga and Kiester teamed up to promote the new breed, which they named the American Curl. With Judge Nancy Grimm's help and advice, Nancy Kiester and Grace Ruga wrote the first breed standard and created a breeding program. Both hair lengths and all patterns and colors were included in the original standard. They chose domestic long and shorthairs as the only acceptable outcrosses; no pedigreed breeds were allowed, since this could have created opposition from other breeders in the cat fancy.

They first exhibited the American Curl in October 1983 at a CFA show in Palm Springs, California. Cat fanciers immediately recognized that the Curl's unparalleled ears were unique to the cat fancy.

In 1986 TICA granted the Curl championship status. Later the same

Seven-month old American Curl kitten.

year, CFF accepted the breed for experimental status, and CFA accepted the Curl for registration. In February 1991 the CFA granted the breed Provisional status. In a comparatively short time, all North American associations accepted the American Curl for championship, although at first some cat associations accepted only the American Curl longhair because Shulamith, the breed's foundation cat, had long hair.

To insure the breed's health and genetic diversity, outcrossing to domestic longhairs and shorthairs will continue for litters born before January 1, 2015. Outcrossing to other pedigreed breeds is not allowed. As of 2015, the gene pool will be closed, unless the deadline is again extended. The origi-

GENERAL	The distinctive feature of the American Curl is their attractive, uniquely curled-back ears. Elegant, well balanced, moderately muscled, slender rather than massive in build; proper proportion and balance are more important than size.
BODY	Semi-foreign rectangle; length one and one half times height at shoulder, medium depth of chest and flank. Size intermediate; moderate strength and tone, flexible.
HEAD	Modified wedge without flat planes, moderately longer than wide, smooth transitions. Nose straight and moderate in length; slight rise from bottom of eyes to forehead; gentle curve to top of head, flowing into neck, without a break. Size medium in proportion to body. Muzzle rounded with gentle transition; no pronounced whisker break. Chin firm, in line with nose and upper lip.
EARS	Minimum 90 degree arc of curl, not to exceed 180 degrees. Firm cartilage from ear base to at least one third of height. Shape wide at base and open, curving back in smooth arc when viewed from front and rear. Tips rounded and flexible. Size moderately large. Erect, set equally on top and sides of head. Furnishings desirable.
EYES	Walnut shape, oval on top and round on bottom. Set on slight angle between base of ear and tip of nose, one eye width apart. Moderately large. Clear, brilliant, color no relation to coat color except blue eyes required in colorpoint class.
LEGS AND PAWS	Length medium in proportion to body, set straight when viewed from front or rear. Medium boning, neither fine nor heavy. Paws medium and rounded.
TAIL	Flexible, wide at base, tapering; equal to body length.
COAT— LONGHAIR DIVISION	Texture fine, silky, laying flat. Undercoat minimal. Coat length semi-long. Tail full and plumed.
COAT— SHORTHAIR DIVISION	Texture soft, silky, laying flat; resilient without a plush dense feel. Undercoat minimal. Coat length short. Tail coat same length as body coat.
COLOR	All colors and patterns, including pointed pattern, pointed with white, ticked tabby, shaded, smoke, chinchilla, van, and bicolor.
DISQUALIFY	Extreme curl in adult where tip of ear touches back of ear or head. Ears that are straight, severely mismatched, thick, or having inflexible tips. Lack of firm cartilage in base of ear. Tail faults.

| **ALLOWABLE OUTCROSSES** | Domestic longhair or shorthair for litters born before January 1, 2015. |

nal deadline was January 1, 2010, but since the breed still had a fairly small gene pool, fanciers decided this was too soon to close the gene pool. Even with careful selection of outcrosses, however, different body styles, head shapes, hair types and personalities will be added. It will take time for the breed to settle into a consistent type that approaches the ideal outlined in the standard.

PERSONALITY

Curls have qualities other than the whimsical ears to make them attractive pets. They are people cats that do not show any of the stereotypical aloofness, and are affectionate without harassing their humans for attention the way some breeds can. They delight in perching on laps and love to pat and nuzzle their owners' faces. Curls are easily taught to play fetch and never lose their love of play. They are also noted for their affinity with children.

While not as active as the Abyssinian or Siamese, American Curls are plenty frisky and energetic. They also display the typical cat curiosity and want to be right there to investigate any changes in their environment.

CONFORMATION

At birth, American Curls look like any other kittens, but between one and seven days the ears get firmer and start to plump up and curve back— if they're going to. Since the degree of curl can change dramatically over a short period, kittens should not be purchased until they are between four and four and one-half months of age, when the curl of the ear settles down into the form the cat will carry throughout its life. Curl cats take two to three years to reach maturity.

The degree of ear curl can vary from a minimum of 90 degrees to a maximum of 180 degrees, or from first degree to the show-favored third degree curl. The ears should not curl back so far as to touch the back of the ears or head, however; this is cause for disqualification, as is any ear lacking firm cartilage from the base to at least one-third of its height.

If you are buying a Curl as a pet, you may be offered a straight-eared Curl. Such cats are common in many Curl breeding programs, particularly when straight-eared domestic cats are used as outcrosses. When a Curl possessing one copy of the curl gene is bred to a cat without the curl gene, approximately fifty percent of the kittens won't possess the curl gene and therefore will have straight ears. They are still pedigreed American Curls; however, they can't be shown except as household pets. Still, they have the same body style and charming personality as the curly-eared cats, and are considerably less expensive to purchase.

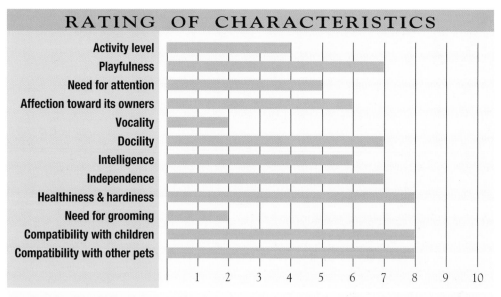

HISTORY

No one knows exactly when domestic cats first set paw in America. However, it's clear that cats arrived with the Europeans settlers, since America has no indigenous cat species from which domestic cats could have developed. Since cats were often kept aboard ships to protect the grain and other foodstuffs from rodents, it's not surprising that domestic cats first appeared in North America when the Europeans arrived; North America has no indigenous species from which domestic cats could have developed. Domestic cats may have been catting around the New World since the 1500s. Unquestionably, domestic cats were present in Jamestown, the first permanent British colony in the New World, since a written record dating from 1609 mentions the colony's cats. On July 4, 1776, when the members of

Classic silver tabby American Shorthair.

RATING OF CHARACTERISTICS

Characteristic	Rating
Activity level	4
Playfulness	7
Need for attention	5
Affection toward its owners	6
Vocality	2
Docility	7
Intelligence	6
Independence	7
Healthiness & hardiness	8
Need for grooming	2
Compatibility with children	8
Compatibility with other pets	7

1—breed exhibits the least amount of this characteristic, 10—breed exhibits the most of this characteristic

✳ **Championship status in all associations**

the Continental Congress assembled in Philadelphia to adopt the Declaration of Independence, the American Shorthair's ancestors were around to witness the historic event. They were too busy ridding the barns and fields of mice to put their paw print alongside Thomas Jefferson's signature, but they heartily approved of the document. After all, cats declared their independence thousands of years ago and hold the concept dear to their hearts to this day.

Cats became working members of American society, performing that age-old service as the perfect mouser. Function was far more important than form, and folks paid little attention to the color, pattern, and body style of their mousers. Through natural selection—since life in those days was hard on cat and human alike—these feline immigrants developed powerful muscles, strong jaws, and hardy, healthy constitutions.

In time, life became easier, and cats became more than mere mouse-catchers as people began to take an interest in the beauty of the feline form. At first, American Shorthairs were welcomed in the newly formed American cat fancy in the late 1800s. At that time, the breed was merely called Shorthair.

Classic silver tabby, one of the most popular color and pattern combinations for the American Shorthair.

Tabby American Shorthair. Notice the characteristic "M" on the forehead.

Later, the breed was renamed Domestic Shorthair.

The first American Shorthair to be registered in this country was an orange tabby male named Belle that ironically was imported from England in the early 1900s. It wasn't until 1904 when the first American-born American Shorthair (named Buster Brown) was registered under the breed name of Shorthair.

With the import of foreign breeds, the familiarity of the ASH no longer worked in its favor. Early in the 1900s, fanciers became more interested in the imported breeds like the Persian and Angora than in the familiar ASH that had warmed their laps and served them faithfully for so many years. The foreign imports crossed with the ASH, and the pure bloodlines of the American native became diluted.

In the early 1900s, a group of fanciers who loved the sturdy look of their proud all-American cats began a selective breeding program to preserve the natural beauty, mild temperament, and hardiness of the American Shorthair. However, acceptance in the show ring was a long time coming. As late as the 1960s American Shorthairs were still treated like the strays of the cat fancy.

Breeders also battled confusion between their carefully bred American Shorthairs and random-bred domestic cats. While a non-pedigreed domestic cat may look something like a pedigreed American Shorthair, the mix of genes means that a random-bred domestic generally will not breed true; you cannot count on type, temperament, and length of hair as you can with a pedigreed American Shorthair.

In the late 1950s a number of ASH breeders, hoping to "improve" the breed and introduce new colors, began cross-breeding Persians into their American Shorthair lines. As a result, the American Shorthair body style and head type began to change, becoming more Persian in style. The face broadened and flattened, the eyes became rounder, the ears shorter. However, many American Shorthair breeders, who had struggled for decades to promote the natural beauty of the ASH, were dismayed at the changes. The American Shorthair standard was subsequently amended to disqualify any cat showing evidence of hybridization.

In September 1965, breeders voted to change the breed's name to "American Shorthair." With the brand-new name came a brand-new image, and the breed finally received some of the esteem it deserved. The same year, CFA named a silver tabby male (Shawnee Trademark) Best Cat, and the breed finally began to receive some hard-earned respect in the cat fancy. Today, the American Shorthair is one of the most popular shorthairs, a fitting status for America's hometown breed.

PERSONALITY

When describing the American Shorthair, the expression "happy medium" springs to mind. These all-American cats are medium in size, build, type, and temperament; they are neither too big nor too small, not overly cuddly nor distant, neither couch potatoes nor hyperactive. The American Shorthair is the perfect breed for those who want a cat that enjoys being in your lap but not in your face. American Shorthairs are known for their adaptable temperaments and quiet voices; they are sociable, easily trained, and adapt well to other animals and children. They generally do not like to be picked up; like their Pilgrim companions who left England to find freedom, they cherish their independence. Because of the American Shorthair's history as a working cat, they make great companions in terms of health, strength, and vitality.

American Shorthairs enjoy a good romp with their favorite humans, but can amuse themselves with a ball of paper just as well. They tend to remain active and playful well into their old age. Due to their barn cat background, ASHs have strong hunting instincts and enjoy catching and killing catnip mice—and real ones, too, if given access to the great outdoors, something that's discouraged by breeders. Your indoor ASH will put presents on your pillow, usually well-killed catnip mice, and proudly wait for the well-deserved petting and praise.

CONFORMATION

The American Shorthair is known as a healthy, hardy breed with few genetic defects—not surprising since the breed developed from hardy domestic stock. The relatively large gene pool helps keep the breed healthy as well. The standard emphasizes that the American Shorthair should be a "true breed of working cat" and that no part of the anatomy should be exaggerated as to foster weakness. With proper care ASHs enjoy long life spans. However, some lines are known to carry the inherited heart disease feline hypertrophic cardiomyopathy (HMC), and due to the crossbreeding done with Persians, some are prone to polycystic kidney disease (PKD), a serious disease that can cause renal failure. A PKD genetic test is available at the Veterinary Genetics Laboratory at the University of California, Davis, which helps breeders screen out affected breeding stock. Discuss these disorders with your breeder.

The most striking and best known color is the silver tabby; a large percentage of all American Shorthairs exhibit this color. With the black markings set against the brilliant silver background, the pattern is dynamic and memorable.

GENERAL	The American Shorthair is a true breed of working cat. The general effect is that of a strongly built, well balanced, symmetrical cat with conformation indicating power, endurance, and agility.
BODY	Solidly built, powerful, and muscular with well-developed shoulders, chest, and hindquarters. Back broad, straight and level.
HEAD	Large, with full-cheeked face giving impression of an oblong just slightly longer than wide. Sweet, open expression. Forehead forms smooth, moderately convex continuous curve flowing over top of head into neck. No dome between ears. Nose medium length, same width for entire length. Gentle curved rise from bridge of nose to forehead.
EARS	Medium size, slightly rounded at tips, not unduly open at base. Distance between ears, measured from lower inner corners, twice distance between eyes.
EYES	Large and wide with upper lid shaped like half an almond cut lengthwise and lower lid shaped in fully rounded curve. At least width of one eye between eyes. Outer corners set very slightly higher than inner corners. Bright, clear, and alert.
LEGS AND PAWS	Medium in length and bone, heavily muscled. Viewed from rear, all four legs straight and parallel with paws facing forward. Paws firm, full and rounded, with heavy pads. Toes five in front, four behind.
TAIL	Medium long, heavy at base, tapering to abrupt blunt end in appearance but with normal tapering final vertebrae.
COAT	Short, thick, even, and hard in texture. Regional and seasonal variation in coat thickness allowed. Coat dense enough to protect from moisture, cold, and superficial skin injuries.
COLOR	Many colors and patterns including solid; shaded; smoke; particolor; bicolor; tortoiseshell; cameo; van; tabby (classic, mackerel, and patched); tabby and white.
DISQUALIFY	Evidence of hybridization resulting in colors chocolate, sable, lavender, lilac, or point-restricted pattern. Any appearance of hybridization with any other breed including long or fluffy fur, deep nose break, bulging eye set, brow ridge. Kinked or abnormal tail. Locket or button. Incorrect number of toes. Undershot or overshot bite. Any feature so exaggerated as to foster weakness.
ALLOWABLE OUTCROSSES	None.

HISTORY

Like the American Curl, the American Wirehair started as a spontaneous mutation in the domestic cat population; somewhere along the bloodline Mother Nature worked her magic and produced a special litter with distinctive fur. In 1966, Fluffy and Bootsie, two barn cats with no apparent unusual qualities from a small farm in upstate New York, parented a litter in which all five kittens had peculiar wiry hair. Sadly, all but one of the kittens were killed by a weasel. This was particularly unfortunate since subsequent matings between Fluffy and Bootsie produced no more wiry haired kittens. Whatever magic Mother Nature used to create that one exceptional litter apparently was a one-time thing.

White American Wirehair.

RATING OF CHARACTERISTICS

Characteristic	Rating (1–10)
Activity level	6
Playfulness	6
Need for attention	6
Affection toward its owners	8
Vocality	5
Docility	4
Intelligence	7
Independence	6
Healthiness & hardiness	6
Need for grooming	3
Compatibility with children	6
Compatibility with other pets	6

1—breed exhibits the least amount of this characteristic, 10—breed exhibits the most of this characteristic

✳ **Championship status in ACFA, CCA, CFA, and TICA**

However, the one surviving kitten—a red and white bicolor male—lived and prospered. Joan O'Shea of nearby Vernon, New York, an experienced breeder of Siamese, Havana Browns, and Rex cats, heard about the kitten from a friend, who told her the kitten looked just like her Rex cats. O'Shea drove up to look at the kitten and instantly fell in love with the long-legged, big-eared kitten with the strange twisted fur. She also immediately realized that the "just a hair different" kitten, appropriately named Adam, wasn't a Rex at all but likely an entirely new breed.

It took Joan O'Shea several months to convince the owner, Nathan Mosher, to part with Adam, since O'Shea wasn't the only one attached to the little ball of frizzy fur. Eventually persistence and fifty dollars sealed the deal, and O'Shea went home with Council Rock Farm Adam of Hi-Fi—Adam's new official name. Adam mated with Tip-Toe, a neighbor's straight-coated calico cat, who had also come from Mosher's farm. She produced two red and white females with their father's wiry hair, and two straight-coated kittens.

O'Shea acquired the two wired females and named them Abby and Amy. Aby died young but Amy carried on in her father's tradition. Since Tip-Toe was related and might possess the gene that governed the wiry coat,

American Wirehairs are similar in personality to the American Shorthair.

O'Shea wasn't yet sure how the coat was inherited. However, subsequent matings to unrelated cats proved the gene was dominant; only one parent needed the gene to produce Wirehair offspring. To make sure the breed wasn't related to one of the existing Rex breeds, O'Shea sent samples of Adam's hair to noted British cat geneticists Antony G. Searle and Roy Robinson for analysis. Robinson told her the hair samples showed the coat was unique and not related to either the Cornish or Devon Rex. All three types of hair (guard, down, and awn) were twisted, and the awn hairs were hooked at the tip.

O'Shea sold Amy to Rex breeders Bill and Madeline Beck, who became instrumental in helping the breed into the cat fancy limelight. Amy gave birth to a number of Wirehairs, including a female named Barberry Ellen, the first homozygous Wirehair (she possessed two copies of the Wirehair gene), a boon to the breed because even when bred with an unrelated outcross all offspring had wiry hair. All of today's American Wirehairs are descendants of Adam or Amy.

When O'Shea and the Becks first mapped out a breeding program for the newly named American Wirehair, they thought it would be best to use an outcross that would contribute hybrid vigor, since the breed sprang from the domestic cat population. American Shorthairs were chosen as the outcross, and O'Shea and the Becks decided the standard should reflect the American Shorthair's conformation with a specific standard written for the coat. Since then, the standard has changed only slightly.

CFA accepted the American Wirehair for registration in 1967 and granted championship status in 1978. O'Shea stopped working with the breed around 1970; the Becks did not work with the breed for much longer than O'Shea. However, by then other dedicated breeders and exhibitors had picked up the Wirehair torch and kept the breed going, and have also worked to improve the original body style by selectively breeding for a more American Shorthair type. The breed is still relatively rare, even though it is now accepted for championship by the four largest North American cat associations.

PERSONALITY

The American Wirehair's hair may be abrasive and unruly, but its personality is anything but. Wirehairs are people cats that enjoy human attention and affection and are loyal and playful. They are active without being hyper, and affectionate without being clingy. Similar in personality to the American Shorthair due to the crossbreeding that was and still is being done, Wirehairs are mild-mannered, middle-of-the-road cats. Not demanding cats, they enjoy human attention but retain their independent spirit. Agile and fun-loving, they enjoy playing fetch and are a bit more playful and active than the American Shorthair. They enjoy interactive toys in which their human companions take an active role but can entertain themselves if necessary. They generally get along well with other pets and children. Fanciers say that they seem particularly in tune with their humans' feelings and try to offer com-

The American Wirehair's scruffy fur is springy, tight, and medium in length.

fort and companionship when their chosen humans are feeling blue. That's when they turn on the purrs and sit beside them to offer their support.

CONFORMATION

At first sight, this scruffy, wide-eyed feline might look like an American Shorthair that stuck an unwary claw into an electrical outlet, with hair-frizzing effect, but the American Wirehair's unruly coat is an all-natural gift from Mother Nature. In the show hall, the unique, wiry coat is of supreme importance; CFA's standard allots a full 45 points out of the possible 100 to the Wirehair's coat, more than for any other breed. The Cornish Rex is second with 40 points. (Some of the other associations, such as ACFA allot only 40 points for the Wirehair's coat, however.)

The coat differs from the Cornish Rex's coat in that the Wirehair possesses all three hair types. In addition, the Wirehair gene is dominant, unlike the Cornish and the Devon Rex's recessive coats. The Wirehair's hairs are crimped, hooked, or bent, resulting in a dense, resilient coat that leads to ringlet formation rather than waves. At present, significant variation exists in the texture and length of the individual coats. The preferred coat is short, very dense, and coarse to the touch.

GENERAL	The American Wirehair is a spontaneous mutation. The coat, which is not only springy, dense, and resilient, but also coarse and hard to the touch, distinguishes the American Wirehair from all other breeds.
BODY	Medium to large. Back level, shoulders and hips same width, torso well-rounded and in proportion.
HEAD	In proportion to the body. Underlying bone structure is round with prominent cheekbones and well-developed muzzle and chin. There is a slight whisker break. In profile, the nose shows a gentle concave curve.
EARS	Medium, slightly rounded at tips, set wide and not unduly open at the base.
EYES	Large, rounded, bright, and clear. Set well apart. Aperture has slight upward tilt. The color should reflect intensity, and complement the color of the cat.
LEGS AND PAWS	Legs medium in length and bone, well-muscled and proportionate to body. Paws firm, full and rounded, with heavy pads. Toes, five in front and four behind.
TAIL	In proportion to body, tapering from the well-rounded rump to a rounded tip, neither blunt nor pointed.
COAT	Springy, tight, medium in length. Individual hairs are crimped, hooked, or bent, including hair within the ears. The overall appearance of wiring and coarseness and resilience of coat is more important than crimping of each hair. Density of wired coat leads to ringlet formation rather than waves. Coat that is very dense, resilient, crimped, and coarse is most desirable, as are curly whiskers.
COLOR	Any color or pattern acceptable except those showing evidence of hybridization resulting in the colors chocolate, lavender, the pointed pattern, or these combinations with white.
DISQUALIFY	Incorrect coat. Kinked or abnormal tail. Long or fluffy fur. Incorrect number of toes. Evidence of hybridization resulting in colors chocolate, lavender, the Himalayan pattern, or these combinations with white.
ALLOWABLE OUTCROSSES	American Shorthair.

BALINESE

In the early 1900s, longhaired kittens began appearing spontaneously in otherwise shorthaired Siamese litters. Breeders of the time weren't trying to create a longhaired version of the Siamese; in fact, they were horrified to find these longhaired renegades in their pedigreed Siamese lines. Some fanciers believe the recessive gene for long hair was introduced into the European Siamese gene pool after World War I. Since the Siamese was nearly obliterated during the war, other breeds and some random-bred domestic cats were used to revitalize the breed. The Turkish Angora, a breed with a silky semi-long fur similar to the Balinese coat, was thought to have been one of the breeds used. Other fanciers believe that the recessive gene for long hair is simply a naturally occurring mutation. Both hypotheses have been disputed, and both have their reputable pro-

Blue point Balinese.

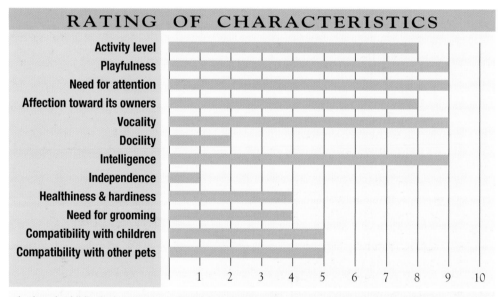

RATING OF CHARACTERISTICS

Characteristic	Rating
Activity level	8
Playfulness	9
Need for attention	8
Affection toward its owners	8
Vocality	9
Docility	2
Intelligence	8
Independence	1
Healthiness & hardiness	4
Need for grooming	4
Compatibility with children	5
Compatibility with other pets	4

1—breed exhibits the least amount of this characteristic, 10—breed exhibits the most of this characteristic

✳ **Championship status in all associations**

ponents, but no one really knows for sure. Regardless of how the long hair gene was acquired—forbidden trysts, or Mother Nature's tinkering—early Siamese breeders quietly gave away these occasional longhairs, fearing other breeders would think they were using crossbreeding in their cattery programs.

No one began a serious effort to turn these longhaired rebels into a breed until the 1940s. At that time, fanciers recognized these cats might make a worthy addition to the cat fancy. New York breeder Helen Smith and California breeder Sylvia Holland began working with the longhaired cats born in their pedigreed Siamese litters. Soon after, other breeders joined in to help develop the breed and bring it recognition in the cat fancy.

To say Siamese breeders were not excited about the new breed is a vast understatement. Much hissing and spitting occurred before the Balinese gained any acceptance; Siamese breeders were worried that the new breed would damage the Siamese's pure bloodlines. However, the Balinese fanciers were persistent. Since the name "Siamese Longhair" would anger already angry Siamese breeders, Helen Smith came up with the name Balinese, comparing the cat's graceful movements and flowing lines to those of the colorful dancers of Bali. The breeders wrote the first breed standard to resemble the Siamese in all but hair length, and in the same point-restricted pattern and four colors accepted in the Siamese. Crossbreeding was allowed only with the Siamese.

In those early days, Balinese cats often had heavier boning and thicker coats than the standard called for, and frequently fell short of meeting the standard in head type and ear set as well. Hampered by Siamese breeders who wouldn't sell top-quality breeding stock to them, the Balinese breeders struggled to refine the body type by crossbreeding back to the Siamese. After years of frustrating work, the Balinese improved in type. By 1970, when CFA granted championship, all major North American associations that existed at that time had accepted the Balinese.

THE JAVANESE

When the Balinese was first recognized, the breed standard allowed only the four original Siamese point-restricted colors: seal point, chocolate point, blue point, and lilac point. In the 1970s, however, fanciers developed a new breed by crossing the Balinese to the Colorpoint Shorthair (see Colorpoint Shorthair, page 123). This combined the semi-long Balinese coat with the Colorpoint's myriad colors.

This new breed, Siamese in body style but with the longer coat of the Balinese and the wider range of point-restricted colors of the Colorpoint Shorthair, was at first called "new-color Balinese." Like the Balinese breeders before them, these breeders had an uphill battle convincing both Siamese and Balinese fanciers that this colorful cross would make a good addition to the cat fancy. Their perseverance paid off, and in 1979 the CFA board granted registration status to the new breed. However, CFA told the fanciers to come up with a new name, since the breed would not be considered a color division of the Balinese. The Balinese was created solely from Siamese bloodlines, but the Javanese was a hybrid because it was created by crossing the Balinese with the Colorpoint Shorthair, which was created by crossing Siamese with red domestic shorthairs, Abyssinians, and American Shorthairs. The breed was renamed the Javanese after the Isle of Java, an island in Indonesia to the west of Bali. The Javanese isn't from Java any more than the Balinese is from Bali, but the name lent a nice romantic sound to the new breed. A separate breed standard was written as well. In May of 1986, CFA accepted the Javanese for championship competition. At that time, allowable outcrosses were Siamese, Balinese, Colorpoint Shorthair, and certain limited outcrossings with the Oriental Longhair.

However, many of the other cat associations merely extended the accepted colors of the Balinese to include the Javanese colors. By 2008, only CFA considered the Javanese a separate breed. Because the Javanese and the Balinese are identical except for color and since the hybridization happened so long ago, many breeders felt CFA should combine the two breeds, as the other associations had done. Breeders petitioned CFA to change the breed's status. At last, CFA's board voted to make the Javanese a color division of the Balinese breed, ending a long-standing policy that confused cat lovers and

frustrated breeders. On May 1, 2008, the Javanese became a color division of the Balinese, and in 2010 a single standard was adopted, fully combining the two breeds. In addition to sealpoint, chocolate point, blue point, and lilac point, the Balinese palette now includes twenty-two additional colors (see conformation). Lynx point is also known as tabby point since the face, legs, and tail have tabby markings; tortie point is a mixture of black and red or their dilute colors, blue and cream.

PERSONALITY

Since the Balinese and the Siamese are closely related, they share many traits. Like the Siamese, Balinese are curious, outgoing, intelligent cats with excellent communication skills. They are known for their chatty personalities and are always eager to tell you their views on life, love, and what you've served them for dinner. They often keep up a running monologue; they are not for those who think cats should be seen and not heard. Balinese are in tune with your moods and will be right there to cheer you up if you're sad or to share your joy when you're happy. Vocal themselves, they respond to your tone of voice, and harsh scoldings for minor infractions hurt their sensitive feelings. A coaching tone and positive reinforcement are more effective for correcting unwanted behavior.

Balinese are agile and athletic, and if allowed will hitch a ride on the shoulder of any willing human. They love to play and easily learn to fetch, bringing the ball or toy back for repeated throwing. They keep you entertained with their antics, but have a loving, devoted disposition as well. They can be quite assertive in their requests for attention, but also possess a special dignity particular to the Balinese and Siamese breeds.

CONFORMATION

The Balinese standard is almost identical to the Siamese and the Colorpoint Shorthair standards. The main differences are color and hair length. In addition to sealpoint, chocolate point, blue point, and lilac point, CFA accepts the Balinese in red point, cream point, cinnamon point, blue-cream point, red-cream point, fawn-cream point, lilac-cream point, and in these colors in the patterns lynx point, tortie lynx point, parti-color point, and tortie parti-color point. While having the same conformation as the Siamese, the Balinese appears to have softer lines and less extreme body type because of the longer hair. Because the fur is only semi-long and lacks the downy undercoat, the coat doesn't tangle and even show cats require little grooming.

Fanciers have two body styles from which to choose: the Extreme and the Old-Style Balinese. The Extreme Balinese is the one you'll usually see at cat shows. The Old-Style Balinese, recognized by UFO, while still slender and refined, is not as extreme in head or body type. The old-style versions of the Siamese breeds are making comebacks among cat lovers who remember with affec-

Seal lynx point Javanese. The hair is longest on the tail.

tion yesterday's Siamese, less svelte and sleek, fewer health issues, and with the same sparking, chatty personality as today's Extreme Siamese. UFO also accepts the Old-Style Siamese and the Old-Style Colorpoint Shorthair, CFF accepts the Old Style Siamese, and TICA accepts the Old-Style Siamese under the name "Thai."

Although Extreme Balinese are generally healthy and long-lived if kept inside, the breed has a few inheritable conditions and diseases. In particular, hereditary liver amyloidosis has been found in some Balinese lines. In addition, incidences of dilated cardiomyopathy, an enlargement of the heart muscle that decreases heart function, have been found in some lines, but they seem to be at a lower risk for the often-fatal feline hypertrophic cardiomyopathy (HCM) than some other breeds. Some Balinese are also prone to plaque buildup, tartar formation, and gingivitis, which can lead to periodontitis.

GENERAL	The ideal Balinese is a svelte cat with long tapering lines, very lithe but strong and muscular. The Balinese is unique with its distinct range of colors and silky coat that hides a supple and athletic body.
BODY	Medium size. Graceful, long, and svelte; a combination of fine bones and firm muscles. Shoulders and hips continue same sleek lines of tubular body. Hips never wider than shoulders. Abdomen tight.
HEAD	Long, tapering wedge; medium size in good proportion to body. Wedge starts at nose and flares out in straight lines to tips of ears forming a triangle, with no break at the whiskers. Muzzle fine, wedge-shaped. Nose long and straight, a continuation of the forehead. No less than the width of an eye between the eyes.
EARS	Large, pointed, wide at base, continuing the lines of the wedge.
EYES	Almond shaped; medium size; neither protruding nor recessed. Slanted toward nose in harmony with lines of wedge and ears. Uncrossed. Eye color deep vivid blue.
LEGS AND PAWS	Leg bone structure long and slim; hind legs higher than front. In good proportion to body. Paws dainty, small, and oval. Five toes in front and four in back.
TAIL	Bone structure long, thin, tapering to a fine point. Tail hair spreads out like a plume.
COAT	Medium length, longest on the tail; lying close to the body. Fine, silky, and without downy undercoat, may appear shorter than it is.
COLOR	Body even with subtle shading when allowed. Allowance made for darker color in older cats, but there must be definite contrast between body color and points. Mask, ears, legs, feet, tail dense and clearly defined, and all of the same shade. Mask covers entire face including whisker pads and is connected to ears by tracings; should not extend over top of head. No ticking or white hairs in points.
DISQUALIFY	Any evidence of illness or poor health; weak hind legs; mouth breathing due to nasal obstruction or poor occlusion. Malocclusion resulting in either undershot or overshot chin. Emaciation. Visible kink in tail. Eyes other than blue. White toes and/or feet. Incorrect number of toes. Definite double coat (i.e., downy undercoat).
ALLOWABLE OUTCROSSES	Siamese, Colorpoint Shorthair, and certain limited outcrossing to Oriental Longhair for litters born on or prior to 12-31-2015.

HISTORY

The Bengal breed originated as a human-made hybrid of a domestic cat (*Felis silvestris catus*) and a leopard cat (*Prionailurus bengalensis*). The leopard cat looks very much like a domestic cat, except for the larger, snapping eyes, pronounced whisker pads, longer legs, and brilliant leopard-style markings. It looks, in fact, like a miniature leopard.

The Bengal began its journey toward becoming a recognized breed in 1963 when breeder Jean Mill of Covina, California, bought a female leopard cat from a pet store. At that time, leopard cats could be purchased at pet stores in the United States; today, it's more difficult to get a license to import or own them. Jean Mill wasn't trying to create a new breed of cat—she just wanted a unique pet.

After several years, Mill thought her little leopard cat looked lonely, so she put a male domestic cat in the cat's pen to keep her company. She wasn't expecting a romantic relation-

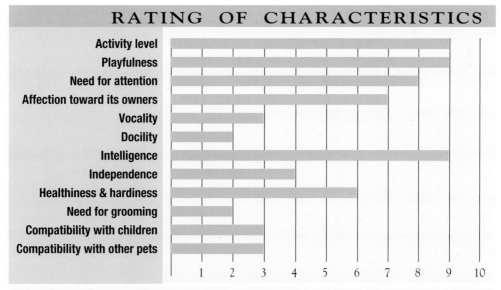

Bengals are an active breed.

RATING OF CHARACTERISTICS

Characteristic	Rating (1–10)
Activity level	9
Playfulness	9
Need for attention	8
Affection toward its owners	7
Vocality	3
Docility	2
Intelligence	9
Independence	4
Healthiness & hardiness	6
Need for grooming	2
Compatibility with children	3
Compatibility with other pets	2

1—breed exhibits the least amount of this characteristic, 10—breed exhibits the most of this characteristic

ship, but to Mill's surprise, in 1965 her leopard cat produced a litter. Only one kitten survived, a female hybrid that Mill named Kin-Kin. Mill contacted Cornell University College of Veterinary Medicine in Ithaca, New York, for advice on how to handle the hybrid, and was told that Kin-Kin was probably sterile. That proved to be not the case, since Kin-Kin grew up, mated with her domestic father, and produced two kittens. One was all black and had inherited the wild leopard cat temperament; as an adult it was a nervous recluse that refused to let anyone near it. The other, a spotted male, inherited the sweet domestic disposition of his father.

Bengals are very active and enjoy interactive play with their human companions.

After some consideration, Mill decided that creating a crossbred breed would benefit the plight of the leopard cats. Mill was dismayed by the predicament of orphaned leopard cat cubs taken by hunters and sold to American pet stores. When the cubs grew to adulthood and reverted to their wild ways, they generally ended up in zoos, or dumped out on the streets to fend for themselves. Mill wanted to provide the American market with an acceptable spotted substitute.

In the first crossings of leopard cat to domestic, the male kittens were infertile, as is the case with many hybrids. The females were usually fertile as were the male kittens in generations farther from the leopard cat ancestor. However, many of those first hybrid kittens grew up to be nervous cats of uncertain temperament, similar to their wild relatives. It was only after the cats were three or four generations away from the leopard cat that the Bengal's temperament became more predictably domestic.

Unfortunately, in 1965 Mill's husband died and she abandoned her breeding program for a time to put her life back in order. It wasn't until 1980 after she had remarried that she began breeding Bengals again. Most of her breeding stock this time was provided by Dr. Willard Centerwall, a geneticist at the University of California at Davis. Dr. Centerwall had been studying leopard cats because, due to their genetic makeup, they seemed resistant to the feline leukemia virus. Mill provided a home for the hybrid female kittens Dr. Centerwall had used in his experiments.

Since only the hybrid females were fertile, Mill needed domestic males to use in the bloodline. After a long search, Mill selected a spotted brown tabby male acquired at a local shelter (appropriately named "Finally Found"), and a semi-feral red tabby domestic with dark brown rosetted spots. The red male came all the way from India to add his genes to Mill's recipe; when visiting a zoo in Delhi, Mill found a litter of spotted kittens living in a rhinoceros cage. Entranced by the kittens' appearance, she managed to get a male (named Toby in honor of the zoo's curator, Dr. Toby Nainan) imported to America.

Many obstacles had to be overcome along the way. Those first hybrid kittens (first generation cats are called F1s) often grew up to be nervous, shy cats similar to their wild relatives. Only after the cats were several generations away from the leopard cat that the temperament became sweet and predictable. Another factor that slowed the breed's progress was that for several generations the breed could only develop via the female kittens born, since the male kittens are sterile, as is true of many hybrids. Second generation males (F2s) are sterile as well, and only about 50% of the third generation males (F3s) are fertile.

Mill persisted and encouraged other breeders to join her in her, and by 1985, she had sufficient generations to show the Bengal. She began taking her Bengals to cat shows sponsored by

TICA. The breed sparked immediate controversy among breeders and fanciers because of the hybridization. Some fanciers felt that the breed could pose a hazard in the show hall, and others felt breeding domestics with wildcats was unwise from a conservation standpoint. However, the cat lovers visiting the shows were immediately entranced by the breed's beauty, and Mill didn't have trouble recruiting breeders for her select group. In 1988, The International Bengal Cat Society (TIBCS) was formed, and soon became the largest club for Bengal enthusiasts and breeders in the world. The members were dedicated to promoting and preserving the Bengal of domestic cat.

In 1991, TICA accepted the Bengal for championship status. TICA requires the cats be bred Bengal to Bengal for at least four generations (F4 or better) to be shown to ensure the mild, docile temperament. However, in CFA the Bengal is still considered the party crasher at the cat fancy cocktail party. CFA's long-standing policy has been to disallow any breeds created from domestic cat/wild cat crosses, and that policy seems not likely to change. Not only are Bengals not allowed to be shown at CFA-sponsored shows, they are not permitted in the same building. They are not allowed to compete in any other events, such as agility trials, at any CFA-sponsored activity, for fear of liability issues connected with the temperament of cats with wild blood, even when the wild blood admixture was many years in the past.

All other associations have fully accepted the Bengal—even ACFA who had reservations in the beginning and accepted Bengals for registration but not exhibition because of temperament concerns. Bengal breeders and fanciers have proven to their satisfaction that the Bengal is fully domestic in temperament and no danger to judges, exhibitors, or the show-going public.

Only Bengals well removed from the leopard cat are eligible to be shown for championship. To be shown in TICA, for example, a Bengal must be what's called a SBT (Stud Book Traditional), which means the cat must show at least three generations of Bengal-to-Bengal breeding on its pedigree, with no cats of unknown registry or of leopard cat or part-leopard cat heritage within that three generation period. This means SBT Bengals are at least four generations away from the original leopard cat/domestic cat mating. Most pet Bengals are F4s (filial 4, or fourth generation) or SBTs; although Bengals closer to the wild blood are available from some breeders. F1 Bengals (filial 1, or first generation) have a parent that's a leopard cat; F2 Bengals have a leopard cat grandparent; F3 Bengals have a leopard cat great-grandparent; F4 Bengals have a leopard cat great-great-grandparent, and so on. Therefore, it's important to know what you're buying when acquiring a Bengal as a pet or to show. Before purchasing a Bengal that's an F2 (second generation) or F3 (third generation) as a pet, be sure the cat is domestic in temperament and uses the litter box appropriately. Generally, only experienced breeders and fanciers are appropriate owners of F1 and F2 Bengals. Leopard cats are very difficult to litter box train because in the wild they eliminate in running water to prevent larger predators from tracking them. That's only one of the reasons leopard cats make poor pets.

Today, the exotic look and lively personality have won the Bengal an enthusiastic following. Mill and the other dedicated breeders are working to better the Bengal. Although the associations require show Bengals to be at least four generations away from the leopard cat, occasionally some breeders still create new lines by crossing domestics with leopard cats to improve the body or coat type. The leopard cat (*Prionailurus bengalensis*), a small wild cat about the size of the domestic, is one of the most widespread felid species, found throughout India, China, the Korean peninsula, and Far East Russia, and most of Southeast Asia including Sumatra, Java, Borneo, Taiwan, and the Philippines. Considered of least concern among endangered wildcat species, it's possible to obtain the licensing to own and breed them in the United States, depending upon your state, county, and city. Once used to begin a new line, however, that particular line must start over and the descendants can't be shown for championship for another four generations.

PERSONALITY

The Bengal may look like a wild cat, but fanciers say this breed is as lovably friendly as any full-blooded domestic. Full of life and very people-oriented, Bengals as playful, gregarious, energetic cats with a generous dose of feline curiosity. Bengal enthusiasts rave about the breed's personality and playful antics.

Bengals form strong bonds of love and loyalty with their human companions, and become faithful, affectionate, fun-loving friends, provided you meet them halfway and give them the love they need in return. Athletic and agile, Bengals love to climb and will gravitate toward the highest point in any room. Bengals are great sources of entertainment; turn off the TV, and watch your Bengal; they're the best show around.

One of the main characteristics that make them so special as companions is their intelligence. It's not surprising Bengals are sharp as furry tacks since surviving in the jungle takes wit as well as strong jaws, sharp claws, and lightning reflexes. Bengals learn very quickly, and enjoy learning new behaviors like walking their human companions on leads, and teaching their humans how to play fetch. Yes, Bengals are skillful teachers of humankind, and are particularly adept at instructing their human friends on dinnertime and what the favored cuisine should be. In fact, they learn tricks you'd rather they didn't, such as turning on and off light switches, opening doors, and flushing toilets. The curious Bengal will get into everything, and changes in the environment provoke a quick response from the Bengal. Open a cupboard and your Bengal will dive in for a look-see, and will rearrange the contents if they're not up to Bengal standards.

Because of the leopard cat's habit of eliminating in water to hide their scent from larger predators, some Bengals learn to use the toilet. Like their wild relatives, Bengals relish their freedom; they dislike being held or restrained. This isn't unique to Bengals but to most very active breeds.

Bengals form strong bonds with their human companions.

Bengals love water, particularly if it's running. Some only dip an occasional paw under the faucet, while others will join you for a romp in the tub or shower—as long as it's their idea. Some fanciers report that their cats' fascination with water borders on obsession, and steps must be taken to keep floods to a minimum; Bengal owners quickly learn to keep the toilet lid down.

CONFORMATION

Part of the fascination with spotted breeds in general and the Bengal in particular lies in the wild appearance. Bringing home a mini leopard, one with a lithe, feral body and vivid spotted coat, reminds us that our feline

GENERAL (TICA STANDARD)	The goal of the Bengal breeding program is to create a domestic cat that has physical features distinctive to the small forest-dwelling wildcats, and with the loving, dependable temperament of the domestic cat. Keeping this goal in mind, judges shall give special merit to those characteristics in the appearance of the Bengal that are distinct from those found in other domestic cat breeds.
BODY	Torso long and substantial, not oriental or foreign. Medium to large, but not quite as large as the largest domestic breed. Boning is sturdy and firm; never delicate. Very muscular, especially in the males; one of the most distinguishing features.
HEAD	Broad modified wedge with rounded contours. Longer than it is wide. Slightly small in proportion to body, but not to be taken to extreme. Skull behind the ears makes a gentle curve and flows into neck. Overall look of head should be as distinct from the domestic cat as possible. Strong chin, aligns with tip of nose in profile. Muzzle full and broad, with large, prominent whisker pads and high, pronounced cheekbones. Slight muzzle break at the whisker pads. Nose large and wide; slightly puffed nose leather.
EARS	Medium to small, relatively short, with wide base and rounded tops. Set as much on side as top of head, following the contour of the face in the frontal view, and pointing forward in the profile view. Light horizontal furnishings acceptable; but lynx tipping undesirable.
EYES	Oval, almost round. Large, but not bugged. Set wide apart, back into face, and on slight bias toward base of ear. Eye color independent of coat color except in the lynx points. The more richness and depth of color the better.
LEGS AND PAWS	Legs medium length, slightly longer in the back than in the front. Feet large, round, with prominent knuckles.
TAIL	Medium length, thick, tapered at end with rounded tip.
COAT	Length short to medium. Texture dense and luxurious, close-lying, unusually soft and silky to the touch. Patterns spotted or marbled. Spots shall be random, or aligned horizontally. Rosettes showing two distinct colors or shades. Contrast with ground color must be extreme, giving distinct pattern and sharp edges. Belly must be spotted.
COLOR	Brown tabby, seal sepia tabby, seal mink tabby, seal lynx point, black silver tabby, seal silver sepia tabby, seal silver mink tabby, seal silver lynx point. Spotted or marbled patterns only.

DISQUALIFY	Spots on body running together vertically forming a mackerel tabby pattern on spotted cats; circular bulls-eye pattern on marbled cats; substantially darker point color (as compared to color of body markings) in seal sepia, seal mink, or seal lynx point cats. Any distinct locket on the neck, chest, abdomen or any other area. Withhold all awards: belly not patterned.
ALLOWABLE OUTCROSSES	None.

companions walked on the wild side only a few thousand years ago and still retain many of their wild instincts. We caress the spotted coat and marvel at the mysterious feline nature. The Bengal's spots are aligned horizontally rather than in random or tabby configuration. Rosettes in a semicircle around a redder center is the preferred look. Emphasis is put on the contrast between the spots and the background color; the edges should be sharp and pattern distinct for a show-quality cat. In the marbled pattern, the markings are derived from the classic tabby gene, but the overall look is random, giving the impression of marble.

Bengals sometimes possess a "glitter gene" that gives the fur an iridescent glow, as if covered with warm frost. Three recessive coat variations have been developed: the snow leopard, the marbled, and the snow marbled. These types are still quite rare.

The standard for the Bengal, unlike most other cat breeds, includes a description of the cat's ideal temperament, describing it as confident, alert, curious, and friendly. Any sign of definite challenge disqualifies the cat in order to prevent temperament problems from being perpetuated in the breeding stock. TICA requires that show cats be bred Bengal to Bengal for at least three generations to ensure a docile temperament.

Bengals are hardy, healthy cats with few known breed-related genetic problems. Breeders have worked hard to keep the Bengal free of the genetic problems found in some other breeds. The most serious known disease is feline hypertrophic cardiomyopathy (HCM), the most common feline heart disease; the first noticeable symptom is often sudden death. While it's possible for any cat to have this disease, ask your breeder if any affected cats are known in the pedigree or the cattery, and ask if breeding cats are screened. Look for a breed who screens his or her Bengals for cardiomyopathy, polycystic kidney disease (PKD), and pyruvate kinase (PK) deficiency.

Note: before considering purchasing a domestic cat with wildcat ancestors, be sure to check your state's laws regarding the owning of hybrids. It's also strongly recommended that you research your county and city laws, and your homeowner association rules if applicable, prior to buying hybrid animals. More information can be found online at www.hybridlaw.com.

HISTORY

According to the centuries-old legend, pure white cats resided in the Buddhist temples of the country of Burma (now Myanmar), and were revered as the feline carriers of the souls of priests who had departed the mortal plain. (The term for this process is transmutation, which means to change from one form to another.) The Goddess of transmutation, Tsim-Kyan-Kse, was worshipped in these temples, represented by a golden statue with glowing sapphire eyes.

Mun-Ha, a priest and worshipper of Tsim-Kyan-Kse, served at the temple of Lao-Tsun. Every evening Mun-Ha's faithful companion Sinh, one of the 100 sacred white cats that lived at the temple, joined Mun-Ha for his evening prayers in front of the golden statue.

Seal point Birman.

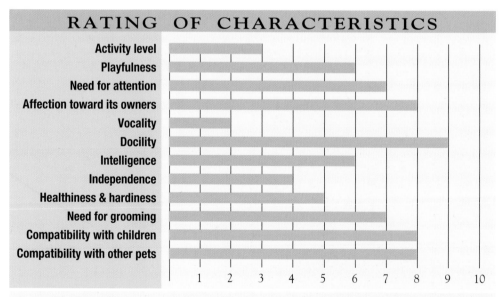

RATING OF CHARACTERISTICS

Characteristic	Rating
Activity level	3
Playfulness	6
Need for attention	7
Affection toward its owners	8
Vocality	2
Docility	9
Intelligence	6
Independence	4
Healthiness & hardiness	5
Need for grooming	7
Compatibility with children	8
Compatibility with other pets	8

1—breed exhibits the least amount of this characteristic, 10—breed exhibits the most of this characteristic

One day, marauders from Siam raided the temple for its riches and struck down Mun-Ha. As Mun-Ha lay dying, Sinh put his paws on Mun-ha's head and faced the statue of Tsim-Kyan-Kse. Suddenly, Sinh's white fur changed to a beautiful golden hue, his face, tail, and legs darkened to the color of the earth, and his eyes changed from yellow to a deep, sapphire blue. Sinh's paws, however, remained white as a symbol of Mun-Ha's pure spirit. The next morning, all the temple cats had undergone the same transformation. For the next seven days Sinh refused all food and finally died, carrying Mun-Ha's spirit into paradise.

The more scientific, and less romantic, story of this breed, also called the Sacred Cat of Burma, begins in 1919, when a pair of Birman cats arrived in France. Two different accounts are associated with this pair of cats and, like the legend, neither can be documented. The first one alleges that around the beginning of the twentieth century, the temple of Tsim-Kyan-Kse was again raided. Two Westerners, Auguste Pavie and Major Gordon Russell, helped some of the priests and their sacred cats escape to Tibet. When the two returned to France in 1919, they were given a pair of Birman cats by the grateful priests.

In the second and less heroic account, an individual named Mr. Vanderbilt bought the pair of Birmans from a disgruntled servant of the temple of Lao-Tsun. In both accounts, the male cat, Maldapour, died on the ocean voyage to France, but the female, Sita, arrived in France pregnant with Maldapour's offspring, and became the European foundation of the Birman breed.

The breed flourished, and in 1925 the Birman was formally recognized in France and the first breed standard was written. The breed was further developed and refined in that country until the chaos of World War II, when the breed almost became extinct. At one point, the Birman breed again dwindled to a single pair of cats. It took many years of careful crossbreeding to reestablish the Birman; the breeds used to refurbish the breed were likely Persians and Siamese (and possibly others, such as the Turkish Angora), but by 1955 the breed had achieved its former glory and began to be exported to other countries. Birmans were officially recognized as a purebred breed in Britain in 1966.

In 1959, the first pair of Birman cats arrived in the United States, and in 1967 CFA officially accepted the Birman for championship. Since then, the Birman has flourished in North America and has become a popular and well-known breed. Today, the Birman is one of the most popular longhaired breeds, and all North American cat associations recognize the Birman for championship.

PERSONALITY

Birmans are affectionate, gentle, and faithful companions with an air of dignity that seems to invite adoration by their human attendants. As former temple cats, Birmans seem to have become accustomed to adoration. They are very

GENERAL	A cat of mystery and legend, the Birman is a colorpointed cat with long silky hair and four pure white feet. It is strongly built, elongated and stocky, neither svelte nor cobby. The distinctive head has strong jaws, firm chin, and medium length nose.
BODY	Elongated and stocky, with a good muscular feel.
HEAD	Skull strong, broad, and rounded; a slight flat spot just in front of each ear, and a slight flat spot on forehead in between the ears. Forehead slopes back and is slightly convex. Nose is medium in length and width, in proportion to size of the head; nose starts just below eyes and is Roman (slightly convex) in shape and profile; nostrils are set low on nose leather. Cheeks full with somewhat rounded muzzle; muzzle neither short and blunted nor pointed and narrow. Jaws heavy. Chin strong and well-developed.
EARS	Medium in length; almost as wide at the base as tall. Modified to a rounded point at tip; set as much to the side as to the top of the head.
EYES	Almost round with sweet expression. Set well apart, with the outer corner tilted very slightly upward. Blue in color, the deeper and more vivid blue the better.
LEGS AND PAWS	Legs medium in length and heavy. Paws large, round, and firm; five toes in front, four behind. Paw pads: pink preferred but dark spot(s) on paw pad(s) acceptable because of two colors in pattern.
TAIL	Medium in length, in pleasing proportion to the body.
COAT	Medium long to long, silken in texture, with heavy ruff around the neck; slightly curly on stomach. Fur does not mat.
COLOR	Seal point, blue point, chocolate point, and lilac point. Body color even; strong contrast between body color and points. Points of mask, ears, legs, and tail dense and clearly defined, all the same shade. Mask covers entire face including whisker pads and connects to ears by tracings. No ticking or white hair in points. Front paws have white gloves ending in even line across paw at, or between, second or third joints. Upper limit of white is metacarpal (dew) pad. Glove on back paws covers all toes; may extend higher than front gloves. Gloves extend up back of hock, called laces. Laces end in point or inverted "V" and extend ½ to ¾ of the way up hock. Lower or higher laces acceptable, but must not extend beyond hock. Ideally, front gloves match, back gloves match, and laces match.

DISQUALIFY	Lack of white gloves on any paw. Kinked or abnormal tail. Crossed eyes. Incorrect number of toes. Areas of pure white in the points, if not connected to gloves and part of or extension of gloves. Discrete areas of point color in the gloves, if not connected to point color of legs (exception, paw pads). White on back legs beyond hock. Eye color other than blue. White tail tips or chin spots.
ALLOWABLE OUTCROSSES	None.

intelligent and affectionate, according to fanciers, and very people-oriented. They will generally greet visitors with curiosity rather than fear. Because of their gentle temperaments, Birmans are easy to handle, care for, and show, and they make ideal pets for anyone who wants quiet companions that will offer love and affection in return for just a little well-deserved worship.

CONFORMATION

In the ideal Birman, the matching white gloves on the front paws should end at or between the second and third joints of the paw. On the back paws, the gloves should cover all the toes and may extend up higher than the gloves on the front paws. The gloving must extend up the back of the hock and in this area are called laces. Ideally, the laces end in a point or inverted "V" and extend one-half to three-quarters of the way up the hock. Symmetry of the laces is desirable.

In a perfect Birman, the front gloves match, the back gloves match, and the laces match.

Ideally, the front gloves should match, the back gloves should match, and the laces should match. However, getting well-gloved Birmans is the thorn in the paw of every Birman breeder.

Birmans are born pure white, and then develop color on the points. The shading of the legs comes later, so the period of waiting for the glove markings to appear is an anxious one for Birman breeders, since the glove markings are the most difficult to perfect. The gene governing the trait is the dominant white spotting factor, which is very difficult to control.

HISTORY

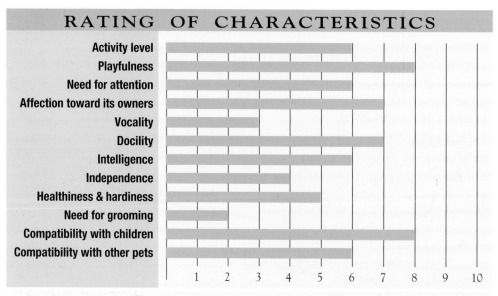

The Bombay was created in the 1950s by the late Nikki Horner of Louisville, Kentucky, an American breeder who wanted to develop a cat that possessed the conformation of the Burmese but with a sleek black coat and copper eyes instead of brown fur and yellow eyes—sort of a pint-sized panther. A breeder and exhibitor since the age of 16, Horner bred a number of breeds including American Shorthairs, Burmese, Himalayans, Persians, and Siamese over her long, prosperous cat fancy career. However, Horner wanted to create a living legacy before she left for the great show hall in the sky. She named the breed after Bombay, India, land of the black leopard. She first attempted to breed a female Burmese to a black American Shorthair. The results were disappointing; they looked more like poor American Shorthairs than anything else.

For her second try Horner chose her cats more carefully. She shopped around until she found a black American Shorthair male that had the rich eye color she wanted and bred him to one of her best champion Burmese. After much trial

Bombays have brilliant copper eyes.

RATING OF CHARACTERISTICS

Characteristic	Rating (1–10)
Activity level	6
Playfulness	8
Need for attention	6
Affection toward its owners	7
Vocality	3
Docility	7
Intelligence	6
Independence	6
Healthiness & hardiness	5
Need for grooming	2
Compatibility with children	8
Compatibility with other pets	6

1—breed exhibits the least amount of this characteristic, 10—breed exhibits the most of this characteristic

✳ **Championship status in all associations**

and error, Horner finally produced the results she was looking for: a cat with the conformation and short polished coat of the Burmese, and the American Shorthair's copper-colored eyes and black color.

However, Horner soon found that creating a breed, even one as striking as the Bombay, doesn't mean cat fancy acceptance. Her many years in the cat fancy and her past winning ribbons didn't help her bypass any of the pesky steps; Burmese breeders and the cat associations didn't make exceptions for her new kid on the block. Since the breed had not been accepted for championship, Horner had no champion Bombays with which to catch the attention of the cat-buying public—a new and not very pleasant feeling for Horner after so many years as a show-stopping top exhibitor.

It wasn't until 1970 that the breed was accepted for registration by the CFA. Advancing from registration to provisional status meant Horner had to form at least one breed club, register 100 examples of the breed, and provide a list of 25 active breeders. Horner worked hard to recruit new breeders and fanciers to her breed.

Eighteen years after Horner began her efforts, the breed finally earned CFA championship status on May 1, 1976. By then, other breeders had joined Horner. However, the cat fancy was still unimpressed with the Bombay's conformation. Breeders Herb and Suzanne Zwecker were instrumental in improving the breed and bringing

the Bombay into the cat fancy limelight. They started over with new stock because they felt the original lines had become too inbred. They bred a non-pedigreed black domestic shorthair male to one of their best sable Burmese females. In time they produced the breakthrough cat for the breed—a Bombay named Road to Fame's Luv It Black, who in 1985 was named CFA's Second Best Cat and Best Shorthair. This brought the breed new respect and interest in the cat fancy.

Before long, the Bombay caught the interest of cat fanciers in the United Kingdom as well. In the United Kingdom, Bombays are classified as part of the Asian group of cat breeds, a group that includes the Burmilla and the Tiffanie. The Bombay is considered an Asian self-colored shorthair, and is accepted for competition by the Governing Council of the Cat Fancy (GCCF). While still uncommon in both the United Kingdom and in North America, the breed has a dedicated following.

PERSONALITY

If an aloof, independent cat is what you're craving, this breed isn't for you. The Bombay is an endearing breed: playful, loving, lighthearted, and agreeable to just about any suggestion from its human companion, particularly if that includes an invigorating game of fetch or a cuddle on the couch. Due to their hybrid heritage, Bombays strike a pleasing balance between the moderate American Shorthair and the frisky, vocal Burmese. However, since the American Shorthair is rarely used as an outcross today, Bombays tend to be more like the Burmese than like the American Shorthair. They are very clever and people-oriented (thanks to the Burmese background), but won't talk your ear off every second of the day (thanks to the American Shorthair). However, Bombays will get their thoughts across if they have something vital to impart, and you can count on them to stare you down with those hypnotizing copper eyes and repeat the message until you give them your full attention. They want constant attention, and they are clever in their attempts to gain your notice. When you sit down, don't be surprised to see your Bombay sitting beside you moments later. Bombays are very attached to their humans, and tend to love the entire family rather than bond with one person. Fanciers say they are particularly good with well-behaved children.

Known for their curiosity and high intelligence, Bombays love to follow their human companions all over the house. They love to keep an eye on every move and help with every chore. This doesn't get the chores done faster, but it's certainly entertaining.

CONFORMATION

Black to the roots, the Bombay's coat invites caressing with its fine, satin-like texture and shimmering "patent leather" sheen. Bombays develop slowly, gaining their eye color and gleaming coat well after they are four months old. Some prospective buyers tend to think the kittens look rather ordinary. Bombays, like fine wine, improve with age.

Bombay breeders outcross to the Burmese to maintain the head and body type and short satin-like texture. Very few outcross to American Shorthairs now that the dominant black coloration is well established. In fact, in TICA the American Shorthair is no longer an acceptable outcross.

However, the Bombay inherited one defect from the Burmese, a genetic disorder that affects the development of the fetus' skull. This recessive mutation that causes a congenital craniofacial defect in Burmese and Bombay cats is common in contemporary lines of Burmese, and has been identified by the Lyons Feline Genetics Research Laboratory at UC Davis, California. One copy of the Burmese head defect mutation doesn't cause the craniofacial defect but can produce a foreshortened facial structure. Kittens that inherit two copies of the

Notice the glossy "painted on" coats of these beautiful Bombays.

GENERAL	The Bombay is a medium-size cat, well-balanced, friendly, alert, and outgoing; muscular and having a surprising weight for its size. The body and tail should be of medium length, the head rounded with medium-sized, wide-set ears, a moderate nose stop, which is visible (not a break), large rounded wide-set eyes, and an overall look of excellent proportions and carriage.
BODY	Medium in size, muscular in development, neither compact nor rangy.
HEAD	Pleasingly rounded with no sharp angles. Face full with considerable breadth between the eyes, blending gently into a broad well-developed moderately rounded muzzle that maintains rounded contours of the head. In profile there is a moderate visible stop; however, it should not present a "pugged" or "snubbed" look. Moderate stop not considered a break, but a slight indentation at bridge of nose between the eyes providing change of direction from rounded head to medium, rounded muzzle. End of nose is slightly rounded down completing roundness of head.
EARS	Medium in size and set well apart on a rounded skull, alert, tilting slightly forward, broad at the base, and with slightly rounded tips.
EYES	Set far apart with rounded aperture. Color ranging from gold to copper, the greater the depth and brilliance the better.
LEGS AND PAWS	Legs in proportion to the body and tail. Paws round, toes five in front, four in back.
TAIL	Straight, medium in length; neither short nor whippy.
COAT	Fine, short, satin-like texture; close-lying with a shimmering patent leather sheen.
COLOR	Mature specimen black to the roots. Kitten coats should darken and become more sleek with age.
DISQUALIFY	Kinked or abnormal tail. Lockets or spots. Incorrect number of toes. Nose leather or paw pads other than black. Green eyes. Improper bite. Extreme break that interferes with normal breathing and tearing of eyes.
ALLOWABLE OUTCROSSES	Black American Shorthair, Sable Burmese.

mutation are stillborn or must be euthanized at birth. The Veterinary Genetics Laboratory at UC Davis, California now offers the DNA test for this defect to help breeders identify cats that carry the gene. Breeders can use the test to avoid breeding carriers together, and to eliminate the gene from their bloodlines.

Blue British Shorthair.

HISTORY

The British Shorthair is native to Great Britain in the same way that the American Shorthair is native to America—long ago it was transported there from somewhere else. However, the progenitor of the Brit, as it's affectionately called, is probably Great Britain's oldest natural breed of cat, and was roaming around Great Britain for centuries before its cousin journeyed to the New World. In many ways, the British Shorthair's struggle for recognition resembles the American Shorthair's fight for acceptance in North America. Both began as working cats and weren't appreciated as the special breeds they are for many years.

The Brit's progenitor was a common street cat once called the European Shorthair. This breed, whose conformation is much different from the Brits you'll see in show halls today, came to Great Britain some 2,000 years ago, courtesy of the Roman Empire. As they conquered and colonized other lands, the Romans brought cats along with them to control

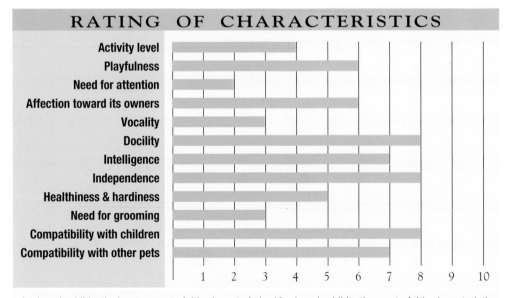

RATING OF CHARACTERISTICS

Characteristic	Rating (1–10)
Activity level	4
Playfulness	6
Need for attention	4
Affection toward its owners	6
Vocality	3
Docility	7
Intelligence	7
Independence	7
Healthiness & hardiness	7
Need for grooming	3
Compatibility with children	8
Compatibility with other pets	7

1—breed exhibits the least amount of this characteristic, 10—breed exhibits the most of this characteristic

✳ **Championship status in all associations**

rodent populations. These cats had been obtained from the Egyptians, who were very tight-pawed with their treasured felines. Eventually, however, Phoenician caravans transported them along trade routes, and Roman armies smuggled them out of Egypt and carried them along to many lands. Although the Phoenicians first introduced cats to England, the Romans were most likely responsible for their widespread establishment when Rome invaded the British Isles. Eventually, the Romans were driven from the Isles, but the cats they had brought with them remained.

The cats left behind didn't look like today's British Shorthair. Lithe with long, elegant bones, these cats were sandy brown or yellow-gray in color, with ticked coats like the Abyssinian and tabby markings on the face, legs, and tail. They were probably members of, or closely related to, the African wildcat, *Felis silvestris lybica*, the progenitor of all domestic cats. After arriving in Europe, however, they interbred with the European wildcat, *Felis silvestris silvestris*, a local wildcat subspecies inhabiting most of Europe. This caused a shift in both coat and body style, since the European wildcat has a broad head, small wide-set ears, a sturdy, muscular body, and short, thick fur. Some European wildcats bear the mackerel tabby pattern; this common tabby pattern found today in so many breeds and random-bred cats may have arisen from the European wildcat.

Because of the colder and wetter conditions, the cats in Europe developed stocky, muscular body styles and thicker, water-repelling coats that were favorable to the climate. For hundreds of years, these cats earned their livings as perfect mousetraps in Great Britain's barns, granaries, alleys, gardens, and households. Cats were largely considered all-natural pest control rather than pampered house pets.

From these working cats, the British Shorthair developed into a stalwart, substantial breed. British cat owners began to change their attitudes in the 1800s, when they started to appreciate these hardy alley cats for their beauty, strength, personality, and their value as companions.

British Shorthairs are affectionate but not clingy.

Blue British Shorthairs, at first simply called "Shorthairs," were favorites of cat enthusiast Harrison Weir, who is considered the father of the cat fancy. Mr. Weir was instrumental in getting the British Shorthair recognized as a breed in its own right. When he held his now-famous first modern-day cat show in 1871 at The Crystal Palace in Sydenham, London, England, Weir wrote the standards by which each breed should be judged, and elevated Britain's common garden cat to the lofty and patriotic name of "British Shorthair." At that first show, Weir's own 14-year-old female blue tabby British Shorthair was awarded Best in Show. The show was such a success that exhibiting pedigreed cats suddenly became all the rage in the United Kingdom, and through Weir's efforts, British Shorthairs became popular with the British cat fancy.

Just before the turn of the century, longhaired exotics caught the cat fancy's eye and British Shorthairs declined in popularity. Nevertheless, Brits held their own until the chaos of World War II decimated the breed, along with most other European breeds as well.

After the war, breeders dedicated to preserving the British Shorthair gained grudging permission from the Governing Council of the

British Shorthair.

Cat Fancy (GCCF) to crossbreed their Brits with other breeds to rebuild the gene pool. Domestic shorthairs, Russian Blues, Burmese, Korats, Chartreux, and Persians were bred into the remaining bloodlines to rejuvenate what was left of the breed. It took many generations to bring the breed back to its former glory, but eventually breeders attained the conformation they wanted—one that reflected the powerful build, hardiness, muscular strength, and adaptability that had allowed the cat to survive all the years of hardship and persecution. Because of the number of Russian Blues, Chartreuxes, and blue Persians used in the bloodlines, blue became the dominant color, and for a number of years the breed was called the British Blue.

American cat fanciers took little notice of the British Shorthair until the 1960s; the breed was first accepted for championship in the United States by the American Cat Association (ACA) in 1967. In 1970, ACFA recognized the breed for championship in only one color—solid blue—and under the now obsolete name "British Blue." Blue was, and still is, the most common color both here and in Great Britain, due to the large number of Russian Blue, Chartreux, Korats, and blue Persians bred into the bloodlines after the war. In ACFA, Brits of other colors had to be shown as American Shorthairs. Other associations refused to accept British Shorthairs under any condition; because of the many outcrosses after the war, most organizations considered the breed a hybrid.

However, a solid black British Shorthair named Manana Channaine earned so many ACFA wins as an American Shorthair that the ASH breeders pushed to have the interloping Brit removed from the American Shorthair classes. This brought new attention to the British Shorthair, and made it apparent that quality Brits came in other colors besides blue. In the 1970s, Brit breeders campaigned for the Brit's recognition in all its myriad colors and patterns. The breed slowly earned supporters, and between 1970 and 1980 the North American cat associations accepted the Brit for championship in all the many colors of the breed. Today, the Brit has an active following, and Brits have earned acceptance in all North American cat registries. In Great Britain, the breed also has many fans; in the GCCF the British Shorthair is accepted in many colors and patterns.

PERSONALITY

If you're looking for a cat that will loot your refrigerator and swing dizzily from your chandeliers, then the British Shorthair is not for you. Fanciers say the British Shorthair is the perfect household companion if you like a breed that's undemanding, not always underfoot or in your face. British shorthairs like to keep a low profile; they are affectionate but not clingy, playful but not overactive. They are quiet, even-tempered, and undemanding with a bit of typical British reticence, particularly when they're first introduced. When they get over their initial reserve, however, they become extremely faithful companions. Brits do need love and attention if they are to become the loyal, loving companions they can be; the more attention and affection you give them, the more they will repay you in kind. Once they get to know and trust you, Brits are confident and devoted, and enjoy following you from room to room to keep an eye on your activities. They are calm, quiet companions, appreciating quality time without demanding your total attention. Brits make great apartment cats, being alert and playful without being hyper or destructive.

British Shorthairs tend to show their loyalty to the entire family rather than select one person with whom to bond. They tend to be more independent than many breeds and usually adapt well to most situations. Brits tend not to be vocal cats; they make tiny squeaking sounds rather than meows, which is quite humorous coming from those burly bodies. They make up for it by some of the loudest purring you've ever heard; Brits are known for their motor boat type purrs.

One thing Brits are not, however, is lap cats. They'd much rather sit beside you, or curl up at your feet, than cuddle on your lap. Brits dislike being picked up, and tolerate it with legs stiffly stretched out to push you away. They detest being kissed, too, but head presses are acceptable, and they accept petting with great enthusiasm and mighty purrs of appreciation. They get along with other animals in the home, including dogs as long as the proper introductions are made. British Shorthairs are at their very best with children, and children love these plush smiling friends.

CONFORMATION

In CCA and TICA, the British Long-hair is accepted as a championship breed. The body and head conformation is the same; only the coat conformation is different. The standard calls for semi-long, straight, dense fur that stands away from the body, and is not long and flowing. A ruff and britches are desirable. A fluff-plush texture is desired, dense, with a natural protective appearance. The texture may differ slightly in colors other than blue.

Like the American Shorthair, the British Shorthair is known for its health and vigor. The only major health problem is the inherited polycystic kidney disease (PKD). PKD causes multiple cysts to develop on both kidneys, resulting in renal failure. Fortunately, a PKD genetic test is available from the UC Davis School of Veterinary Medicine Veterinary Genetics Laboratory, which can help breeders screen out affected breeding stock. Currently the VGL recommends the PKD1 test for British Shorthairs, Persians, Exotics, Scottish Folds, Burmillas, Himalayans, and Persian out-crosses. Be sure to talk to your breeder about this and any other health concerns, and buy from a breeder who tests for PKD and provides a written health guarantee.

In addition, both A and B blood types exist in British Shorthair bloodlines, which is only a problem if you plan to breed your Brit. Type B is usually very rare; researchers estimate that less than one percent of U.S. domestic cats have type B blood. However, some purebred breeds have higher percentages of type B blood because of inbreeding or line-breeding, and British Shorthairs have about 35 percent type B blood, according to a study conducted by the University of Pennsylvania. Queens with type B blood, when bred to toms with type A blood, can produce litters with both type B and type A kittens. The kittens with type A blood are born apparently healthy but fade rapidly and die 24 to 72 hours after birth. This is sometimes called "fading kitten syndrome," but actually is due to the natural antibodies that occur, causing neonatal isoerythrolysis (NI). The A-type kittens absorb the anti-A antibodies from the colostrum when they nurse, which attacks and destroys the kitten's red blood cells, causing death. Fortunately, a DNA test has been developed for the gene and mutation associated with the B blood group at the UC Davis. British Shorthair and other high risk breeds can be tested so compatible mates can be selected to avoid blood type conflict in the kittens.

GENERAL	The British Shorthair is a compact, well-balanced, and powerful cat, with a short, very dense coat. Individuals convey an overall impression of balance and proportion in which no feature is exaggerated to foster weakness or extremes.
BODY	Medium to large, well-knit, and powerful. Level back and a deep broad chest.
HEAD	Round and massive. Round face with round underlying bone structure well set on short thick neck. Forehead should be rounded with slight flat plane on top of head. Forehead should not slope. Nose is medium, broad. In profile there is a gentle dip. Chin is firm, well-developed in line with nose and upper lip. Muzzle is distinctive, well-developed, with definite stop beyond large, round whisker pads.
EARS	Medium in size, broad at the base, rounded at the tips. Set far apart, fitting into (without distorting) rounded contour of the head.
EYES	Large, round, well opened. Set wide apart and level. Eye color depends upon coat color.
LEGS AND PAWS	Legs short to medium, well-boned, and strong. In proportion to the body. Forelegs are straight. Paws round and firm. Toes five in front
TAIL	Medium length in proportion to the body, thicker at base, tapering slightly to a rounded tip.
COAT	Short, very dense, well bodied and firm to the touch. Not double coated or woolly.
COLOR	Any other color or pattern with the exception of those showing evidence of hybridization resulting in the colors chocolate, lavender, the Himalayan pattern, or these combinations with white.
DISQUALIFY	Incorrect eye color, green rims in adults. Tail defects. Long or fluffy coat. Incorrect number of toes. Locket or button. Improper color or pigment in nose leather and/or paw pads in part or total. Any evidence of wryness of jaw, poor dentition (arrangement of teeth), or malocclusion.
ALLOWABLE OUTCROSSES	None.

HISTORY

The Burmese as we know and love it today can be traced back to a single female domestic cat named Wong Mau. In 1930, Wong Mau was transported into the United States from Rangoon, Burma (now Yangon, Myanmar), by Dr. Joseph Thompson of San Francisco. As the story goes, an unnamed sailor gave the feline to Dr. Thompson, who brought her home to the City by the Bay. Wong Mau was a small, fine-boned cat with a compact body, a rounded, short-muzzled head, round eyes set far apart, and a short, walnut-brown coat with darker brown on her face, ears, feet, and tail. Dr. Thompson was very taken with Wong Mau, since she looked like cats he'd seen in Tibet. Dr. Thompson had served as a U.S. Navy doctor for some

The Burmese body and head styles have changed over the years.

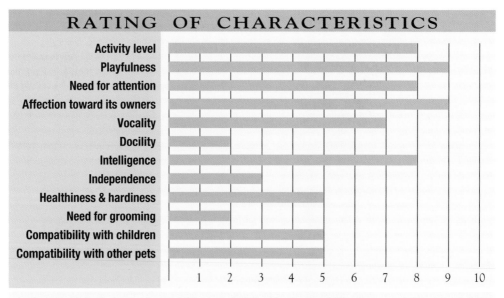

RATING OF CHARACTERISTICS

Characteristic	Rating
Activity level	9
Playfulness	9
Need for attention	8
Affection toward its owners	9
Vocality	7
Docility	2
Intelligence	8
Independence	3
Healthiness & hardiness	5
Need for grooming	5
Compatibility with children	5
Compatibility with other pets	5

1—breed exhibits the least amount of this characteristic, 10—breed exhibits the most of this characteristic

※ **Championship status in all associations**

years and developed a strong interest in Southeast Asia. He spent time in a monastery in Tibet and was enchanted by the shorthaired, solid brown cats in the area. These felines, called "copper cats" in their native land for their rich brown color, have existed in Southeast Asia for centuries. They were depicted and described in the ancient text *The Cat-Book Poems*, a manuscript of verses and paintings written in the city of Ayutthaya, Siam, some time between 1350 C.E. when the kingdom was founded, and 1767 C.E. when the city was destroyed by invaders. As the legend goes, the Burmese is a descendant of a breed once worshipped in Burmese temples as embodiments of gods. *The Cat-Book Poems* also shows pictures of Siamese and what is likely Korat cats,

suggesting these cats existed as separate, definable breeds for centuries.

Dr. Thompson was so taken with Wong Mau's beauty and personality that the doctor wanted to create a breeding program to isolate Wong Mau's distinguishing characteristics so he could reproduce her type and color. He enlisted the help of two eminent breeders, Virginia Cobb of Newton Cattery, and Billie Gerst of Gerstdale Cattery, and also recruited the help of noted geneticist Dr. Clyde E. Keeler of Harvard University. Between them, they developed a breeding program, which included the Siamese as the first outcross; the Siamese was considered the closest in conformation, since at that time the Siamese and the Burmese were similar in head and body type.

Devoted, loving cats, Burmese are loyal and people-oriented.

Over the years, the Siamese became more extremely svelte in body and head shape through selective breeding.

Wong Mau was bred to a sealpoint Siamese male named Tai Mau. The resulting kittens showed three different colors and patterns: beige, sable brown, and pointed. In the process, Dr. Thompson discovered that Wong Mau herself was a Siamese hybrid—half Siamese and half Burmese, what we would call a Tonkinese today (see the Tonkinese profile on page 276). Since the pointed pattern is a recessive trait and a cat must inherit a copy of the gene from both parents to have the pattern, Wong Mau herself must have possessed the gene for the pointed pattern.

The sable brown kittens were then crossed with one another and back to their mother Wong Mau. After several generations, he had identified three color variants: some looked like Wong Mau (medium brown with slightly darker points), some looked like Tai Mau (sealpoint Siamese), and some were a solid, dark chocolate brown that the doctor called the "dark color phase." Dr. Thompson thought this variety was the most beautiful and striking, and he and his team of breeders worked to isolate the gene governing this trait. The sable cats were crossed with each other or back to Wong Mau. The points were somewhat darker in color, most noticeable in Burmese kittens and becoming less apparent in adult cats. Later, it was discovered that the Burmese gene responsible for the sable color is a member of the albino series of gene alleles (see Chapter Four). The Burmese gene causes solid black to appear dark sable brown by reducing the amount of pigment in the hair. Today, the point-restricted color is not noticeable in adults, but it is notable in Burmese kittens to a certain extent.

The Contemporary Burmese has a rounded head and large, rounded eyes.

In 1936, CFA accepted the Burmese for registration, and Burmese cats were an immediate hit when they were introduced into North America's show halls in the late 1930s and early 1940s. Siamese breeders hissed over the acceptance of the Burmese, since they were afraid the Burmese would adulterate their Siamese stock, but most cat lovers and fanciers took an immediate liking to these beautiful brown cats. The results of the original breeding program were published in the April 1943 *Journal of Heredity*, written by Dr. Thompson, Virginia Cobb, Billie Gerst, and Dr. Clyde E. Keeler. Unfortunately,

Dr. Thompson died of a heart attack while the paper was in publication.

The paper brought the Burmese more attention and new breeders. Demand was much greater than supply, and to increase the gene pool, breeders continued to breed back to the Siamese, creating many hybrids, which some breeders sold as pedigreed Burmese. This caused much confusion over what comprised a pedigreed Burmese. CFA suspended registration of the Burmese in 1947, and insisted three generations of Burmese-to-Burmese breeding was necessary for cats to be registered as Burmese. The other associations that accepted the Burmese did not, but since only three North American cat associations existed at the time, it was a major setback to be excluded from the largest. Nevertheless, Burmese breeders got to work to regain their lost status. In 1953, CFA reinstated the Burmese for registration, and in 1957 CFA again granted championship status. In 1958, the breed club United Burmese Cat Fanciers wrote a single breed standard for Burmese breeders, to avoid such problems in the future. Adopted in 1959, the new standard added the words "somewhat compact" to the description. This was a very important change, since today's Contemporary Burmese are extremely compact. The word "somewhat" was later removed from the standard. Such changes showed that breeders were actively differentiating the Burmese from the Siamese, particularly because Siamese breeders were actively moving toward an increasingly svelte breed.

The actual look of the Burmese has changed over the years, achieving the diversity and current appearance through years of selective breeding. Almost thirty years ago, two distinct head types emerged: the Contemporary Burmese and the European Burmese.

PERSONALITY

Breeders and fanciers report that Burmese are amusing, playful, and super-smart, the perfect interactive cats for home, office, shop—any place people are in need of love and amusement. Devoted, loving cats, Burmese are loyal and people-oriented. Burmese will give you unconditional love even when you are not your most loveable. Burmese never grow up; they are as entertaining at 16 weeks as they are at 16 years. These streaks of brown lightning love to perform animated antics for your amusement and theirs. Full of high-spirited playfulness, they love to entertain their favorite humans by performing daring leaps to the top of the bookcase, pausing only to make sure their audience is watching. If their antics go unnoticed, they hop right down and fix you with an unflinching stare, demanding attention or else. Burmese are a very determined breed, and will win just about any battle of wills.

Fanciers report temperament differences between adult males and females. Spayed females are intelligent, highly curious, active, and deeply emotionally involved with their human companions. Altered males are wholly devoted to their humans too, but are a bit more moderate in temperament. After a game of fetch or hide and seek (they hide, you seek), they like to lounge about, usually on top of whatever you're doing. The only issue about which they are passionately concerned is the selected cuisine and how soon it will be served.

Burmese have a unique rasp to their voices and sound a bit like cats going hoarse from too much talking. However, Burmese are not as talkative as their Siamese neighbors, unless they have something important to express. Then they'll reiterate the message repeatedly until you get out your universal feline/human translator and take care of whatever is troubling them.

CONFORMATION

The Burmese's body style has changed over the years. The 1953 standard described the Burmese as "medium, dainty, and long." By 1957 the standard was changed to "midway between Domestic Shorthair and Siamese." The words "somewhat compact" were added to the standard in 1959; the word "somewhat" was dropped from the standard somewhat later. Since then, the standard has remained almost unchanged.

Over the last 20 years or so a difference of opinion has developed among breeders and fanciers as to the favored conformation of the breed. One group favors the European Burmese—longer, narrower muzzles with a less pronounced nose break and a slightly narrower head. The other favors the Contemporary Burmese—shorter, broader muzzle, pronounced nose break, and broader, rounder head shapes. Both conformation types can be seen in today's show halls. In ACFA and CFA, the European Burmese has been accepted for championship as a

breed in its own right. In CCA, CFF, and UFO, the breed is recognized under the name "Foreign Burmese." In TICA, the European Burmese is accepted as an experimental breed.

One of the main differences between the two breeds, besides the head and body type, is that the European Burmese comes in additional colors. Because the Burmese was crossbred with European Siamese lines that possessed the red gene, the colors red and cream were introduced, producing six additional colors.

The Contemporary Burmese has an inherited genetic disorder that affects the development of the fetus' skull. This recessive mutation that causes a congenital craniofacial defect is common in Contemporary Burmese, and the gene has been identified by the Lyons Feline Genetics Research Laboratory at UC Davis, California. One copy of the recessive head defect mutation doesn't cause the craniofacial defect but can produce a foreshortened facial structure. Kittens that inherit two copies of the mutation are stillborn or may need to be euthanized at birth. However, the Veterinary Genetics Laboratory at UC Davis, California now offers the DNA test for this defect to help breeders identify cats that carry the gene. Breeders can use the test to avoid breeding carriers together, and to eliminate the gene from their bloodlines.

Burmese also can be prone to gingivitis. Feeding a high quality tartar-control dry food will remove some of the tartar, but Burmese should get a dental checkup with their yearly physical and professional teeth cleanings as needed. If your Burmese needs it and will allow it, brush

GENERAL	The overall impression of the ideal Burmese would be a cat of medium size with substantial bone structure, good muscular development, and a surprising weight for its size. This together with a rounded head, expressive eyes, and a sweet expression presents a totally distinctive cat which is comparable to no other breed.
BODY	Medium in size, muscular in development, and presenting a compact appearance. Allowance to be made for larger size in males. An ample, rounded chest, with back level from shoulder to tail.
HEAD	Pleasingly rounded without flat planes whether viewed from the front or side. The face is full with considerable breadth between the eyes and blends gently into a broad, well-developed short muzzle that maintains the rounded contours of the head. In profile there is a visible nose break. The chin is firmly rounded, reflecting a proper bite. The head sits on a well-developed neck.
EARS	Medium in size, set well apart, broad at the base and rounded at the tips. Tilting slightly forward, the ears contribute to an alert appearance.
EYES	Large, set far apart, with rounded aperture.
LEGS AND PAWS	Legs well-proportioned to body. Paws round. Toes five in front and four behind.
TAIL	Straight, medium in length.
COAT	Fine, glossy, satin-like texture; short and very close lying.
COLOR	Sable, champagne, blue, platinum.
DISQUALIFY	Kinked tail, lockets or spots. Blue eyes. Crossed eyes. Incorrect nose leather or paw pad color. Malocclusion of the jaw that results in a severe underbite or overbite that visually prohibits the described profile and/or malformation that results in protruding teeth or a wry face or jaw. Distinct barring on the torso. Any color other than the four accepted colors of sable, champagne, blue, and platinum.
ALLOWABLE OUTCROSSES	Tonkinese through December 31, 2021.

your cat's teeth regularly with cat toothpaste and a child's size toothbrush; ask your veterinarian for instructions. Left untreated, gingivitis can lead to periodontal disease, which can cause tissue, tooth, and bone loss, and can undermine your cat's health and affect his nervous system, kidneys, liver, and heart.

Brilliant eye color is important in the show Chartreux.

HISTORY

The Chartreux (pronounced shär-TRUE), a true blue cat with a Mona Lisa smile and an amiable temperament, is France's contribution to the cat fancy. Since the Chartreux has been around for so many centuries, it's hard to say with certainty just where and when it first developed. Like most breeds with long histories, the Chartreux tale is the stuff of legends.

The most popular account tells that the Chartreux was bred by monks at the Grande Chartreuse Monastery, the chief monastery of the Carthusian order, located north of Grenoble in southeastern France. As the story goes, the Carthusian order of monks at the monastery, in their spare time between praying, liqueur-making, and weapon-forging, bred Chartreux cats with the same skill and dedication with which they created their world-famous yellow and green Chartreuse liqueurs. Allegedly, they selectively bred the cats

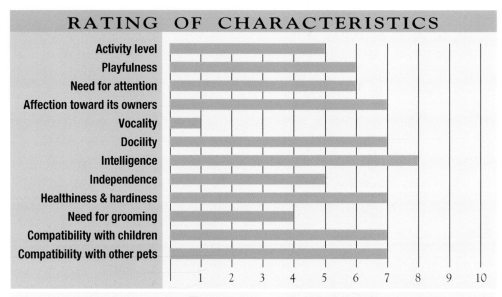

RATING OF CHARACTERISTICS

Characteristic	Rating (1–10)
Activity level	5
Playfulness	6
Need for attention	6
Affection toward its owners	7
Vocality	1
Docility	7
Intelligence	8
Independence	5
Healthiness & hardiness	7
Need for grooming	4
Compatibility with children	7
Compatibility with other pets	7

1—breed exhibits the least amount of this characteristic, 10—breed exhibits the most of this characteristic

✳ **Championship status in all associations**

to have quiet voices so as not to disturb the monks' meditations. It's a lovely, romantic tale, but a tale is likely all it is, since the monastery's records do not mention cats, blue or any other color. A mention of the Chartreux breed, however, is found in the 1749 36-volume *Histoire Naturelle* (Natural History) by French biologist Comte de Buffon, who lists four cat breeds common in Europe at that time: Domestic, Angora, Spanish, and Chartreux.

According to Jean Simonnet's definitive 1980 book *The Chartreux Cat*, the Chartreux probably came from the Near East, and the cat described as the Cat of Syria by the Italian naturalist Ulisse Aldrovandi (1522–1605), was likely its ancestor. In Jean Simonnet's book, an illustration of the Cat of Syria shows a stocky cat with solid blue coloring and vivid, slightly almond-shaped copper colored eyes. Beside the cat, a brown mouse cowers, a testament to the Chartreux's strong hunting instincts, and one of the reasons the breed was so highly prized.

Brought to Europe from the Near East countries in merchant ships, the Chartreux became established as a French breed. That the Chartreux survived at all is a testament to the breed's endurance and flexibility, since for many centuries members of the breed weren't treated with the kindness and love they've earned today. Primarily street cats, they were prized for their rat-catching prowess and, for a time, for their luxurious pelts. As Jean

Simonnet notes, "One can truly say that the Chartreux cats beloved to us formerly did not have the 'best of times' with our countrymen."

The modern history of the breed began in the 1920s when two sisters, Christine and Suzanne Leger, discovered a colony of plush, shorthaired blue cats in the city of Le Palais on Belle Ile Island off the coast of Brittany in northwest of France. These free-roaming cats lived on the grounds of a hospital and matched the description of the Chartreux. (The hospital was run, coinciden-

The Chartreux' coat comes in one color—blue.

tally, by a religious order.) The people of Le Palais called them "hospital cats," and the Leger sisters were taken with their beauty and thick blue coats. Christine and Suzanne Leger were the first to work seriously with the breed, and in 1931 they exhibited the cats in Paris. The breed became popular, and the Leger sisters and several other breeders were making good progress breeding and showing the cats, when World War II intervened, decimating the country and the breed.

After the war, the few remaining Chartreux breeders bred the few remaining Chartreux cats with blue British Shorthairs, Russian Blues, and Persians, to keep the bloodlines going. As soon as the breed was well established, breeders worked to bring the breed back to its former look and standard. In 1970, Fédération Internationale Féline (FIFe) made the decision to combine the Chartreux and the British

Shorthair into a single breed category; fanciers felt strongly that this would lead to the elimination of the Chartreux breed they'd worked so hard to protect. The breed club du chat des Chartreux (The Chartreux Cat Club) was formed to protect the breed; club members and other breeders worked so hard to get this decision overturned that in 1977 FIFe reversed its decision and adopted separate standards for the two breeds. Chartreux breeders worked hard to restore their "Carthusians," as they're known in France, to their former conformation. Today, du chat des Chartreux works to preserve, promote, and protect the Chartreux. In European cat shows today, the Chartreux is shown in its own breed category; crossbreeding with the British Shorthair or the Russian Blue is not allowed. The breed is accepted by all associations except the Governing Council of the Cat Fancy (GCCF).

The Chartreux made its journey to the United States in 1970, when the late Helen Gamon of La Jolla, California, imported the first Chartreux from France. She brought back three cats—Tornade, Taquin, and Thilda—that became the foundation for the North American Chartreux. Gamon and other dedicated breeders were instrumental in establishing and advancing the Chartreux in the United States and Canada. The breed achieved CFA championship status in 1987; today, all North American associations accept the Chartreux as a breed in its own right. Because of careful breeding and since the

The Chartreux is known as the smiling cat of France.

120

British Shorthair has never been used as an outcross as it has in some European countries, the North American Chartreux gene pool is now thought to be one of the purest in the world.

Chartreux breeders generally follow the French tradition of naming all their kittens born in a particular year starting with a particular letter of the alphabet. In 2013 kittens will have names beginning with "I"; in 2014 kittens will have names beginning with "J." In 2015, however, breeders will bypass "K" and jump to "L"; Chartreux breeders omit the letters K, Q, W, X, Y, and Z.

PERSONALITY

Chartreux cats may have been invited in by monks to rid the monastery of vermin. Today, however, Chartreux cats are popular because they make terrific companions. Who can resist a cat that greets you with a mighty purr and an enigmatic smile? They are amiable, loyal, loving, and adaptable, and when you sit down next to your Chartreux, you invariably end up with an exquisitely soft lapful of adoring blue feline.

Chartreux are the strong silent types of the cat fancy; they keep their comments to themselves, even when standing beside empty food dishes. Chartreux may open their mouths as if to meow, but no sound comes out. When they do vocalize, it's usually with small chirps or trills—it's amazing to hear tiny chirps come out of those large, powerful bodies and strong jaws. They do purr with the greatest enthusiasm, however, particularly when you're serving up their favorite snack. In addi-tion, quality time with their preferred persons always make them smile.

Nevertheless, Chartreux cats have a quiet but well-developed sense of humor, and enjoy a good joke, particularly if it's at your expense. Known for their hunting prowess and their strong hunting instinct, they love toys that move, preferably by human power. Feathered toys that whirl through the air are particular favorites. They easily learn to play fetch and enjoy frolicking with other felines and sometimes even an agreeable dog—and their human friends, of course. They are very intelligent cats; they quickly learn their names and if you like a good challenge you can even teach them to come when you call—if they're in the mood, of course. This cat is the perfect feline friend; in return for a bowl of food, a clean litterbox, and a soft bed (yours) to sleep on, you get a constant companion that entertains, loves, and cheers you up with its angelic smile and sweet devotion.

CONFORMATION

The Chartreux is generally a healthy and hardy breed, but some lines are known to possess the recessive gene for hereditary patellar luxation (kneecap dislocation). The kneecap occasionally pops out of its track when the joint is moved; this condition can cause lameness and pain. The dislocation may occur repeatedly if the track in which the kneecap rests is malformed or is too shallow; rarely the kneecap will dislocate permanently. Reputable breeders screen their breeding cats for this inheritable problem and provide a written health guarantee.

GENERAL	The Chartreux is a sturdy, shorthaired French breed coveted since antiquity for its hunting prowess and its dense, water repellent fur. Its husky, robust type is sometimes termed primitive, neither cobby nor classic. Though amply built, Chartreux are extremely supple and agile cats; refined, never coarse nor clumsy.
BODY	Robust physique: medium-long with broad shoulders and deep chest. Strong boning; muscle mass is solid and dense.
HEAD	Rounded and broad but not a sphere. Powerful jaw; full cheeks, with mature males having larger jowls. High, softly contoured forehead; nose straight and of medium length/width; with a slight stop at eye level. Muzzle comparatively small, narrow, and tapered with slight pads. Sweet, smiling expression. Neck short and heavy set.
EARS	Medium in height and width; set high on the head; very erect posture.
EYES	Rounded and open; alert and expressive. Color range is copper to gold; a clear, deep, brilliant orange is preferred.
LEGS AND PAWS	Legs comparatively short and fine-boned; straight and sturdy. Feet are round and medium in size; may appear almost dainty compared to body mass.
TAIL	Tail of moderate length; heavy at base; tapering to oval tip. Lively and flexible.
COAT	Medium-short and slightly woolly in texture; should break like a sheepskin at neck and flanks. Resilient undercoat; longer, protective topcoat. Note: degree of woolliness depends on age, sex and habitat, mature males exhibiting heaviest coats. Silkier, thinner coat permitted on females and cats under two years.
COLOR	Any shade of blue-gray from ash to slate; tips lightly brushed with silver. Emphasis on color clarity and uniformity rather than shade. Preferred tone is a bright, unblemished blue with an overall iridescent sheen.
DISQUALIFY	White locket, visible tail kink, green eyes; any signs of lameness in the hindquarters.
ALLOWABLE OUTCROSSES	None.

HISTORY

The Colorpoint shares body style, personality, coat length, and color pattern with the Siamese, but in the untraditional colors of red, cream, tortoiseshell, and lynx (tabby) points. Two separate schools of thought exist about the Colorpoint Shorthair: those who think that a breed that walks, talks, and looks like a Siamese should be considered Siamese, and those who deem the Colorpoint a Siamese hybrid.

In the CFA, the Siamese comes in four colors only: seal, blue, chocolate, and lilac points. These traditional colors are considered natural mutations developed and refined by breeders, although evidence shows that quite a lot of outcrossing occurred along the bloodline.

The effort to produce a Siamese-style pointed cat in colors other than the traditional four (sealpoint, chocolate point, blue point, and lilac point) began in Britain and North America in the 1940s. Early in the program, these innovative breeders focused on only red point and cream point (a dilute of red). The breeders

Colorpoints are active and need interactive play with their human companions.

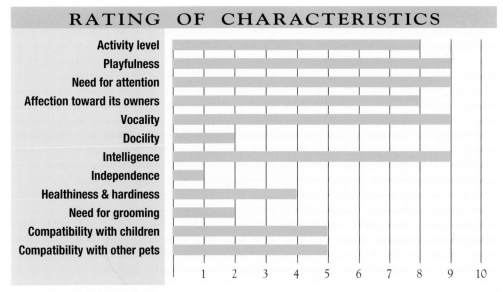

RATING OF CHARACTERISTICS

Characteristic	Rating (1–10)
Activity level	8
Playfulness	9
Need for attention	9
Affection toward its owners	9
Vocality	9
Docility	2
Intelligence	8
Independence	1
Healthiness & hardiness	4
Need for grooming	2
Compatibility with children	3
Compatibility with other pets	3

1—breed exhibits the least amount of this characteristic, 10—breed exhibits the most of this characteristic

* **Championship status in CCA, CFA, and UFO; championship status as color divisions of the Siamese in AACE, ACFA, CFF, and TICA**

crossed Siamese with red domestic shorthairs to obtain the desired colors. Later, Abyssinians and American Shorthairs were used by North American breeders. Initially, the Colorpoint breeders experienced setbacks and failures; in the effort to achieve the proper colors in the proper places, the Siamese body type was often sacrificed.

As the new breed gained acclaim, breeders introduced another color, lynx (tabby) point, which added another ten colors and patterns to the list of accepted color varieties. The third and last color class, parti-color (tortie) point, added four more varieties; the pointed areas are decorated with one of the four traditional Siamese colors-seal, chocolate, blue, or lilac-randomly mottled with red and/or cream. The pattern is particularly striking when, instead of mottled, the face has a blaze, with one side of the face red or cream and the other side one of the four Siamese colors. Because the color red is carried on the sex-linked X chromosomes, particolor cats are almost always female (see Chapter Four).

Once the color and pattern were achieved by linebreeding, the lines were then crossed back to the Siamese to reestablish the body style, personality, and coat texture and length. While technically a hybrid, the Colorpoint now has very little non-Siamese gene inheritance, based on a ten-generation bloodline bred back to the Siamese after the color had been achieved.

The new colors grew in popularity, and the next step was to gain recognition from the registering associations. However, many Siamese breeders were upset about the new colors, afraid the colors would pollute their pedigreed lines. In order to appease the Siamese breeders, the North American breeders suggested the name Colorpoint Shorthair to distinguish it from the Siamese. CFA saw the appeal of the colorful cats, and agreed the new breed was a hybrid, not a natural breed like the Siamese. In 1964, the CFA board of directors accepted the Colorpoint Shorthair for registration as a separate breed, and in 1974, the breed was accepted for CFA championship. CFA recognizes the Siamese in only the four traditional colors, but most other associations have accepted the new range of colors as part of the Siamese breed. Today, only CCA, CFA, and UFO consider the Colorpoint Shorthair a separate breed.

PERSONALITY

It's easy to see why the Siamese and their look-alikes are popular. Their outgoing, friendly demeanor makes them popular in any crowd. Never at a loss for words, they'll keep the conversation rolling at the dullest party. Colorpoints are good-natured and loving, but they can be determined. Once a Colorpoint gets an idea into its furry little head, you might as well just give in and spare yourself the lengthy discussion.

Colorpoints are outgoing, talkative, and intelligent.

Colorpoints have a great need to play and enjoy playing a good game of fetch with their favorite humans. They can be mischievous and action-packed when they're in the mood. Colorpoints love practicing their pounce, on scraps of paper or unsuspecting human toes—whatever catches their eye. When in movement, which is most of the time, Colorpoints seem to sail right off the floor in their daring dashes to catch that catnip mouse.

Although they are a very active breed, they are also loving and affectionate and will seek you out for a good, long session of purring, petting, and pampering. They are outgoing, talkative, intelligent, and very sensitive to their owner's moods and needs. If you're watching a sad movie and crying, the Colorpoint will be the first to jump up to give you a nudge and a cuddle.

CONFORMATION

The body type of the Colorpoint Shorthair is almost identical to that of the Siamese. Head shape, body conformation, ear and eye placement, and size are the same in both standards.

The Colorpoint Shorthair is essentially a Siamese cat in colors other than the traditional four accepted Siamese colors, so the similarity of the breed standards isn't surprising. The notable difference is in the color and pattern.

Colorpoint Shorthairs are generally healthy and long-lived if kept inside. However, since they are closely related to, and still crossbred with, the Sia-

GENERAL	The Colorpoint Shorthair is a medium-sized, svelte, refined cat with long tapering lines, very lithe, but muscular. Balance and refinement are the essence of the breed, where all parts come together in a harmonious whole, with neither too much nor too little consideration given to any one feature. The ideal is a cat with type identical to the Siamese, but with its own distinct and unique colors.
BODY	Medium sized. Graceful, long, and svelte. A distinctive combination of fine bones and firm muscles. Shoulders and hips continue same sleek lines of tubular body. Hips never wider than shoulders. Abdomen tight.
HEAD	Long tapering wedge. Medium in size in good proportion to body. The total wedge starts at the nose and flares out in straight lines to the tips of the ears forming a triangle, with no break at the whiskers. No less than the width of an eye between the eyes. When the whiskers are smoothed back, the underlying bone structure is apparent. Skull flat. In profile, a long straight line is seen from the top of the head to the tip of the nose. No bulge over eyes. No dip in nose. Neck long and slender. Nose long and straight. A continuation of the forehead with no break. Muzzle fine, wedge shaped.
EARS	Strikingly large, pointed, wide at base, continuing the lines of the wedge.
EYES	Vivid blue in color, no other shades or colors allowed. Almond shaped. Medium size. Neither protruding nor recessed. Slanted towards the nose in harmony with lines of wedge and ears. Uncrossed.
LEGS AND PAWS	Legs long and slim. Hind legs higher than front. In good proportion to body. Paws dainty, small, and oval. Toes five in front and four behind.
TAIL	Long, thin, tapering to a fine point.
COAT	Short, fine textured, glossy. Lying close to body.
COLOR	Pointed pattern; red point, cream point, seal lynx point, chocolate lynx point, blue lynx point, lilac lynx point, red lynx point, cream lynx point, seal-tortie point, chocolate-tortie point, blue-cream point, lilac-cream point, seal-tortie lynx point, chocolate-tortie lynx point, blue-cream lynx point, lilac-cream lynx point.

DISQUALIFY	Weak hind legs. Mouth breathing due to nasal obstruction or poor occlusion. Emaciation. Visible kink. Eyes other than blue. White toes and/or feet, white spots or white marking anywhere on the cat except as appropriate for the tabby pattern on lynx points. Clearly defined white undercoat in the points. Incorrect number of toes. Malocclusion resulting in either undershot or overshot chin.
ALLOWABLE OUTCROSSES	Colorpoint Shorthair or Siamese.

mese, the breed shares some of the same inheritable conditions and diseases. In particular, hereditary liver amyloidosis has been found in some Colorpoint bloodlines.

Like Siamese, Colorpoints are prone to plaque buildup, tartar formation, and gingivitis. Gingivitis can lead to the dental disease periodontitis (an inflammatory disease affecting the tissues surrounding and supporting the teeth), which can cause tissue, bone, and tooth loss. Untreated, dental disease can undermine a cat's overall health. Colorpoints need annual veterinary checkups, periodic teeth cleaning by your veterinarian and, if your cat will tolerate it, regular tooth brushing using cat toothpaste and a cat toothbrush. Be sure to talk to your breeder about any health concerns and buy from a breeder who offers a written health guarantee.

The Colorpoint's head is a long tapering wedge; the neck is long and slender.

HISTORY

The first known Cornish Rex was born on July 21, 1950, on a farm in Bodmin Moor, Cornwall, England, when a tortoiseshell and white random-bred cat named Serena gave birth to five kittens. The litter contained one curly-coated orange and white male kitten, which Nina Ennismore, Serena's owner, named Kallibunker. Kallibunker was noticeably different from his littermates. His hair was short and curly and, instead of possessing the cobby body like that of his littermates and mother, Kallibunker's body was long and lithe. He had large ears, a slender tail, and a foreign wedge-shaped head.

Interested in this mini-mutant mouser, Ennismore recognized that Kallibunker's fur was similar to the wavy fur of the Astrex rabbit, since Ennismore had previously raised and exhibited rabbits. She got in touch with British geneticist A. C. Jude, who agreed that the fur of Kallibunker was similar to the Astrex rabbit's fur. On the advice of Jude, Ennismore backcrossed Kallibunker to his mother.

The Cornish coat feels like warm suede;
Rexes make perfect winter lap warmers.

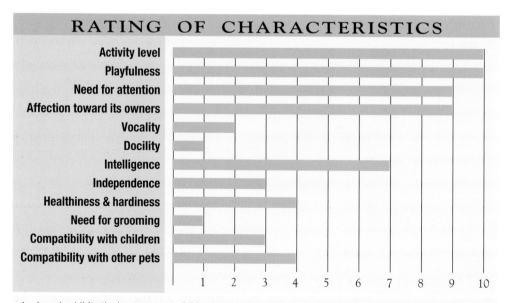

RATING OF CHARACTERISTICS

Characteristic	Rating (1–10)
Activity level	10
Playfulness	10
Need for attention	9
Affection toward its owners	9
Vocality	2
Docility	1
Intelligence	7
Independence	2
Healthiness & hardiness	4
Need for grooming	1
Compatibility with children	2
Compatibility with other pets	4

1—breed exhibits the least amount of this characteristic, 10—breed exhibits the most of this characteristic

✳ **Championship status in all associations**

This mating produced a litter containing one straight-coated kitten and two curly-coated kittens. A second mating was arranged for Kallibunker and his mom, and again curly-coated kittens were produced. The name Cornish Rex was decided upon for the new breed because of the breed's Cornish origin and the resemblance to the Astrex rabbit. A. C. Jude suggested a few other tests to determine the coat's inheritance; Kallibunker was test-mated to Burmese, Siamese, and British domestic shorthairs. The coat mutation was determined to be recessive. For a trait governed by a recessive gene to manifest in the appearance of a cat, the cat must inherit two copies of the gene—one from each parent. These test matings proved that Kallibunker's mother Serena must have possessed one copy of the Rex gene.

Two Cornish Rexes arrived in North America in 1957, courtesy of fancier Fran Blancheri. One died shortly after arrival, but the other, LaMorna Cove, who was pregnant by Poldhu (one of the kittens sired by Kallibunker), survived and produced a Rex litter. LaMorna and family became the foundation cats for the Cornish Rex in America.

Since the gene pool was small, breeders outcrossed to other breeds to maintain genetic diversity. Siamese, Havana Browns, American Shorthairs, and domestic shorthairs were among the outcrosses used. This not only provided genetic diversity, but also supplied a wide variety of colors and patterns from which to choose.

Outcrossing has since been disallowed because there's now enough diversity to keep the breed healthy. The CFA accepted the Cornish for championship in 1964; all the North American registries now accept the Cornish Rex. The Governing Council of the Cat Fancy (GCCF) and the Fédération Internationale Féline (FIFe) in Europe also accept the Cornish Rex.

PERSONALITY

Cornish Rexes are good for folks who like having their lives run by active, inquisitive, gazelle-like felines that love a good joke, as long as it's not on them. Everything is a game to the Cornish Rex, and they can be hard to ignore when they're in a sociable mood, which is most of the time. Rexes are determinedly outgoing with their favorite humans. With their warm suede feel, they make the perfect winter lap warmer, too. They are intelligent, alert, and usually easy to handle. Extremely affectionate, Rexes are particularly so around dinnertime, so devoted, in fact, that you can't keep them out of your plate without a squirt bottle. Dinner will never be the same again with a purring Cornish stealing your food as soon as your back is turned, or even while you're looking.

Some Rexes enjoy retrieving and will bring back objects for you to toss again and again. They are adept climbers, leapers, and sprinters, and have marvelously agile paws. No shelf or cupboard is safe from a persistent Cornish.

CONFORMATION

Some people who are mildly allergic to cats are able to own Cornish Rex cats, but the reason for this is not that Rexes are hypoallergenic, as some people claim. The Cornish and the Devon do shed less than other cat breeds (they can't shed hair they don't have), which is great if keeping hair off the couch is important to you. However, cat hair itself is not what causes allergic symptoms in humans. An allergenic protein called Fel d1, secreted via saliva and sebaceous glands, produces the symptoms. When cats groom, they spread Fel d1 onto their fur. Cornish Rexes produce this protein, too. They just don't deposit as much allergen-laced hair all over the house. Since Cornish Rex cats are easy to bathe (the soap penetrates the short coat easily and their fur dries quickly), regular bathing can reduce the Fel d1 covering the Rex's fur, and can reduce allergic symptoms. However, be sure to spend a good deal of time around adult Rexes before agreeing to buy if you or a family member is allergic. Some people can tolerate them, and others can't.

The Cornish Rex shares similarities, and differences, with the Devon Rex. The Rex coats of both the Cornish and the Devon are governed by recessive genes (see Chapter Four, page 42). Both create similar changes in the coat. The mutation seems to affect the body type as well, since Rex kittens have a different conformation than their straight-coated littermates. The Cornish Rex completely lacks guard hairs. The soft awn hairs make up the Cornish coat and form a tight, uniform wave that lies close to the body. The awn wave extends from the top of the head, down across the back, sides, and hips, and continues to the tip of the long, tapering tail.

The Cornish Rex completely lacks guard hairs; often their whiskers are stunted or missing.

GENERAL	The Cornish Rex is distinguished from all other breeds by its extremely soft, wavy coat and racy type. It is surprisingly heavy and warm to the touch. All contours of the Cornish Rex are gently curved.
BODY	Small to medium in size; never coarse. Torso long and slender, not tubular, showing a deep, but not broad chest. Outline is comprised of graceful arches and curves without any sign of flatness. The back is naturally arched and evident when the cat is standing naturally. The underline gently curves upward from the ribcage to form waistline (tucked up in appearance). Hips and thighs muscular and feel somewhat heavy in proportion to the rest of body.
HEAD	Comparatively small and egg shaped. Length about one third greater than the width. A definite whisker break, oval with gently curving outline in front and in profile. Muzzle narrowing slightly to a rounded end. Nose Roman. In profile a straight line from end of nose to chin with considerable depth and squarish effect. Cheek bones high and prominent, well chiseled. Chin strong, well-developed.
EARS	Large and full from the base, erect and alert; set high on the head.
EYES	Medium to large in size, oval in shape, and slanting slightly upward. A full eye's width apart. Color should be clear, intense, and appropriate to coat color.
LEGS AND PAWS	Legs very long and slender. Thighs well-muscled, somewhat heavy in proportion to the rest of the body. The Cornish Rex stands high on its legs. Paws dainty, slightly oval. Toes five in front and four behind.
TAIL	Long and slender, tapering toward the end and extremely flexible.
COAT	Short, extremely soft, silky, and completely free of guard hairs. Relatively dense. A tight, uniform marcel wave, lying close to the body and extending from the top of the head across the back, sides, and hips continuing to the tip of the tail. Size and depth of wave may vary. The fur on the underside of the chin and on chest and abdomen is short and noticeably wavy.
COLOR	All colors and patterns. Cats with no more white than a locket and/or button shall be judged in the color class of their basic color with no penalty for such locket and/or button.
DISQUALIFY	Kinked or abnormal tail, incorrect number of toes, coarse or guard hairs, signs of lameness in the hindquarters, signs of poor health.
ALLOWABLE OUTCROSSES	None.

The Cornish is a generally healthy breed, but it does have one genetic problem; both A and B blood types exist in Cornish Rex bloodlines, which is only a problem if you plan to breed your Cornish. Type B is usually very rare; researchers estimate that less than one percent of U.S. domestic cats have type B blood. However, some pedigreed breeds have higher percentages of type B blood because of inbreeding or line-breeding, and Cornish Rex can have up to 60 percent type B blood, according to a study conducted by the University of Pennsylvania. Queens with type B blood, when bred to toms with type A blood, can produce litters with both type B and type A kittens. The kittens with type A blood are born apparently healthy but fade rapidly and die twenty-four to seventy-two hours after birth. This is sometimes called "fading kitten syndrome," but actually is due to the natural antibodies that occur, causing neonatal iso-erythrolysis (NI). The A-type

kittens absorb the anti-A antibodies from the colostrum when they nurse, which attacks and destroys the kitten's red blood cells, causing death. Fortunately, DNA test has been developed for the gene and mutation associated with the B blood group at the University of California, Davis. Cornish Rex and other high risk breeds can be tested so compatible mates can be selected to avoid blood type conflict in the kittens.

An inquisitive Cornish Rex.

The Cymric is a longhaired Manx.

HISTORY

Presumed by researchers to have been introduced to the Isle of Man by human settlers and explorers, the Manx has existed there for many centuries. The Isle, located in the Irish Sea between England and Ireland, has no indigenous domestic cat species, and several theories exist about the introduction of domestic cats. Speculated sources include arrival with the Spanish Armada, Phoenician traders, or Viking settlers who colonized the Isle of Man. Many fanciers believe the British Shorthair was later added to the Manx mix. Given the proximity of the regions and the similarity in body styles, that's a reasonable hypothesis.

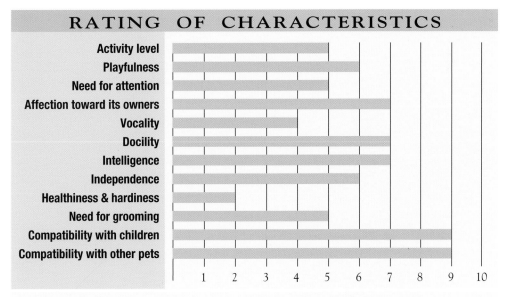

RATING OF CHARACTERISTICS

Characteristic	Rating
Activity level	5
Playfulness	6
Need for attention	7
Affection toward its owners	7
Vocality	4
Docility	7
Intelligence	7
Independence	6
Healthiness & hardiness	2
Need for grooming	5
Compatibility with children	9
Compatibility with other pets	9

1—breed exhibits the least amount of this characteristic, 10—breed exhibits the most of this characteristic

✳ **Championship status in AACE, ACFA, CCA, TICA, and UFO under the name Cymric; Championship status in CFA in Manx longhair division**

Solid white rumpy Cymric. This tail type is prized in the show ring.

Records have been found that describe the cat as a mutation among the island's domestic cats, rather than a cat that arrived with its tail already absent. In this case, the lack of tail is governed by a dominant gene, unlike most other breeds with short tails. This indicates that the Manx and the Cymric (KIM-ric) are not related to breeds, such as the Japanese Bobtail whose tails are governed by recessive genes.

Wherever they came from and whatever their genetic makeup, fanciers took note of the Manx, and it soon became a popular breed in the earliest days of the cat fancy. Manx cats are noted in early American cat registry records as well.

Although a relative newcomer to the cat fancy, the Cymric apparently has been around as long as the Manx itself. Fanciers insist that the Cymric is not a human-made hybrid as has been suggested (Manx to Persian outcrossing apparently occurred in the 1930s and 1940s), but rather a variation of the Manx breed with a history as long and rich as that of the Manx. Since the Isle of Man possessed both shorthaired and longhaired cats, it's presumed that the longhair gene passed around by inbreeding on the Isle itself, just as was the Manx gene. Unlike the Manx gene, however, long hair is a recessive trait, and the gene could be carried unnoticed through generations of Manx.

While the Cymric was shown in ACA as early as 1963, the breed didn't really begin to take hold until the mid-1970s. First shown under the name Longhaired Manx, the name was changed to Cymric during this period. The word is the Welsh name for Wales and was chosen by pioneer Cymric breeders Blair Wright and Leslie Falteisek. In 1976, CCA was the first to accept the Cymric for championship status; it now has full championship standing in most associations. CFF is the only association that does not accept the Cymric; however, the reason they have not done so is that no group of fanciers has campaigned for acceptance.

In May 1994, CFA changed the name from Cymric to Longhair Manx; both hair lengths share a single breed standard. Because only hair length separates the two breeds, CFA breeders campaigned for the Cymric to be considered part of the Manx breed. Longhaired kittens born to Manx parents (possible when both parents carry the recessive gene for long hair) can be registered as Cymrics in all associations except CFF. This eliminates the previous status problems with "split litters" in which both hair lengths are present.

The Cymric and the Manx are two of the most challenging to breed because of the Manx gene.

Cymric embryos that are homozygous (inheriting the Manx gene from both parents) die in the womb. Homozygous kittens comprise roughly one

fourth of the kittens conceived; therefore, Cymric litters are usually small (see Manx profile, page 187). Even heterozygous kittens can have deformities such as, spina bifida, fusions of the spine, and defects of the colon. Careful breeding helps minimize the defects.

PERSONALITY

The personality of the Cymric has won a strong following despite the breeding challenges. Cymrics are intelligent, fun-loving cats, and they get along well with other pets, including dogs. Cymrics are particularly noted for their loyalty to their humans and enjoy spending quality time with them. As cats go, they can be easily taught tricks. Despite their playful temperament, they are gentle and nonaggressive. Their playful yet tractable dispositions make the Cymric a good choice for families with children.

Cymrics are powerful jumpers and if sufficiently motivated will manage to breach the most secure shelf. They are also fascinated by water, as long as you don't dunk them in the nasty stuff. Perhaps this fascination comes from originating on a small piece of land surrounded by it.

CONFORMATION

Cymrics come in a variety of tail lengths. The tail types are broken into four classifications: rumpy, rumpy-riser, stumpy, and longy. Since the tailless gene is dominant, all Cymrics that possess the Manx gene will have one of the four tail types. Rumpies are completely tailless and are prized because

GENERAL (TICA STANDARD)	The overall appearance should be that of a medium-sized, compact, muscular cat. The Cymric has a round head with a firm muzzle and prominent cheeks, short front legs, height of hindquarters, great depth of flank, and a short back, which forms a smooth continuous arch from the shoulders to the round rump. The Manx and Cymric are essentially the same in all respects, the Cymric having a longer coat. The Cymric has a medium/semi-long coat with a silky texture, which varies with coat color. Britches, tufts of hair between the toes and full furnishings in the ears distinguish the Cymric.
BODY	Compact; well-balanced; solidly muscled; medium size; sturdy bone structure; broad chest; short back forming smooth, continuous arch from shoulders to rump; rump extremely broad and round.
HEAD	Rounded and slightly longer than broad. Medium size. Cheeks are prominent and stud jowls in the mature stud cat. Chin strong. Muzzle slightly longer than broad with definite muzzle break. Round whisker pads. In profile gentle nose dip with a moderately rounded forehead. Neck short and thick.
EARS	Rather wide at base, tapering to rounded tip. Medium sized, set wide apart; when viewed from behind, they resemble the rocker of a cradle. Hair may be tufted with full furnishings in the Cymric.
EYES	Rounded and large angled, slightly higher at the outer edge of the eye. Color conforms to coat color but should only be considered if all other points are equal.
LEGS AND PAWS	Legs sturdy boning and well-muscled. Forelegs shorter than hind legs. Hind legs with substantial musculature, should be straight when viewed from behind. Feet round shape of medium size. Suggestion of toe tufts in the Cymric.
TAILLESSNESS	Appears tailless. No penalty for a rise of bone or cartilage which does not stop the judge's hand when the palm is stroked down the back and over the rump.
COAT	Medium double coat. Texture silky. Texture can vary with the coat color. The coat should have a well-padded quality due to the open outer coat and thick close under coat. Seasonal changes in coat length and texture are allowed.

COLOR	Any color or pattern.
DISQUALIFY	Any congenital deformity. Weak hindquarters causing inability to stand or walk properly.
ALLOWABLE OUTCROSSES	Manx.

they can compete successfully in the show ring. They often have a dimple at the base of the spine where the tail would be if it were present. Rumpy-risers that possess a short knob of tail, stumpies that have an often curved or kinked tail stump, and longies that have tails almost as long as that of an average cat, are used for breeding or are sold as pets. Many breeders dock the tails of the longies to make it easier to find homes for them. Docked Cymrics have a short tail stub; they are not completely de-tailed as this might damage their spines. Docked Cymrics cannot be shown for championship competition, although they can be shown in the HHP category of most associations.

Cymrics have long, strong hind legs and are powerful jumpers.

HISTORY

The Devon Rex can be traced back to a single cat in 1960. The father of the Devon breed, a feral, curly-coated tom, lived around an abandoned tin mine near Buckfastleigh, a small town in the county of Devon in southwest England, which borders Cornwall, the birthplace of the Cornish Rex.

The curly-coated tom mated with a straight-coated calico female, producing a litter of kittens in the garden of cat lover Beryl Cox. One of the kittens, a brownish-black male that Cox named Kirlee, had the same short, curly coat as his father. At first, Beryl Cox thought Kirlee was a Cornish Rex, since the Cornish's birthplace was not far away from her county of Devon.

Subsequent matings between Kirlee and the cats of Cornish Rex breeder Brian Stirling-Webb resulted in only straight-coated offspring, from which Cox and Webb concluded that the two breeds were unrelated. Fanciers now think that Kirlee's

Devons shed less than most breeds and need little grooming.

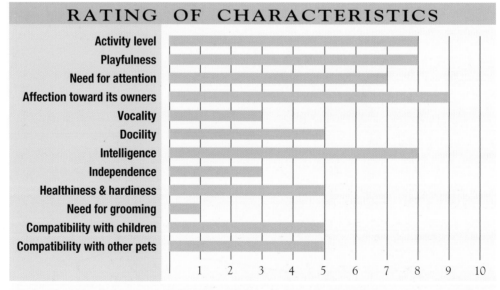

RATING OF CHARACTERISTICS

Characteristic	Rating (1–10)
Activity level	8
Playfulness	8
Need for attention	8
Affection toward its owners	9
Vocality	3
Docility	5
Intelligence	8
Independence	3
Healthiness & hardiness	5
Need for grooming	1
Compatibility with children	5
Compatibility with other pets	5

1—breed exhibits the least amount of this characteristic, 10—breed exhibits the most of this characteristic

✳ **Championship status in all associations**

calico mother and the curly-coated feral male that was her father must have been related, since the Devon Rex gene that governs the curly coat is recessive and must be inherited from both parents to manifest in offspring. Kirlee must have inherited one copy of the gene from each of her parents. The name Devon Rex was adopted for the new breed, and a breeding program was established.

The first Devon was imported to the United States in 1968. In 1972, ACFA became the first U.S. association to accept the Devon for championship. The Devon was accepted by TICA in 1979 (the year TICA was formed). The CFA accepted the Devon for championship in 1983. Today all North American cat associations accept the Devon for championship. In addition, the Devon is accepted for championship in Europe by The Governing Council of the Cat Fancy (GCCF) and the Fédération Internationale Féline (FIFe).

Through careful outcrossing, breeders have expanded the Devon Rex gene pool while retaining the integrity of the breed. While it has never quite caught up to the Cornish Rex in popularity, the Devon has made great strides and is seen more and more frequently in the show halls and judging rings of North America and Europe.

PERSONALITY

Devons have been compared to pixies, elves, and, of course, space aliens for their jumbo-sized satellite-dish ears, large, mischievous "window-to-the-soul" eyes, and ethereal appearance. Fanciers laud the playful "poodle cat," as the breed is affectionately called, as people-oriented snugglers that love nothing better than to cuddle up with you at night and wake you in the morning with hugs, kisses, and purrs of affection. Moreover, since the Devon sheds less than other breeds, you can snuggle back without fear of covering yourself in as much cat hair.

Devon Rex guard hairs are fragile and break easily; their whiskers are often missing altogether.

GENERAL	The Devon Rex is a breed of unique appearance. Its large eyes, short muzzle, prominent cheekbones, and huge, lowset ears create a characteristic elfin look. A cat of medium fine frame, the Devon is well covered with soft, wavy fur; the fur is of a distinctive texture, as the mutation that causes its wavy coat is cultivated in no other breed.
BODY	Hard and muscular, lithe, and of medium length. Broad in chest and medium fine in boning, with medium fine but sturdy legs. Carried high on the legs with the hind legs somewhat longer than the front. Allowance to be made for larger size in males, as long as good proportions are maintained.
HEAD	Modified wedge. In the front view, the wedge is delineated by a narrowing series of three distinct convex curves: outer edge of ear lobes, cheekbones, and whisker pads. Head to be broad but slightly longer than it is broad. Face to be full-cheeked with pronounced cheekbones and a whisker break. In profile, nose with a strongly marked stop; forehead curving back to a flat skull. Muzzle is short, well-developed. Prominent whisker pads. Chin strong, well-developed. In profile, chin shall line up vertically with nose, being neither undershot nor overshot.
EARS	Strikingly large and set very low, very wide at the base, so that the outside base of ear extends beyond the line of the wedge. Tapering to rounded tops and well covered with fine fur. With or without earmuffs and/or ear-tip tufts.
EYES	Large and wide set, oval in shape, and sloping toward outer edges of ears. Any eye color is acceptable, as no points are assigned to eye color, although colorpoints generally will have blue and minks generally will have aqua eyes.
LEGS AND PAWS	Legs long and slim. Paws small and oval, with five toes in front and four behind.
TAIL	Long, fine, and tapering, well covered with short fur.
COAT	Cat is well covered with fur, with greatest density occurring on the back, sides, tail, legs, face, and ears. Slightly less density is permitted on the top of head, neck, chest, and abdomen. Bare patches are a fault in kittens and a serious fault in adults. Coat is soft, fine, full-bodied, and rexed. Coat is short on back, sides, upper legs, and tail. It is very short on the head, ears, neck, paws, chest, and abdomen. A rippled wave effect should be apparent when the coat is smoothed with one's hand. The wave is most evident where the coat is the longest, on body and tail.

COLOR	All colors and patterns including bi-color and the pointed pattern.
DISQUALIFY	Extensive baldness, excessively long, and/or shaggy coat; long hair on the tail; kinked or abnormal tail, incorrect number of toes, crossed eyes, weak hind legs; any evidence of illness or poor health.
ALLOWABLE OUTCROSSES	American Shorthair or British Shorthair. Kittens born on or after May 1, 2028 may have only Devon Rex parents.

However, there are many other reasons to acquire a Devon besides their curly coats. Their loyalty, devotion, playfulness, courage, and intelligence set them apart from other breeds, just to name a few of the qualities that make them a good choice for the cat-obsessed. Devons are shoulder perchers, lap sitters, tail waggers, and retrievers of tossed cat toys. They have a well-developed sense of curiosity and want to be involved in whatever you're doing, whether it's peeling potatoes for dinner or taking a quick dip in the shower. Your Devon will hop into the bathtub before it's dry, just to see what you were up to; a bit of water can't dampen your Devon's curiosity, or its thirst to constantly be by your side.

CONFORMATION

While the Cornish's coat lacks guard hairs, the Devon's coat contains all three hair types (guard, awn, and down), but the guard hairs are typically fragile and stunted, and the whisker hairs are often missing altogether. The hairs break easily and therefore this breed can develop bald patches that remain until the next hair growth cycle (typically fall and spring). Devons need very little grooming; their favorite grooming tool is your hand, applied on their heads and down their backs.

Some people who are mildly allergic to cats are able to own Devon Rex cats, but the reason for this is not that Rexes are hypoallergenic, as some people claim. The Cornish and the Devon do shed less than other cat breeds (they can't shed hair they don't have), which is great if keeping hair off the couch is important to you. However, cat hair itself is not what causes allergic symptoms in humans. An allergenic protein called Fel d1, secreted via saliva and sebaceous glands, produces the symptoms. When cats groom, they spread Fel d1 onto their fur. Devon Rex produce this protein, too. They just don't deposit as much allergen-laced hair all over the house. Since Devon Rex cats are easy to bathe (the soap penetrates the short coat easily, and their fur dries quickly), regular bathing can reduce the Fel d1 covering the Rex's fur, and this may reduce allergic symptoms. However, be sure to spend a good deal of time around adult Devon Rexes (not only kittens, who will not yet produce much Fel d1) before agreeing to buy

Blue Point Devon Rex, Devons come in all patterns and colors, including the pointed pattern.

if you or a family member is allergic. Some people can tolerate the Devon, and some people can't.

The Devon Rex is generally a healthy breed, but is does have one genetic problem; both A and B blood types exist in Devon Rex bloodlines, which is only a problem if you plan to breed your Devon Rex. Type B is usually very rare; researchers estimate that less than one percent of U.S. domestic cats have type B blood. However, some pedigreed breeds have higher percentages of type B blood because of inbreeding or line-breeding, and the Devon Rex can have up to 60 percent type B blood, according to a study conducted by the University of Pennsylvania. Queens with type B blood, when bred to toms with type A blood, can produce litters with both type B and type A kittens. The kittens with type A blood are born apparently healthy but fade rapidly and die twenty-four to seventy-two hours after birth. This is sometimes called "fading kitten syndrome," but actually is due to the natural antibodies that occur, causing neonatal iso-erythrolysis (NI). The A-type kittens absorb the anti-A antibodies from the colostrum when they nurse, which attacks and destroys the kitten's red blood cells, causing death. Fortunately, a DNA test has been developed for the gene and mutation associated with the B blood group at the University of California, Davis. Devon Rex and other high risk breeds can be tested so compatible mates can be selected to avoid blood type conflict in the kittens.

HISTORY

The ancient Egyptians are the first people to leave extensive evidence of their alliance with domestic cats—an affiliation that developed at least 5,000 years ago, according to Egyptian writings, statues, and bas-reliefs. Presumably, cats were first welcomed for their ability to keep rodents away from stores of grain and thus prevent famine, and for their ability to kill snakes. However, later Egyptian domestic cats became beloved household companions, and then sacred animals associated with the gods. Evidence in the form of depictions, paintings, and sculptures shows that spotted cats existed during the time of the Egyptian cat cult, and some believe that the predecessor of the Mau was the same cat worshipped by the ancient Egyptians. A papyrus painting dating around 1100 B.C.E. shows Ra in the form of a spotted cat beheading the evil serpent Apep. In 1580 B.C.E., a papyrus record quotes a spotted cat as saying, "I am the cat which fought near the Persea Tree

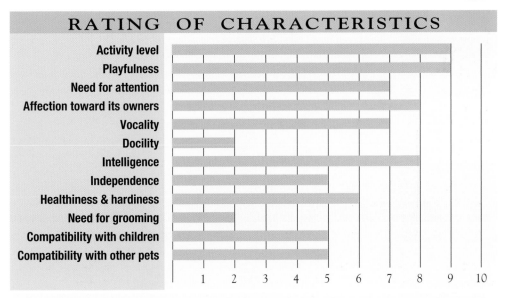

Silver Egyptian Mau. The tabby "M" on the forehead is sometimes called a scarab beetle mark.

RATING OF CHARACTERISTICS

Characteristic	Rating
Activity level	9
Playfulness	9
Need for attention	7
Affection toward its owners	7
Vocality	7
Docility	2
Intelligence	8
Independence	5
Healthiness & hardiness	6
Need for grooming	2
Compatibility with children	5
Compatibility with other pets	5

1—breed exhibits the least amount of this characteristic, 10—breed exhibits the most of this characteristic

✳ **Championship status in all associations**

in Annu on the night when the foes of Neb-er-tcher were destroyed!" In addition, a 1400 B.C.E. tomb painting found in Thebes depicts a spotted cat retrieving a duck for an Egyptian hunter, showing that cats were not only worshipped but played an important role in everyday life as well.

If, as some fanciers believe, the Egyptian Mau is a living artifact of that ancient era, then the Mau is one of the oldest breeds of domestic cat. Characteristics common to modern Maus can be seen in papyrus paintings, right down to the random spots. However, that's not proof of anything except that spotted cats lived in ancient Egypt.

Smoke Egyptian Mau. All markings are jet black with a pale silver undercoat.

Egyptian Maus joined the European cat fancy in the early 1900s. Fanciers in Italy, Switzerland, and France worked to develop the breed; however, as it did many pedigreed breeds, World War II decimated the Egyptian Mau population, and by the mid-1940s the Mau was almost extinct.

The efforts of the exiled Russian Princess Nathalie Troubetskoy brought the Mau back from the brink of extinction. While in Italy, she rescued some of the few remaining specimens. She was also instrumental in importing at least one Mau from Egypt via the Syrian Embassy.

In 1956, Troubetskoy immigrated to the United States, bringing with her three Maus bred from her original stock. Upon arrival, Troubetskoy established the Fatima Egyptian Mau Cattery, and began to promote the breed. The Mau soon collected a following of fanciers who wanted to preserve the rare, beautiful, historically significant breed.

Because of the small gene pool and because additional Maus were almost impossible to obtain from Egypt, a certain amount of inbreeding and out-crossing were required to continue the breed in North America. Selective breeding for temperament was also a priority, since disposition problems were noted in some bloodlines. Finally, in the 1980s breeder Cathie Rowan brought thirteen additional Maus into the United States, paving the way for more imports. In 1991, breeder J. Len Davidson imported four more. This widening of the gene pool was vital to the breed's health and well-being.

In 1968, CFF was the first to accept the Egyptian Mau for championship status. CCA soon followed, and the CFA granted championship in 1977. Today, all major associations accept the Mau. In addition, the Mau is accepted for championship in Europe by The Governing Council of the Cat Fancy (GCCF).

PERSONALITY

While fanciers might at first be attracted to the Egyptian Mau's beautiful spotted coat, most become enthusiasts because of the breed's temperament and personality. Maus, like their ancestors that were invited along on the duck hunts of their Egyptian companions, love to fetch. In fact, they love any play activity that mimics hunting behavior, and if allowed outside will become very competent (some might say savage) hunters. Indoor-only Maus, the only kind recommended by most breeders, will sometimes leave gifts of well-killed catnip mice on the pillows of their favorite people. Be sure to give your Mau lots of pettings and praise, and perhaps a treat or two, for these presents; Maus will be upset, and quite confused, if their generous gifts are coldly rejected.

While not overly talkative, Maus will let their humans know if some-thing is amiss, particularly if that something concerns food dishes. Their voices are usually melodious and quiet. When engaged in conversation with their human companions, Maus wag their tails, tread with their feet, and make a variety of sounds that fanciers call "chortling."

Maus are devoted to the humans who pay them the proper homage. If you show your Mau you can be trusted, your Mau will shower you with love and loyalty. Fanciers describe them as fiercely loyal cats that generally don't take to strangers. Once they bond with their preferred persons, they want to be worshiped by their chosen family rather than by the entire human race.

CONFORMATION

One of this breed's most striking features is its random, distinctive spots. Considerable variety exists in placement and shape. The spots can be small or large, round, oblong, or irregular shaped. Any of these are of equal merit, but the spots, however shaped or whatever size, should be distinct, with good contrast between pale ground color and deeper markings. The cheeks bear tabby markings including the characteristic "M" on the forehead, which is sometimes described as a scarab beetle mark. Mascara lines grace the cheeks. The first begins at the corner of the eye and continues along the cheek's contour. As the story goes, ancient Egyptian women patterned their elaborate eye makeup after the Mau's markings.

GENERAL	The Egyptian Mau is the only natural domesticated breed of spotted cat. The Egyptian's impression should be one of an active, colorful cat of medium size with well-developed muscles.
BODY	Medium long and graceful, showing well developed muscular strength. Loose skin flap extending from flank to hind leg knee. General balance is more to be desired than size alone. Allowance to be made for muscular necks and shoulders in adult males.
HEAD	Slightly rounded wedge without flat planes, medium in length. Not full-cheeked. Profile showing a gentle contour with slight rise from the bridge of the nose to the forehead. Entire length of nose even in width when viewed from the front.
EARS	Medium to large, alert and moderately pointed, continuing the planes of the head. Broad at base. Slightly flared with ample width between the ears. Hair on ears short and close lying. Inner ear a delicate, almost transparent, shell pink. May be tufted.
EYES	Large and alert, almond shaped, with a slight slant towards the ears. Skull apertures neither round nor oriental. Eye color gooseberry green. Allowance is made for changing eye color, with some discernible green by eight months of age and full green eye color by one and one half years of age. Preference given at all ages for greener eyes.
LEGS AND PAWS	Legs and feet in proportion to body. Hind legs proportionately longer, giving the appearance of being on tip-toe when standing upright. Feet small and dainty, slightly oval, almost round in shape. Toes five in front and four behind.
TAIL	Medium long, thick at base, with slight taper.
COAT	Medium in length with a lustrous sheen. In the smoke color the hair is silky and fine in texture. In the silver and bronze colors, the hair is dense and resilient in texture and accommodates two or more bands of ticking separated by lighter bands.
COLOR	Silver, bronze, smoke.
DISQUALIFY	Lack of spots. Blue eyes. Lack of green in eye color in cats over the age of one year six months. Mottled or pink paw pads. Kinked or abnormal tail. Incorrect number of toes. White locket or button distinctive from other acceptable white-colored areas in color sections of standard.
ALLOWABLE OUTCROSSES	None.

HISTORY

The European Burmese shares much of its history with the Burmese, and both came from the same foundation stock. A U.S. Navy doctor named Dr. Joseph Thompson brought a female cat named Wong Mau to the United States from Rangoon, Burma (now Yangon, Myanmar), a country which borders Thailand, formerly Siam. Some sources say she was given to the doctor by notable wild animal collector Buck Wilson, while others say Dr. Thompson found Wong Mau himself in Southeast Asia when he was serving as a ship's doctor.

When Dr. Thompson arrived back home in the United States, Thompson set out to determine Wong Mau's genetic makeup and establish a breeding program for her. He bred Wong Mau to a sealpoint Siamese named Tai Mau. After several generations, he had identified three color variations: some looked like Wong Mau (medium brown color and darker points), some like Tai Mau (sealpoint Siamese), and some were solid, dark chocolate brown. Dr. Thompson decided that the dark chocolate brown kitties were the most striking and

Active and people-oriented, European Burmese thrive on human attention.

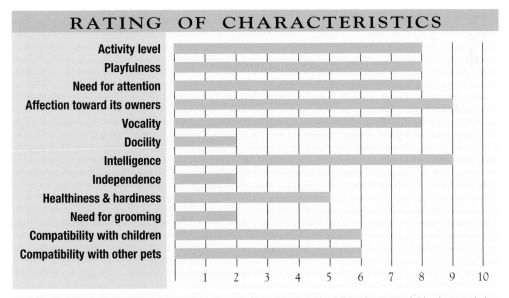

RATING OF CHARACTERISTICS

Characteristic	Rating
Activity level	8
Playfulness	8
Need for attention	8
Affection toward its owners	9
Vocality	8
Docility	2
Intelligence	9
Independence	2
Healthiness & hardiness	5
Need for grooming	2
Compatibility with children	6
Compatibility with other pets	6

1—breed exhibits the least amount of this characteristic, 10—breed exhibits the most of this characteristic

✳ **Championship status in: ACFA, CFA, and UFO under the name European Burmese; Championship status in CCA and CFF under the name Foreign Burmese; experimental status in TICA**

beautiful, and he set out to isolate the genes governing this color. He crossed these sable cats with each other or back to Wong Mau. The points were somewhat darker in color, most noticeable in Burmese kittens and becoming less apparent in adult cats.

The histories of the Burmese and the European Burmese diverge in 1949, when a pair of Wong Mau's descendants was imported to England by Siamese breeder Lilian France. The male was named Casa Gatos da Foong, and the female was called Chindwin's Minou Twm. Minou was already pregnant by an unrelated male, but lost her kittens while she was confined for the six month quarantine. (Cats and other companion animals entering the United Kingdom are quarantined for at least six months to prevent introducing rabies to the United Kingdom.)

Minou suffered from poor health after that, so France imported another female Burmese from the United States, Laos Cheli Wat, who had already proved herself healthy and fertile. Two years later France imported another male, Casa Gatos Darkee. From these cats the breed quickly gained popularity, and other fanciers began breeding programs. Since the gene pool was limited in Europe, Siamese were included in Burmese breeding programs.

The European Burmese breeding program began by accident in 1964 when a Burmese female in heat escaped and mated with a shorthaired red tabby. Another breeder deliberately mated a brown Burmese female with a red-point Siamese. A third color line was created when a tortie and white farm cat that carried the recessive Siamese gene mated with a brown Burmese tom carrying the recessive blue gene. Additional colors were added accidentally and intentionally. Many breeders contributed to developing additional colors for the breed. Not only does the European Burmese come in ten colors outside the four original hues decorating the Burmese, the conformation is distinctively different as well. While the Burmese is stocky and compact with a substantial bone structure, rounded head, and short muzzle, the European is an elegant cat of moderate type with a slightly rounded head.

Despite the long European history, the European Burmese is a fairly recent addition to the North American cat fancy. When the breed was brought to North America dressed in its new colors and body style, breeders began the long and difficult road toward acceptance. Since most associations didn't accept colors beyond the original Burmese colors of sable, champagne, blue, and platinum, a new standard was written. In addition, the European Burmese has a different head and body style from the Burmese. CFA accepted the breed for registration in 1994, first in the miscellaneous class.

The European Burmese comes in many additional colors, while the Burmese is accepted in only four.

The breed has made great strides since then. The majority of North American associations accept the Burmese and the European Burmese for championship, but as separate breeds. Some call the breed the European Burmese, while others call it the Foreign Burmese. Regardless of the name, they are the same breed. The European Burmese is popular with fanciers who prefer its moderate type over the compact cobby body, round head, and foreshortened face of the North American contemporary Burmese. The associations that don't accept the European type accept the contemporary Burmese, although today most associations accept both types. Most European Burmese breeders breed the European Burmese.

PERSONALITY

Euro-Burms are people-oriented cats that form strong bonds with the humans who love them. They have never met a stranger, and usually play host or hostess when visitors come to call. Full of high spirits and friskiness even as adults, they love to entertain, and will execute daring leaps to the top of the TV, the drapes, or anywhere else they can catch human attention, pausing to make sure their audience is watching the performance. If their humans are so rude as to stop admiring their antics, these heart and lap warmers materialize in any available lap, demanding undivided attention—or else. If you want a cat that isn't the center of attention, don't get a European Burmese. They crave and thrive on human attention, lots of it, and have a ready purr for the human who provides it. Although playful and spirited well into adulthood, they enjoy a good snooze in warm laps, and caresses from loving hands. A good petting session is about all the grooming necessary for this sleek and sassy breed.

A European Burmese should not be left alone for extended periods. Unless the household has more than one cat—or a friendly, companionable dog—a Euro-Burm may not do well if its favorite people are away at work all day. This breed can become unhappy, bored, even depressed or destructive if left on its own all day. Make sure you can provide enough companionship for a European Burmese before buying.

European Burmese are the proverbial curious cats. Intelligent and inquisitive, they follow you wherever you go, wanting to be involved in every moment of your day and night. They love to "help" with the chores, diving under crisp covers as you try to make the bed, and standing in front of the computer screen as you try to read your email. It's hard to get annoyed with their extreme loyalty; loving gazes from those wide innocent eyes always win the day. Watch those dishwashers and clothes dryers—your Euro-Burm will want to get in and investigate. Refrigerators are another appliance of interest; if you're not watching (and sometimes when you are), your Euro-Burm will crawl inside to grab a quick snack.

CONFORMATION

The European Burmese is an elegant, medium-sized cat of foreign type. Foreign, by the way, means slender—not anorexic and not chubby, but somewhere in between. Any resemblance to either the svelte Siamese or the cobby British Shorthair is regarded a fault.

The ACFA, CFA, and UFO standards call for an elegant cat of moderate type with gently rounded contours. In CCA and CFF, however, the breed is called the Foreign Burmese, and the standard calls for an elegant cat of a foreign type. Whether you call the body type moderate or foreign, however, both note that any resemblance to either the svelte Siamese or the cobby British Shorthair is regarded a fault. The breed medium in size, has a hard, muscular body, alert ears, and has a sweet, appealing expression in those slightly oriental eyes. Eye color is bright yellow to amber; deeper color is preferred. The coat is short, fine, close-lying, and very glossy with a satin-like texture. The fur is almost without undercoat, which makes grooming a breeze; a once a week grooming is usually enough.

One of the main differences between the Burmese and the European Burmese, besides head and body type, is that the European Burmese comes in many additional colors. Because the Burmese was crossbred with European Siamese lines that possessed the red gene, the colors red and its dilute cream were introduced, producing additional colors. With the acceptance of tortoiseshell, the number of colors doubled.

In CFF, lilac tortie is not a recognized color, but champagne tortie and platinum tortie are. In all colors, the cat's underside is slightly paler than the back. Though not a pointed pattern breed, the points may show some contrast, left over from the Siamese heritage.

The European Burmese has recently been accepted as a breed in its own right in the United States. In the CFA, they are shown in the miscellaneous class, except in International Division

GENERAL	The European Burmese is an elegant, unique cat breed of far eastern origin, moderate type with gently rounded contours. Any oriental elongation or excessive cobbiness is incorrect and should be regarded as a fault.
BODY	Medium length and size. Hard and muscular. Heavier than it looks. Chest strong and rounded in profile. Back straight from the shoulder to the rump.
HEAD	Top slightly rounded. Good breadth between the ears. Wide cheekbones, tapering to a short blunt wedge. Jaw wide at the base; strong lower jaw; strong chin. Visible nose stop in profile.
EARS	Medium in size; set well apart; slight forward tilt; broad at the base. Slightly rounded tips. The outer line continues the shape of the upper face, except as that may not be possible in mature, full-cheeked males.
EYES	Large, alert, set well apart. Top line slightly curved, with an oriental slant toward the nose. Lower line rounded. Eye color yellow to amber; the deeper the color, the better. Lustrous and bright.
LEGS AND PAWS	Legs rather slender, but in proportion to the body. Hind legs slightly longer. Feet small and oval.
TAIL	Medium length; not thick at the base; tapering slightly to a rounded tip.
COAT	Short, fine, and close-lying; very glossy; satin-like in texture. Almost without undercoat.
COLOR	Brown, blue, chocolate, lilac, red, cream, seal tortie, blue tortie, chocolate tortie, lilac tortie.
DISQUALIFY	White patches. Noticeable numbers of white hairs. Visible tail kink. Excessive tabby markings.
ALLOWABLE OUTCROSSES	None.

shows, where they are eligible for championship. In CFF, CCA, and UFO, the breed is accepted for championship under the name Foreign Burmese.

Because the European Burmese facial type is not as extreme as the Burmese, the breed lacks some the physical problems of the Burmese, such as cranial deformities, eye tearing, and breathing problems. However, some lines are prone to tartar buildup and gingivitis, which can lead to the dental disease periodontitis and can cause tissue, tooth, and bone loss.

EXOTIC SHORTHAIR

HISTORY

In the late 1950s American Shorthair breeders, motivated by the popularity of the Persian, secretly began to mix Persians into their American Shorthair bloodlines to improve body type and to introduce the beautiful and favored silver Persian color into the American. (At that time and until 1965 American Shorthairs were known as Domestic Shorthairs.) Because of this hybridization, the American Shorthair conformation went through a period of remodeling in the 1960s. The boning of the American grew heavier, the head rounder, and the nose shorter, and the coat denser and longer. Because the Persian's conformation was popular (and still is), the hybrids did well in the shows, although known in CFA and CCA as the Exotic they were not a recognized breed at the time.

Other American Shorthair breeders, appalled at the changes occurring in the breed, became determined to disallow any Americans that showed signs of hybridization. Exotic Shorthairs might have faded away into cat fancy history if it wasn't for the efforts of CFA judge Jane Martinke. She was the first to

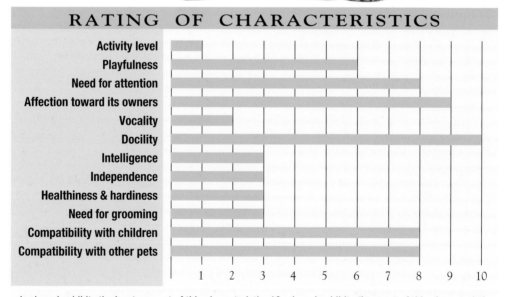

Exotic Shorthair.

RATING OF CHARACTERISTICS

Characteristic	Rating
Activity level	1
Playfulness	6
Need for attention	8
Affection toward its owners	9
Vocality	2
Docility	10
Intelligence	3
Independence	3
Healthiness & hardiness	3
Need for grooming	3
Compatibility with children	8
Compatibility with other pets	8

1—breed exhibits the least amount of this characteristic, 10—breed exhibits the most of this characteristic

✳ **Exotic Shorthair accepted for championship status in all associations**
✳ **Exotic Longhair accepted for championship in AACE, CCA, CFF, and UFO; Longhair Exotic accepted for championship in ACFA and CFA; accepted for championship in TICA as the Persian/Himalayan/Exotic Shorthair breed group**

suggest that these American Shorthair/Persian mixes should have a room of their own, rather than be allowed to rearrange the furniture in the American Shorthair's suite.

The Exotic Shorthair was first accepted for championship status by the CFA in 1967. CFA breeders were then allowed to shift their American Shorthair/Persian hybrids into the newly formed Exotic Shorthair classification.

Few breeders chose to transfer their cats to the new class, however, and the breeders who did decide to work with the Exotic had a long road ahead of them. Because of the initial resistance to the new breed and because few Persian breeders would allow their cats to be used in the Exotic breeding programs, progress was very slow.

At first, Exotic breeders used Burmese and Russian Blues in addition to American Shorthairs to introduce the shorthair gene. The breeders used the shorthaired breeds just often enough to keep the shorthair gene in the bloodline.

As the breed began to gain in popularity, and as the gene pool grew larger, the CFA began limiting the outcrosses. In 1987 the CFA closed the Exotic to shorthair outcrosses altogether, leaving the Persian as the CFA's only allowable outcross.

Even with the slow start, the Exotic made steady progress with the help of the devoted advocates of the breed who saw that a Persian in a Shorthair's clothing would make a valuable addition to the cat fancy. In 1971, the first Exotic Shorthair achieved the status of grand champion. In 1991, an Exotic was CFA's Cat of the Year, and in 1992 CFA's Best Kitten was also an Exotic. Today, the Exotic is one of the most popular shorthair breeds, and has a large following among cat fanciers.

EXOTIC LONGHAIR

The Persian was, and still is, used in breeding programs; it's necessary to breed back to the Persian to maintain the proper cobby body conformation, rounded head type, and thick coat. This does cause some difficulty, however. If the Exotic parent carries a copy of the recessive longhair gene—which the majority does—approximately 50 percent of kittens from Exotic/Persian matings will have long hair. Even when Exotic is bred to Exotic, the litters will contain on average 25 percent longhaired kittens when the recessive gene for long hair is carried by both parents. These kittens are longhaired versions of shorthaired Persians—the oxymoron of the cat fancy. This slows the process of reproducing Exotic Shorthairs and can be frustrating because of the number of Exotic Longhairs produced. Exotic Longhairs look and act exactly like Persians, but are technically

GENERAL	The ideal Exotic should present an impression of a heavily boned, well balanced cat with a sweet expression and soft, round lines. The large, round eyes set wide apart in a large round head contribute to the overall look and expression. The thick, plush coat softens the lines of the cat and accentuates the roundness in appearance.
BODY	Cobby type, low on the legs, broad and deep through the chest, equally massive across the shoulders and rump, with a well-rounded midsection and level back. Good muscle tone, with no evidence of obesity. Large or medium in size. Quality the determining consideration rather than size.
HEAD	Round and massive, with great breadth of skull. Round face with round underlying bone structure. Well set on a short, thick neck. Skull structure to be smooth and round to the touch and not unduly exaggerated from where the forehead begins at the top of the break to the back of the head, as well as across the breadth between the ears. When viewed in profile, the prominence of the eyes is apparent and the forehead, nose, and chin appear to be in vertical alignment. Nose is short, snub, and broad, with "break" centered between the eyes. Cheeks full. Muzzle not overly pronounced, smoothing nicely into the cheeks. Chin full, well-developed, and firmly rounded, reflecting a proper bite.
EARS	Small, round tipped, tilted forward, and not unduly open at the base. Set far apart, and low on the head, fitting into (without distorting) the rounded contour of the head.
EYES	Large, round, and full. Set level and far apart, giving a sweet expression to the face. Brilliant in color; eye color depends upon coat color.
LEGS AND PAWS	Legs short, thick, and strong. Forelegs straight. Hind legs are straight when viewed from behind. Paws large, round, and firm. Toes carried close, five in front and four behind.
TAIL	Short, but in proportion to body length. Carried without a curve and at an angle lower than the back.
COAT— SHORTHAIR (EXOTIC STANDARD)	Dense, plush, soft and full of life. Standing out from the body due to a rich, thick undercoat. Medium in length. Acceptable length depends on proper undercoat.
COAT— LONGHAIR (EXOTIC STANDARD)	Long and thick, standing off from the body. Of fine texture, glossy and full of life. Long all over the body, including the shoulders. The ruff immense and continuing in a deep frill between the front legs. Ear and toe tufts long. Brush very full.

COLOR	All patterns and colors, including the pointed pattern.
DISQUALIFY	Locket or button. Kinked or abnormal tail. Incorrect number of toes. Any apparent weakness in the hind quarters. Any apparent deformity of the spine. Deformity of the skull resulting in an asymmetrical face and/or head. Crossed eyes.
ALLOWABLE OUTCROSSES	Persian.

hybrids like their Exotic parents. In the beginning, this was a major problem for Exotic Shorthair breeders, because the longhairs they produced could not be registered or shown as either Exotics or Persians.

Because of these difficulties, all North American associations now recognize the Exotic Longhair either as a breed in its own right or as a division of the Exotic or the Persian so that the longhair kittens born to Exotic Shorthair parents or Exotic Shorthair/Persian crosses can be registered and shown as either Exotic Longhairs or as Persians, depending upon the breed they resemble.

For example, in CFA, Longhair Exotics that meet Persian color descriptions are eligible to compete in Persian color classes. The Exotic Shorthair parentage is indicated by particular registration prefixes. The longhair division for Exotics was created for scoring pur-

Exotics are relaxed, easygoing cats that enjoy a playful romp in between naps.

poses, and national and regional points accumulated by Longhair Exotics shown in Persian color classes count toward Longhair Exotic breed and color class wins, not toward Persian wins. This is fair for the Persians that are completing, and gives the Exotic breeders a way of exhibiting and earning points for the outstanding examples of Exotic Longhairs.

In AACE, ACFA, CCA, CFF, and UFO, the Exotic Shorthair and the Exotic Longhair are accepted for cham-

pionship competition as separate breeds, with crossbreeding allowed. ACFA recognizes the Exotic Longhair under the name Longhair Exotic; in CCA, the two breeds are judged separately but share a single breed standard under the name "Exotic." In TICA, the Exotic Shorthair, Persian, and Himalayan share a single standard and are part of the Persian Breed Group; these breeds may be bred with one another and are judged according to their appearance and hair length; an Exotic with the others in their breed group.

PERSONALITY

Some folks who don't appreciate that laid-back, mellow personality label Persians and their relatives "furniture with fur," but in truth Exotics are playful and enjoy a good game of catching the catnip mouse between bouts of catching a few ZZZs. Because of the American Shorthair influence, Exotics are reported to be somewhat livelier than Persians, although some breeders say that the two breeds are indistinguishable. Undoubtedly, the Exotic personality is, if not identical, very much like the Persian's—laidback, loyal, sweet, and affectionate. They want to be involved in their favorite humans' lives and will quietly follow them from room to room just to see what they are doing. They also enjoy hugs and cuddles, and lavish their humans with purrs and licks of affection until the thick coat drives them away to lounge on cool kitchen linoleum or cold fireplace bricks. Fanciers point out that because of the short coat, they can spend more time playing with their Exotics than grooming them.

CONFORMATION

The Exotic is a shorthaired Persian, and still crossed with Persians, so it's hardly surprising the Exotic shares the same health issues with the Persian. These include sinus and breathing problems caused by the foreshortened face, snub nose, abridged sinus cavities, and perpetually running eyes. Some Exotics need daily face washing with a warm cloth to eliminate excess tearing. In addition, some lines are prone to plaque, tartar buildup, and gingivitis. Gingivitis can lead to the dental disease periodontitis, which can cause tissue, tooth, and bone loss.

However, the most serious inherited problem is polycystic kidney disease (PKD), which is very common in Persians, Himalayan, Exotics, and related breeds. PKD causes multiple cysts to develop on both kidneys, resulting in renal failure. According to the School of Veterinary Medicine in Davis, California, an estimated 37 percent of Persians have PKD, a breed that accounts for nearly 80 percent of the cat fancy's pedigreed cats. When you add the Exotic and the Himalayan, the percentage is even higher. Fortunately, a PKD genetic test is available from the UC Davis School of Veterinary Medicine Veterinary Genetics Laboratory, which can help breeders screen out affected breeding stock. Currently the VGL recommends the PKD1 test for British Shorthairs, Persians, Exotics, Scottish Folds, Burmillas, Himalayans, and Persian out-crosses. Be sure to talk to your breeder about this and any other health concerns, and buy from a breeder who tests for PKD and provides a written health guarantee.

HISTORY

The Havana Brown, a cat the color of chocolate kisses, is another breed that comes from the mysterious land of Siam. Solid brown cats were described and depicted in *The Cat-Book Poems*, a manuscript of verses and paintings written in the city of Ayutthaya, Siam, some time between 1350 C.E. when the kingdom was founded, and 1767 C.E. when the city was destroyed by invaders from Burma. These brown cats appear in the manuscript alongside royal Siamese, black and white bicolors, and silver-blue Korats. The people of Siam considered the burnished brown cats very beautiful and believed they protected their human companions from evil. Solid brown (self-brown) cats were among the first felines to come to England from Siam (now Thailand) in the late 1800s. Early records describe these cats as "Siamese, with coats of burnished chestnut, and greeny-blue eyes." It is believed that these imports were not all of the same genetic types, but rather represent what today would be

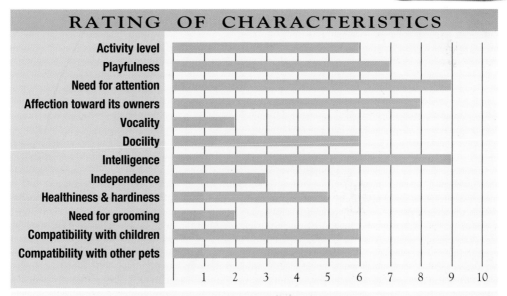

Havana Browns are intelligent and affectionate.

RATING OF CHARACTERISTICS

Characteristic	Rating
Activity level	6
Playfulness	7
Need for attention	9
Affection toward its owners	8
Vocality	2
Docility	5
Intelligence	9
Independence	3
Healthiness & hardiness	5
Need for grooming	2
Compatibility with children	6
Compatibility with other pets	6

1—breed exhibits the least amount of this characteristic, 10—breed exhibits the most of this characteristic

✳ Championship status in all associations; called the Havana in TICA and CFF

called Burmese, chocolate point Siamese, Tonkinese (Burmese/Siamese hybrids), and Havana Browns. It's hard to tell one from another from mere descriptions.

Solid brown cats were exhibited in Europe during the late 1800s and the early 1900s. A self-brown took first

Green eyes are a must for the show Havana Brown.

prize at a show in England in 1888, indicating that, at that time, fanciers valued and treasured brown cats. At a 1928 cat show, the British Siamese Cat Club gave a special award to the cat with "the best chocolate body." Writers of the day described these cats as "chocolate-colored Siamese, that is, the same color all over."

Soon after, however, self-browns fell from grace. In 1930 the Siamese Cat Club announced, "The club much regrets it is unable to encourage the breeding of any but blue-eyed Siamese." Solid brown cats lacking blue eyes were accordingly banned from competition and disappeared from the cat fancy.

Self-browns made their comeback in the early 1950s when a handful of English breeders decided brown was still beautiful. Working first separately and then together, these breeders studied chocolate gene inheritance and then started a breeding program, apparently using Siamese, domestic shorthairs, and Russian Blues. The breeders were striving to produce a solid-colored cat in the chocolate point coloring of the Siamese, rather than the sable coloring of the

Burmese. At that time in England, the only recognized foreign breeds other than the Siamese were the Abyssinian and the Russian Blue.

In 1952 the first solid chocolate kitten to be registered in England was born. This kitten, Elmtower Bronze Idol, became the foundation cat for the new breed. Bronze Idol was produced by mating a seal point Siamese that carried the chocolate gene with a solid black cat also carrying chocolate. The black cat was the offspring of a black cat bred to a seal point Siamese. Since chocolate coloration is governed by a recessive gene, Bronze Idol had to receive the gene from both parents to express the trait.

In 1958, the Governing Council of the Cat Fancy accepted the breed for championship competition under the name Chestnut Brown Foreign. Later, the breed was renamed Havana. Two stories exist regarding the naming of the breed. One claims that the Havana was named after a rabbit breed of the same color. The other maintains the Havana was named after the Havana tobacco because it has the color and matt appearance of a Havana cigar.

The first Havanas reached America in the mid-1950s. The breed was recognized in 1959 under the name Havana Brown, and in 1964 CFA granted the Havana Brown championship status.

In 1974, the gene pool was closed in North America, which many breeders felt was much too early in the breed's development, given that the breed was, and still is, quite rare. By the early 1990s, Havana Brown numbers were dwindling, and breeding closely related cats was necessary because no unrelated cats were available. Breeders became very

concerned about the Havana's future as a viable breed, and they contacted Dr. Leslie Lyons Ph.D. at the Veterinary Genetics Laboratory at University of California, Davis for help in developing an outcross program. The Winn Feline Foundation, a non-profit organization that supports studies to improve cat health, funded the project so Veterinary Genetics Laboratory could analyze the Havana Brown's genetic makeup. The study showed the Havana badly needed outcrosses to maintain the breed's health and diversity.

Breeders petitioned CFA to open the breed to outcrossing. In 1997, CFA voted to allow the Havana Brown certain limited outcrosses to chocolate point and seal point Siamese, certain colors of Oriental Shorthairs (breeders favor solid ebony and solid chestnut), and unregistered solid black and solid blue domestic shorthairs. Kittens from a Havana Brown and an allowable outcross could then be mated back to a Havana Brown, at which point the offspring were considered registrable and showable Havana Browns provided they met the color standard. To date, breeders report the program has been successful in enlarging the gene pool and keeping the breed healthy.

PERSONALITY

More distinctive than the muzzle, ears, or minklike coat is the Havana Brown's personality. Although still quite rare and for years one of the cat fancy's best kept secrets, Havanas have built a solid following of enthusiastic fanciers. Havana Browns are affectionate, gentle, highly intelligent, and, unlike their Siamese compatriots, quiet.

GENERAL	The overall impression of the ideal Havana Brown is a cat of medium size with a rich, solid color coat and good muscle tone. Due to its distinctive muzzle shape, coat color, brilliant and expressive eyes, and large forward tilted ears, it is comparable to no other breed.
BODY	Torso medium in length, firm, and muscular. Adult males tend to be larger than their female counterparts. Overall balance and proportion rather than size to be determining factor. The neck is medium in length and in proportion to the body. The general conformation is mid-range between the short-coupled, thick set and svelte breeds.
HEAD	When viewed from above, the head is longer than it is wide, narrowing to a rounded muzzle with a pronounced break on both sides behind the whisker pads. The somewhat narrow muzzle and the whisker break are distinctive characteristics of the breed and must be evident in the typical specimen. When viewed in profile, there is a distinct stop at the eyes; the end of the muzzle appears almost square; this illusion is heightened by a well-developed chin, the profile outline of which is more square than round. Ideally, the tip of the nose and the chin form an almost perpendicular line. Allow for sparse hair on chin, directly below lower lip.
EARS	Large, round-tipped, cupped at the base, wide-set but not flaring; tilted forward giving the cat an alert appearance. Little hair inside or outside.
EYES	Shape: aperture oval in shape. Medium sized; set wide apart; brilliant, alert and expressive. Color: any vivid and level shade of green; the deeper the color the better.
LEGS AND PAWS	Ideal specimen stands relatively high on its legs for a cat of medium proportions in trunk and tail. Legs are straight. The legs of females are slim and dainty; slenderness and length of leg will be less evident in the more powerfully muscled, mature males. Hind legs slightly longer than front. Paws are oval and compact. Toes: five in front and four behind.
TAIL	Medium in length and in proportion to the body; slender, neither whip-like nor blunt; tapering at the end. Not too broad at the base.
COAT	Short to medium in length, smooth and lustrous.
COLOR	Rich and even shade of warm brown throughout; color tends toward red-brown (mahogany) rather than black-brown. Nose leather brown with a rosy flush. Paw pads rosy toned. Whiskers brown, complementing the coat color.

DISQUALIFY	Kinked tail, locket or button, incorrect number of toes, any eye color other than green, incorrect color of whiskers, nose leather or paw pads.
ALLOWABLE OUTCROSSES	Certain limited outcrossing is permissible for the Havana Brown; contact the CFA Central Office for details.

They are remarkably adaptable and agreeable cats, and adjust to almost any situation with poise and confidence.

Havanas must have human interaction if they are to live happy, healthy lives. They crave attention from their human companions and are not content unless they can be by your side, helping you with your household tasks. Havanas love to reach out and touch their favorite humans; they often nudge their human friends with an out-stretched paw as if asking for attention.

Fetch is a favorite Havana game, and they can often be found carrying toys and stray objects around in their mouths. If you've misplaced a sock or some other small, easily carried object, check your Havana's cat bed. You might find that it has magically found its way there.

CONFORMATION

Rather than attempt a Siamese body style as British breeders have done, American breeders have favored a more moderate body and head type for their Havana Browns. The European Havana Brown is considerably more Siamese in conformation than North American Havanas. The North American Havana Brown's distinctive muzzle, rich color, expressive eyes, and large ears make it distinctive and exceptionally striking among the American cat breeds.

The Havana's coat is also distinctive. Color is very important to this breed: the coat should be a rich, even shade of warm brown, tending toward red-brown or mahogany rather than black-brown. Allowance is made for ghost tabby markings in kittens and youngsters. In CFF and TICA the breed is called "Havana," since lilac (lavender in CFF), a dilute of brown, is an accepted color.

Havana Brown kitten at 15 weeks.

HISTORY

The first deliberate cross between a Siamese and a Persian was made in 1924 by a Swedish geneticist, but it wasn't until 1935 that the first pointed pattern longhair was born. In the early 1930s, two Harvard medical researchers crossed a Siamese female with a black Persian male, not to create a new breed, but to establish how certain characteristics were inherited. This mating produced a litter of black, shorthaired kittens. They then bred a black Persian female with a Siamese male. The outcome was the same. This is not surprising, since longhair and the colorpoint pattern are both governed by recessive genes. Both parents have to possess the genes in order for the traits to be expressed in the offspring.

By crossing a female from the second litter with a male from the first, they produced Debutante, a cat that possessed the Siamese body type and color pattern and the long hair of the Persian. Debutante looked more like today's Balinese

The Himalayan's facial structure is the same as the Persian's.

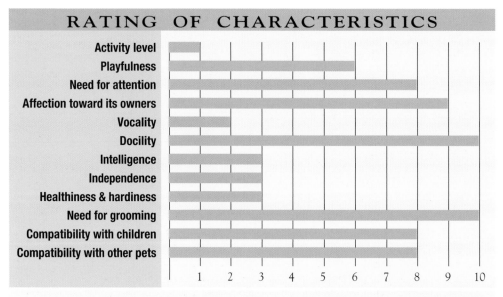

RATING OF CHARACTERISTICS

Characteristic	1	2	3	4	5	6	7	8	9	10
Activity level	▓									
Playfulness	▓	▓	▓	▓	▓	▓				
Need for attention	▓	▓	▓	▓	▓	▓	▓	▓		
Affection toward its owners	▓	▓	▓	▓	▓	▓	▓	▓	▓	
Vocality	▓	▓								
Docility	▓	▓	▓	▓	▓	▓	▓	▓	▓	▓
Intelligence	▓	▓	▓							
Independence	▓	▓	▓							
Healthiness & hardiness	▓	▓	▓							
Need for grooming	▓	▓	▓	▓	▓	▓	▓	▓	▓	▓
Compatibility with children	▓	▓	▓	▓	▓	▓	▓	▓		
Compatibility with other pets	▓	▓	▓	▓	▓	▓	▓	▓		

1—breed exhibits the least amount of this characteristic, 10—breed exhibits the most of this characteristic

❋ **Championship status in AACE, ACFA, CCA, CFF, and UFO under the name Himalayan; championship status in CFA as a color division of the Persian breed; championship status in TICA as part of the Persian Breed Group.**

than today's Himalayan. At this point, the Harvard medical researchers, having learned what they wanted to know about genetics, ended their experiment. During the same year, however, British fanciers formed a breeders' club, hoping to produce a pointed pattern breed with the Persian hair type and conformation. Breeders in America showed interest in the same goal.

World War II interfered with the breeding program, both in Europe and in the United States. Finally, in 1950 American breeder Marguerita Goforth succeeded in creating the long awaited Persian-like colorpoint. CFA and ACFA recognized the breed in 1957 under the name Himalayan, named for the color pattern found in other animals such as the Himalayan rabbit. By 1961, all major U.S. cat associations recognized the Himalayan.

While this was going on in the States, British breeders were also working to create the breed. In 1955, the Governing Council of the Cat Fancy (GCCF) recognized the Himalayan under the name Colorpoint Longhair, a name that remains to this day.

In 1984, the CFA united the Himalayan and the Persian breeds, reasoning that the body and coat type was the same for both breeds. In addition, since the Himalayan requires occasional outcrosses to the Persian to preserve the type, no registration or status problems would occur for the Himalayan/Persian hybrids if they were considered varieties of the same breed. This policy continues today. Himalayans are considered part of the Persian breed and are called Pointed Pattern Persians. Persians that carry the colorpoint gene are called colorpoint carriers.

The decision was controversial, and not all breeders welcomed the new policy. Some Persian breeders were concerned about the introduction of hybrids into their Persian bloodlines, while Himalayan breeders were concerned about losing the breed that they had worked so hard and long to perfect. A group of fanciers and breeders split from the CFA and formed the National Cat Fanciers' Association (NCFA) because they so strongly disagreed with the new policy.

However, other associations soon adopted similar policies; TICA combined the Exotic, Himalayan, and Persian into one breed group governed by a single standard. In AACE, ACFA, CCA, CFF, and UFO, the Himalayan is considered a separate breed and has its own breed standard. However, because Himalayans are regularly crossed with Persians, these associations have special rules for Himalayan-Persian hybrids, usually allowing them to be shown either as Himalayans or Persians, depending upon their appearance. For example, in ACFA, non-pointed Himalayans are included in the Himalayan standard, allowing them to be shown for championship as that breed. CFF has a similar stan-

GENERAL (TICA STANDARD)	The Himalayan is a man-made hybrid breed identical to the Persian, but distinguished by the points on the cats' extremities (the facial mask, feet, ears, and tail) which results in a Persian-type cat with the coloring and deep blue eyes of the Siamese-patterned cat. The ideal Himalayan is a strong cat with excellent boning and musculature, a well-balanced cat, giving the impression of robust power.
BODY	Cobby, firm, well-rounded mid-section, in proportion. Medium to large in size. Back short and level. The chest is to be deep; equally massive across the shoulders and rump with a short, well-rounded abdomen and ribs; boning heavy, sturdy and in proportion. Musculature firm and well developed, not overly fat.
HEAD	Round, broad, smooth domed, with great breadth. Should be medium to large in size and in proportion to body. Jaws broad and powerful with perfect tooth occlusion. Cheeks should be full and prominent. Overall sweet expression. Chin strong, full, well-developed, fitting into the face. Nose almost as broad as long with open nostrils. Muzzle should be short, broad and full. In profile short, snub nose, definite break directly between eyes. Forehead, nose, and chin in straight line. Neck short, thick, and well-muscled.
EARS	Small and round tipped, not unduly open base. Set wide apart, fitting into contour of head.
EYES	Large, round, and full. Set level and far apart giving a sweet expression to the face, eye color has equal importance to size and shape. Deepest blue preferred, but light to medium blue is acceptable.
LEGS AND PAWS	Legs: large bones, well-developed and with firm musculature. In front view, the forelegs should be short and straight from breadth of chest adding to sturdy appearance, not to have a bull dog appearance. When viewed from the rear, the legs should be straight. Feet round and large.
TAIL	Short and straight. In proportion to body length.
COAT	Long all over the body. Full of life. Dense undercoat giving the coat full volume. Ruff should be immense. Seasonal variations in coat shall be recognized.
COLOR	All pointed colors and pointed patterns. Clear color preferred with subtle shading allowed. Allowance should be made for darker shaded areas on coats of mature cats. There must be a definite contrast between the body and point color. The points, comprising of the ears, legs, feet, tail, and mask, must show the basic color of the cat.

| **DISQUALIFY** | Kinked tail. Severe malocclusion or extremely asymmetric face structure; crossed, slanted or improperly focusing eyes. Severe overshot or undershot jaw. |
| **ALLOWABLE OUTCROSSES** | Persian. |

dard. This makes it easier for breeders and avoids ending up with kittens that can't be bred or shown for championship either as Himalayans or Persians. Whatever you call it, the Himalayan remains a popular breed with a solid following of fanciers.

PERSONALITY

Himmies, as fanciers call them, are perfect indoor cat companions. They are gentle, calm, and sweet-tempered, but they possess a playful side as well. Like the Siamese, Himalayans love to play fetch, and a scrap of crumpled paper or a kitty toy will entertain them for hours, or until their next nap.

Himalayans are devoted and dependent upon their humans for companionship and protection. They crave affection and love to be petted and groomed, which is fortunate, since every Himalayan owner will spend part of each day doing just that. Like their Persian siblings, they are docile and won't harass you for attention the way some breeds will. They possess the same

Himalayan owners spend time each day combing that long fur to prevent mats. Fortunately, most Himmies enjoy being groomed.

165

Seal point Himalayan. Notice the contrast in color between the pointed areas and the body.

activity level as the Persian, and they are not vocal like the Siamese.

CONFORMATION

The Himalayan shares the same health issues with the Persian. Some lines are prone to plaque, tartar buildup, and gingivitis. Gingivitis can lead to the dental disease periodontitis, which can cause tissue, tooth, and bone loss.

The most serious inherited problem is polycystic kidney disease (PKD), which causes multiple cysts to develop on both kidneys, resulting in renal failure. The disease is very common in Persians, Himalayan, Exotics, and breeds in which the Persian was used as an outcross. According to the School of Veterinary Medicine in Davis, California, an estimated 37 percent of Persians have PKD, a breed that accounts for nearly 80 percent of the cat fancy's pedigreed cats. Add the numbers of Himalayans and Exotics, and the percentage is even higher. Fortunately, a genetic test for PKD has been developed and is available from the Veterinary Genetics Laboratory at the UC Davis School of Veterinary Medicine, which helps breeders screen their breeding stock for affected or carrier cats. Currently the VGL recommends the PKD1 test for Himalayans, Persians, Exotics, Scottish Folds, Burmillas, British Shorthairs, and Persian outcrosses. Be sure to talk to your breeder about this and any other health concerns, and buy from a breeder who tests for PKD and provides a written health guarantee.

The current show trend is toward a more extremely flat facial type, with a nose placed high between the eyes. This troubles some fanciers, who think the extremely flat face is harmful and creates health problems for the breed. Reported difficulties include malocclusions, sinus trouble, breathing problems and wheezing caused by the foreshortened face and nose, and perpetually runny eyes caused by the shortened tear ducts. Some Himalayans need daily face washing with a warm cloth to control the excess tearing and prevent permanent under-eye stains. In addition, some Himalayans have birthing difficulties because of the large, round head.

Some breeders breed and sell the Doll Face Himalayan, which has a less extreme facial type and tends to have fewer health issues related to the foreshortened facial type. No standard exists for the Doll Face; however, such cats can and are registered with TICA and CFA, and some of the other associations as well. Since no standard of perfection exists, buyers must be even more careful when choosing a breeder.

HISTORY

No one knows for sure when and where the Japanese Bobtail originated, but it is believed that the ancestors of today's JBT traveled from Korea and China to Japan around the beginning of the sixth century. They most likely were kept aboard ships to protect precious silk goods and documents being transported from port to port. Whether these sea-faring cats had bobbed tails or not is not known; the origin of the JBT's bobbed tail mutation will probably never be known. It's clear, however, that the breed has been bobbing around the Far East for many centuries, since early Japanese folklore contains numerous references to short-tailed cats. Bobtailed cats can be found in Japanese woodcut prints and silkscreen paintings from the Edo period (1603–1867), so they were not only well known in Japan but by the fifteenth century were prized for their grace and beauty, and were kept in the temples and homes of the Imperial Japanese families for many years. It's safe to say the Japanese Bobtail is one of the oldest existing cat breeds with a history as rich with legends and folklore as the country in which it developed.

Japanese Bobtail Shorthair.

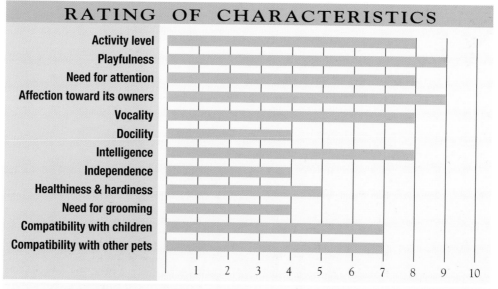

RATING OF CHARACTERISTICS

Characteristic	Rating
Activity level	8
Playfulness	9
Need for attention	8
Affection toward its owners	9
Vocality	4
Docility	4
Intelligence	8
Independence	4
Healthiness & hardiness	5
Need for grooming	4
Compatibility with children	7
Compatibility with other pets	7

1—breed exhibits the least amount of this characteristic, 10—breed exhibits the most of this characteristic

⚹ **Championship status in all associations (shorthair); championship status for Japanese Bobtail Longhair in all associations except CFF**

Bobtailed cats born with a particular pattern of red, black and white markings were called Mi-Ke (pronounced mee-kay, meaning "three fur" in Japanese) were considered lucky; such cats were particularly treasured. The most famous story about the Mi-Ke is the legend of Maneki Neko, which means "beckoning cat" in Japanese. As the tale goes, a bobtailed, tri-colored cat named Tama lived at the poor Kotoku temple in Setagaya, Tokyo. The monk often shared his meager food with his beloved cat to make sure she got enough to eat. One day, Lord Ii Natotaka was caught in a rain storm near the temple. While he sought shelter under a nearby tree, he noticed Tama beckoning to him from the temple gate. A moment after he left the tree in response to the cat's welcoming gesture, the tree was struck by lightning. Since Tama had saved his life, Lord Ii Natotaka took the temple as his family's own, bringing it great prosperity. The lord renamed the temple Gotokuji and built a large new temple building. Tama, revered for bringing such good fortune, lived out her life in comfort and was buried with honors in the temple cemetery.

Other legends about Maneki Neko abound, but all associate the cat with good luck and prosperity. Maneki Neko silkscreen paintings and other artwork were particularly popular in the Edo period. Today, figurines of Maneki Neko can be found in many Japanese shops, restaurants, and other businesses as charms to bring good fortune and success. These figurines clearly show the bobbed tail, the tri-colored pattern, and the raised beckoning paw.

Japanese Bobtails possess a personality that will make you purr.

Japanese Bobtails might have remained pampered royal cats if not for the Japanese silk industry. Around the fifteenth century, when growing rodent populations threatened to destroy the silkworms and their cocoons from which the precious silk was harvested, the Japanese government ordered cats be set free to protect the silk industry. Afterward, Japanese Bobtails became street and farm cats, and after many years of survival on Japan's streets and farms, natural selection turned the Japanese Bobtail into a hardy, intelligent, adaptable cat. Until quite recently, the Japanese Bobtail was considered a common working cat in its native land.

The Japanese Bobtail came to North America in 1968. Abyssinian breeder Elizabeth Freret saw a Japanese Bobtail at a Maryland pet show and, enchanted by the cat's beauty and personality, she began the year-long process of obtaining Bobtails from Japan. With the help of CFA Japanese Judge Bess Higuchi and Judy Crawford, an American JBT breeder living in Japan, Freret obtained three Japanese Bobtail kittens a year later in August 1968. These three—a Mi-Ke female, a red and white male, and a cinnamon tabby female—became the breed's foundation stock in North America.

Around the same time, judge and breeder Lynn Beck imported three male and five female Japanese Bobtails through a Tokyo agent. She saw her first Bobtail at a CFA show in Japan during a judging assignment, and fell in love with the appealing, graceful breed.

Elizabeth Freret and Lynn Beck were instrumental in gaining recognition for the breed. Together they wrote the first breed standard, and frequently exhibited Bobtails in the experimental classes so judges and fanciers could see and handle them. They also founded the Japanese Bobtail Cat Club, to attract new breeders and exhibitors to the Japanese Bobtail. More cats were imported to widen the gene pool and keep the breed healthy, and soon new breeders signed on to advance the breed. In 1969, CFA accepted Japanese Bobtails for registration. In 1971, the breed was granted provisional status, and in 1976, the Japanese Bobtail was granted CFA championship status. Today, all North American associations accept the breed for championship.

PERSONALITY

As elegant and clever as a Haiku, Japanese Bobtails are living works of art with their sculptured bodies, pert bobbed tails, alert ears, and large window-to-the-soul eyes. But they're not just for admiring; they also possess a personality that will make you purr. Bobs make outstanding companions. Fearless and fierce as samurai warriors when on the hunt for a roving rodent or catnip mouse, Japanese Bobtails nevertheless passionately adore their human families and spend much of their waking hours at their favorite human's side, chirping quiet queries and sticking curious noses into everyone's business. They're bold, intelligent, and energetic, and easily adjust to new people, situations, and animals, making them good show cats. Bobtails are very active; they are ever-present companions that stop short of being

GENERAL	Japanese Bobtail presents overall impression of medium-sized cat with clean lines and bone structure, well-muscled but straight and slender rather than massive in build. The unique set of its eyes, combined with high cheekbones and a long parallel nose, lend a distinctive Japanese cast to the face. Its short tail resembles a bunny tail with the hair fanning out to create a pom-pom appearance, which effectively camouflages underlying bone structure of the tail. Overall type, composed of balance, elegance, and refinement is essence of Japanese Bobtail breed.
BODY	Medium in size, torso long, lean, and elegant, not tubular, showing well developed muscular strength without coarseness. No inclination toward flabbiness or cobbiness. General balance of utmost importance. Neck neither too long nor too short, in proportion to the length of the body.
HEAD	Long and finely chiseled, head forms almost a perfect equilateral triangle (does not include the ears) with gentle curving lines, high cheekbones, and a noticeable whisker break; the nose long and well-defined by two parallel lines from tip to brow with a gentle dip at, or just below, eye level. Muzzle fairly broad and rounding into the whisker break; neither pointed nor blunt. Chin full, neither undershot nor overshot.
EARS	Large, upright, and expressive, set wide apart but at right angles to the head rather than flaring outward, and giving the impression of being tilted forward in repose.
EYES	Large, oval rather than round, but wide and alert; set into the skull at a rather pronounced slant when viewed in profile. The eyeball shows a shallow curvature and should not bulge out beyond the cheekbone or the forehead.
LEGS AND PAWS	Legs in keeping with the body, long, slender, and high, but not dainty or fragile in appearance. The hind legs noticeably longer than the forelegs, but deeply angulated to bend when the cat is standing relaxed so the torso remains nearly level rather than rising toward the rear. When standing, the cat's forelegs and shoulders form two continuous straight lines, close together. Paws oval. Toes five in front and four behind.
TAIL	Tail is unique not only to the breed, but to each individual cat. This is to be used as a guideline, rather than promoting one specific type of tail out of the many that occur within the breed. The tail must be clearly visible and is composed of one or more curves, angles, or kinks or any combination thereof. The furthest extension of the tail bone from the body should be no longer than three inches. The direction in which the tail is carried is not important. The tail may be flexible or rigid and should be of a size and shape that harmonizes with the rest of the cat.

COAT— SHORTHAIR	Shorthair: medium length, soft and silky, but without a noticeable undercoat.
COAT— LONGHAIR	Longhair: length medium-long to long, texture soft and silky, with no noticeable undercoat in the mature adult. Frontal ruff desirable. Coat may be shorter and close lying over the shoulders, gradually lengthening toward the rump, with noticeable longer hair on the tail and rear britches. Ear and toe tufts desirable. Coat should lie so as to accent the lines of the body.
COLOR	No color or pattern is preferred over any other. In the dominant colored bi-colors and tri-colors (Ml-KE) any color may predominate with preference given to bold, dramatic markings and vividly contrasting colors. In the dilute colored bi-colors and tri-colors (MI-KE), any color may predominate, with preference given to soft, muted markings and gently contrasting colors. In the solid color cat the coat color should be of uniform density and color from the tip to the root of each hair and from the nose of the cat to the tail. Nose leather, paw pads, and eye color should harmonize generally with coat color. Blue eyes and odd eyes are allowed. All colors with the exception of those showing evidence of hybridization resulting in the colors chocolate, lavender, point restricted (i.e. pointed pattern) or unpatterned agouti (i.e., Abyssinian coloring) or those colors with white.
DISQUALIFY	Tail bone absent or tail bone extending more than 3 inches from the body. Tail lacking in pom-pom or fluffy appearance. Delayed bobtail effect (i.e., the pom-pom being preceded by an inch or two of normal tail with close-lying hair rather than appearing to commence at the base of the spine).
ALLOWABLE OUTCROSSES	None.

clingy. They want to be involved with their human companions and are more than willing to lend a paw when you need it—and even when you don't. Bobtails also enjoy a good conversation; they have chirping voices that produce a wide range of tones; some breeders describe this as "singing."

Because of their high intelligence, Bobtails readily learn behaviors usually reserved for the canine crowd, such as fetching and learning to walk on a lead. Be careful what you teach them, however; if jumping on your stomach at three in the morning gets you up to feed them even once, they'll jump on your stomach in the wee hours forevermore. Their intelligence can get them into mischief, since they are adept at opening cupboards and getting into off-limit rooms—and out of closed off rooms as well. At their most mischievous, how

Black, red, and white Japanese Bobtail Shorthair. This color combination is called "Mi-Ke."

ing bone structure, which varies greatly from cat to cat. The tail is usually about four inches (10 cm) long, but curls into a corkscrew shape so it appears much shorter.

Since the Bobtail was a street cat for so long, it is likely that somewhere along the bloodline they acquired the recessive gene for long hair. Longhaired Mi-Ke cats appear in seventeenth century Japanese artwork alongside depictions of their shorthaired kin. Although Japanese Bobtail Longhairs are not as common as their shorthaired compatriots, they've been noted in Japan's street cat populations. In the cold provinces of Japan's northernmost islands, where a long coat is an important survival trait, longhaired short tailed cats have been seen in the street cat populations for centuries. However, the Japanese Bobtail Longhair wasn't accepted for championship by North American cat associations until 1991. Breeders worked hard to gain championship status for the longhaired Bobtails that kept appearing in otherwise shorthaired litters. Their persistence paid off; today, the Japanese Bobtail Longhair is accepted for championship by every association except CFF.

Two copies of a recessive gene are required for the trait to be expressed in a cat's physical appearance; the longhair gene can be passed down in shorthaired lines for many generations before appearing. Even when both parents possess one copy of the longhair gene, the ratio of shorthaired over longhaired offspring is approximately 3 to 1.

ever, they are loads of fun to watch. You'll need no better excuse for neglecting the housework than watching the antics of your Japanese Bobtail at play.

CONFORMATION

The gene responsible for the pompom tail is a simple recessive; to have the bobbed tail each Bobtail must have two copies of the bobbed tail gene. Therefore, Bobtail to Bobtail crosses produce 100 percent Bobtail offspring. The Bobtail gene is not related to the dominant Manx gene or to the American Bobtail, and isn't associated with any known genetic defects. The tail's fur camouflages the underly-

HISTORY

The earliest illustrations and descriptions of the Korat (pronounced ko-RAHT) can be found in *The Cat-Book Poems*, a manuscript of verses and paintings written in the city of Ayutthaya, Siam, some time between 1350 C.E. when the kingdom was founded, and 1767 C.E. when the city was destroyed by invaders from Burma. When the book was written can't be more accurately determined since back then manuscripts were handwritten on palm-leaf or bark parchment. When a manuscript became too old, it was painstakingly reproduced by hand onto new materials. This makes it difficult to date the original documents. Still, it's likely the oldest document about cats in existence. The manuscript illustrates and describes in verse seventeen kinds of lucky cats, including the Siamese, Burmese, Havana Brown, and Korat. The artists and writers of the document, whose names have long been forgotten, describe the Korat as a good

Luminous green eye color is preferred in the show Korat.

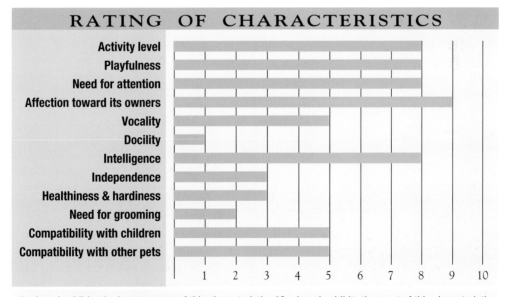

RATING OF CHARACTERISTICS

Characteristic	Rating (1–10)
Activity level	8
Playfulness	8
Need for attention	8
Affection toward its owners	9
Vocality	5
Docility	1
Intelligence	8
Independence	3
Healthiness & hardiness	3
Need for grooming	2
Compatibility with children	5
Compatibility with other pets	5

1—breed exhibits the least amount of this characteristic, 10—breed exhibits the most of this characteristic

luck cat, with eyes the color of new rice that shine like dewdrops on a lotus leaf, and a body the color of rain clouds and silver. Unlike Siamese cats that were primarily owned by Thailand's royalty, Korats were (at least originally) cats of the common people, and were highly prized as living good luck charms. Called Si-Sawat (si meaning color and sawat meaning the silver-blue seed of a fruit plant of the same name), Korats were never sold, but rather were given as special expressions of respect, honor, and esteem. As the story goes, new brides were given a pair of Si-Sawat cats to ensure happy, fortunate marriages. Other tales associate the Korat with ceremonies to bring critical rainfall to the new rice crops. One story tells how Korats were paraded through northeast Thai villages, being sprinkled with water to assure rain would fill the rice paddies with much-needed water. Whether these stories are true or not isn't known, but they add to the mystique of the good luck cat of Siam.

Whether *The Cat-Book Poems* was produced during the mid-fourteenth century or the mid-eighteenth makes little difference. Either way, the Korat can be deemed among the oldest of the domestic cat breeds, along with its compatriots, the Siamese, Burmese, and Havana Brown, also described in the manuscript. The Korat is also considered one of today's purest pedigreed breeds.

Jean Johnson of the Cedar Glen Cattery is credited with bringing the first Korat cats to America. Johnson, who lived in Bangkok with her husband for six years, tried unsuccessfully to buy a pair of Korats. During her time there, she saw only a handful of Korats, and all were owned by members of the Thai government, Thai nobility, or high-ranking representatives of foreign gov-

Korats are affectionate, active, and playful.

174

ernments. Johnson was told they had been given and received "under terms of highest honor, esteem, or respect, and endowed by the giver with the attribute of bringing good health and fortune to the recipient." She was told they were not for sale, nor could she, a mere American woman, ever hope to be so esteemed as to be given one. When she left Thailand in 1954, she was no closer to owning a single Korat, let alone a breeding pair. However, in 1959, Jean Johnson received two Korats, Nara and Darra, from a friend in Bangkok, who had obtained the cats from the Mahajaya cattery of Khunying Abhibal Rajamaitri, a widely known and esteemed Thai breeder. Nara and Darra are the first Korats known to have been exported from Thailand for breeding purposes.

The pair, Nara and Darra, became North America's foundation Korats. To avoid inbreeding, Johnson cross-bred Nara and Darra to Siamese cats also from Thailand. She then eliminated from her breeding program kittens with Siamese characteristics.

In 1962, Gail Lankenau Woodward imported a female Korat named Mahajaya Dok Rak of Gala, also from the Mahajaya cattery and bred by Khunying Abhibal Rajamaitri, and a male Korat named Nai Sri Sawat Miow of Gala from Cholburi, the capital of Chonburi Province in Thailand. Soon after, Gertrude Gecking Sellars imported a female Korat named Me-Luk of Tru-Lu, bred by Colonel Chompoo Arthachinda. These Korats widened the Korat gene pool and provided new enthusiastic breeders in North America.

In 1966, the American Cat Association (ACA) became the first North American association to recognize the Korat, followed by CFA later the same year. Today the Korat is recognized by all the North American registries and, while still quite rare, is promoted by a committed, passionate group of breeders and fanciers. The Korat is also accepted for championship by Fédération Internationale Féline (FIFe) and Governing Council of the Cat Fancy (GCCF), and has an active following of fanciers in the United Kingdom, France, Germany, Finland, Norway, and Denmark. GCCF also accepts the Thai Lilac (solid lilac Korats) and the Thai Blue Point (blue pointed pattern Korats).

In its native land today, the Korat is hard to find and harder to export. They are still rare in their native country and remain highly prized by the Thai people, who still consider the cat a symbol of good luck. A recent anecdote tells of a Thai man who used his Korat's cat show entry number when choosing numbers for a lottery ticket, and won. Korats are still generally given as signs of esteem; given how rare the cats are, the esteem must be great to earn such a precious gift.

PERSONALITY

Korats are not as vocal as their Siamese comrades; they have other ways of getting their wishes across. At dinnertime they'll wrap themselves around your ankle, clamber up onto your shoulder, and perhaps give you a gentle love-bite on the shin if you don't hurry up with the cat food—but

GENERAL	The Korat's general appearance is of a silver blue cat with a heavy silver sheen, medium sized, hard bodied, and muscular. All smooth curves with huge eyes, luminous, alert, and expressive. Perfect physical condition, alert appearance.
BODY	Semi-cobby, neither compact nor svelte. The torso is distinctive. Broad chested with good space between forelegs. Muscular, supple, with a feeling of hard coiled spring power and unexpected weight. Back is carried in a curve.
HEAD	When viewed from the front, or looking down from just back of the head, the head is heart-shaped with breadth between and across the eyes. The eyebrow ridges form the upper curves of the heart, and the sides of the face gently curve down to the chin to complete the heart shape. Profile well-defined with a slight stop between forehead and nose which has a lion-like downward curve just above the leather. Chin and jaw strong and well-developed, making a balancing line for the profile and properly completing the heart-shape. Neither overly squared nor sharply pointed, nor a weak chin that gives the head a pointed look.
EARS	Large, with a rounded tip and large flare at base, set high on head, giving an alert expression. Inside ears sparsely furnished. Hairs on outside of ears extremely short and close.
EYES	Large and luminous. Particularly prominent with an extraordinary depth and brilliance. Wide open and oversized for the face. Eye aperture, which shows as well-rounded when fully open, has an Asian slant when closed or partially closed. Eye color luminous green preferred, amber cast acceptable. Kittens and adolescents can have yellow or amber to amber-green eyes; the color is not usually achieved until the cat is mature, usually two to four years of age.
LEGS AND PAWS	Legs well-proportioned to body. Distance along back from nape of neck to base of tail appears to be equal to distance from base of tail to floor. Front legs slightly shorter than back legs. Paws oval. Toes five in front and four behind.
TAIL	Medium in length, heavier at the base, tapering to a rounded tip. Non-visible kink permitted.
COAT	Single. Hair is short in length, glossy and fine, lying close to the body. The coat over the spine is inclined to break as the cat moves.
COLOR	Silver-tipped blue all over, the silver should be sufficient to produce a silver halo effect. The hair is usually lighter at the roots with a gradient of blue which is deepest just before the tips, which are silver. Adults should be without shading or tabby markings. Allow for ghost tabby markings in kittens. Where the coat is short, the sheen of the silver is intensified.

| **DISQUALIFY** | Visible kink. Incorrect number of toes. White spot or locket. Any color but silver-tipped blue. |
| **ALLOWABLE OUTCROSSES** | None. |

given something important to say, they will speak their minds.

On the cat activity level scale, they are an 8: social, playful, and full of life, but not bouncing-off-the-walls hyper. They also possess high intelligence. Like the Siamese, Korats are fetchers of tossed toys, chasers of sunbeams and paper scraps, cats whose favorite game is the one in which their esteemed human companions take an active part. Korats crave affection from their humans, and will use their brainpower to gain possession of your lap, your arms, and your heart.

CONFORMATION

Coat and color, as well as a muscular and semi-cobby body type, set this breed apart. The coat is a solid, even, silver-blue color with no tabby markings or shading, but the hair shafts themselves are lighter at the roots and shade to a darker blue just before the tips. The fur is tipped with silver, giving a silvery sheen or "halo effect" to the coat. The Korat goes through an ugly duckling phase and doesn't attain its true beauty until two to four years of age. The green eye color is not usually true until the cat matures.

Korats are healthy cats and only two inherited diseases are known to exist in some lines: gangliosidosis GM1 and GM2, both of which are fatal. Gangliosidoses are degenerative neurological diseases caused by abnormal accumulation of lipids known as gangliosides in the nervous system, and particularly in nerve cells. Affected cats die young from progressive neurologic dysfunction; in GM2, the disease progression is more rapid. Both diseases are governed by recessive genetic mutations, so a cat must inherit the faulty gene from both parents to develop either disease. However, cats who possess one copy become carriers that pass on the mutation to offspring; since the Korat gene pool is relatively small, both diseases have become widespread both in North America and in Europe and Asia.

Fortunately, by-mail DNA tests now exist that allow breeders to identify affected and carrier cats. Breeders can use these tests to cull carriers from breeding programs, and to avoid breeding carriers together, which would produce about 25 percent affected kittens. The Veterinary Genetics Laboratory at UC Davis School of Veterinary Medicine, California, offers DNA tests for GM1 and GM2 in Korats (www.vgl.ucdavis.edu/services/index.php). Testing and culling carrier cats has done much to reduce the spread of the diseases. Still, it's wise to buy from a breeder who tests for these diseases and provides a written health guarantee.

LaPERM

HISTORY

At first glance, the LaPerm looks like the cat just back from a grooming salon. However, Mother Nature is this breed's only stylist. Also called the Dalles LaPerm, the LaPerm is one of the newly accepted breeds, and although it's been around since the 1980s, the LaPerm has made great strides in the last few decades. This "new wave" cat has steadily gaining fanciers because an appealing personality comes with the unique curly locks.

The LaPerm's journey began in a cherry orchard in The Dalles, Oregon. In early March of 1982, an ordinary brown tabby barn cat named Speedy, who earned her living catching rodents in the orchards and barns, gave birth to six kittens. The owners, Linda and Richard Koehl, noticed one of the kittens looked very different from her littermates. Instead of the fine down that covered the bodies of her siblings, she was entirely bald. In addition, she was smaller than her littermates and had larger ears and a longer body. Linda Koehl thought the ugly kitten would surely curl up and die.

LaPerm longhair. The breed has made great strides in the last few decades.

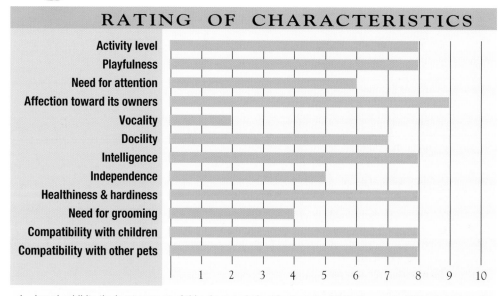

RATING OF CHARACTERISTICS

Characteristic	Rating
Activity level	8
Playfulness	8
Need for attention	6
Affection toward its owners	9
Vocality	2
Docility	7
Intelligence	8
Independence	5
Healthiness & hardiness	8
Need for grooming	4
Compatibility with children	8
Compatibility with other pets	8

1—breed exhibits the least amount of this characteristic, 10—breed exhibits the most of this characteristic

❋ **Championship status in long and short hair lengths in ACFA, CFA, and TICA; NBC status in long and short hair lengths in UFO**

The kitten didn't die, but she soon curled up. When the kitten was about eight weeks old, soft curly hair sprouted from her hairless body, and as she grew, she developed a soft wavy coat. Appropriately, Linda Koehl named the cat Curly. Not being knowledgeable about cat breeds, Linda Koehl accepted Curly as extraordinary and thought no more about it. When Curly matured, Linda Koehl discovered her soft fur felt so inviting to touch that Koehl found herself picking up and cuddling the cat. Not only was Curly's coat unique, she had such a sweet, gentle, trusting personality that Koehl found herself becoming a bonafide cat lover, quite a leap for someone who previously owned cats only for their efficient, all natural pest control.

Curly, a tabby like her dam, soon went into heat, mated with one of the male mouse catchers on the farm, and produced her own litter of five male tabby kittens, all of whom were bald at birth. Like their mother, all soon sprouted coats of curly hair. This intrigued Koehl enough to do bit of research on cat breeds, and Koehl decided she had somehow acquired cats with Rex genes. She thought that was strange, but it didn't occur to her that these cats might be a unique new breed.

As soon as they were old enough, Curly's five sons zealously set about to increase the curly crowd. One of the males walked across the street to woo the neighbor's shorthaired black female kitty. This resulted in five more curly-haired kittens; Linda Koehl obtained them all to add to her ever-increasing curly-coated clowder of cats.

During the next ten years, Linda Koehl made no attempt to control the breeding or keep track of the curly litters. Left on their own, Curly and her progeny did what unaltered cats do best; the Koehls' orchard soon had a large and diverse colony of curly-coated cats in both short and long hair and in a plethora of colors and patterns. Although Koehl didn't know it at the time, the curly coat is governed by a dominant gene, which means only one parent need possess the gene in order to produce curly-coated offspring. Because of this, and because the gene pool was relatively small, the number of curly-coated cats grew rapidly.

Visitors to the cherry grove were fascinated by the curly cats. After doing

The LaPerm is content to sit in your lap for some quality pampering.

LaPerms are agile and active.

and started the long and involved process of gaining recognition for the LaPerm. Not all associations currently recognize the breed, but it's likely only a matter of time since the three largest North American associations, ACFA, CFA, and TICA, accept the LaPerm for championship.

PERSONALITY

LaPerms are gentle, people-oriented cats that are affectionate without being overly demanding or clingy. They adore human companionship and adapt well to indoor or apartment living as long as they get the requisite amount of playing and pampering. Like most cats, LaPerms develop the closest bond with their human friends when they get regular human interaction and affection.

LaPerms are agile and active. Like their barn cat ancestors, they enjoy a good game of chase, and love pouncing on the catnip mouse. They particularly enjoy interactive toys in which you take an active role. Inquisitive by nature, they always want to stick their noses into all household activities. Unlike many active breeds, the LaPerm is quite content to sit in your lap for some quality petting and pampering after they're done racing about the house.

Vocally quiet, LaPerms speak up only when they have something of extreme importance to say, such as bringing your attention to their empty food dishes. However, they enjoy an occasional quiet chat with their favorite people, particularly if their human

more research, Linda Koehl realized her cats might be unique. In 1992, ten years after Curly's birth, Koehl entered four of her curly cats into a CFA show in Portland, Oregon, to see what professional exhibitors and judges had to say. A breed name was required in order to register for the show, so Koehl named Mother Nature's new creation the LaPerm, since the coat looks like it has a permanent wave. Her cage of LaPerms was soon surrounded by a crowd of curious cat fanciers. Koehl was astonished by the enthusiastic reception her cats received, and she was completely unprepared when the judges told her the breed was unknown to the cat fancy and should be preserved, selectively bred, and advanced as a new breed.

With advice from judges and exhibitors, Koehl wrote the first LaPerm breed standard and set up her cattery. Koehl regularly took her cats to shows and exhibited them so judges, exhibitors, and cat lovers could see and inspect them. With the help of other breeders who started their own LaPerm catteries, Koehl developed a breeding program companions are doing most of the chatting.

CONFORMATION

The coat will be curly if a kitten has inherited the dominant gene for curly hair. If a kitten does not inherit at least one copy of the LaPerm gene from its parents, it will have ordinary straight hair. A kitten that inherits two copies of the gene is a boon to breeders, because even when bred to a normal-coated outcross, all the kittens will have curly hair.

LaPerm kittens can be born hairless, but many have short wavy hair or straight hair at birth. At about two weeks of age, kittens begin to grow curly hair. Conversely, kittens may be born with curly or straight hair and then lose it, and they can go through varying stages of hair and hairlessness during the first four months or so. In addition, many LaPerms go through an ugly duckling period before their first birthday during which they lose most or all of their fur. The fur usually grows back curlier and thicker than before. The coat changes so much in the first six months that it's nearly impossible to tell what the kitten will look like as an adult, so if you plan to show it's wise not to agree to buy a LaPerm until the coat settles down. Some of the straight-haired kittens grow up to become pet quality straight-haired cats, but some sprout curls as they mature.

The LaPerm comes in both long- and shorthaired varieties and in every color and pattern genetically possible. In the shorthaired LaPerm, the coat is soft and wavy over the shoulders, back, and undersides. In the longhaired variety, the hair is medium long, and the curls range from tight ringlets to long corkscrew curls, resembling the "Gypsy Shag" hairstyle. The coat may vary in length and fullness according to the season and the cat's maturity. At times, the coat will part naturally down the middle of the back. The coat's feel may vary from cat to cat and between individual colors.

According to some breeders, the LaPerm is hypoallergenic and therefore better tolerated by the cat-allergic. However, no breed of cat is hypoallergenic. Some of our uniquely coated breeds do shed less than other cat breeds, which is helpful in keeping your house free of hair, but cat hair itself does not cause allergic symptoms. The culprit is a protein called Fel d1, which is secreted in the cat's saliva and by the sebaceous glands. When cats groom, they spread this protein onto their fur, regardless of whether it's straight, curly, wavy, or absent altogether. If you are allergic to cats, be cautious of any breeder who insists her cats are hypoallergenic; never buy a cat sight unseen based upon such claims. In addition, keep in mind that cats can produce less Fel d1 when they are kittens; make sure you spend time with adult cats from your chosen cattery before you agree to buy.

In both CFA and TICA, outcrossing with domestic longhairs and domestic shorthairs is allowed to keep the gene pool large and the breed healthy. In CFA, LaPerm kittens born on or after January 1, 2015, can have only LaPerm parents. Since the breed developed from hardy barn cats, this breed has few health problems specific to the breed.

GENERAL	The LaPerm is a naturally occurring mutation producing curly coats in both long- and shorthaired cats. Medium sized, with moderate type. All parts of body are in harmony with size of cat. This breed matures in two to three years.
BODY	Moderate in size with medium fine to medium boning. Hips are slightly higher than shoulders. Allowances are made for larger size in males, as long as they remain balanced and in proportion.
HEAD	Modified wedge, slightly rounded with gentle contours. Whisker pads appear full and rounded, with long, flexible whiskers. Muzzle broad with rounded contours, and moderate to strong whisker pinch. Chin strong and firm. Slight dip to nose just below bottom of eye, continuing straight to tip of nose.
EARS	Continue modified wedge of head; slightly flared and cupped; medium to large. Full furnishings and earmuffs with lynx tipping preferred on longhair; not required on shorthair.
EYES	Medium large and expressive; almond shape at rest, rounder when alert; set moderately far apart; slightly slanted toward base of ear. Color can be copper, gold, yellow, green, blue, aqua (for mink colored cats), or odd eyes; no correlation between coat color and eye color.
LEGS AND PAWS	Medium long to match body length; forelegs may be slightly shorter than hind legs. As with body, medium fine boning; rounded feet.
TAIL	In proportion to body; tapering from base to tip.
COAT— LONGHAIR	Semi-longhair; coat loose, bouncy, springy; light and airy enough to part with a breath. Stands away from body; curls preferred over waves; unkempt appearance ("Gypsy Shag" look); neck ruff at maturity. Longest curls at base of ears and tail, and in ruff; tightest curls in ruff and at base of ears; tail plumed with some curling.
COAT— SHORTHAIR	Short to approximately medium-long; coat springy, curly or wavy; stands away from body with waves over most of cat. Tail like bottle-brush, not plumed; may be wavy. No ruff, ringlets, or earmuffs. Texture may be harder than longhair.
COLOR	All genetically possible colors and patterns. Cats with no more than a locket and/or button shall be judged in the color class of their basic color, with no penalty for such locket or button.
DISQUALIFY	Cobby body, short legs, crossed eyes, incorrect number of toes, visible and non-visible tail faults, straight hair.
ALLOWABLE OUTCROSSES	Domestic longhairs and domestic shorthairs. Kittens born on or after January 1, 2015 can have only LaPerm parents.

HISTORY

Maine Coons, like American Shorthairs, are considered native to America because they've been on this continent since the colonial days, and perhaps longer. How they got here in the first place and where their progenitors came from, however, is anyone's guess, since none of the local colonists happened by with their camera phones to record the event.

Many imaginative stories exist about the origin of the breed (some more believable than others), but hard proof is as elusive as a cat at bath time. One story alleges that the breed is a raccoon/domestic cat hybrid, thus the name Maine Coon. Even though both raccoons and Maine Coons have lush, long tails and the tendency to dunk their food into their drinking water, such a union is biologically impossible. Another anecdote, unlikely but at least possible, holds that the Maine Coon was produced by bobcat/domestic cat trysts, which would explain the ear and toe tufts and the impressive size of the breed.

A more imaginative story claims that Maine Coons are descendants of longhaired cats belonging to Marie Antoinette. The Queen's cats and other belongings were smuggled to America by a captain

Maine Coons are devoted, playful, and loving.

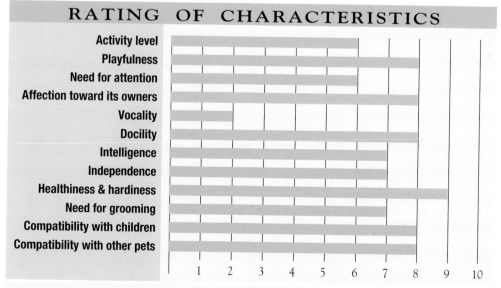

1—breed exhibits the least amount of this characteristic, 10—breed exhibits the most of this characteristic

✳ **Championship status in all associations**

named Clough, who was preparing to rescue the Queen from her rendezvous with the guillotine. Unfortunately, the Queen lost her head, and the cats ended up staying with Clough in Maine.

Last, but not least, is the tale of a sea captain named Coon who, in the 1700s, brought longhaired cats with him on his excursions to America's northeastern coast. Allegedly, these longhaired buccaneers mated with the local population while on shore leave. This last story has at least a ring of truth. Seafarers who used cats to control rodent populations on their sailing ships probably brought some longhaired cats with them to the New World. Some of the cats went ashore when they reached the northeastern coast and established themselves on the farms and in the barns of the early settlers. Given Maine's severe climate, those initial years must have been tough on cat and human alike. Only the breed's strongest and most adaptable survived. Through natural selection, the Maine Coon developed into a large, rugged cat with a dense, water-resistant coat and a hardy constitution.

Regardless of where the breed came from, the Maine Coon was one of the first breeds to be recognized by the late nineteenth-century cat fancy, and became an early favorite. Maine Coons were shown in local cat shows as early as the 1860s, and were prized for their beauty, size, intelligence, and mellow temperaments. When cat shows became all the rage in the late 1800s, Maine Coons, then called Maine Cats,

were right there to show off their beautiful, thick coats and wide palette of colors and patterns. Mrs. F. R. Pierce, who owned Maine Coons as early as 1861, wrote the chapter on Maine Cats in Frances Simpson's 1903 *The Book of the Cat*, and noted that a brown tabby Maine Cat won Best Cat at the first American allbreed cat show in 1895 at Madison Square Garden, New York City. The Maine Coon did very well in shows in Boston and Chicago as well.

However, in the early 1900s, as new and more exotic breeds were imported into the country, the cat fanciers of the era abandoned Maine Coons for Persians, Angoras, and other imports. By 1950, the breed had all but vanished and in fact was declared extinct in the 1950s.

Fortunately, the announcement of the Maine Coon's demise was greatly exaggerated. A small group of dedicated breeders kept this undercat from going under. Breeders held Maine Coon-only cat shows for a time, and in 1968 breeders founded the Maine Coon Breeders and Fanciers Association (MCBFA). The associations that had snubbed the Maine Coon accepted them for championship competition again, and today the Maine Coon has regained its former glory, second only to the Persian in popularity.

PERSONALITY

No breed has a monopoly on love and affection, but there's got to be some good reason that the Maine Coon has clawed its way up from near extinction to the prized place of America's second most popular breed (according to the CFA's registration totals). Maine Coon fanciers say that the popularity is due to the breed's large size, intelligence, luxuriant coat, hardy disposition, and devotion to their human family. Maine Coons are kittens in big cat suits, gentle giants who are playful well into old age, as well as jumbo-sized packages of loving devotion.

Maine Coons can also be reserved around people with whom they're not familiar, probably due to their jumbo-sized brains. Given time, however, even the most cautious adapt. Breeders note that this initial adjustment period is actually a decision-making process; Maine Coons are deciding if these new humans have proven themselves worthy of trust. As soon as they make up their minds, however, they form close bonds with the entire household and become loving and devoted. Most want to be near you but not on your lap.

They are true family members and participate in all family routines, whether watching you channel surf from the comfort of the couch, or following you from room to room.

As befits a former seafarer, Maine Coons are fascinated by water, perhaps because their thick coats are water-repellent and won't become annoyingly soaked as easily as a thinner coat would. Some will join their humans in the shower briefly, or at least walk around on the wet floor after you get out. They prefer to stand on the edge of the tub, however, and touch the water with a curious paw.

Maine Coons are the gentle giants of the cat fancy.

CONFORMATION

One of the largest domestic breeds, male Maine Coons weigh in at twelve to eighteen pounds (5.4 to 8 kilos), while the females fall into a "petite" ten to fourteen pound (4.5 to 6.3 kilos) range. Slow to mature, the Maine Coon takes three to four years to develop fully. Although brown tabby is the most common color and pattern, Maine Coons come in a wide variety of colors and patterns.

The heavy all-weather coat, shorter on the shoulders and longer on the stomach and britches, makes the cat appear larger than it really is. The texture is smooth and silky rather than cottony, so the coat doesn't mat as easily as the coats of some longhaired breeds. Breeders usually recommend a twice-weekly combing with a good steel comb.

GENERAL	The Maine Coon is solid, rugged, and can endure a harsh climate. A distinctive characteristic is its smooth, shaggy coat. A well-proportioned and balanced appearance. Quality should never be sacrificed for size. It has adapted to varied environments.
BODY	Muscular, broad-chested. Size medium to large. The body should be long with all parts in proportion to create a well-balanced rectangular appearance with no part of the anatomy being so exaggerated as to foster weakness. Allowance should be made for slow maturation.
HEAD	Medium in width and slightly longer in length than width with a squareness to the muzzle. Cheekbones high. Muzzle visibly square, medium in length, and blunt ended when viewed in profile. It may give appearance of being a rectangle but not appear to be tapering or pointed. Length and width of the muzzle proportionate to the rest of the head and present a pleasant, balanced appearance. The chin should be strong, firm, and in line with the upper lip and nose. Head should exhibit a slight concavity when viewed in profile.
EARS	Large, well-tufted, wide at base, tapering to appear pointed. Set approximately one ear's width apart at the base; not flared.
EYES	Large, expressive, wide set with an opened oval shape. Slightly oblique setting with slant toward outer base of ear. Eye color can be shades of green, gold, green-gold, or copper. Blue eyes or odd eyes are also allowed for white- or bicolor- (including vans) patterned cats.
LEGS AND PAWS	Legs substantial, wide set, of medium length, and in proportion to the body. Forelegs are straight. Back legs are straight when viewed from behind. Paws large, round, well-tufted. Five toes in front; four in back.
TAIL	Long, wide at base, and tapering. Fur long and flowing.
COAT	Heavy and shaggy; shorter on the shoulders; longer on the stomach and britches. Frontal ruff. Texture silky with coat falling smoothly.
COLOR	Any color or pattern with the exception of those showing hybridization resulting in the colors chocolate, lavender, the Himalayan pattern; the unpatterned agouti on the body (Abyssinian-type ticked tabby) or these combinations with white.
DISQUALIFY	Delicate bone structure. Undershot chin. Crossed eyes. Kinked tail. Incorrect number of toes. White buttons, white lockets, or white spots. Cats showing evidence of hybridization.
ALLOWABLE OUTCROSSES	None.

HISTORY

The Manx has existed for many centuries on the Isle of Man, located in the Irish Sea between England and Ireland. Since the Isle did not have an indigenous feline species from which the Manx could develop, it is surmised that domestic cats were introduced by human settlers and explorers. Exactly who and when is uncertain.

One story has it that the cats were aboard a ship of the Spanish Armada that was wrecked on the Isle of Man in 1588. The resourceful cats supposedly swam ashore at Spanish Point and set up mousekeeping on the Isle. Another story claims that the Manx was introduced by Phoenician traders who transported the cats from Japan. Still another says that cats arrived with the Viking settlers who colonized the Isle of Man.

Regardless of how cats got on the Isle, they presumably arrived with their tails intact. Geneticists believe that the Manx's taillessness is the result of a spontaneous mutation within the Isle's domestic cat population. Genetically, the Manx and other short-

Calico rumpy Manx; this champion cat is entirely tailless.

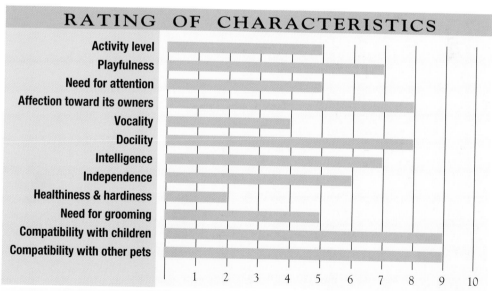

RATING OF CHARACTERISTICS

Characteristic	Rating
Activity level	5
Playfulness	7
Need for attention	5
Affection toward its owners	5
Vocality	4
Docility	8
Intelligence	7
Independence	5
Healthiness & hardiness	4
Need for grooming	3
Compatibility with children	9
Compatibility with other pets	9

1—breed exhibits the least amount of this characteristic, 10—breed exhibits the most of this characteristic

✳ **Championship status in all associations**

Colorpoint Max. Pointed pattern Manx are not accepted for championship in many associations; TICA is one of the few that does.

tailed domestic felines are quite different. The Manx's tail, or lack thereof, is governed by a dominant gene, while most other short-tailed breeds, such as the Japanese Bobtail, have tails governed by recessive genes. Given the Isle's closed environment and small gene pool, the dominant gene easily passed from one generation to the next.

Inhabitants of the Isle, unaware of or unimpressed by boring scientific theory, invented more interesting tales to account for the Manx's lack. One contends that the Manx is an impossible cross between a cat and a rabbit. Another claims that Irish invaders stole the cats' tails to use for their hel-

met plumes. A third says two Manx cats were passengers on Noah's Ark, but as they were the last to board Noah slammed the door on their tails.

The modern history of the Manx is better documented, if more mundane. The Manx was a well-established and popular breed before the earliest days of the cat fancy, supported by an enthusiastic group of Manx owners. King Edward VIII was reportedly a Manx fancier and often attended cat shows featuring the breed. British fanciers formed the first Manx club in 1901.

The Manx had made its journey to America by the 1880s (and probably earlier), and began appearing in cat shows soon after. Manx cats are noted in earliest American cat registry records.

Manx cats were at first exported from the Isle of Man but, as the demand grew, the supply waned. Fanciers had to rely on British and American sources for their cats and, since Manx cats are difficult to breed, demand exceeded supply. Today, show-quality Manx cats are in great demand because of their rarity, but pet quality can be obtained fairly easily.

PERSONALITY

The Manx's personality is probably the reason the breed has won such a strong following despite the physical difficulties and breeding challenges. Manx cats make great household companions. They are intelligent, fun-loving cats that manage to express themselves very well without tails to swish around. Manx are particularly noted for their strong bonds of devotion and loyalty to their chosen humans and enjoy spending quality time with them, whether it's sitting beside their humans enjoying quiet time, or racing around the house after a tossed sponge ball or a whirling feather-tufted toy. Manx are exceptional jumpers because of the powerful back legs. If sufficiently motivated, they will find a way into the most secure cupboard. No shelf is safe from the high-flying Manx.

They get along particularly well with other cats and well-behaved dogs and enjoy romps with these compatible companions. Despite their playful temperament, they are gentle and nonaggressive. Their playful yet trac-table dispositions make them good pets for families with children. They are fascinated by water; perhaps this fascination comes from originating on a small piece of land surrounded by the liquid. However, if you dunk them in the nasty stuff they quickly lose their fascination.

CONFORMATION

Some Manx are known for their unusual rabbitlike gait, known as the "Manx hop." While some fanciers consider the walk to be a result of skeletal abnormalities related to the Manx gene, others consider it merely a result of the short back and the long hind legs as noted in the Manx standard.

The Manx is one of the most challenging cats to breed because of the Manx gene. Homozygous Manx kittens (kittens that inherit the Manx gene from both parents) die in vivo early in their development. Since homozygous kittens comprise roughly one quarter of kittens conceived from Manx to Manx matings, Manx litters are generally small, averaging two or three, sometimes four kittens.

Even the heterozygous kittens (kittens that inherit the Manx gene from one parent) have a higher than average mortality rate, because the Manx gene can cause deformities, such as spina bifida, fusions of the spine, and defects of the colon. Because of the possible physical problems, the Manx standard calls for disqualification of any cat with congenital deformities. Careful breeding helps minimize the defects.

Since all Manx cats can possess only one copy of the Manx gene, and since

GENERAL	The overall impression of the Manx cat is that of roundness; round head with firm, round muzzle and prominent cheeks; broad chest; substantial short front legs; short back which arches from shoulders to a round rump; great depth of flank and rounded, muscular thighs.
BODY	Solidly muscled, compact and well-balanced, medium in size with sturdy bone structure. The Manx is stout in appearance with broad chest and well-sprung ribs. The constant repetition of curves and circles give the Manx the appearance of great substance and durability, a cat that is powerful without the slightest hint of coarseness. Flank has greater depth than in other breeds, causing considerable depth to the body when viewed from the side. The short back forms a smooth, continuous arch from shoulders to rump, curving at the rump to form the desirable round look. Length of back is in proportion to the entire cat, height of hindquarters equal to length of body.
HEAD	Round head with prominent cheeks and a jowly appearance that enhances the round appearance of the breed. In profile, head is medium in length with a gentle dip from forehead to nose. Well-developed muzzle, very slightly longer than it is broad, with a strong chin. Definite whisker break with large, round whisker pads. Short, thick neck.
EARS	Wide at the base, tapering gradually to a rounded tip. Medium in size in proportion to the head, widely spaced and set slightly outward. When viewed from behind, the ear set resembles the rocker on a cradle. The furnishings of the ears are sparse.
EYES	Large, round and full. Set at a slight angle toward the nose; outer corners slightly higher than inner corners. Color is gold to copper, odd eyed, blue eyed, green, or hazel as appropriate to the coat color.
LEGS AND PAWS	Legs heavily boned, forelegs short and set well apart to emphasize the broad, deep chest. Hind legs much longer than forelegs, with heavy, muscular thighs and substantial lower legs. Longer hind legs cause the rump to be considerably higher than the shoulders. Hind legs are straight when viewed from behind. Paws are neat and round with five toes in front and four behind.
TAILLESSNESS	Appearing to be absolute in the perfect specimen. A rise of bone at the end of the spine is allowed and should not be penalized unless it is such that it stops the judge's hand, thereby spoiling the tailless appearance of the cat. The rump is extremely broad and round.
COAT	Double coat is short and dense with a well-padded quality due to the longer, open outer coat and the close cottony undercoat. Coat may be thinner during the summer months. Texture of outer guard hairs is somewhat hard, appearance is glossy. A softer coat may occur in whites and dilutes due to color/texture gene link.

COLOR	All colors and patterns with the exception of those showing evidence of hybridization resulting in the colors chocolate, lavender, the Himalayan pattern, or these combinations with white.
DISQUALIFY	Evidence of poor physical condition; incorrect number of toes; evidence of hybridization; evidence of weakness in the hindquarters; in profile, pronounced stop or nose break. Transfer to AOV: definite, visible tail joint.
ALLOWABLE OUTCROSSES	None.

heterozygous cats cannot breed true, Manx cats come in a wide variety of tail lengths. It's thought that modifying polygenes are responsible for the variety of tail types. The tail types are broken into four classifications: rumpy, rumpy-riser, stumpy, and longy.

Rumpies compete in the championship show ring and are highly prized by fanciers. They are completely tailless and often have a dimple at the base of the spine where the tail would be if it were present. Rumpy-risers have a short knob of tail that consists of one to three vertebrae connected to the last bone of the spine, and are allowable in the show ring as long as the vertical rise of the bones does not stop the judge's hand when stroked down the cat's rump (judges are allowed to examine a cat's tail with the palm of the hand only). Stumpies have a short tail stump that is often curved or kinked. In CFA, Manx cats with a definite, visible

tail joint are transferred to the non-champion Any Other Variety class.

Longies have tails that are almost as long as an average cat's. Many breeders dock the tails of these pet-quality kittens to make finding homes for them easier, although not all fanciers approve of this practice. Docked Manx have a short tail stub; they are not completely de-tailed as this might damage their spines. Docked Manx cannot be shown for championship competition, although they can be shown in the HHP category of most associations.

Since the Manx gene is dominant, all Manx cats that possess the Manx gene will have one of the four types of tail. With all these variables, show-quality Manx cats are hard to come by. Even a Manx with a perfect tail is not necessarily a show cat. It must also have the proper body and head type, legs, ear set, and coat quality to compete for those coveted titles.

NORWEGIAN FOREST CAT

HISTORY

The Norwegian Forest Cat, called the *skogkatt* (forest cat) in Norway, is a natural breed and despite its feral appearance is not a descendant or a hybrid of any wild cat species. Forest Cats probably arrived in Norway from Europe, descendants of domestic cats introduced to northern Europe by the Romans. It is supposed that the Norwegian Forest Cat has existed for a long time, since several mentions of large, longhaired cats exist in Norse mythology. Estimates of when these cat tales were written vary greatly. Most Norse myths were passed down by oral tradition and were finally recorded in what was called the Edda poems, written sometime between 800 C.E. and 1200 C.E. These myths suggest that domestic cats have been in Norway for hundreds, possibly thousands, of years. Whether the cats portrayed in the myths are Forest Cats is subject to debate.

When cats arrived in the northern countries, most likely with human settlers, traders, or crusaders, the breed's progenitors were probably shorthaired, since

Notice the long, dense mane on this impressive Norwegian Forest Cat.

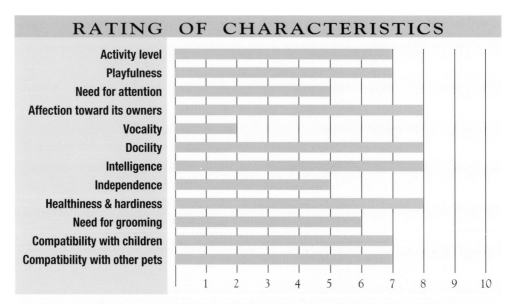

RATING OF CHARACTERISTICS

Characteristic	Rating
Activity level	7
Playfulness	7
Need for attention	5
Affection toward its owners	8
Vocality	2
Docility	8
Intelligence	8
Independence	5
Healthiness & hardiness	8
Need for grooming	6
Compatibility with children	7
Compatibility with other pets	7

1—breed exhibits the least amount of this characteristic, 10—breed exhibits the most of this characteristic

✳ **Championship status in all associations**

the cats transported by the Romans came from Egypt (generally) and were shorthaired varieties. The cats survived and in time adapted to the severe climate. Northern Norway, where the sun never sets from May 12 to August 1, and where the winter nights are correspondingly long and dark, proved a harsh test for these cats. Over the centuries of prowling the Norwegian forests, they developed long, dense, water-resistant coats, hardy constitutions, quick wits, and well-honed survival instincts.

The first efforts to have the Forest Cat recognized as a distinct breed began in the 1930s. The first Norwegian cat club was founded in 1934, and in 1938 the first Forest Cat was exhibited at a show in Oslo, Norway. World War II, however, put a damper on all cat breeding and showing, and after the war the breed came close to extinction. Interbreeding with Norway's shorthaired domestic cat (called the *hauskatt*) threatened the Forest Cat's existence as a pure breed. It wasn't until the 1970s that the cat fanciers of Norway started a serious breeding program to preserve the Norwegian Forest Cat.

Wegies (as Norwegian Forest Cats are affectionately known) arrived in the United States in 1980. The same year, the Norwegian Forest Cat Fanciers' Association (NFCFA) was founded in Wilmington, Delaware, by a group of breeders and fanciers dedicated to preserve and protect the Norwegian Forest Cat. This group began working to get

The Norwegian Forest Cat's coat length varies according to the season.

the Forest Cat recognized by North American cat registries. TICA, the first to recognize the breed, accepted the Norwegian Forest Cat for championship competition in 1984. The breed

GENERAL	The Norwegian Forest Cat is a sturdy cat with a distinguishing double coat and easily recognizable body shape. It is a slow maturing breed, attaining full growth at approximately five years of age.
BODY	Solidly muscled and well-balanced, moderate in length, substantial bone structure, with powerful appearance showing a broad chest and considerable girth without being fat. Flank has great depth. Males should be large and imposing; females may be more refined and may be smaller.
HEAD	Equilateral triangle, where all sides are of equal length as measured from the outside of the base of the ear to the point of the chin. The neck is short and heavily muscled. Nose is straight from the brow ridge to the tip of the nose without a break in the line. The flat forehead continues into a gentle curved skull and neck. Chin is firm and should be in line with the front of the nose. It is gently rounded in profile. Muzzle is part of the straight line extending toward the base of ear without pronounced whisker pads and without pinch.
EARS	Medium to large, rounded at the tip, broad at base, set as much on the side of the head as on top of the head, alert, with the cup of the ear pointing a bit sideways. The outsides of the ears follow the lines from the side of the head down to the chin. The ears are heavily furnished. Lynx tips are desirable but not required.
EYES	Large, almond shaped, well-opened, and expressive, set at a slight angle with the outer corner higher than the inner corner. Eye color should be shades of green, gold, green-gold, or copper. White cats and cats with white may have blue or odd eyes.
LEGS AND PAWS	Medium, with hind legs longer than front legs, making the rump higher than the shoulders. Thighs are heavily muscled; lower legs are substantial. When viewed from the rear, back legs are straight. When viewed from the front the paws appear to be "toe out." Large round, firm paws with heavy tufting between toes.
TAIL	Long and bushy. Broader at the base. Desirable length is equal to the body from the base of tail to the base of neck. Guard hairs desirable.
COAT	Distinguishing double coat, consisting of a dense undercoat, covered by long, glossy, and smooth water-resistant guard hairs hanging down the sides. The bib consists of three separate sections: short collar at neck, side mutton chops, and frontal ruff. Britches are full on the hind legs. The coat may be fuller in the winter than the summer because the dense undercoat has its full development in the winter. Softer coats are permitted in shaded, solid, and bicolor cats. Type and quality of coat is of primary importance; color and pattern are secondary.

COLOR	Every color and pattern is allowable with the exception of those showing hybridization resulting in the colors chocolate, sable, lavender, lilac, cinnamon, fawn, point-restricted (Himalayan type markings), or these colors with white. Color and pattern should be clear and distinct. In the case of the classic, mackerel, and spotted tabbies the pattern should be well-marked and even.
DISQUALIFY	Severe break in nose, square muzzle, whisker pinch, long rectangular body, cobby body, incorrect number of toes, crossed eyes, kinked or abnormal tail, delicate bone structure, malocclusion resulting in either undershot or overshot chin, cats showing evidence of hybridization.
ALLOWABLE OUTCROSSES	None.

attained CFA championship status in 1993.

PERSONALITY

Natural athletes, Norwegian Forest Cats love to investigate counters, bookcases, and the loftiest peaks of their cat trees. Wegies are active and playful and retain their fun-loving spirit well into adulthood, but don't be fooled by the breed's impressive muscles and all-weather exterior. They are sweet, friendly, and family-oriented, and they love their human companions. Despite the wild years in the forests of Norway—or perhaps because of it—they would much rather cuddle than prowl.

Perhaps, because of years spent in Norway's harsh climate, nothing fazes them much, either. They take new people and new situations in stride; as cats go, Forest Cats are the strong, silent types. They are conversely great purrers, particularly when perched beside their favorite humans. Outgoing and gregarious, they tend not to bond with one person, but rather love everyone unconditionally and enthusiastically.

CONFORMATION

The Norwegian Forest Cat's distinguishing double coat varies in length according to the time of year. The cat goes through a spring molting, when the winter coat is shed, and a fall shedding, when the summer coat departs. At these times of year, thorough daily combing is necessary unless you want seasonal layers of cat hair on everything. The rest of the year the Forest Cat requires only weekly grooming since it tends to hang onto its coat, perhaps remembering those harsh winters.

HISTORY

The first Ocicat was created in 1964 when breeder Virginia Daly of the Dalai Cattery in Berkley, Michigan, interested in new and unusual varieties of cats, tried to create a Siamese with Abyssinian-colored points. Daly developed a breeding plan that called for a mating between ruddy Abyssinian male Dalai Deta Tim of Selene (son of the famous Champion Raby Chuffa of Selene, the longhair-carrying Aby that fathered many Somalis), and a large seal point Siamese female, Dalai Tomboy Patter. Since the Abyssinian pattern and coloration is dominant over the Siamese pattern, the kittens looked like Abyssinians, but all of them carried the recessive gene for the Siamese pointed pattern. Daly then bred one of the female Aby/Siamese hybrid kittens, Dalai She, to a chocolate point Siamese male, Champion Whitehead Elegante Sun. This litter produced Daly's objective—an Aby-pointed Siamese that Daly named Dalai Driftwood. The same litter produced a happy surprise—an ivory male kitten with golden

Spots run along the spine from shoulder blades to tail, ending in a dark tip.

RATING OF CHARACTERISTICS

Characteristic	Rating
Activity level	9
Playfulness	9
Need for attention	7
Affection toward its owners	7
Vocality	7
Docility	7
Intelligence	7
Independence	4
Healthiness & hardiness	5
Need for grooming	2
Compatibility with children	7
Compatibility with other pets	8

1—breed exhibits the least amount of this characteristic, 10—breed exhibits the most of this characteristic

* **Championship status in all associations**

spots and copper eyes. Daly named the unusual kitten Tonga.

Tonga was adorable and unique, but Daly's goal was to create Aby-pointed Siamese, so she sold Tonga as a pet. However, Daly mentioned Tonga to geneticist Clyde Keeler of Georgia University, who was elated about her accidental find because he'd long wanted to recreate the extinct Egyptian spotted fishing cat, and Tonga sounded spot-on. Keeler sent Daly a detailed breeding plan, featuring Tonga as the sire of the new breed. Keeler was distressed to discover Tonga had already been sold. However, Tonga's parents produced another spotted male, Dalai Dotson, and the breeding plan was officially launched, with Dalai Dotson as the sire of the new breed. Additional matings between Tonga's parents, She and Sunny (Elegante Sun), produced more Tonga look-alikes, and the breed was officially launched. Daly's daughter suggested the name Ocicat because they reminded her of the spotted wild cat called the ocelot.

In 1965, the first Ocicat was exhibited at a CFA show, to considerable interest and acclaim. In 1966, CFA accepted the Ocicat for registration status, and Daly registered Dalai Dotson with CFA. Being accepted for registration doesn't guarantee a breed will go on to become an accepted new breed, but Daly was hopeful since the Ocicat was striking and unique. Other breeders, charmed by the active, personable spotted cats, signed on to become Ocicat breeders and began their own breeding programs.

In the minutes of the CFA annual meeting recognizing the Ocicat for registration, the breed was mistakenly described as a cross between the Abyssinian and the American Shorthair. When the error was brought to their attention, Siamese was added to the wording, without removing American Shorthair from the list. This error turned out to be a happy accident for the Ocicat; breeders added American Shorthairs into their Ocicat lines, and the handsome silver coloration of the American Shorthair was added to the Ocicat gene pool. The American Shorthair influence also added size and musculature to a breed that originally resembled the lithe Abyssinian and the svelte Siamese.

Even with the early enthusiastic reception in CFA, the Ocicat didn't achieve championship status until 1987. A combination of factors was responsible, the main reason being that Daly took an 11-year break from breeding and promoting Ocicats to care for an ailing family member. Since Daly was the impetus behind the breed, the Ocicat developed slowly for the next decade.

In the early 1980s, however, Daly returned to breeding Ocicats, and her efforts and those of other Ocicat breeders and enthusiasts brought the breed back in the spotlight. The word got around about the beauty and personality of the breed, and some other breeders joined the Ocicat fan club, either purchasing breeding stock from Daly or other breeders, or trying to duplicate Daly's results. This helped widen the gene pool and also brought the breed the numbers it needed for recognition. In May of 1986, the Ocicat attained CFA provisional status, and only one year later was granted championship status. TICA granted championship in 1987 as well. Today, all North American cat associations recognize the Ocicat for championship. The breed has gained in popularity and has a strong following.

PERSONALITY

Ocicats have the untamed look of a spotted wildcat but possess the temperament of the housecat, and without a drop of wildcat blood and therefore none of the problems of a wildcat/domestic cat cross. Ocicats may look like they walk on the wild side, but they are affectionate, adaptable, curious, and playful, and possess strong devotion to their human companions. Highly intelligent, active, and social, Ocicats quickly learn to respond to their names and can be taught a variety of tricks, including coming on command. Begging for food is another trick that Ocicats master with very little prompting.

The Ocicat personality is active, affectionate, and very social and adaptable. Ocicats tend to bond with only one person and prefer that person's company to all others, although they are friendly and affectionate to others in the household. They get along well with other animals and people, and appreciate an animal companion to keep them company if left alone for any length of time.

Like their Abyssinian ancestors, Ocicats love to perform daring tap dances on top of your bookcases for your amusement. They are an active breed and require a good deal of space and plenty of toys and diversions to keep them occupied. Like their Siamese ancestors, Ocicats are vocal, but not annoyingly so. They want to tell you about their day when you come home at night, but they won't bore you with every detail. In addition, their voices lack the Siamese rasp that some people find annoying. However, because they are a vocal breed, they are highly tuned to tone of voice, and harsh verbal reprimands can hurt their sensitive feelings, or even damage the trust they've placed in their favored humans.

CONFORMATION

The Ocicat is ordinarily a very robust, healthy breed; Ocis live fifteen to eighteen years if kept inside. The close-lying, short coat is lustrous, smooth, satiny, and long enough to carry several bands of ticking. The Ocicat is an agouti breed, like the Abyssinian; if you look closely at the spots, you'll see each hair has bands of alternating color. Ideally, rows of spots run along the spine from the shoulder blades to the tail. Spots are also scattered across the shoulders and hindquarters and extend down the legs. Large thumbprint-shaped spots on the sides of the torso give the subtle suggestion of the classic tabby bull's eye pattern. All hairs are ticked except the tip of the tail.

The Ocicat was created by crossing three pedigreed breeds, all of which have had some inheritable health problems that the Oci could have inherited. Most Ocicat breeders, however, have been careful to choose outcrosses for their health as well as their conformation, and when possible to screen them for hereditary diseases to keep their bloodlines free of genetic disorders. Nevertheless, since Abyssinians are still used as outcrosses in CFA, and both Abys and Siamese are allowable outcrosses in TICA, it's possible that some Ocicat lines have inherited hereditary diseases such PK deficiency, which typically causes anemia, and has been found in Aby lines.

Progressive retinal atrophy (PRA), an inherited late-onset blindness characterized by progressive degeneration of rods and cones in the retina, has been found in Abyssinian, Somali, and some Ocicat lines. More seriously, the inherited heart disease feline hypertrophic cardiomyopathy (HCM) has been found in some Siamese lines. The most common feline heart disease, HCM's first symptom is often sudden death at a relatively early age. In addition, both Siamese and Abyssinians are prone to plaque, tartar, and gingivitis, which can lead to the dental disease periodontitis and cause tissue, tooth, and bone loss.

Fortunately, DNA tests are available by mail for PK deficiency and PRA from the Veterinary Genetics Laboratory at the UC Davis (www.vgl.ucdavis.edu/services/index.php). Breeders can use these tests to eliminate affected and carrier cats from their breeding programs. Talk to your breeder about these and any other health concerns you have, and buy from a breeder who tests their breeding stock and offers a written health guarantee.

Ocicats are active, affectionate, social, and adaptable. They tend to bond with only one special person.

GENERAL	The Ocicat is a medium to large, well-spotted agouti cat of moderate type. It displays the look of an athletic animal: well-muscled and solid, graceful and lithe, yet with a fullness of body and chest. This powerful, athletic, yet graceful spotted cat is particularly noted for its "wild" appearance.
BODY	Solid, hard, rather long-bodied with depth and fullness but never coarse. The Ocicat is a medium to large cat with substantial bone and muscle development, yet with an athletic appearance, and should have surprising weight for its size. There should be some depth of chest with ribs slightly sprung, the back is level to slightly higher in the rear, and the flank reasonably level. Preference is given to the athletic, powerful, and lithe, and objection taken to the bulky or coarse. It should be noted that females are generally smaller than males. The overall structure and quality of this cat should be of greater consideration than mere size alone.
HEAD	The skull is a modified wedge showing a slight curve from muzzle to cheek, with a visible, but gentle, rise from the bridge of the nose to the brow. The muzzle is broad and well defined with a suggestion of squareness and in profile shows good length. The chin is strong, and the jaw is firm with a proper bite. The moderate whisker pinch is not too severe. The head is carried gracefully on an arching neck. An allowance is made for jowls on mature males.
EARS	Alert, moderately large, and set so as to corner the upper, outside dimensions of the head. If an imaginary horizontal line is drawn across the brow, the ears should be set at a 45 degree angle, i.e., neither too high nor too low. When they occur, ear tufts extending vertically from the tips of the ears are a bonus.
EYES	Large, almond shaped, and angling slightly upwards toward the ears with more than the length of an eye between the eyes. All eye colors except blue are allowed. There is no correspondence between eye color and coat color. Depth of color is preferred.
LEGS AND PAWS	Legs should be of good substance and well-muscled, medium-long, powerful, and in good proportion to the body. Feet should be oval and compact with five toes in front and four in back, with size in proportion to legs.
TAIL	Fairly long, medium slim with only a slight taper and with a dark tip.
COAT	Texture short, smooth, and satiny with a lustrous sheen. Tight, close lying, and sleek, yet long enough to accommodate the necessary bands of color. No suggestion of woolliness. All hairs except the tip of the tail are banded. Within the markings, hairs are tipped with a darker color, while hairs in the ground color are tipped with a lighter color.

| **COLOR** | Tawny spotted, cinnamon spotted, chocolate spotted, blue spotted, fawn spotted, lavender spotted, ebony silver spotted, cinnamon silver spotted, chocolate silver spotted, blue silver spotted, fawn silver spotted, lavender silver spotted. All colors should be clear and pleasing. The lightest color is usually found on the face around the eyes, and on the chin and lower jaw. The darkest color is found on the tip of the tail. distinctive markings should be clearly seen from any orientation. Those on the face, legs, and tail may be darker than those on the torso. Ground color may be darker on the saddle and lighter on the underside, chin, and lower jaw. The determining factor in answering any and all questions as to the correct color of an Ocicat will be the color of the tail tip. |

| **DISQUALIFY** | White locket or spotting, or white anywhere other than around eyes, nostrils, chin, and upper throat (except white agouti ground in silvered colors). Kinked or otherwise deformed tail. Blue eyes. Incorrect number of toes. Long hair. Due to the spotted patched tabby (torbie) cats resulting from the sex-linked O gene, no reds, creams, or torbies are allowed. Very rufous cinnamons and fawns may resemble red or cream, but never produce female torbies. |

| **ALLOWABLE OUTCROSSES** | Abyssinian for litters born before 1/1/2015. |

HISTORY

In the past, so the story goes, blue-eyed, pointed pattern cats were owned by royalty and were kept in the Royal Palace of Siam. The Siamese breed, however, is only one of several varieties native to the area. *The Cat-Book Poems*, a manuscript of verses and paintings written in the city of Ayutthaya, Siam, some time between 1350 C.E. when the kingdom was founded and 1767 C.E. when the city was destroyed by invaders, describes and shows a variety of cats native to the area. These include solid black cats, black-and-white bicolor,

Orientals are natural entertainers.

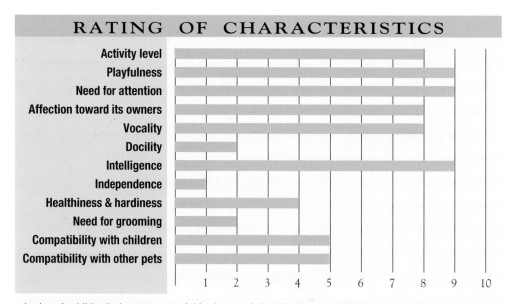

RATING OF CHARACTERISTICS

Characteristic	Rating (1–10)
Activity level	8
Playfulness	8
Need for attention	9
Affection toward its owners	8
Vocality	5
Docility	2
Intelligence	9
Independence	1
Healthiness & hardiness	4
Need for grooming	1
Compatibility with children	5
Compatibility with other pets	5

1—breed exhibits the least amount of this characteristic, 10—breed exhibits the most of this characteristic

✳ **Championship status in all associations in both long and short hair lengths**

solid brown, and solid blue, as well as cats bearing the point-restricted color pattern. The point-restricted cats portrayed in the book had slim bodies and legs, large ears, and tapered muzzles, similar to today's Siamese and its related breeds.

The first cats imported to England from Thailand were often solid brown or solid blue, or black-and-white bicolor, as well as colorpointed. These blue, brown, and bicolor cats were shown in Europe in the 1890s, and were becoming very popular with the developing cat fancy. However, in the 1920s, Britain's Siamese Cat Club dealt them a deathblow by issuing the following statement, "The club much regrets it is unable to encourage the breeding of any but blue-eyed Siamese." Without the club's support and funds, interest in the other varieties dwindled. The blue-eyed pointed pattern cat became the Siamese norm in Britain. World War II interrupted the breeding programs of even the most popular cat breeds, so it wasn't until after the war that people had time to think about the colors and patterns of their cats.

The Oriental seen in the show halls today is not a direct import from Thailand, but rather a Siamese hybrid developed in the 1950s and 1960s. The breed's creation was deliberate—breeders with a flair for

exterior decorating set out to create a cat breed that looked and acted like the Siamese but were lavishly adorned in a wide range of colors and patterns. In the 1950s, British breeders crossed Siamese cats with domestic shorthairs and Russian Blues. In the late 1960s American breeders, fascinated by the British Orientals, took up the torch and crossed Siamese, domestic shorthairs, and Abyssinians to create a new look. Body style was not sacrificed for color and pattern, and backcrosses to the Siamese preserved type and personality traits.

The Oriental breeders met with initial hissing and spitting from Siamese breeders who were resistant at best to the idea of another Siamese-type hybrid, but, since the way had already

The personality of this breed is as distinctive as its multicolored exterior.

Ebony Oriental Shorthair.

been paved by breeders of the Color-point Shorthair, which gained CFA acceptance in 1964, the opposition didn't stop Orientals from gaining ground. Fanciers took to the Orientals very quickly, and demand rose.

At first, breeders worked only with shorthairs; the idea to add a longer coat to the mix came later. In 1972, CFA accepted the Oriental Shorthair for registration, and granted full championship status in 1977. Since then, the Oriental Shorthair rapidly increased in popularity; it speedily became one of CFA's most popular shorthaired breeds.

The Oriental Longhair was developed from Oriental Shorthairs; the fanciers involved wanted a breed that

had the same wide range of colors and patterns as the Shorthair but with a semi-long coat like the Balinese. Since the Siamese and the Colorpoint had the longhaired Balinese, it seemed only fair that the Oriental Shorthair should have its own longhaired variant—a breed with a long, lean, classy chassis, silky fur, and a full palette of colors and patterns from which to choose. The Oriental Longhair was developed in the late 1970s by breeders who crossed the Oriental Shorthair with the Balinese. The breed achieved official recognition in 1985 when TICA accepted them for championship status, and they were accepted for registration by the CFA in February 1988. The breed grew in popularity, appealing to cat lovers who want the elegant body type and personality of the Siamese, the wash-and-wear hairdo of the Balinese, and the myriad colors and patterns of the Oriental Shorthair.

In 1995, two major changes occurred in CFA that impacted the Oriental Shorthair. First, the Oriental Shorthair and the Oriental Longhair became a single breed called the Oriental. Before that time, the Oriental Longhair was a separate breed and therefore if two Oriental Shorthairs produced long-haired kittens (possible if both parents possessed the recessive longhair gene), those kittens could not be shown as either Oriental Longhairs or Oriental Shorthairs. Now offspring from Long-hair and Shorthair matings could be registered as Orientals and shown in whatever division their hair length dictated for them.

Secondly in 1995, CFA accepted a new color class for the Oriental— bicolor. Bicolors were previously relegated to the nonchampion Any Other Variety (AOV) class. Now cats of this color and pattern class could be shown for CFA championship. This decision doubled the number of accepted colors and patterns to over 300.

PERSONALITY

The personality of the Oriental is as distinctive as the multicolored exterior. They are natural entertainers, full of enthusiasm, energy, and the belief that the world should revolve around them. Haughty and royal one minute, they are animated and inquisitive the next. They are highly curi-

ous, and will go to great lengths to be involved in your activities. This is not the breed for you if you work all day and have an active night life. The Oriental shouldn't be left alone for long periods and need other cats as playmates and company for those times you can't be with them. The Oriental craves attention; this breed needs quality time with their preferred persons. They have a real need for play, and retain that need well into adulthood. It's wise to have lots of toys for your Oriental, or they will create their own, sometimes out of household items you'd rather they didn't.

Orientals are extremely social, loving, and loyal, and their feelings are easily hurt if you ignore or scold them. Orientals don't just want attention— they need it desperately if they are to live happy, healthy lives. If you provide the tender loving care they need, they'll do just about anything to please you. Ignore them, and they become unhappy and depressed. However, when given their full share of affection, Orientals will repay you with a lifetime of love, affection, and intelligent conversation. They usually bond with one person and become extremely devoted to and dependent upon their chosen human. Expect them to be at your side, on your shoulder, and at the door to interrogate you about where you've been, why you went there, and what you brought back for "me-orrr."

The breed is just as vocal as the Siamese, but range, frequency, and inflection can vary from cat to cat, and bloodline to bloodline. However, like their Siamese relatives, they are never at a loss for words on any subject.

GENERAL	The ideal Oriental is a svelte cat with long, tapering lines, very lithe but muscular. Excellent physical condition. Eyes clear. Strong and lithe, neither bony nor flabby. Not fat. Because of the longer coat the Longhair Division appears to have softer lines and less extreme type than the Shorthair Division.
BODY	Long and svelte. A distinctive combination of fine bones and firm muscles. Shoulders and hips continue the same sleek lines of tubular body. Hips never wider than shoulders. Abdomen tight. Neck long and slender.
HEAD	Long tapering wedge, in good proportion to body. The total wedge starts at the nose and flares out in straight lines to the tips of the ears forming a triangle, with no break at the whiskers. No less than the width of an eye between the eyes. When the whiskers (and face hair for the Longhair Division) are smoothed back, the underlying bone structure is apparent. Allowance must be made for jowls in the stud cat. Skull flat. Nose long and straight. A continuation of the forehead with no break. Muzzle fine, wedge-shaped. Chin medium size. Tip of chin lines up with tip of nose in the same vertical plane.
EARS	Strikingly large, pointed, wide at the base, continuing the lines of the wedge.
EYES	Almond shaped, medium size. Neither protruding nor recessed. Slanted towards the nose in harmony with lines of wedge and ears. Uncrossed. Eye color green; pointed and white blue; white and bi-color blue, green or odd eyed.
LEGS AND PAWS	Legs and slim. Hind legs higher than front. In good proportion to body. Paws dainty, small, and oval. Toes five in front and four behind.
TAIL	Long thin at the base, and tapered to a fine point. Longhair Division: tail hair spreads out like a plume.
COAT— SHORTHAIR	Short, fine textured, glossy, or satinlike, lying close to body.
COAT— LONGHAIR	Medium length, fine, silky, without downy undercoat, lying close to the body, the coat may appear shorter than it is. Hair is longest on the tail.
COLOR	Orientals come in solid, smoke, shaded, bicolor, particolor, tabby color classes, and pointed with white, making over 300 color and pattern combinations. The Oriental's reason for being is the coat color.
DISQUALIFY	Any evidence of illness or poor health. Weak hind legs. Mouth breathing due to nasal obstruction or poor occlusion. Emaciation. Visible kink in tail. Miniaturization. Lockets and buttons. Incorrect number of toes. Longhair Division: definite double coat (i.e., downy undercoat).

ALLOWABLE OUTCROSSES	Shorthair Division: Siamese or Colorpoint. Effective with Oriental litters born after June 15, 2010, no Oriental litters that result from a pointed to pointed breeding (i.e., any cross between a pointed Oriental (shorthair division) and Siamese or a Colorpoint Shorthair or a pointed Oriental), will be permitted. Such matings will not be registrable for litters born after June 15, 2010.
	Longhair Division: Siamese, Colorpoint, Balinese. The above restrictions will not be placed on individual cats imported from other associations or registries. Such cats may be registered in CFA as Oriental AOVs.

CONFORMATION

The Oriental comes in every color you can imagine, and likely some you can't. Sometimes playfully called "Ornamentals" because of the color and pattern combinations, this breed is essentially a Siamese not confined to the colorpoint pattern. Orientals are likely the most colorfully decorated cat breed on the planet. The Oriental is available in over 300 color and pattern combinations, and two hair lengths. Shorthairs have coats that look almost painted on; longhairs have single-coated, semi-long fur. Some colors and patterns are more common than others; solid ebony and solid white are two common favorites. Chestnut, blue, and ebony tabby are also popular. So many combinations are possible that all breeders specialize in a chosen few; no one breeder can produce all varieties, so if you have your heart set on a particular color or pattern, you may need to do some asking around to find the right breeder. In CFA, pointed Oriental Shorthairs that meet Colorpoint Shorthair color descriptions can compete in Colorpoint Shorthair color classes.

The Oriental is in general a healthy breed but can suffer from the same defects as the Siamese, since they are closely related. The inherited heart disease feline hypertrophic cardiomyopathy (HCM) has been found in some Siamese lines. The most common feline heart disease, HCM's first symptom is often sudden death at a relatively early age. In addition, both Siamese and Orientals are prone to plaque, tartar, and gingivitis, which can lead to the dental disease periodontitis and cause tissue, tooth, and bone loss. If not treated, periodontitis can undermine the cat's overall health.

HISTORY

Persians have enjoyed a long reign in the cat fancy and have featured prominently in shows since 1871, the year of the first modern cat show held at London's Crystal Palace. At this famous affair, organized by Harrison Weir, commonly known as the "father of the cat fancy," many representatives of the breed were present, starting a supremacy that continues today.

Persians have been around for much longer than 125 years. Long-haired cats, including the ancestors of the modern Persian and Angora breeds, were first seen in Europe in the mid-to-late 1500s, introduced by Roman and Phoenician caravans from Persia (now Iran) and Turkey, according to documents of the era. Researchers believe the recessive gene for long hair appeared spontaneously via mutation in the cat population in the cold mountainous areas of Persia. An Italian traveler by the name of Pietro della Valle (1586–1652) is credited with bringing Persian cats to the European world in the 1600s. Both Angora and Persian cats are mentioned in the manuscript Voyages de Pietro della Valle. He

Persians love to play between periods of regal lounging.

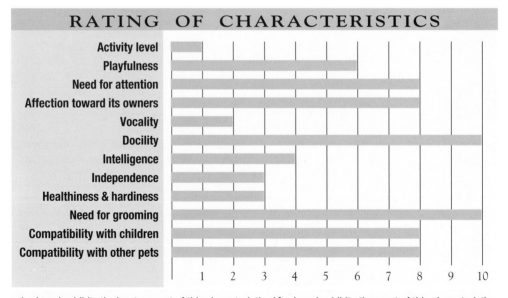

RATING OF CHARACTERISTICS

Characteristic	Rating (1–10)
Activity level	1
Playfulness	6
Need for attention	8
Affection toward its owners	8
Vocality	2
Docility	10
Intelligence	4
Independence	3
Healthiness & hardiness	3
Need for grooming	10
Compatibility with children	8
Compatibility with other pets	8

1—breed exhibits the least amount of this characteristic, 10—breed exhibits the most of this characteristic

✳ Championship status in all associations

described the Persians as gray with very long, silky, glossy fur. He noted that the cats resided in the province of Khorazan in Persia, and that they came from India with the Portuguese.

Other travelers brought Persian and Angora cats into France and then into England, causing them to be called "French cats" for a number of years. These cats quickly became popular in Britain. During this time and for centuries after, the Turkish Angora and Persian varieties (among others) were commonly crossed.

At first, Angoras were preferred for their silky white coats. Eventually, however, the British fanciers came to favor the stockier Persian conformation. By the time of Harrison Weir's cat show in 1871, distinct differences between the Persian and the Angora could be seen, the former being stockier with small, rounded ears, and the latter being slender and tall eared. By the early 1900s, the Persian had become overwhelmingly popular. Blue Persians were particularly prized, probably because Queen Victoria owned two.

In the early 1900s, the Governing Council of the Cat Fancy decided that the Persian, as well as the Angora and Russian Longhairs, would be known simply as Longhairs, a policy that continues today. Each color is considered a separate breed in the British cat fancy.

Persians were imported to America in the late 1800s, where they were enthusiastically received. The Persian quickly shoved aside the competition and quickly took its place as the top

cat. Using British standards as a starting point, American breeders began their own breeding programs to refine the coat, color, and conformation. Soon the American Persian developed a style of its own and evolved into the type we see today. They are by far the most popular pedigreed breed in the North American cat fancy. In North America, the Persian is considered one breed, regardless of color. Colors and patterns are divisions within the breed.

PERSONALITY

If you want your cats bouncing around like hyperactive popcorn, don't buy a Persian. Persians are perfect companions, if you like placid, sweet-tempered cats. Don't count on using your Persian pal as a furry doorstop, however. They love to play between periods of regal lounging on your favorite davenport. Proponents say that Persians do not deserve their furniture-with-fur reputation; they are intelligent, just not as inquisitive as some breeds, and not as active.

Persians are devoted to their humans, but can be selective in conferring that honor. You must earn their trust and love. They crave affection and love to be petted and fussed over, but won't harass you for attention the way some breeds will. They will, however, let their feelings be known if they are not getting the requisite amount of attention.

Owning a Persian requires a significant time commitment. That beautiful coat requires daily grooming to keep

That beautiful coat requires daily grooming.

it in good condition and free of mats. Because of the long coat and docile temperament, Persians should be considered indoor-only pets. Many Persian fanciers keep at least part of the coat clipped, particularly the hindquarters and around the anus to avoid the accumulation of feces. However, this should be done only if the cat will not be shown.

CONFORMATION

Over the years, the show trend has been toward a flatter, more extreme facial type in the Persian and its related breeds the Exotic Shorthair and Himalayan (see pages 152 and 162). Sometimes called the Peke-face after the Pekingese dog, the extreme facial type with a nose placed high between the eyes is the one you'll generally see in the show halls. This trend troubles some fanciers, who feel the extreme type can be harmful to the breed. Reported problems include upper respiratory problems, wheezing, constantly runny eyes, malocclusions, and birthing difficulties. For those who like a less extreme facial arrangement, the Doll Face Persian is bred and promoted by some breeders. This type possesses a less extreme look and emphasizes the sweet expression.

Persians come in many colors and patterns. The various colors, along with the breed itself, have a long history of selective breeding. Breeders have worked hard to perfect each, and breeders usually specialize in a few choice favorites. Within the divisions are a multitude of colors and pattern varieties. The body and face type does differ slightly from one color to the next, and therefore judges have some leeway in judging.

GENERAL	Should present an impression of a heavily boned, well-balanced cat with a sweet expression and soft, round lines. Large round eyes set wide apart in a large round head. The long thick coat softens the lines of the cat and accentuates the roundness in appearance.
BODY	Cobby type, low on the legs, broad and deep through the chest, equally massive across the shoulders and rump, with a well-rounded mid-section and level back. Good muscle tone. Large or medium in size. Quality the determining consideration rather than size.
HEAD	Round and massive, with great breadth of skull. Well set on a short, thick neck. Skull structure to be smooth and round to the touch and not unduly exaggerated from where the forehead begins at the top of the break to the back of the head, as well as across the breadth between the ears. When viewed in profile, the prominence of the eyes is apparent and the forehead, nose, and chin appear to be in vertical alignment. Nose short, snub, and broad, with "break" centered between the eyes. Cheeks full. Muzzle not overly pronounced, smoothing nicely into the cheeks. Jaws broad and powerful. Chin full, well-developed, and firmly rounded, reflecting a proper bite.
EARS	Small, round tipped, tilted forward, and not unduly open at the base. Set far apart, and low on the head, fitting into (without distorting) the rounded contour of the head.
EYES	Brilliant in color, large, round, and full. Set level and far apart, giving a sweet expression to the face. Eye color depends upon coat color.
LEGS AND PAWS	Legs short, thick, and strong. Forelegs straight. Hind legs are straight when viewed from behind. Paws large, round, and firm. Toes carried close, five in front and four behind.
TAIL	Short, but in proportion to body length. Carried without a curve and at an angle lower than the back.
COAT	Long and thick, standing off from the body. Of fine texture, glossy and full of life. The ruff immense and continuing in a deep frill between the front legs. Ear and toe tufts long. Brush very full.
COLOR	Solid, silver and golden, smoke and shaded, tabby, parti-color, calico and bicolor, and Himalayan divisions.
DISQUALIFY	Locket or button. Kinked or abnormal tail. Incorrect number of toes. Any apparent weakness in the hind quarters. Any apparent deformity of the spine. Deformity of the skull resulting in an asymmetrical face and/or head. Crossed eyes. Incorrect eye color.
ALLOWABLE OUTCROSSES	None.

The Pixiebob is intelligent and is playful without being destructive.

HISTORY

Conflicting stories exist about the origin of this breed. The most commonly told tale is that the Pixiebob traces its roots to trysts between American bobcats and random-bred domestic barn cats; these cats are frequently called "Legend Cats" because the bobcat-domestic cat matings are neither documented nor proven. While domestic cats have been known to mate with small, closely related felids, such hybrids are known for producing sterile males for at least the first several generations.

Carol Ann Brewer of Stoneisland Cattery in Washington State is credited with the creation of the Pixiebob breed. In spring of 1985, Carol Ann Brewer purchased a spotted polydactyl male kitten with a short tail from a couple who lived near Puget Sound in the foothills of the Cascade Range in Washington State. In January 1986, she rescued a bobbed tail classic tabby male that reportedly stood as tall as her knees. She named this cat Keba. He mated with a neighbor's domestic female cat named Maggie, and a litter was produced in April 1986. Brewer took one of the female kit-

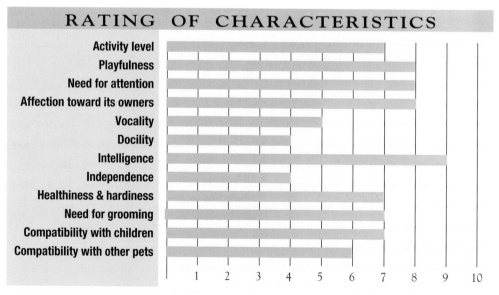

RATING OF CHARACTERISTICS

Characteristic	Rating
Activity level	7
Playfulness	8
Need for attention	8
Affection toward its owners	8
Vocality	5
Docility	4
Intelligence	9
Independence	4
Healthiness & hardiness	7
Need for grooming	4
Compatibility with children	6
Compatibility with other pets	6

1—breed exhibits the least amount of this characteristic, 10—breed exhibits the most of this characteristic

❋ **Championship status in ACFA, CCA, TICA, and UFO in both long and short hair lengths**

tens from that litter; the kitten had a reddish-fawn coat with subdued spotting and a face with a wild appearance, although the cat was domestic in temperament. Brewer named her Pixie. Pixie became the foundation female of the breed.

In 1987, Brewer began looking for more bobtailed cats with the distinctive wild appearance. She wanted to create more cats like Pixie. In 1989 she wrote the first breed standard, which included the consistently reproduced traits of these bobtailed cats, and named the breed the Pixiebob, in honor of Pixie and because of the defining trait of the breed—its bobbed tail.

When Brewer began seeking association acceptance for the breed, she discovered how difficult it would be to register a wildcat hybrid, even a merely suspected one; CFA doesn't accept any breeds with wildcat blood, not even the popular Bengal. In 1993, Brewer approached TICA and submitted the first standard in preparation to begin the process of recognition for the breed. The breed was presented to TICA as a purely domestic breed and DNA testing for wildcat markers revealed that the cats tested possessed none. No proof existed that the Pixiebob was anything but a short-tailed domestic cat. The stated goal of the Pixiebob breeding program, according to the TICA breed standard, is to create a domestic cat with a visual similarity to the North American Bobcat. In 1994, TICA accepted the Pixiebob for exhibition. Brewer began

the necessary steps to gain recognition, which included recruiting new breeders. Effective May 1, 1996, TICA advanced the breed to New Breed or Color (NBC) status. In 1998, the Pixiebob achieved TICA championship status.

While some Pixiebob fanciers still firmly believe the breed has bobcat ancestors, others think it's more likely the breed is simply a domestic cat with a tail mutation. Pixiebobs can have tails of varying lengths, and some have ordinary long tails. Breeders say the tail is unlike the Manx tail types; Pixiebobs are not born completely tailless like the Manx, although rarely a tail will be so short that the cat appears tailless. Some breeders dock Pixiebobs with long tails to make the cats easier to sell, since few prospective owners want ordinary tails on a breed characterized by its bobbed tail.

PERSONALITY

The Pixiebob's wild look does not reflect the breed's personality, which is loving, trustworthy, and tractable. While Pixiebobs vary in temperament depending upon their bloodlines and outcrosses, most are intelligent, social, people-oriented, and curious and playful. Some tend to be more laidback with sweet and devoted personalities.

The Pixiebob is intelligent, bonds well with its adoptive family, and is playful without being destructive. Pixiebobs tend to get along well with both children and other pets. They can be

The Pixiebob is the cat fancy's only polydactyl breed.

leash trained easily, and love to take walks with their humans.

In general, fanciers say Pixiebobs become attached to the entire family and get along well with everyone. They usually don't bond with one special person. Some Pixiebobs are sociable with people outside the family as well, while others love their families but hide under the bed when strangers come to call. Most Pixiebobs like to be close to their human families, and follow their owners around the house. They also enjoy children who play nicely, and usually get along well and enjoy playing with other cat-friendly companion animals, as long as the proper introductions are made.

Most are quiet; their vocalization is usually limited to chirps and twitters, although they will meow occasionally when they have something essential to say to their favorite humans. Some will have conversations with their people in quiet meows. Fanciers say Pixiebobs are highly intelligent and quickly learn the meaning of useful words and phrases. Now that the breed is closed to random-bred domestic outcrosses, the personality and temperament will likely settle down to a consistent type.

CONFORMATION

The Pixiebob is the only pedigreed breed that allows polydactyly—cats with more than the usual five toes on the front paws and four on the back. The Pixiebob is allowed up to seven toes per paw. Polydactyly usually occurs only on the front paws in cats, but on occasion the back paws will also have extras. For all other breeds, polydactyly is a disqualifying fault.

According to breeders, Pixiebobs have no known breed-related inherited diseases or health problems, and breeders are working to keep it that way. Breeding Pixiebobs with recognized breeds is forbidden for that reason, since some breeds have a higher incidence of certain inheritable diseases. Particularly, breeding Bobs with Manx is prohibited, since the Manx gene is known to be associated with serious health problems. Nevertheless, it's wise to buy from a breeder who will guarantee the cat's health in writing.

GENERAL (TICA STANDARD)	The goal of the Pixiebob breeding program is to create a domestic cat with a visual similarity to the North American Bobcat.
BODY	Substantial and rangy. Medium to large in size. Prominent shoulder blades. Back not level, slight upward slope toward hips. Hips medium width, prominent, slightly higher than shoulder sloping downward to tail. Deep flank, broad chest. Primordial belly pouch.
HEAD	Medium to large inverted pear. Chin well-developed. Full broad muzzle. Fleshy gently rounded whisker pads. Definite whisker break. Nose wide, slightly convex. Slight nose bump. Slightly rounded forehead; concave curve, eye ridge to bridge of nose.
EARS	Medium height, wide, deep base. Set as much on side as top of head, slight outward tilt. Lynx tipping desirable, more prominent on longhair.
EYES	Medium-sized, heavily hooded soft triangle. Bushy brow. Deep set, one eye width apart. Eye color gold, brown, or gooseberry green.
LEGS AND PAWS	Legs long, hind legs slightly longer. Muscular with heavy boning. Feet large, long, wide almost round, large fleshy toes. All toes except dew claws must rest on floor pointing forward. Seven toes maximum.
TAIL	Tail bone must be two inches minimum, maximum length to hock with leg extended. Articulated tail, kinks and curls acceptable.
COAT— SHORTHAIR	Short stand-up coat. Belly hair longer. Texture soft and wooly, having loft. Is resilient to the touch. Coat, color, and pattern secondary to type. Both coats facial hair is full and bushy, with downward growth pattern. Coat separates easily and is weather resistant.
COAT— LONGHAIR	Medium, under two inches (5 cm). Belly hair longer. Texture soft, lying closer to the body than shorthair. Semi-dense. Coat, color, and pattern secondary to type. Both coats' facial hair is full and bushy, with downward growth pattern. Coat separates easily and is weather resistant.
COLOR	All shades of Brown Spotted Tabby; mouse coat; reversed ticking; light color throat to belly; paw pads/hocks dark brown/black; tail tip should be dark brown/black; white or cream band must surround eye; mascara marking from outer corner down through cheek. Pattern small to medium spots; muted by ticking; random spotting preferred.
DISQUALIFY	Any color/pattern not described. Lack of ticking or pattern throughout coat. Ruff around neck for longhair. Round eyes. Fine boning. Tail under 1 inch or full length tail.
ALLOWABLE OUTCROSSES	None.

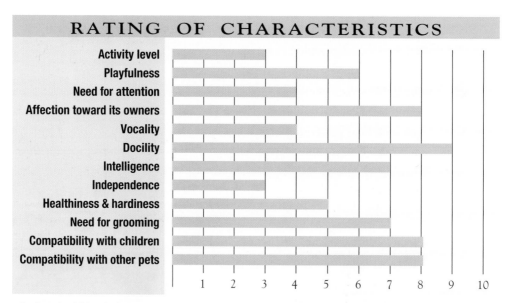

The RagaMuffin is a people-oriented breed that is cuddly and affectionate.

HISTORY

RagaMuffin breeders say that the RagaMuffin is not a new breed, but rather is as old as the better-known Ragdoll. The history of the RagaMuffin is intertwined with the history of the Ragdoll breed. The Ragdoll was developed in the 1960s by the late Ann Baker of Riverside, California, a former Persian breeder. In fact, who, where, and when are just about the only details involving the breed's origins that are known for a fact. Now that Baker has passed on, the full facts probably never will be known. The foundation cat from which the breed originated, Josephine, was a longhaired white female of unknown parentage. According to Ann Baker, Josephine produced unremarkable kittens until she was struck by a car in the early 1960s; after the accident Josephine was taken to a laboratory where she was genetically altered in a secret government experiment. This genetic alteration, said Baker, caused Josephine forever after to produce kittens with the traits for which the Ragdoll is famous. All subsequent offspring possessed non-matting fur, docile nature, larger size, impervious-

RATING OF CHARACTERISTICS

Characteristic	Rating (1–10)
Activity level	3
Playfulness	6
Need for attention	4
Affection toward its owners	8
Vocality	4
Docility	9
Intelligence	7
Independence	3
Healthiness & hardiness	5
Need for grooming	7
Compatibility with children	8
Compatibility with other pets	8

1—breed exhibits the least amount of this characteristic, 10—breed exhibits the most of this characteristic

ness to pain, and the tendency to go limp like a child's rag doll—thus the breed's name. However, this couldn't be confirmed, Baker claimed, since the government covered up all the evidence. This story, needless to say, is hard to believe.

Josephine's offspring, however they came to be produced, became the foundation of the Ragdoll breed. The Ragdolls of America Group (RAG, a group formed to gain acceptance for the Ragdoll in the Cat Fanciers' Association) says that Josephine was a semi-feral solid white Turkish Angora-type cat that resided on the property of Mrs. Pennels in Riverside, California, a neighbor of Ann Baker's. After her car accident, Josephine mated with a feral black-and-white mitted longhaired tom and produced a mitted seal point longhair with a white blaze and a white tail tip named Daddy Warbucks and a seal pointed bicolor female named Fugianna. Daddy Warbucks went on to become one of the foundation males of the breed. Another litter followed, sired by a solid brown longhaired tom. This tryst produced a seal point female named Tiki and a black-and-white-mitted male named Buckwheat. The breed's founder, the late Ann Baker, came into possession of these cats, and all subsequent generations can be traced back to them. After years of selective breeding, the Ragdoll developed into the breed known today. This seems to be a credible story for the breed's creation; however, this lineage cannot be confirmed with certainty, since the trysts between these feral cats were not documented by Baker or anyone else.

Ann Baker came into possession of these cats (Josephine apparently never belonged to her), and Baker gave the cats the name Cherubim. Many of these Cherubim cats had the pointed pattern and mitted feet, but others came in a variety of solid and bi-color patterns. Baker called the non-pointed and non-mitted cats Miracle Ragdolls. In 1971, Ann Baker trademarked the name Ragdoll and, in an attempt to protect her interests and keep control over the breed, formed her own registry, The International Ragdoll Cat Association (IRCA). She sold Ragdoll franchises, and required her IRCA breeders to sign license agreements, pay licensing fees, and breed according to her carefully controlled breeding program; she told the breeders which cats would be allowed to mate, and to whom. She kept all breeding records in her head, which made it difficult to know the exact lineage of the cats. The breeders also had to pay a 10 percent commission on the sale of each kitten they bred and sold. In addition, Ragdolls could only be registered with IRCA, and were not allowed to be registered or exhibited with any other cat association.

Some breeders were very displeased with these arrangements, and they wanted to distance themselves from the questionable claims being made about their beloved breed. Baker allegedly claimed Ragdolls had been outcrossed with skunks to improve their tails, and contained implanted human

Although RagaMuffins are not overly vocal, they will speak up if they have something vital to tell you.

continued to make all marketing and breeding decisions, and kept the breeding records to herself. The IRCA breeders didn't object to the financial arrangement, but they were embarrassed by Baker's treatment of the other Ragdoll breeders, who she constantly harassed by sending out accusations and vicious stories in which she accused the breeders of killing her cats and making attempts on her own life, among other wild claims. Even her most loyal breeders eventually became very uncomfortable with Baker's strange behavior.

The breeders also worried about the health of the cats at Baker's cattery, which according to IRCA breeders at the time, were often infested with fleas, ear mites, and fungus. Cases of feline leukemia were reported at her cattery. The breeders felt the head of their organization should have healthy and well cared for cats and kittens.

In July 1993, Ann Baker told a group of IRCA breeders that she was going to retire and turn over IRCA to them. Baker said she would act as an advisor, and she would turn over all records, pedigrees, and breeding program information. The breeders were delighted by this news, but later Baker changed her mind and refused to give up command. The group voted to quit IRCA at this point and try for recog-

genes, and represented a link between humans and extraterrestrials. In 1975, these breeders split from IRCA, formed the Ragdoll Fanciers' Club International (RFCI), and began the long process to gaining acceptance for the Ragdoll breed. Only colorpointed cats in mitted, bicolor, and van patterns were developed.

Other breeders stayed with Baker and IRCA because of their love for their breed, and either agreed with Baker or were daunted by the lawsuits Baker filed and the harassment she unleashed at the breeders who took their cats and left. For the next 20 years or so, IRCA was supported by breeding license fees of $150.00 a year, plus the 10 percent commission from every kitten sold. Baker

nition with the associations that had already accepted the Ragdoll. Since they had signed contracts agreeing not to use the Ragdoll name outside of IRCA, the breeders chose a name for their breed to avoid violating their contracts and Baker's trademark. Curt Gehm of Liebling Cats in Virginia is credited with the name RagaMuffin.

In 1994, some of the former IRCA breeders formed the RagaMuffin Associated Group (RAG) to preserve the breed and promote it with the mainstream associations. Curt Gehm wrote the first breed standard with the help of ACFA. Breeders had to start from scratch, because the associations wouldn't grant them the same acceptance they'd already granted the Ragdoll. The breeders were representing the RagaMuffin as a new breed, not as a new Ragdoll color division, and therefore the RagaMuffin had to go through each phase of acceptance and meet each association's requirements as a new breed. However, the breeders persisted, and today all associations except CCA recognize the RagaMuffin, although TICA has yet to accept the breed beyond registration status. The RagaMuffin has a solid base of fans who believe the breed is the cat's meow.

The RagaMuffin is similar, but not identical, in conformation to the Ragdoll because of the many years of separation between the two breeds. The RagaMuffin comes in a wider variety of colors, and the body type is slightly different. RagaMuffin breeders note that the RagaMuffin is not a new breed but an old one with a new name. Although Ragdolls and RagaMuffins are both descendants from the original blood-lines that Baker developed, RagaMuffin breeders split away from IRCA much more recently than Ragdoll breeders. Some RagaMuffin breeders believe that if the breed's history is put into proper perspective, the RagaMuffin is the parent breed, and the Ragdoll is simply a division of the original. According to some breeders, the Ragdoll breeders who "abandoned the originator of the breed" took only a few colors and patterns, and the breed is just a small part of what the Ragdoll was intended to be.

On the other paw, there is a certain amount of resentment from the early abandoners of the originator of the breed toward the more recent abandoners of the originator of the breed. Since Ragdoll breeders endured years of Baker's lawsuits and wrath and worked very long and hard to bring the Ragdoll into the spotlight, some Ragdoll breeders feel RagaMuffin fanciers have no cause to criticize, and in fact are using the Ragdoll's hard-won success to advance the RagaMuffin.

PERSONALITY

Fanciers who raise both Ragdolls and RagaMuffins claim that their temperaments are very similar. Very lovable and attentive, the RagaMuffin is a people-oriented breed that's cuddly and affectionate, with a tendency to go limp when held in your arms. While not overly active, they enjoy playing with their preferred people, and some will retrieve tossed toys, before settling down for a cuddle in your lap. They greet family members at the door and follow their favorite humans around the house, just to keep an eye on their

GENERAL	The overall impression of the RagaMuffin is one of sweetness and robust health. They are a large cat with substantial bone structure and full bodies. The large, expressive eyes strongly contribute to the overall sweet look. The only extremes in this cat are large size, large expressive eyes, and docile nature. RagaMuffins attain full maturity at approximately four years of age. The cat should have an overall balance, with quality and conformation given preference over size.
BODY	Rectangular, broad chest and broad shoulders, and moderately heavy muscling in the hindquarters with the hindquarters being equally as broad as the shoulders. There is a fatty pad in the lower abdomen. These cats are fully fleshed and upon palpation should feel well covered with flesh. The cat should have an overall balance in body size, shape, and distribution of weight, with quality and conformation given preference over size.
HEAD	Broad modified wedge with a rounded appearance. The forehead should be moderately rounded. Muzzle is round, slightly shorter than moderate in length, tending to broadness. The chin is firmly rounded, reflecting a proper bite. There is puffiness to the whisker pad, which results in the characteristic "sweet look" of the RagaMuffin. Cheeks are full. In profile, there is an obvious nose dip, giving the impression of a scoop rather than a break. Neck is short, heavy, and strong.
EARS	Medium in size, set as much on the side of the head as on the top of the head with slight flaring, tilted slightly forward. Ears are rounded with moderate furnishings, in pleasing proportion to the head.
EYES	Large, walnut shaped and expressive, moderately wide set, the eyes contribute to the characteristic sweet look. A slight oriental slant to the eye is acceptable. The more intense the eye color, the better. All eye colors are allowed, including odd eyed. Exception: mink colors must be aqua, and sepia colors must be yellow to gold.
LEGS AND PAWS	Legs should be heavily boned, medium in length with the back legs slightly longer than the front legs, yet in proportion to the body. The paws should be large and round, able to support the weight of the cat without splaying, and with tufts beneath and between the paws.
TAIL	Long, in proportion to the body. It is fully furred, similar in look to a plume or soft bottlebrush, medium at the base with a slight taper.
COAT	Fur is to be medium to medium-long. Texture is to be soft, dense, and silky. Texture will vary slightly with color. Fur length is to be slightly longer around neck and outer edges of face, resulting in the appearance of a ruff, and increasing in length from top of head down through shoulder blades and back, with the coat on the sides and stomach being medium to medium-long. The fur on the front legs is thick and short to medium in length. The fur on the hind legs is medium to medium-long and thick with the appearance of a wispy frill on the hindquarters.

COLOR	Every genetically possible color and pattern allowable with or without white, except pointed colors. Any amount of white is allowed, e.g., white spots on paws, back, chest, or belly; blaze, locket, etc. The degree of symmetry whether in the pattern or the white spotting is of no importance. Nose leather and paw pads are accepted in all colors and in any color combination, not necessarily related to coat color, listed colors are preferred, not required. Cats with white on feet may have pink paw pads or they may be bicolored or multi-colored.
DISQUALIFY	Penalize extreme cranial doming, nose break, Roman nose, small ears, pointed ears. Cobby body, short tail, cottony undercoat. Disqualify poor health or condition, crossed eyes, tail kink, polydactyl or pointed colors. Short hair on the body and/or tail, giving the impression of a short-haired cat.
ALLOWABLE OUTCROSSES	None.

activities. Although they are not an overly vocal breed, they will speak up if they have something vital to tell you, such as the empty state of their food dishes. These cats adapt easily to a variety of environments and household situations, and are generally very good with other cats, dogs, and well-behaved children. Because of their value and gentle nature, it's wise to keep RagaMuffins indoors.

CONFORMATION

As a rule, RagaMuffins are strong, healthy cats with no known genetic health problems affecting the breed. The RagaMuffin is similar, but not identical, in conformation and temperament to the Ragdoll. The main difference is in accepted colors and patterns. While the Ragdoll is accepted in six colors and three patterns in CFA, the RagaMuffin comes in any genetically possible color or pattern with the exception of pointed colors. In CFF and ACFA, every color and pattern is allowable with and without white, including the pointed colors and pattern. In ACFA, the IRCA Ragdoll and Miracle Ragdoll are the foundation cats of the RagaMuffin and are the only cats allowed to be foundation registered.

RagaMuffins attain full maturity at approximately four years of age.

221

RAGDOLL

The Ragdoll is a breed whose origins are surrounded by mystery, controversy, and tall tales. Instead of facts, we have colorful stories, speculation, conjecture, and plain old fiction. Telling one from the other is easier said than done.

The Ragdoll was developed in the 1960s by the late Ann Baker of Riverside, California, a former Persian breeder. In fact, who, where, and when are just about the only details involving the breed's origins that are not subject to debate.

The foundation cat from which the breed originated, Josephine, was a semi-feral longhaired white female of unknown parentage. According to Ann Baker, Josephine produced unremarkable kittens until she was struck by a car in the early 1960s; after the accident Josephine was taken to a laboratory where she was genetically altered in a secret government experiment. This genetic alteration, said Baker, caused Josephine forever after to produce kittens with the traits for which the Ragdoll is famous. All subsequent off-

Docile, mild-mannered, and congenial, Ragdolls make ideal indoor companions.

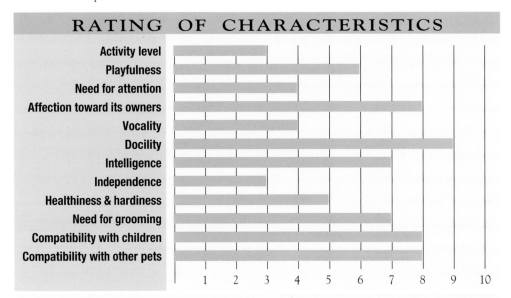

RATING OF CHARACTERISTICS

Characteristic	Rating (1–10)
Activity level	3
Playfulness	6
Need for attention	4
Affection toward its owners	8
Vocality	4
Docility	9
Intelligence	7
Independence	3
Healthiness & hardiness	5
Need for grooming	7
Compatibility with children	8
Compatibility with other pets	8

1—breed exhibits the least amount of this characteristic, 10—breed exhibits the most of this characteristic

* **Championship status in all associations**

spring possessed non-matting fur, docile nature, larger size, imperviousness to pain, and the tendency to go limp like a child's rag doll—thus the breed's name. However, this couldn't be confirmed, Baker claimed, since the government covered up the evidence. According to those who knew her, Ann Baker truly believed it happened just this way.

According to TICA's genetics committee chairperson, Dr. Solveig Pflueger M.D. Ph.D., this kind of genetic engineering did not exist in the 1960s. It's more likely, she notes, that the foundation cat possessed some exceptional genes, either recessive or masked by her dominant white color, so that when she coupled with mates that enhanced her latent genes, some striking offspring were produced.

These striking offspring, however they were produced, became the foundation of the Ragdoll breed. The Ragdolls of America Group (a group formed to gain acceptance for the Ragdoll in the Cat Fanciers' Association) says that Josephine was a feral white Turkish Angora-type cat that resided on the property of Mrs. Pennels in Riverside, California, a neighbor of Ann Baker's. After she recovered from her car accident, Josephine mated with a feral black-and-white mitted longhaired tom and produced two kittens: a mitted sealpoint longhaired male with a white blaze and a white tail tip named Daddy Warbucks, and a sealpointed bicolor female named Fugianna. Daddy Warbucks went on to become one of

the foundation males of the breed; Ann Baker called him "the father of the Ragdoll look." Another litter followed, sired by a longhaired brown tom. This tryst produced a sealpoint female named Tiki and a black-and-white mitted male named Buckwheat. Ann Baker came into possession of these cats, and all subsequent generations can be traced back to them. After years of selective breeding, the Ragdoll developed into the breed known today. This seems to be a likely story for the breed's creation; however, this lineage cannot be confirmed with certainty, since the trysts between these feral cats were not documented by Baker or anyone else. Baker passed away in January 1997, so the details of the breed's history will probably never be known. However, what's not in debate is that Ann Baker, despite her strange claims, was the founder of the Ragdoll breed.

The first Ragdoll breeding pair, Buddy and Rosie, was sold to Denny and Laura Dayton in 1969. The Daytons were instrumental in establishing the Ragdoll breed, and in the beginning tried to work with Baker to get the breed accepted by the mainstream associations. Baker, however, wasn't interested. In 1971, Ann Baker trademarked the name Ragdoll and, in an attempt to protect her interests and keep control over the breed, set up her own registry, The International Ragdoll Cat Association (IRCA), and sold breeder franchises. Baker required her IRCA breeders to pay a licensing fee and breed according to her carefully controlled breeding program—she directed which cats would be allowed to mate, and with whom. The breeders also had to pay a 10 percent commission on the sale of each kitten. In addition, Ragdolls could only be registered with IRCA, and were not allowed to be registered or exhibited with any cat association. The mainstream cat associations, in their turn, didn't recognize IRCA Ragdolls—or any Ragdolls for quite a long time.

When a new breed is created or discovered, it is generally one person or a few people who do the initial work of developing the breed and getting it recognized. It's understandable for that person or persons to feel a certain possessiveness toward the breed, and want to have some say as to the breed's future direction. This can lead to disagreement as others become involved in the breed's development, as other breeders must for a breed to grow and flourish, but it usually doesn't lead to all-out war. However, nothing was usual about the origin of the Ragdoll.

In the mid-1970s, a group of breeders unhappy with Baker's restrictions and fees, and who wanted to gain recognition for the Ragdoll with the cat associations and to distance themselves from the incredible claims Baker was making about the breed, split from Baker and in 1975 formed the Ragdoll Fanciers' Club (RFC). Founded by Denny and Laura Dayton, this group was dedicated to developing the breed and achieving recognition with the mainstream national cat associations. The club's name was later changed to the Ragdoll Fanciers' Club International (RFCI). Although the Daytons had purchased their Ragdolls before the creation of IRCA and had signed no franchise agreement with Baker, disputes over ownership followed, and litigation from Baker ensued. She also made it difficult for RFCI breeders to be taken seriously by the mainstream cat associations due to the increasingly unbelievable claims about the cats, and due to letters Baker sent to the cat associations, the media, and to everyone else she could think of, charging the Daytons with stealing and/or killing her cats and making attempts upon her life, among other charges.

Later, other breed groups affiliated with the mainstream cat associations formed to promote the Ragdoll, such as the CFF-affiliated Ragdoll Fanciers' Club, TICA-affiliated Ragdoll International, and CFA-affiliated Ragdolls of America Group. It took many years of effort to overcome the strange tales and controversy, but with the Ragdoll's hard-won CFA championship status granted in February 2000, the breed was finally recognized for championship by every major North American cat association. The Ragdoll has earned its place in the spotlight, just as it has earned its place in the laps and hearts of fanciers everywhere.

PERSONALITY

Docile, mild-mannered, and congenial, Ragdolls make ideal indoor companions. One of the nicest features of these cats is their laid-back, sweet personality. They are devotion wrapped in silky fur, loving loyalty with gentle white paws. Very in tune with their

Mitted Ragdolls may have a white blaze on the nose or the forehead.

human's routines and emotions, Ragdolls are there when you come home at night to greet you with a leg rub, a forehead kiss, and a big purr. If you've had a bad day, they'll cuddle into your lap to offer gentle comfort so that soon you'll be smiling again. A better friend you couldn't have.

They are playful but are not overactive. Known to adapt easily to almost any environment, Ragdolls get along well with children and adults, as well as other cats and dogs. They are easily trained to stay off the counter and are affectionate without being overly demanding. They have soft, polite voices, even at dinnertime, even though they are renowned for their enthusiasm for food. One thing Ragdolls are not, however, is impervious to pain. If you accidently step on their tails, they'll shriek and eye you reproachfully, just as any other cat will.

CONFORMATION

The Ragdoll comes in six point colors: seal, blue, chocolate, lilac, red, and cream. Point colors may be solid, lynx, tortie-lynx, and parti-colored, or tortie. All Ragdolls are pointed, but points are partially overlaid with white in the mitted, bicolor, and van patterns. Solid division Ragdolls have dense and clearly defined masks, ears, legs, feet, and tails that are all of the same shade. The mask covers the entire face including whisker pads, and is connected to the ears by tracings. Body color is even, with subtle shading permissible but clear color preferred. Mitted Ragdolls have well-defined points on legs (except the feet), ears, masks, and tails. They may have a white blaze in the shape of a star, diamond, hourglass, or line located anywhere from the top of the nose leather to the forehead. Chin is white and extends into white belly stripe. The front feet have evenly matched white mittens on both feet, preferably going up to and around the wrist joint. On the back legs the white must go up to and around the hocks entirely, extending no higher than mid-thigh. In the van pattern, point color is restricted to the ears, tail, and mask. Ear and tail color is dense and clearly defined, with minor white spotting allowed. The mask may be limited to the upper part of the mask, which may show gradual fading of color.

Body, legs, and feet are a pure, glistening white with minor spotting allowed.

Ragdolls are hardy, healthy cats. The only major inherited disease is hypertrophic cardiomyopathy (HCM). HCM is the most common cardiac disease in cats. The symptoms of affected cats are usually sudden death due to increased left ventricular heart muscle thickness. In Ragdolls, the condition is caused by an inherited mutation. The Ragdoll mutation for HCM produces an early onset of the disease, with an average age of fifteen months at diagnosis. In addition, Ragdolls that inherit two copies of the gene for the disease have an even earlier onset. Fortunately, the Veterinary Genetics Laboratory at UC Davis offers a DNA test for the Ragdoll breed-specific HCM mutation. Breeders can use this as a tool to screen out affected and carrier cats and eliminate them from their breeding stock. The tests are done with DNA collected from cheek swabs and sent in via mail, avoiding the inconvenience and invasiveness of blood collection.

All Ragdolls have large, vivid blue eyes.

GENERAL	The ideal Ragdoll is a well-balanced cat with no extreme features. They are a medium to large, moderately longhaired, blue-eyed pointed cat. The point markings may be covered by a range of white overlay patterns. Ragdolls are slow maturing, reaching full coat and color at about three years of age. The Ragdoll is an affectionate and intelligent cat, giving the impression of graceful movement and subdued power, striking in appearance.
BODY	Large and long, broad and solid, with heavy boning. Rectangular in shape, with a full chest and equal width across shoulders and hindquarters. Body firm and muscular, not fat. Moderate stomach pad on lower abdomen acceptable. Females may be substantially smaller than males. Allow for slow maturation in young adults.
HEAD	Proportionately large with a broad, modified wedge that is equilateral in shape, where all sides are of equal length as measured from the outside of the base of the ear to the end of the gently rounded muzzle. Appearance of a flat plane between ears. Cheeks in line with wedge. When whiskers and fur are smoothed back, the underlying bone structure is apparent. Slightly curving; ending in straight, medium-length nose. Chin well-developed, strong, in line with nose and upper lip. Neck heavy and strong.
EARS	Medium sized. Wide set and moderately flared, continuing the line of wedge. Wide at base with rounded tips, and tilted forward.
EYES	Large, vivid blue ovals. Wide set and moderately slanted, complementing wedge. Color blue.
LEGS AND PAWS	Legs substantial and medium length; medium heavy musculature; hind legs slightly heavier; paws round, large, with tufting desirable.
TAIL	Long, medium at base with slight taper; in proportion to body.
COAT	Semi-long, silky, plush, with medium undercoat; coat lies with body and breaks as cat moves; medium ruff.
COLOR	Sealpoint and white; blue point and white; all other pointed and white colors including lilac, chocolate, all lynx colors, red, cream, tortie and all van colors; all mitted point colors including chocolate, seal, lilac, blue, all lynx colors, red, cream and tortie; all colorpoint colors including chocolate, seal, lilac, blue, all lynx colors, red, cream, and tortie.
DISQUALIFY	Eye color other than blue; any white on pointed colors; lack of white chin on mitted colors; any dark markings on area of white mask in bicolor.
ALLOWABLE OUTCROSSES	None.

HISTORY

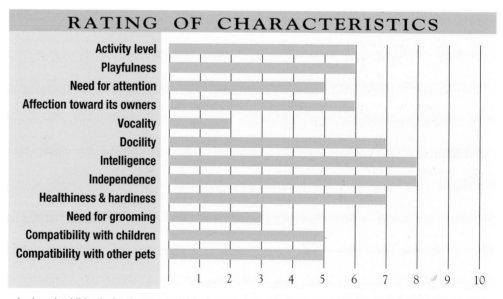

The most commonly held theory regarding this breed's origin is that Russian Blues were brought to Great Britain in 1860 by British sailors from the White Sea port town of Archangel (Arkhangelsk) in northern Russia. Whether this story is true—and if true, whether the cats really originated in that area—is anyone's guess. Their thick coats give credence to the theory that they developed in a cold climate, and, according to accounts, blue shorthairs still exist in Russia.

The Russian Blue is not believed to be related to the other three shorthaired solid blue breeds: Thailand's Korat, France's Chartreux, and Britain's British Blue (now called the British Shorthair). The four breeds have distinct differences in coat type, conformation, and personality, although the Korat, Chartreux, and Russian Blue share a similar silver-blue sheen. Since all four of these breeds have been around for so long that their ancestries are shrouded in legend and conjecture, a common ancestor is possible.

In 1871 a Russian Blue was shown at the first cat show at the Crystal Palace in London, under the name Archangel Cat. At this point, Russian Blues were

Russian Blues are lithe and graceful cats.

RATING OF CHARACTERISTICS

Characteristic	Rating
Activity level	6
Playfulness	6
Need for attention	6
Affection toward its owners	6
Vocality	2
Docility	7
Intelligence	8
Independence	8
Healthiness & hardiness	6
Need for grooming	3
Compatibility with children	5
Compatibility with other pets	5

1—breed exhibits the least amount of this characteristic, 10—breed exhibits the most of this characteristic

228

※ **Championship status in all associations**

shorthaired, solid blue felines with foreign body types. From photos and published sources of the time, the original coat was thick, dense, glossy, and colored a light silver-blue.

Russian Blues competed in the same class with all other shorthaired blues, despite obvious differences in type. Since the round-headed, cobby British Blues were favored in the show halls, the slender Russian Blues rarely won. Finally, the Governing Council of the Cat Fancy (GCCF) acknowledged the breed, and in 1912 the Russian Blue was granted a class of its own. The breed then made progress until World War II when it almost became extinct, as did many other breeds.

During the 1940s and 1950s two independent groups of breeders worked to resurrect the Russian Blue by crossbreeding the few hardy survivors with other blue breeds. In Britain, breeders crossed the Russian Blue with bluepoint Siamese and British Blues. Because of the Siamese influence, the British Russian Blue's moderate foreign body style became more extreme.

At the same time, Scandinavian breeders attempted to recreate the breed by crossing blue cats from Finland with Siamese cats that carried color factors that would enhance the solid blue coloration. These cats were larger and had larger heads and shorter, denser coats than British Russian Blues.

In 1965, a group of British breeders, not pleased with all the changes, began efforts to restore the Russian Blue to its original condition. In 1966, the show standard was again changed, now stating that the Siamese type was undesirable. By breeding the Scandinavian cats, with their good head type and vivid green eye color, with the British Russian Blues, with their silver-blue coat color and graceful body style, the breeders finally achieved consistency.

The Russian Blue arrived in America in the early 1900s, but it was not until 1947 that serious attempts at breeding and promoting in the United States began. Because of the inconsistency in the breeding stock, and because three other blue breeds existed upon which fanciers could focus their esteem, the Russian Blue didn't get as much attention as it might otherwise have received. However, imports from Britain gradually improved the bloodlines, and the Russian Blue gained much needed stability.

Hard work by dedicated breeders has improved the Russian Blue bloodline to the point that American Russian Blues have even been exported to Europe to improve their bloodlines. Russian Blues are now accepted for championship in all North American cat associations.

PERSONALITY

Russian Blues are quiet, gentle, genteel cats, and are usually reserved or absent when strangers come to call. When they're with their own beloved and trusted humans, however, they are playful and affectionate. Russian Blues are active but not annoyingly so. They like nothing better than to spend time

Show-quality Russian Blues have vivid green eyes.

pouncing on a favorite toy or chasing sunbeams. They willingly entertain themselves, but prefer games in which their preferred people take an active role. When you're home, they follow you around, unobtrusive but ever-present companions. The slight upturn to the corners of the mouth make Russian Blues appear to be forever smiling.

Members of this breed are polite, quiet, and well-behaved, for cats. It's quite easy to teach them to stay off counters and out of off-limit areas; usually a simple "No" will do. However, Russian Blues seem to think politeness should go both ways and take offense at being made to look silly. A dignified breed, Russian Blues can be trusted to know when you're making fun of them—and they won't soon forget this breach in manners, either.

Russian Blues like their daily routine to be just so, and dislike household changes more than the average cat—and the average cat dislikes household changes a lot. They particularly dislike changes to their dinner schedule, and will make you aware of their displeasure. They are also fastidious about their litter boxes and will complain or even go elsewhere if they're not spic and span.

CONFORMATION

This breed's most distinctive feature, its beautiful silver-tipped blue coat, is silky, plush, and so dense it stands out from the body. You can literally draw pictures in the fur with your fingers. The coat's guard hairs bear silver tipping that reflects light, giving the coat a silver sheen. Combined with vivid green eyes, the Russian Blue is a strikingly beautiful breed. Even though it's short, the dense double coat does require some grooming to keep it looking its best. Twice or three times a week is best, and more during the spring and fall shedding seasons.

Although blue is the only color accepted by the North American registries, in Europe, Great Britain, Australia, and New Zealand other colors are recognized. In the Governing Council of the Cat Fancy (GCCF), Australian Cat Federation (ACF), and New Zealand Cat Fancy (NZCF), the breed is simply called "Russian" and is accepted in solid blue, white, and black. The Fédération Internationale Féline (FIFE), however, accepts only blue. In addition, the European Russian Blue tends to be larger and more heavily built than the American Russian Blue.

GENERAL	The good show specimen has good physical condition, is firm in muscle tone, and alert.
BODY	Fine boned, long, firm, and muscular; lithe and graceful in outline and carriage without being tubular in appearance.
HEAD	Smooth, medium wedge, neither long and tapering nor short and massive. Muzzle is blunt, and part of the total wedge, without exaggerated pinch or whisker break. Top of skull long and flat in profile, gently descending to slightly above the eyes, and continuing at a slight downward angle in a straight line to the tip of the nose. Medium in length. No nose break or stop. Length of top-head should be greater than length of nose. The face is broad across the eyes due to wide eye-set and thick fur. Muzzle smooth, flowing wedge without prominent whisker pads or whisker pinches. Neck long and slender, but appearing short due to thick fur and high placement of shoulder blades.
EARS	Rather large and wide at the base. Tips more pointed than rounded. The skin of the ears is thin and translucent, with little inside furnishing. The outside of the ear is scantily covered with short, very fine hair, with leather showing through. Set far apart, as much on the side as on the top of the head.
EYES	Set wide apart. Aperture rounded in shape. Color vivid green.
LEGS AND PAWS	Legs long and fine boned. Paws small, slightly rounded. Toes five in front and four behind.
TAIL	Long, but in proportion to the body. Tapering from a moderately thick base.
COAT	Short, dense, fine, and plush. Double coat stands out from body due to density. It has a distinct soft and silky feel.
COLOR	Even bright blue throughout. Lighter shades of blue preferred. Guard hairs distinctly silver-tipped giving the cat a silvery sheen or lustrous appearance. A definite contrast noted between ground color and tipping. Free from tabby markings. Nose leather slate gray. Paw pads lavender, pink, or mauve. Eye color vivid green.
DISQUALIFY	Kinked or abnormal tail. Locket or button. Incorrect number of toes. Any color other than blue. Long coat.
ALLOWABLE OUTCROSSES	None.

Scottish Fold Longhair, also known as the Longhair Fold and Highland Fold.

HISTORY

All Scottish Folds can trace their pedigrees back to a barn cat named Susie found in 1961 on the McRae farm near Coupar Angus, a town in Perth and Kinross, Scotland. This white female farm feline had unique, folded down ears, and British Shorthair breeders William and Mary Ross, upon seeing this unusual cat, recognized her potential as a new breed. William Ross asked the McRaes if he could purchase the cat, and was promised a kitten from Susie's first litter. Susie's mother was a straight-eared white cat, and her father was unknown, so it's unclear whether Susie was one of the first of her kind or whether the folded ears had never been noticed before. One of Susie's brothers also had folded ears, but he wandered off never to be seen again.

In 1963, Susie produced two folded-ear kittens, and as promised William and Mary Ross were given one—a folded-ear white beauty like her mother that they named Snooks. On the advice of British geneticist Peter Dyte, the Rosses started a breeding program using as outcrosses the British Shorthairs that were close on hand in their cattery, and random-bred domestics. They took the name

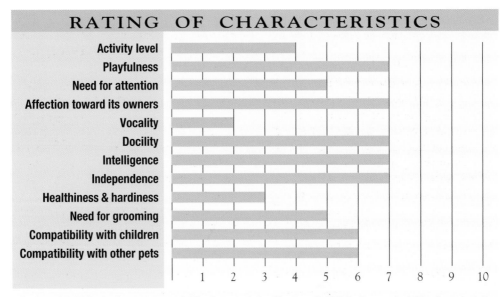

RATING OF CHARACTERISTICS

Characteristic	Rating
Activity level	4
Playfulness	7
Need for attention	7
Affection toward its owners	7
Vocality	2
Docility	7
Intelligence	7
Independence	7
Healthiness & hardiness	3
Need for grooming	5
Compatibility with children	6
Compatibility with other pets	5

1—breed exhibits the least amount of this characteristic, 10—breed exhibits the most of this characteristic

* **Championship status for Scottish Fold Shorthair in all associations**
* **Championship status for Scottish Fold Longhair in AACE, ACFA, and UFO under the name Highland Fold**
* **Championship status for Scottish Fold Longhair in CFF under the name Longhair Fold**
* **Championship status for the Scottish Fold Longhair in CFA and TICA as a division of the Scottish Fold breed**
* **Championship status for the Scottish Fold Shorthair, Scottish Fold Longhair, Scottish Straight Shorthair, and the Scottish Straight Longhair in CCA under the name Scottish**

Denisla as their Fold cattery named after the two rivers, the Den and the Isla, which flowed past their cottage. Snooks was first bred to a red tabby random-bred male. In that litter one kitten, a white male named Snowball, had folded ears. Snowball was mated with a white British Shorthair named Lady May, and five folded-ear kittens were produced in that litter. Snooks was next bred to a blue British Shorthair named Ryelands Regal Gent, and two folded-ear kittens named Hester and Hector were produced in this litter. Snooks, Snowball, and Lady May's kittens became the foundation of the breed.

William and Mary Ross quickly realized that the gene governing the folded ears was dominant; only one parent needed the gene in order to pass along the unique trait. Any cat possessing one copy of the fold gene produced or sired about fifty percent of Fold kittens.

Originally, the Rosses called their new breed Lops after the lop-ear type of rabbit. In 1966, however, they changed the name to Scottish Fold, in honor of its most extraordinary trait and the country in which the breed was found. The same year, the Rosses registered their Scottish Fold cats with the Governing Council of the Cat Fancy (GCCF). Along with

other enthusiasts they gathered along the way, the Rosses began the process of achieving acceptance for their folded friends. At first, a number of breeders and fanciers were enthusiastic about this new and different breed, but soon GCCF became concerned about potential health problems. At first, they were worried about ear infections, ear mite infestations, and deafness, but these concerns were proven unfounded. However, GCCF soon became concerned about genetic problems, which were, unfortunately, very real difficulties. By 1971, GCCF closed registration to Scottish Folds and banned further registration in their registry.

To continue toward the show ring, the Scottish Fold had to pack up its kilts and move to North America. The Fold was first introduced to the United States in 1970 when three of Snooks' offspring, Judy, Joey, and Hester, were sent to New England geneticist Neil Todd, who was researching spontaneous mutations in cats at the Carnivore Genetics Research Center in Newtonville, Massachusetts. Joey and Judy produced two litters while he was conducting his research. He eventually abandoned the project, but found homes for the Folds. Well-known

The Scottish Fold was first introduced to the United States in 1970.

Manx breeder Salle Wolf Peters of Pennsylvania acquired one of the cats, Hester, daughter of Snooks and the blue British Shorthair Ryelands Regal Gent, from Lynn Lamoreux, a doctoral student of Dr. Todd's.

Salle Wolf Peters was the first of many U.S. breeders to fall in love with the Fold's appearance and pleasant personality, and she was instrumental in recruiting other breeders and developing the breed. Other Folds were later imported to the United States. All genuine Scottish Folds can be traced back to Susie and Snooks.

The Scottish Fold was accepted for CFA registration in 1973; in May 1977 Scottish Folds were given CFA provisional status. In 1978, the Fold became a CFA champion breed. In an amazingly short period, the Fold earned acceptance in all the North American cat associations and a place among North America's most popular breeds.

The longhaired version of the breed was not officially recognized until the mid-1980s, although longhair kittens had been cropping up in Scottish Fold litters since the genesis of the breed. Suzie may have carried the recessive gene for long hair, being a barn cat of uncertain origin. The use of a number of Persians in early outcrosses also helped establish the longhair gene. Today, all associations have accepted the Scottish Fold Longhair for championship, although many associations have a separate standard for the longhair and call it the Highland Fold or the Longhair Fold.

The Scottish Fold Longhair is known by three different monikers, depending on the association. AACE, ACFA, and UFO call the breed the Highland Fold; CFF refers to the breed as the Longhair Fold. In CFA and TICA, the longhaired Scottish Fold is a division of the Scottish Fold breed and shares one standard in each association. In CCA, the breed is called Scottish, and both hair lengths share one standard, although the two hair lengths are judged as separate breeds. In addition, CCA accepts the Scottish Straight Shorthair and the Scottish Straight Longhair under the name Scottish; these are Scottish Folds that don't possess folded ears. The Scottish Shorthair, also called the pert-ear, has the same personality and body type as the Scottish Fold; they just don't have folded ears. Since the Fold doesn't breed true, the pet-quality pert-ear can be bought relatively inexpensively. In the Australian Cat Federation (ACF), the Scottish Shorthair is accepted as a breed in its own right.

PERSONALITY

Scottish Folds are intelligent, sweet-tempered, soft-spoken, and easily adaptable to new people and situations. They are loyal and tend to bond with one person in the household. While they will usually allow others to cuddle and pet them, their primary attachment becomes quickly clear as they single out their chosen human. They thrive on attention, but it must be on their own terms.

Despite their devotion, they are not clingy, demanding cats and usually prefer to be near you rather than on your lap. They enjoy a good game of catch the catnip mouse now and then as well, and keep their playful side well into adulthood.

Despite being folded, the Fold's ears are still expressive and swivel to listen, lay back in anger, and prick up when a can of food is opened. The fold in the ear can become less pronounced when the cat is in heat, upset, or ill. Although some Fold owners report an increased production of wax buildup in their cats' ears, the folded ears do not make the cat more susceptible to mites or ear infections. The previously reported susceptibility to deafness may be related to the fact that some early Scottish Folds were white, and white cats can be prone to a type of deafness that's unrelated to the Fold gene.

CONFORMATION

The Scottish Fold's folded ears are produced by a gene that affects the cartilage of the ears, causing the ears to fold forward and downward, giving the head a rounded appearance. The gene is believed to be incompletely dominant; all Scottish Fold cats must have one folded-ear parent to have folded ears themselves. When a heterozygous Fold is bred to a straight-eared cat, approximately fifty percent of the kittens will have folded ears, although the number of Folds in any given litter can vary, sometimes greatly.

Breeding Fold to Fold increases the number of Fold kittens, but also greatly increases the chances of skeletal deformities. Homozygous Folds (Folds that inherit the folded ear gene from both parents) are much more likely to develop a genetic disorder called congenital osteodystrophy, a genetic condition that causes distortion, deformities, or enlargement of the bones, particularly fused tail vertebrae and thickened legs. Early warning signs include a thickness or lack of mobility of the legs or tail. Responsible breeders never breed Fold to Fold; all Scottish Folds must be outbred to prevent the birth of kittens with congenital osteodystrophy. Avoiding Fold-to-Fold breeding reduces this problem but doesn't entirely eliminate it; some controversy still surrounds the breed because of this defect. You can determine tail flexibility by moving your hand down the tail in a very gentle, slightly upward-arching movement. One of the first questions you should ask a prospective breeder is whether the tail is flexible. It's wise to see both parents, or at least their pedigrees.

All Scottish Folds are born with straight ears. At around three weeks of age, the kittens' ears will begin to fold, if they're going to—Scottish Fold

GENERAL	The Scottish Fold cat occurred as a spontaneous mutation in farm cats in Scotland. The breed has been established by crosses to British Shorthair and domestic cats in Scotland and England. In America, the outcross is the American and British Shorthair. All bona fide Scottish Fold cats trace their pedigree to Susie.
BODY	Medium, rounded, and even from shoulder to pelvic girdle. The cat should stand firm with a well-padded body. There must be no hint of thickness or lack of mobility in the cat due to short, coarse legs. Overall appearance is that of a well-rounded cat with medium bone; fault cats obviously lacking in type.
HEAD	Well-rounded with a firm chin and jaw. Muzzle to have well-rounded whisker pads. Head should blend into a short neck. Prominent cheeks with a jowly appearance in males. Nose to be short with a gentle curve. A brief stop is permitted. Profile is moderate in appearance.
EARS	Ears fold forward and downward. Small, the smaller, tightly folded ear preferred over a loose fold and large ear. The ears should be set in a cap-like fashion to expose a rounded cranium. Ear tips to be rounded.
EYES	Wide open with a sweet expression. Large, well-rounded, and separated by a broad nose. Eye color to correspond with coat color. Blue eyed and odd eyed are allowed for all white and bicolor and van patterns.
LEGS AND PAWS	There must be no hint of thickness or lack of mobility in the cat due to short, coarse legs. Toes to be neat and well-rounded with five in front and four behind.
TAIL	Tail should be medium to long but in proportion to the body. Tail should be flexible and tapering which may end in a round tip. Longer, tapering tail preferred.
COAT— SHORTHAIR	Dense, plush, even. Short to medium-short in length. Soft in texture. Full of life. Standing away from body due to density, not flat or close lying. Coat texture may vary due to color and/or regional, seasonal changes.
COAT— LONGHAIR	Medium-long to long hair length. Full coat on face and body desirable, but short hair permissible on face and legs. Britches, tail plume, toe tufts, and ear furnishings should be clearly visible with a ruff being desirable.
COLOR	Any color or pattern with the exception of those showing evidence of hybridization resulting in the colors chocolate, lavender, the Himalayan pattern, or these combinations with white. Eye color appropriate to the dominant color of the cat. Odd eyed and blue eyed allowed in all bicolor and van patterns. Odd eyed will have one blue and one gold eye of equal color depth.

236

DISQUALIFY	Kinked tail. Tail that is foreshortened. Tail that is lacking in flexibility due to abnormally thick vertebrae. Splayed toes, incorrect number of toes. Any evidence of illness or poor health. Palpable nose break. Any color or pattern showing evidence of hybridization resulting in the colors chocolate, lavender, the pointed pattern, or combinations of these colors with white, etc.
ALLOWABLE OUTCROSSES	British Shorthair, American Shorthair.

breedings can result in both straight-eared and fold kittens. It's not readily apparent how many kittens' ears are going to fold in any given litter. Folds that lack the dominant Fold gene will have ordinary straight ears rather than folded ears and are called "straight-ear" or "pert-ear" Folds. Breeders play a waiting game until the ears fold down—or fail to do so. Even if the ears fold correctly, it's often difficult to tell at first if the ears will have the tight folds preferred in the show ring or the looser, pet-quality folds. Generally, three degrees of fold exist—single, double, or triple fold. Single fold is the loosest; generally a loose fold is pet quality rather than show quality. Most desirable is the triple fold—smaller, tightly folded ears that give the head a caplike appearance.

The straight-ear Folds born in Scottish Fold litters share all characteristics of their Scottish Fold ancestry except for the characteristic for which the Fold is named. Since many straight-eared Folds are born, some associations accept straight-ear Folds for championship under the names Scottish, Scottish Shorthair, and Scottish Longhair. These unfolded Folds are considered part of the Scottish Fold breed in the associations that accept the breed, and others accept them for registration and for breeding. Associations that recognize Straight Folds as breeds in their own right include UFO, the Australian Cat Federation (ACF), Livre Officiel des Origines Félines (LOOF), and the Coordinating Cat Council of Australia (CCCA).

The Fold occurred as a spontaneous mutation among barn cats in 1961 in Scotland.

Shorthaired colorpoint Selkirk Rex.

HISTORY

The Selkirk is the newest Rex breed to be recognized by the North American cat associations and has been around a relatively short time compared with the Cornish Rex and the Devon Rex. The Selkirk's development and promotion were due primarily to the efforts of breeder Jeri Newman of the Noface Cattery in Livington, Montana, although many other dedicated breeders lent a hand in furthering the breed.

Newman, a Persian breeder for many years, had always been fascinated by cats in general and feline genetics in particular, made it known to friends and family that she was interested in adopting cats that were in any way out of the ordinary. In 1987, the out-of-the-ordinary came to her. At the For Pet's Sake Animal Shelter in Sheridan, Montana, run out of the home of animal lover Kitty Garrett Brown, an ordinary cat gave birth to a litter of six—five ordinary kittens plus one kitten with a curly coat as plush and huggable as a child's stuffed toy. Peggy Vorrhees of the Bozeman Humane Society of Sheridan, Montana

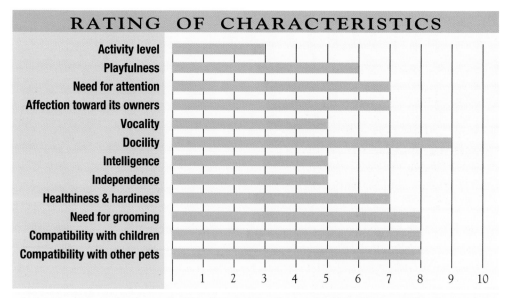

RATING OF CHARACTERISTICS

Characteristic	Rating
Activity level	3
Playfulness	6
Need for attention	7
Affection toward its owners	7
Vocality	5
Docility	9
Intelligence	5
Independence	5
Healthiness & hardiness	7
Need for grooming	6
Compatibility with children	8
Compatibility with other pets	8

1—breed exhibits the least amount of this characteristic, 10—breed exhibits the most of this characteristic

✳ **Championship status in AACE, ACFA, CCA, CFA, TICA, and UFO in both longhair and shorthair varieties**

brought the kitten to Jeri Newman because she thought Newman would be interested in the unusual-coated cat. Indeed she was. The blue-cream and white kitten with the alert green eyes and the extraordinary curly coat resembling lamb's wool caught Newman's immediate attention. At an estimated age of ten months, the cat's whiskers were curly, her ears were full of brillo-like hair, and her coat looked like she'd just had a body wave.

Newman named the cat Miss DePesto because she was always pestering Newman for attention. When "Pest" came of age, Newman bred her to Photo Finish of Deekay, one of her champion black Persian males. The mating produced a litter of six, three of which had the distinctive curly coat. Since Newman had studied genetic inheritance, she knew this meant the gene governing the curly coat was dominant—only one parent needed to possess the gene for the trait to appear in at least some of the offspring.

That litter also included one straight-haired kitten with long hair. Interesting, Newman thought. Not only did Pest carry the dominant curly-coat gene, but also the recessive gene for long hair, since both parents had to possess at least one copy of the longhair gene to produce longhaired offspring.

Newman then bred Pest to Pest's son, a curly black and white male named Oscar Kowalski. The resulting litter of four produced three more curly kittens, including one red point

shorthair male whom Newman named Snowman. This proved that Pest also carried the recessive gene for the pointed pattern, which she had passed on to her son Oscar. Clearly, Pest had a unique and diverse genetic makeup.

Newman named the breed the Selkirk Rex after her stepfather. However, for a time she said the breed was named after the Selkirk Mountains, because they were near where the kittens were born. However, when pointed out to her that the Selkirk Mountains were in British Columbia, she admitted to naming the breed after her stepfather; the Selkirk Rex is the only cat breed named after an individual.

The breed was presented to TICA's board of directors in 1990 and was accepted into the New Breed and Color class. The CFA accepted the breed for registration in the miscellaneous class in 1992. The Selkirk advanced to CFA provisional status on May 1, 1998, and in 2000 achieved the CFA championship status. The breed now has championship status with almost all North American cat associations.

PERSONALITY

One may be at first attracted to the Selkirk's cute and curly exterior, but fanciers say these cats also make champion companions. Selkirks are mellow cats with a generous measure of love and affection for their human companions. Very people-oriented, they stay loyal and loving all their

GENERAL	The Selkirk Rex is the result of a dominant, spontaneous mutation that causes each hair (guard, down and awn) to have a gentle curl giving the coat a soft feel. This is a medium to large cat with heavy boning that gives the cat surprising weight and an impression of power.
BODY	Medium to large and well-balanced. The substantial muscular torso is more rectangular than square, but not long. Back is straight with a slight rise to the hindquarters. Shoulders and hip should appear to be the same width.
HEAD	Skull round, broad, and full-cheeked in both males and females. Skull structure to be smooth and round to the touch from the stop to the back of the head as well as across the breadth of the forehead and between the ears. Muzzle is medium width. The underlying bone structure is rounded with well-padded whisker pads to give the impression of squareness. The length is equal to ½ the width. Profile shows a muzzle, clearly visible beyond the curve of the cheek. The tip of the chin lines up with the tip of the nose and the upper lip in the same vertical plane. Profile reveals a nose stop. The nose has a downward slant with a convex curve and is set below the eye line. Chin firm and well-developed, balanced in proportion to the rest of the head and should be neither receding, protruding, nor excessively massive.
EARS	Medium in size, broad at the base, tapering, set well apart. Should fit into (without distorting) the rounded contour of the head. Furnishings, if present, are curly.
EYES	Large, rounded, set well apart. The eyes should not appear almond or oval shaped. The outside corner is set very slightly higher than the inner corner, giving a sweet open expression to the face.
LEGS AND PAWS	Legs medium to long. Substantial boning. Should be in proportion to the body. Feet large, round, and firm. Toes: five in front, four behind.
TAIL	Medium length, proportionate to body. Heavy at base, neither blunt nor pointed at tip.
COAT— SHORTHAIR	Coat texture is soft, plushy, full, and obviously curly. Coat is dense and full with no bald or thinly covered areas of the body. The coat stands out from the body and should not appear flat or close-lying. Random, unstructured coat, arranged in loose, individual curls. The curls appear to be in clumps rather than as an all over wave. Although curl varies by hair length, sex, and age in an individual, the entire coat should show the effect of the rex gene. Curliness may be evident more around the neck, on the tail and the belly. Allowance should be made for less curl on younger adults and kittens.

COAT—LONGHAIR	Coat texture is soft, full, and obviously curly. It does not feel or appear to be as plush as the shorthair coat, however, should not appear to be thin. Coat is dense and full with no bald or thinly covered areas of the body. The coat may stand out from the body but may appear and feel less than plush, but not close-lying. Random, unstructured coat, arranged in loose, individual curls. The curls appear to be in clumps or ringlets rather than as an all over wave. Although curl varies by hair length, sex, and age in an individual, entire coat should show the effect of the rex gene. Curliness may be evident more around the neck, on the tail, and the belly. Allowance should be made for less curl on younger adults and kittens.
COLOR	All genetically possible colors and patterns. Cats with no more than a locket and/or button shall be judged in the color class of their basic color with no penalty for such locket or button.
DISQUALIFY	Extreme nose break, lack of visible muzzle, malocclusion, tail kinks, crossed eyes, obvious physical deformities, including polydactyl feet, no evidence of curl.
ALLOWABLE OUTCROSSES	British Shorthair, Persian, or Exotic. Kittens born on or after January 1, 2020 may have only Selkirk Rex parents.

lives. They are people-oriented cats that enjoy spending time with their preferred persons. Selkirks make very engaging, tolerant, and loving companions. They are human-oriented, enjoy sleeping with their human companions, and enjoy sitting on or by you. They are not overly demanding of attention, but very social and and love to interact with their people. They don't do well in isolation. Selkirks fit in well with other cats and dogs, and other family members.

The Persians, British Shorthairs, Exotics, and American Shorthairs used in the breeding program have mellowed the Selkirk temperament. Selkirks aren't couch cougars, however; Selkirk breeders, the lifeguards of the gene pool, have done their best to keep the pleasing personality. Breeders have worked hard to produce cats that are not only curly, but also have that wonderful affectionate, playful personality.

CONFORMATION

The Selkirk Rex's coat gene is dominant, meaning only one parent need possess the gene for the curly coat

Selkirk Rex are people-oriented and make champion companions.

The Selkirk Rex has earned championship status in most North American cat associations.

The coat goes through several stages as the cat develops. A Selkirk is curly at birth, then loses its curliness and slowly acquires it again at eight to ten months of age. The coat doesn't fully develop until the cat is two years old. Climate, season, and hormones (particularly in the females) can also influence the coat curl. Unlike the Devon Rex and the Cornish Rex, the Selkirk Rex comes in both long and short hair. Contrary to popular belief, Selkirks are not hypoallergenic and are not for people who are allergic to cats.

Since the Selkirk was developed using established breeds known to have inherited health problems, and is still crossed with these breeds today, it's likely some Selkirk lines have inherited some of these health concerns. In particular, it's vital to buy from a breeder who screens for polycystic kidney disease (PKD), which causes renal failure and is known to exist in Persian, Himalayan, Exotic, and British Shorthair lines. Fortunately, a PKD genetic test is available from the Veterinary Genetics Laboratory at the UC School of Veterinary Medicine, Davis, which can help breeders screen out affected breeding stock. Currently the VGL recommends the PKD1 test for British Shorthairs, Persians, Exotics, Scottish Folds, Burmillas, Himalayans, and Persian out-crosses. Be sure to talk to your breeder about this and any other health concerns, and buy from a breeder who tests for PKD and provides a written health guarantee. A veterinarian's health certificate at the time of sale is not enough, because the majority of these problems do not manifest until later in the cat's life.

to be expressed in the offspring. A cat that has received the Rex gene from one parent will produce Rex kittens at an approximate ratio of one Rex to one straight-coated kitten. The kittens born with straight coats do not carry the Rex gene at all. A cat receiving the gene for the Rex coat from both parents (called homozygous for the Rex gene) is a great boon for breeders, since the cat can be bred with an outcrossing, and all the resulting kittens will have the Rex coat. In addition, the fur of homozygous cats is curlier and softer than the coats of cats that possess only one copy of the gene.

HISTORY

The Siamese is one of the oldest breeds of domestic cat and has a history as long and colorful as the cat itself. The Siamese is also (arguably) the most recognizable breed on the planet. According to accounts, these sleek cats with the brilliant blue eyes and outspoken personality originated in Siam (now Thailand), where they lived in palaces and temples. They were treasured as companions of royalty and religious leaders for generations, and served as guardians of precious documents and valuables in the Buddhist temples. These sacred cats were thought to inherit transmigrated souls en route to the hereafter.

Early legends involving the Siamese are plentiful, including fanciful tales accounting for the cat's traits. One such story tells how a Siamese temple cat, charged with guarding a valuable vase, curled its tail around the vase and stared at it with such intensity that its eyes became permanently crossed. Another tale tells of Siamese cats appointed to guard precious rings; the cats kept the rings on their tails and kinks developed to keep the rings from sliding off.

Siamese are affectionately called Meezers.

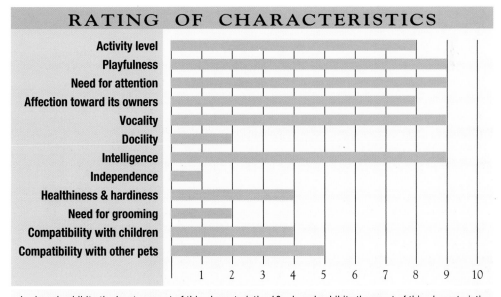

RATING OF CHARACTERISTICS

Characteristic	Rating
Activity level	8
Playfulness	9
Need for attention	8
Affection toward its owners	8
Vocality	9
Docility	2
Intelligence	9
Independence	1
Healthiness & hardiness	4
Need for grooming	1
Compatibility with children	4
Compatibility with other pets	5

1—breed exhibits the least amount of this characteristic, 10—breed exhibits the most of this characteristic

✳ Championship status in all associations

The Cat-Book Poems, a manuscript of verses and paintings written in the city of Ayutthaya, Siam, some time between 1350 C.E. when the kingdom was founded, and 1767 C.E. when the city was destroyed by invaders, clearly show cats with slim bodies and legs, and pale-colored coats with dark coloring on the ears, faces, tails, and feet. When the book was written can't be more accurately determined since these manuscripts were handwritten on palm-leaf or bark parchment. When a manuscript became too old, it was painstakingly copied by hand when the original and subsequent copies became too old and fragile to be usable. This makes it difficult to date. Still, it's likely the oldest document about cats in existence.

Because the Siamese was so valued in its native land the cats were rarely given to outsiders. However, it's clear that by the 1800s the Siamese had been exported to Britain. Siamese cats were exhibited in 1871 in the first modern-style cat show at The Crystal Palace in Sydenham, London. At the event, one journalist of the time disparagingly described the breed as "an unnatural, nightmare kind of cat."

Despite this bad press, the Siamese rapidly became popular among British fanciers. At that time, the Siamese were noted for their crossed eyes and kinked tails; these didn't become conformation faults until later. The first British standard, written in 1892 and rewritten in 1902, described the

Siamese as a "striking-looking cat of medium size, if weighty, not showing bulk, as this would detract from the admired svelte appearance... also distinguished by a kink in the tail."

Siamese must have become used to posh dwellings from its years with royalty; the first Siamese imported to North America lived in the White House. This well-documented account occurred in November of 1878, when David B. Sickels, a U.S. diplomat stationed at the consulate in Bangkok, sent a Siamese cat to first lady Lucy Hayes. In a letter that can be viewed in the Paper Trail archives of the Rutherford B. Hayes Presidential Center, Sickels wrote, "I have taken the liberty of forwarding you one of the finest specimens of Siamese cats that I have been able to procure in this country . . . I am informed that this is the first attempt ever made to send a Siamese cat to America."

By the early 1900s, Siamese cats began appearing in North American cat shows. The breed rapidly clawed its way to the top of the cat fancy's scratching post, and today is one of most popular shorthaired breed in North America. Due to its popularity, the breed has been used in the matrix of many modern cat breeds, including the Ocicat, Himalayan, Burmese, Tonkinese, and Oriental breeds, such as the Oriental Shorthair, Oriental Longhair, and the Balinese.

Although the Extreme Siamese is favored in the show ring, the Old-Style Siamese (known as the Thai in TICA and some of the European associations; see profile on page 270) has an enthusiastic following of breeders and fanciers who prefer this moderate type of Siamese. In some associations, the Thai is synonymous with "Old-Style Siamese"; CFF accepts the Old-Style Siamese for championship, and UFO accepts the Old-Style Siamese, the Old-Style Balinese, and the Old-Style Colorpoint for championship. Other fanciers refer to this type by the term "Applehead," which is more colloquial and informal. These fanciers believe the Old-Style's rounder, heavier body style is closer to the original type that existed before humans began selectively breeding for a svelte body style and elongated head type.

Extreme breeders, on the other hand, believe that the Extreme body style is the original look, which became adulterated through dubious crosses in the early years. They are dedicated to preserving the natural, sleek elegance of the Extreme Siamese. Extreme and Old-Style Siamese fanciers continue to hiss at each other over the difference in style, and it's difficult to say who is correct. The illustrations of the Siamese in the *Cat-Book Poems* show cats with long, slender legs and tails; however, the body type could be interpreted as either Extreme or Old-Style,

Because the Siamese were so valued in their native land, they were rarely given to outsiders.

depending upon one's point of view. Both sides agree on one thing, though: Siamese make wonderful companions. If you're looking for a cat with personality, an impish nature, and a talent for conversation, both the Extreme and the Old-Style will fit the bill. If you're looking for success in the show ring, the Extreme is favored in many associations.

PERSONALITY

Some cats seem to think that a purr or a friendly rub speaks louder than words. Meezers (as Siamese are affectionately called) are not of this school of thought and are known for their talent for clearly communicating their ideas and desires to their human servants. If you can't be drawn into dialogue, they're happy to keep up a running monologue for your enlightenment. No meaningless

245

Siamese are known for their talent for clearly communicating their ideas and desires.

ligent and if you don't give them something to do, they will find something to do that you may not approve of quite as much. This breed needs daily periods of play and interaction; it's critical to the Siamese's emotional and mental health and well-being. They should not be left alone for long periods; this is not a breed you can pat on the head and leave for twelve hours. Siamese will pine and become depressed if left too often alone, and may become destructive out of the frustrated craving for social interaction. The feline companionship of another Siamese or a comparatively active breed will help keep a lonely Siamese happy while you're away, but there is no substitute for human interaction. Moreover, remember two Siamese can think up twice as much mischief to get into while you're out earning the cat food.

This breed is not for those looking for a quiet companion—Siamese need to be treated with patience and require lots of attention and affection if they are to have the close, caring relationship they require with their human companions. For those who want a soul mate cat companion, however, this is your breed. Siamese are usually good family pets and are tolerant of children at least eight and older, as long as the children are taught how to properly handle cats and don't play too rough.

meows, these, but real attempts at communication, according to Siamese fans. To some cat lovers, who prefer their felines seen and not heard, the Siamese rasp (some would say yowl) can be a bit annoying. However, Meezer worshippers wouldn't have it any other way. According to fans, Meezers are the most wonderful, loving, entertaining cats in the known universe.

Siamese are very intelligent, self-assured, playful, determined, curious, and highly active. They love their human companions with a passion; living with the Siamese is a bit like living with exceedingly active children. Except these "children" follow you everywhere, demanding to be involved in whatever you're doing. Determinedly social and very dependent upon their humans, Meezers crave active involvement in your life. They are superintel-

CONFORMATION

Siamese come in four or more colors, depending upon the cat association to which you belong. The CFA recognizes four Siamese colors and one pattern: sealpoint, chocolate point, blue point, and lilac point (called frost in some associations). Solid blues and browns were well documented in *The Cat-Book Poems*, so it's not surprising that the dilute colors chocolate point and lilac point were appearing in Siamese lines early on. Siamese in red point (also called flame point) and cream point, tortie point (mottled mixtures of black and red or their dilute colors in the point areas, also called tortoiseshell), or lynx point (tabby stripes in the point areas) are called Colorpoint Shorthair in CCA, CFA, and UFO, although AACE, ACFA, CFF, and TICA consider these color variations of the Siamese. The red and cream colors were produced by foundation crossings between Siamese, Abyssinians, and red domestic shorthairs. In general, these colors are accepted, depending upon the association: sealpoint, chocolate point, blue point, lilac point, red point, and cream point; lynx point in seal, chocolate, blue, lilac, red, and cream; tortie point in seal, chocolate, blue, and lilac; and tortie lynx point in seal, chocolate, blue, and lilac.

The Himalayan pattern, as the pointed or point-restricted pattern is often called, was named after the rabbit that exhibits the same coat pattern. The color is restricted to the face mask, ears, legs, and tail, while the body remains a lighter color. The concentration of color is kept to the point areas by a temperature-controlled enzyme that creates greater depth of color at the parts of the body farthest away from the cardiovascular system. The cooler the environment, the darker the color becomes.

Siamese kittens are born white, because of the warmth of their mother's body, and develop their point color as they get older.

Siamese are generally healthy, and it's not uncommon for them to live fifteen years or older if kept indoors. However, like most breeds, some lines have genetic problems that have been concentrated through years of selective breeding. In particular, hereditary liver amyloidosis has been found in some Siamese bloodlines. The disease causes an insoluble protein called amyloid to be deposited in the liver, causing lesions, dysfunction, and eventual liver failure.

In addition, incidences of dilated cardiomyopathy, an enlargement of the heart muscle that decreases heart function, have been found in some lines of Siamese, but on the plus side they seem to be at a lower risk than some other pedigreed breeds for the more serious and often fatal feline hypertrophic cardiomyopathy (HCM).

In addition, some Siamese lines are prone to plaque buildup, tartar formation, and gingivitis. Gingivitis can lead to the dental disease periodontitis (an inflammatory disease affecting the tissues surrounding and supporting the teeth), which can cause tissue, bone, and tooth loss. Untreated, dental disease can undermine a cat's overall health. Siamese need annual veterinary checkups, periodic teeth cleaning by your veterinarian and, if your cat will tolerate it, regular tooth brushing using cat toothpaste and a cat toothbrush. Ask your breeder about these and any other concerns you may have, and buy from a breeder who offers a written health guarantee.

GENERAL	The ideal Siamese is a medium-sized, svelte, refined cat with long tapering lines, very lithe but muscular. Males may be proportionately larger. Balance and refinement are the essence of the breed, where all parts come together in a harmonious whole, with neither too much nor too little consideration given to any one feature.
BODY	Medium size. Graceful, long, and svelte. A distinctive combination of fine bones and firm muscles. Shoulders and hips continue same sleek lines of tubular body. Hips never wider than shoulders. Abdomen tight.
HEAD	Long tapering wedge. Medium in size in good proportion to body. The total wedge starts at the nose and flares out in straight lines to the tips of the ears forming a triangle, with no break at the whiskers. No less than the width of an eye between the eyes. When the whiskers are smoothed back, the underlying bone structure is apparent. Skull flat. In profile, a long straight line is seen from the top of the head to the tip of the nose. No bulge over eyes. No dip in nose. Nose long and straight. A continuation of the forehead with no break. Muzzle fine, wedge shaped.
EARS	Strikingly large, pointed, wide at base; continuing the lines of the wedge.
EYES	Almond shaped. Medium size. Neither protruding nor recessed. Slanted towards the nose in harmony with lines of wedge and ears. Uncrossed. Color deep vivid blue.
LEGS AND PAWS	Legs long and slim. Hind legs higher than front. In good proportion to body. Paws dainty, small, and oval. Toes: five in front and four behind.
TAIL	Long, thin, tapering to a fine point.
COAT	Short, fine textured, glossy. Lying close to body.
COLOR	Pointed pattern in seal, blue, chocolate, and lilac point.
DISQUALIFY	Any evidence of illness or poor health. Weak hind legs. Mouth breathing due to nasal obstruction or poor occlusion. Emaciation. Visible kink. Eyes other than blue. White toes and/or feet. Incorrect number of toes. Malocclusion resulting in either undershot or overshot chin. Longhair.
ALLOWABLE OUTCROSSES	None.

HISTORY

This breed may be new to North America, but it's far from new to the world. Longhaired Russian cats have been around for many hundreds of years. Exactly when and how longhaired cats made their way to Siberia is not known, but it is speculated that the breed arrived with Russian emigrants. According to some Siberian fanciers, Russians immigrating (or being exiled) to Siberia brought their cats with them. The mutation for long hair seems to have occurred in three separate areas—Russia, Persia (Iran), and Asia Minor (Turkey). However, it's possible that the long-hair mutation originally occurred in Russia and that Russian Longhairs spread from Russia into Turkey, crossbreeding with local cats to become the Angora, and into Persia, cross-breeding with local cats to become the Persian. If so, all longhairs are derived from the Russian Longhair. Long fur in domestic cats appears to

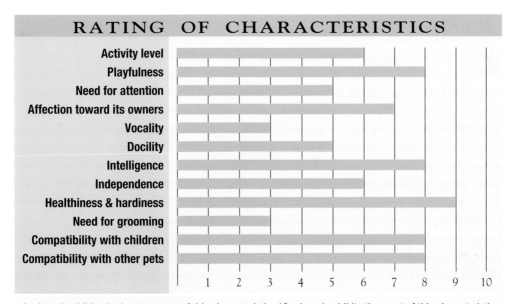

Classic tabby Siberian.

RATING OF CHARACTERISTICS

Characteristic	Rating (1–10)
Activity level	6
Playfulness	8
Need for attention	5
Affection toward its owners	7
Vocality	3
Docility	5
Intelligence	8
Independence	6
Healthiness & hardiness	9
Need for grooming	3
Compatibility with children	8
Compatibility with other pets	8

1—breed exhibits the least amount of this characteristic, 10—breed exhibits the most of this characteristic

✳ Championship status with all cat associations

be an adaptation to cold, and it's certainly cold in Siberia. Due to the merciless climate, these cats developed, or acquired through mating with the local cats, longer hair, all-weather coats, and larger, stockier bodies. The cats survived and developed into a hardy, longhaired breed able to withstand the unforgiving conditions of the region. According to Russian stories, Siberian cats once weighed up to 45 pounds and protected their human companions and households "no worse than a dog."

In Harrison Weir's 1889 book, *Our Cats and All About Them*, he noted in the chapter on longhaired cats the varieties of longhaired cats that existed in his time, and were shown in his famous modern cat show in July 1871 at the Crystal Palace in London, were the Russian, Angora, Persian, and Indian. Weir, known as "the Father of the Cat Fancy," wrote that the Russian Longhair

differs from Angoras and Persians in a number of ways, including its larger size, longer mane, large prominent bright orange eyes, and its long, dense, woolly textured coat including the tail that's thickly covered with very woolly hair. However, the Russian longhairs who shared the limelight at the show may or may not have been Siberians, since apparently no records of these cats were kept in Russia at that time. Harrison Weir wrote that he was not able to discover from where in Russia the cats originated.

Breeder Elizabeth Terrell of Baton Rouge, Louisiana, is credited with bringing the Siberian to the North American cat fancier. As a Himalayan breeder and aficionado of Russian culture, Terrell responded to a 1988 article in a cat publication asking for breeders willing to donate or trade Himalayans to help establish the breed in Russia. Excited about this idea, she contacted Nelli Sachuk, a member of Saint Petersburg's Kotofei (COT-ah-fay) Cat Club, which is a member of the international division of ACFA. Kotofei, named after a fabled Russian character who had the head of a cat, was one of the few Russian cat clubs to extend official pedigrees.

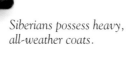

Siberians possess heavy, all-weather coats.

Until the 1980s, the government of the former Soviet Union discouraged its citizens from owning household pets, pedigreed or otherwise, because of housing and food shortages. Most cats living in Russia were working cats that earned their keep by ridding barns, fields, and factories of vermin. In 1987, the government lifted restrictions on house pets, and breeders and fanciers formed cat clubs and began keeping breeding records. In 1988, the first Russian cat show was held in Moscow.

Terrell sent four Himalayans to Nelli Sachuk and in exchange received three Siberians on June 28, 1990—one male (Kaliostro Vasenjkovich) and two females (Ofelia Romanova and Naina Romanova). Soon after, she received the kittens' metrukas (certificates of birth), which detailed their names, dates of birth, and colors and patterns. Before long, the Siberian had captivated Terrell's heartstrings and purse strings. She invested thousands of dollars and expended many hours obtaining more cats and establishing the Siberian as a recognized breed in America.

Just a month after Elizabeth Terrell received her Siberians, breeder David Boehm imported a number of Siberians of his own. Instead of waiting for cats to be sent, he booked a flight to Russia and bought every Siberian he could find. On July 4 he returned with a collection of fifteen cats. His Siberians produced the first litter in North America, and were invaluable in enlarging the Siberian gene pool. Other breeders and fanciers soon joined Terrell and Boehm, and they began the long process of winning association acceptance. Terrell wrote the first North American standard based on the Russian standard, adapted to American cat fancy terms.

Terrell contacted the cat associations to announce her new arrivals and to start the process toward acceptance for the Siberian. She kept careful records over the years, which provided documentation, and asked for help from breeders, fanciers, and judges to support, promote, and propagate the breed. ACFA was affiliated with Russia's Kotofei Cat Club, and this association was the first to accept the breed for registration. Within a few months, other associations followed suit.

Terrell and other breeders formed an inter-registry breed club called Taiga (pronounced Tie-GAH), named after the Taiga forests of Siberia. Their goal is to help maintain the breed's purity and to promote the breed in the cat fancy. Terrell's and other breeders' concern about the breed was that getting true stock was difficult and time-consuming, and not every feline called a Siberian was actually pedigreed. Unless the cat is registered with one of the Russian cat clubs, complete with a certificate of birth, it might be just one of the longhaired random-bred domestics available very inexpensively in the Russian markets. Too, since it had become known that Americans would pay hard cash for Siberians, some cats have been misrepresented. Other people, uninformed about the differences between pedigreed and mixed breeds, will represent their cats as Siberians, just as many Americans will call any longhaired cat Persian or Angora. Buying a Siberian from Russia from now on, says Terrell, will be a little like

GENERAL

The Siberian, Russia's native forest cat, first appeared in recorded history around the year 1000 and hails from the unforgiving climate of Siberia. This is a cat that nature designed to survive, with no extremes in type. The Siberian is a medium to medium large, strong triple-coated cat with surprising heft for its size. The overall appearance should be one of strength, presence, and alertness, with a sweet facial expression. The breed is extremely slow to mature taking as long as 5 years.

BODY

Body is medium in length, and well-muscled with the back arched slightly higher than the shoulders, with a barrel-shaped, firm belly giving the sensation of solid weight. Moderate stomach pad or famine pouch on lower abdomen acceptable. Boning substantial. Musculature substantial, powerful.

HEAD

Modified wedge of medium/large size with rounded contours, in good proportion to the body. The head is broader at the top of the skull and narrows slightly to a full-rounded muzzle. The cheekbones are neither high set nor prominent. There should be a slight doming between the ears and an almost flat area on the forehead. Chin is well-rounded but not protruding, and is in line with the nose. Muzzle is moderately short in length, full and rounded. There is a slight muzzle curvature, but the transition between the side of the head and the muzzle is gentle and inconspicuous. Top of the head is almost flat, with a slight nose curvature of a gentle slope from the forehead to the nose and a slight concave curvature before the tip when viewed in profile. Neck rounded, sturdy, and well-muscled.

EARS

Medium-large, rounded, wide at the base, and tilt slightly forward. The ears should be set as much on the sides of the head as on top. The hair over the back of the ear is short and thin. From the middle of the ear, the furnishings become longer and cover the base of the ear. Ear tipping is allowed.

EYES

Medium to large, almost round. The outer corner angled slightly towards the base of the ear. The eyes should be set more than one eye's width apart and should be open, alert, and expressive. There is no relationship between eye color and coat/color pattern except in the color points which have blue eyes. Eye color should be shades of green, gold, green-gold, or copper. White cats and cats with white may have blue or odd eyes.

LEGS AND PAWS

Legs medium in length. The legs should have substantial boning with the hind legs slightly longer than the front legs. Feet are big and rounded, with toe tufts desirable.

TAIL

Medium in length, being somewhat shorter than the length of the body. It should be wide at the base, tapering slightly to a blunt tip without thickening or kinks, evenly and thickly furnished.

COAT	Moderately long to longhaired cat with a triple coat. The hair on the shoulder blades and lower part of the chest should be thick and slightly shorter. Abundant full collar ruff setting off the head in adults. Allow for warm weather coats. The hair may thicken to curls on the belly and britches, but a wavy coat is not characteristic. Texture varies from coarse to soft, varying according to color. There is a tight undercoat (in mature cats), thicker in cold weather.
COLOR	All colors and combinations are accepted with or without white. White is allowed in any amount and in all areas. White or off-white allowed on chin, breast, and stomach of tabbies. Buttons, spots, and lockets are allowed. Strong colors and clear patterns are desirable. Tarnishing on silvers not penalized.
DISQUALIFY	Kinked tail, incorrect number of toes, crossed eyes. Evidence of illness, poor health, emaciation.
ALLOWABLE OUTCROSSES	None.

playing Russian roulette. Fortunately, a number of North American breeders have established Siberian catteries, so today there's little need to import Siberians from Russia. The Siberian has really caught on with fanciers; it's now accepted for championship in every North American cat association.

PERSONALITY

Siberians are affectionate cats with a good dose of personality and playfulness. They are amenable to handling, and breeders note that Siberians have a fascination with water, often dropping toys into their water dishes or investigating bathtubs before they're dry. Siberians seem very intelligent, with the ability to problem-solve to get what they want. Despite their size, they are very agile and are great jumpers, able to leap tall bookcases in a single bound.

Siberian with green/gold eyes. This breed's eyes are large, alert, and expressive.

Siberians are very people-oriented, and need to be near their owners. They'll meet you at the door when you come home and tell you about their day, and want to hear about yours. Siberians are talkative but not nearly as chatty as Oriental breeds; they express themselves using quiet meows, trills, chirps, and lots of motorboat-type purring. They like sitting on your lap while they're being groomed, an activity they particularly enjoy.

Another favorite game is bringing a toy for you to throw again and again—and again. They love all types of toys—and will make a toy out of just about anything. Nature shows on TV with chirping birds or squeaking mice will bring your Siberians running; they'll put gentle feet on the screen and try to catch the fluttering images.

CONFORMATION

Today's Siberians are gentle giants, one of the largest breeds of domestic cat. Breeders note that Siberian males range between fifteen and twenty-five pounds, and the females range between twelve and seventeen pounds. As befits a cat who has survived the harsh climate of Siberia, the Siberian possesses a long, thick coat with a full ruff and a tight undercoat that becomes thicker in cold weather. The coat's oily guard hairs give the coat its classic water resistance. All colors and patterns are accepted including pointed colors; pointed Siberians in Russia are called Nevsky Masquerades.

This breed is relatively new to North America, but so far the Siberian seems to be a healthy, hardy cat with few known breed-related health problems. The most serious health concern is one that affects many breeds and many random-bred cats as well, the inher-ited heart disease feline hypertonic cardiomyopathy (HMC). HMC is a life threatening heart disease; the first noticeable symptom of HCM is often sudden death. Talk to your breeder about these and any other health concerns and buy from a breeder who offers a written health guarantee. Schools of veterinary medicine, such as UC Davis and organizations, such as the Winn Feline Foundation are working to find ways to treat and find a genetic cure for disease. In 2008, the Winn Foundation funded a study to research familial HCM in the Siberian. Siberian breeder groups raised funds and collected samples to help with the research.

Some breeders claim that Siberians are hypoallergenic, or at least better tolerated than other breeds by people who are sensitive or allergic to cats. Studies have yet to prove this; in fact samples of Siberian fur sent to several laboratories for testing were found to possess Fel d1, the protein which is secreted in the cat's saliva and sebaceous glands and which causes allergic symptoms, although some showed lower levels than average. No breed of cat is hypoallergenic; be wary of anyone who tells you otherwise. Since allergies vary in severity from person to person, it is impossible to say with certainty how a person will react to any particular cat or breed. Spend quality time with fully mature Siberians before agreeing to buy, since kittens may not have begun producing as much Fel d1 as they will when they're older. If you don't live close to a Siberian breeder, try to find a breeder who will send you locks of Siberian hair so you can be tested. Siberians are relatively expensive, so it's wise to be sure.

HISTORY

Singapore, an island spanning 226 square miles (585 sq km) perched off the tip of the Malay Peninsula in Southeast Asia, has scores of feral felines, as do many seaports. These cats make their livings off the leavings of the fishing trade, and in the past were not paid much attention unless they became nuisances, and then they were picked up by the feline police and summarily dealt with. It is a hard life for these nomads and, far from being praised as pedigrees, they were disparagingly known as "drain" or "sewer" cats by the denizens of the island.

Small brown cats with ticked coats have been observed on the isle since at least 1965. This variety, however, is not the only kind of cat found on the island; other varieties include solid-colored cats, deeper-colored ticked cats that often have short, bobbed tails, and cats that display the white spotting factor.

The Singapura breed as we know it in North America has made the Guinness Book of World Records as the smallest breed of domestic cat, had an advertising campaign centered around it to

Singapuras love to be the center of attention.

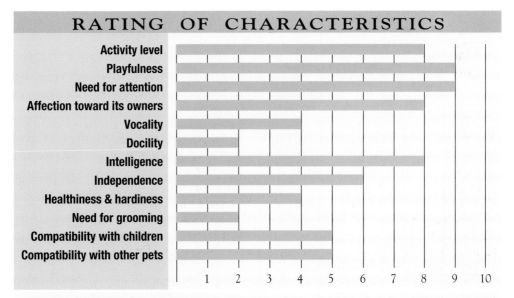

RATING OF CHARACTERISTICS

Characteristic	Rating
Activity level	8
Playfulness	9
Need for attention	9
Affection toward its owners	8
Vocality	4
Docility	4
Intelligence	8
Independence	6
Healthiness & hardiness	3
Need for grooming	2
Compatibility with children	5
Compatibility with other pets	5

1—breed exhibits the least amount of this characteristic, 10—breed exhibits the most of this characteristic

✳ Championship status in all associations

These little lions of love are playful, curious, and almost too intelligent.

promote tourism to the Republic of Singapore, and had the dubious distinction of being caught in the center of a cat controversy.

In 1975, Tommy and Hal Meadow returned from Singapore with three ticked, sepia-colored cats by the names of Tess, Tickle, and Pusse. Tommy Meadow, former CFF judge and Abyssinian and Burmese breeder active in the cat fancy since 1955, wrote a standard for the breed and began a breeding program to weed out undesirable traits and produce consistency in color, coat, pattern, and temperament. The breed was promoted under the name Singapura, the Malaysian name for Singapore.

In 1980, another breeder obtained a fourth cat from the Singapore SPCA that matched the Singapura's description; that cat was also incorporated

into the breeding program. Tommy Meadow founded the United Singapura Society, whose stated goal was to protect, preserve, and promote the Singapura. The CFA accepted the Singapura for registration in 1982, and granted championship status in 1988. The other associations soon followed CFA's lead and accepted the breed.

Singapura breeders not affiliated with the Meadows' United Singapura Society became concerned about the breed's small litter sizes, which they believed was an indication of inbreeding resulting from the four-cat foundation, and worried about the Tommy Meadow's unwillingness to allow other Singapore cats to be imported to widen the gene pool. Because of these and other disagreements, other breed clubs were formed, such as the International Singapura Alliance. Additional Singapore cats were imported by these breeders in the mid-1980s to provide additional Singapura bloodlines.

More controversy arose in 1987, when breeder Jerry Mayes made a Singapura-gathering trip to Singapore. Mayes brought back a dozen Singapore cats, and some surprising news: when Hal and Tommy Meadow entered Singapore in 1974, they already had three cats named Tess, Tickle, and Puss. Mayes alerted Singapore reporter Sandra Davie, and in August 1990, Sandra Davie interviewed Tommy Meadow for an article in Singapore's *The Straits Times*. Tommy admitted to Davie that Tess, Tickle, and Puss, which she originally claimed she found in Singapore in 1974, had been born in America and transported to Singapore when she and her husband Hal moved there in 1974. Tess, Tickle, and Pusse were the grandchildren of Singapore cats Hal sent to Tommy in Galveston, Texas, via a company ship when he was in Singapore on business in 1971.

Tommy explained that after she allowed the cats to mate, she became convinced that the cats could be the foundation of a breed unknown to the North American cat fancy, and decided to breed and promote them as such. However, because of the confidential nature of Hal's work (collecting information for the geophysical company for which he was employed), Hal insisted that Tommy not tell the true origin of Tess, Tickle, and Pusse. Since she did not keep records of the original matings of those first three cats and didn't remember who mated to whom, Tommy maintained that, for all practical purposes, the breed began in 1974, when she began keeping detailed records.

In February 1991, Tommy and Hal Meadow were invited to appear before the CFA Board of Directors to explain the discrepancy, and they reiterated this story to CFA's Board. Hal produced several passports and visas to document his visits to Singapore and said that, since the cats originally came to the United States via a company ship, no import or export papers were filed for the cats.

The CFA board found no probable cause of wrongdoing and took no action against the Meadows; nor did any other association revoke recognition of the breed. The Singapore tour-

ist promotion board apparently came to the same conclusion since they continued with an advertising campaign featuring the Singapura as their national mascot, importing two Singapuras from the United States to serve as models for statues to represent "Singapore's National Treasure."

Other fanciers and breeders, however, were not willing to let the matter go, believing that the Singapura was actually the product of Abyssinian/Burmese crosses produced in Texas and transported to Singapore as a money-making scheme. They pointed to the similarities in type and ticking.

Other fanciers felt that it mattered little whether the Singapura was imported from Singapore in 1971 or in 1975. Proponents pointed out that the Singapura ticked pattern resembling the Abyssinian's does not necessarily prove anything more than a common ancestry, since the Abyssinian is thought to have originated on the Malay Peninsula, swimming distance (if you're a really strong swimmer) from the island of Singapore. The Burmese originally hails from that part of the world as well. However, skeptics pointed out that someone wishing to perpetuate a scam, someone familiar with those breeds, would have chosen the breeds for that reason.

Today, few fanciers worry about the past controversy. The Singapura is accepted by all North American associations, as well as Europe's Governing Council of the Cat Fancy (GCCF). Even those who didn't believe the Meadows's story believe in the charming personality of the Singapura.

PERSONALITY

The Singapura took its name from the Malay word for the Republic of Singapore, Singapura, which means "lion city." That's why Singapuras are known as little lions of love. Puras, happily unaware of the controversy that surrounded their creation, go right on being what they are: pesky people pleasers. At home in any situation, Puras love to be the center of attention, and they don't seem to know the word stranger; they're at the door with you to welcome anyone, whether they're friends and family, or door to door salespeople. They're curious, people-oriented, and remain playful well into old age. Their voices are quiet and unobtrusive even when they're in season, and they trust their humans implicitly.

Puras are not quite as active as Abyssinians, but they are plenty spirited nonetheless. These are busy cats with a daily agenda. They're curious, affectionate, almost too intelligent, and are very much in tune with their favorite humans' moods. They want to help with everything, whether you want them to or not. They help cook, clean, and help you make the beds as long as you don't mind little furry lumps under the covers. Most important, they are as affectionate as they are active. As soon as a human friend provides an empty lap, they stop zipping around and settle in for a good session of petting, purring, forehead kisses, and loving looks from those large, liquid, trusting eyes.

CONFORMATION

The Singapura possesses the dominant ticked tabby gene, which produces alternating bands of color on each individual hair, the same gene that gives the Abyssinian its distinctive coat. The coat color is modified by the Burmese gene, which results in a warm brown color (sepia), alternating with a warm, old ivory ground color. This gives the coat the appearance of refined, delicate coloration. Both of these genes are believed to have originated in Southeast Asia. Unlike the Abyssinian, the Singapura's standard calls for some barring on the inner front legs. Adult male Singapuras weigh in at a flyweight of around six pounds (2.7 kg), and females tip the scales at approximately four pounds (1.8 kg).

Puras have few genetic defects but, like their cousin the Aby, they are prone to plaque, tartar buildup, and gingivitis. Untreated, gingivitis can lead to the dental disease periodontitis that can lead to tooth, tissue, and bone loss, which can undermine a Singapura's overall health. Erythrocyte Pyruvate Kinase Deficiency (PK Deficiency) is an inherited hemolytic anemia that occurs in Abyssinian, Somali, and some other shorthair cats; it has been found in some Singapura lines. The deficiency of this regu-

GENERAL	The appearance of an alert healthy small- to medium-sized muscular bodied cat with noticeably large eyes and ears in proportion to its head. Cat to have the illusion of refined delicate coloring.
BODY	Small to medium overall size cat. Moderately stocky and muscular body, legs, and floor to form a square. Mid-section not tucked but firm. Neck tends toward short and thick.
HEAD	Skull rounded front to back and side to side with rounded width at the outer eye narrowing to a definite whisker break and a medium-short, broad muzzle with a blunt nose. In profile, a rounded skull with a slight curve well below eye level. Straight line nose to chin. Chin well developed.
EARS	Large, slightly pointed, wide open at the base, and possessing a deep cup. Medium set. Outer lines of the ear to extend upward at an angle slightly wide of parallel. Small ears a serious fault.
EYES	Large, almond shaped, held wide open but showing slant. Neither protruding nor recessed. Eyes set not less than an eye width apart. Color hazel, green, or yellow with no other color permitted. Brilliance preferred. Small eyes a serious fault.
LEGS AND PAWS	Legs heavy and muscled at the body tapering to small short oval feet.
TAIL	Length to be short of the shoulder when laid along the torso. Tending toward slender but not whippy. Blunt tip.
COAT	Fine, very short, silky texture, lying very close to the body. Springy coat a fault.
COLOR	Sepia agouti only.
DISQUALIFY	White spotting, barring on tail, top of the head unticked, unbroken necklaces, or leg bracelets. Very small eyes or ears. Visible tail faults. Blue eyes. Any color other than sepia agouti (dark brown ticking on an old ivory undercoat).
ALLOWABLE OUTCROSSES	None.

latory enzyme causes an instability of red blood cells that leads to anemia. Fortunately, a genetic test is available at the Veterinary Genetics Laboratory (VGL) at the University of California, Davis. This tool helps breeders screen out affected or carrier cats. Before you buy, ask if the breeder screens for PK deficiency and provides written health guarantees.

SOMALI

HISTORY

No one knows for sure when and where the first Somali appeared; some proponents think that the long coat was a spontaneous natural mutation in the Abyssinian. Genetic studies indicate, however, that the Somali probably originated around the turn of the century in England when breeders, low on breeding stock, used longhaired cats in their Abyssinian breeding programs. In the late 1910s and in the late 1940s, during the aftermath of World Wars I and II, when so many breeds had dwindled to near extinction, breeders were forced to mix other breeds into their Abyssinian bloodlines to keep the breed going. Raby Chuffa of Selene, a male Abyssinian that came to the United States from Britain in 1953, and that appears on the pedigrees of many Abyssinians, is considered the father of the Somali breed on this continent; all Canadian and American Somalis can be traced back to this cat.

Raby Chuffa's pedigree can be traced back to Roverdale Purrkins, an English Abyssinian female whose dam, Mrs. Mews, was of unknown ancestry and probably carried the

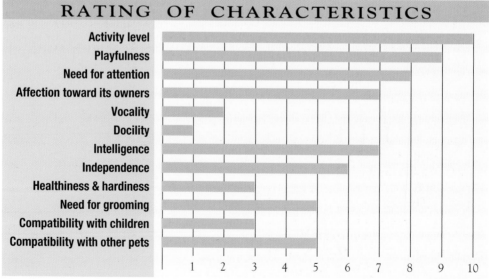

The Somali's ruff and breeches gives the cat a full-coated appearance.

RATING OF CHARACTERISTICS

Characteristic	Rating (1–10)
Activity level	10
Playfulness	9
Need for attention	8
Affection toward its owners	7
Vocality	2
Docility	1
Intelligence	7
Independence	6
Healthiness & hardiness	3
Need for grooming	3
Compatibility with children	4
Compatibility with other pets	5

1—breed exhibits the least amount of this characteristic, 10—breed exhibits the most of this characteristic

260

✳ **Championship status in all associations**

longhair gene. Mrs. Mews was given to breeder Janet Robertson by a sailor during WWII. Mrs. Mews later produced two kittens: Roverdale Purrkins, registered as an Abyssinian, and a black unregistered male. Robertson used Purrkins to start her Roverdale cattery. Her cats and other Abyssinians of British origin were exported to Europe, Australia, New Zealand, Canada, and the United States.

When longhaired kittens cropped up in Abyssinian litters (possible whenever two Abyssinians carrying the recessive gene for long hair were bred together), the kittens were quietly given away, since no breeder wanted to be thought to have Abyssinian lines that were "tainted" with the longhair gene. It wasn't until the 1960s that breeders, seeing the appeal of a longhaired version of a breed that was rapidly gaining popularity in North America, began seriously trying to turn these castaways into a breed of their own. At the same time, breeders in Canada, Europe, Australia, and New Zealand began working with the new breed as well.

Some Abyssinian breeders wanted nothing to do with these longhaired nonconformists and did not want to encourage the connection that the name "Longhaired Abyssinian" would produce. Abyssinian breeder Evelyn Mague, one of the first U.S. breeders to work with the longhaired breed after finding two of her Abyssinians, Lynn-Lee's Lord Dublin and Lo-Mi-R's Trill-By, carried the longhair gene. She came up with the name "Somali" because Somalia borders Ethiopia, the country formerly called Abyssinia for which the Abyssinian was named.

In 1972, Mague founded the Somali Cat Club of America and began bringing the Somali enthusiasts together. In 1975, the CFA-affiliated International Somali Cat Club was founded, and in 1979, the Somali earned championship status in the CFA. Since then, the breed has steadily gained popularity and has won over the opposition. Today, the Somali has championship status in all the North American registries, as well as with the Governing Council of the Cat Fancy (GCCF).

PERSONALITY

Don't get a Somali if you want a cat that can be taken for a furry doorstop, or if you want a cat that's just going to lie around the house all day. With all the virtues of the Abyssinian and adorned by a gorgeous semi-long coat, the Somali is a beautiful and

Ruddy Somali.

GENERAL	The overall impression of the Somali is that of a well-proportioned medium to large cat, firm muscular development, lithe, showing an alert, lively interest in all surroundings, with an even disposition and easy to handle. The cat is to give the appearance of activity, sound health, and general vigor.
BODY	Torso medium long, lithe, and graceful, showing well-developed muscular strength. Rib cage is rounded; back is slightly arched giving the appearance of a cat about to spring; flank level with no tuck up. Conformation strikes a medium between the extremes of cobby and svelte lengthy types.
HEAD	Modified, slightly rounded wedge without flat planes; the brow, cheek, and profile lines all showing a gentle contour. A slight rise from the bridge of the nose to the forehead, which should be of good size with width between the ears flowing into the arched neck without a break. Muzzle shall follow gentle contours in conformity with the skull, as viewed from the front profile. Chin shall be full, neither undershot nor overshot, having a rounded appearance. The muzzle shall not be sharply pointed, and there shall be no evidence of snippiness, foxiness, or whisker pinch.
EARS	Large, alert, moderately pointed, broad, and cupped at the base. Ear set on a line towards the rear of the skull. The inner ear shall have horizontal tufts that reach nearly to the other side of the ear; tufts desirable.
EYES	Almond shaped, large, brilliant, and expressive. Skull aperture neither round nor oriental. Eyes accented by dark lid skin encircled by light colored area. Above each a short dark vertical pencil stroke with a dark pencil line continuing from the upper lid towards the ear. Eye color gold or green, the more richness and depth of color the better.
LEGS AND PAWS	Legs in proportion to torso; feet oval and compact. When standing, the Somali gives the impression of being nimble and quick. Toes five in front and four in back.
TAIL	Having a full brush, thick at the base, and slightly tapering. Length in balance with torso.
COAT	Texture very soft to the touch, extremely fine and double coated. The more dense the coat, the better. Length: a medium- length coat, except over shoulders, where a slightly shorter length is permitted. Preference is to be given to a cat with ruff and breeches, giving a full-coated appearance to the cat.

COLOR	Ruddy, red, blue, and fawn. Warm and glowing. Ticking: distinct and even, with dark colored bands contrasting with lighter colored bands on the hair shafts. Undercoat color clear and bright to the skin. Deeper color shades desired, however, intensity of ticking not to be sacrificed for depth of color. Preference given to cats unmarked on the undersides, chest, and legs; tail without rings. Markings: darker shading along spine continuing through tip of tail; darker shading up the hocks, shading allowed at the point of the elbow; dark lines extending from eyes and brows, cheekbone shading, dots and shading on whisker pads are desirable enhancements, eyes accentuated by fine dark line, encircled by light-colored area.
DISQUALIFY	White locket or groin spot or white anywhere on body other than on the upper throat, chin and nostril area. Any skeletal abnormality. Wrong color paw pads or nose leather. Any other colors than the four accepted colors. Unbroken necklace. Incorrect number of toes. Kinks in tail.
ALLOWABLE OUTCROSSES	Abyssinian

boisterous addition to any household. Like the Abyssinian, the Somali is vigorous and animated, has a keen sense of feline humor, and a real need for play. Everything is a game to a Somali; some will play fetch, but many prefer to chase that ball down the hall and then bat it up and down, around and around, until it rolls back to your feet for you to throw again—and again. If it rolls under something from which they can't retrieve it, then back they'll come and give you a wide-eyed stare or a gentle tap so you'll get up and put the ball back in play. Wands and fishing poles with feathers are a huge hit; you'll need a lockable cupboard for when playtime is over.

Fanciers say the Somali shares more than just a passing resemblance to the wily fox; Somalis know more ways to get into adorable mischief than a barrel of foxes. How adorable you find their mischief often depends upon the hour—it's less adorable when you're jolted awake at 4:00 A.M. by the loud crash of a breakable knickknack hitting the floor.

Like the Abyssinian, Somalis are active, playful, and affectionate.

They are highly intelligent, which contributes to their talent for mischievous amusement.

The Somali is active, curious, and high-spirited, and loves to prance around the house, opening cupboards and generally getting into trouble. Their voices are soft, their minds active, and their food dishes always empty. They also tend to be determined cats; once they get an idea in their furry little heads, there's no dissuading them. They're not belligerent about that idea rolling around between their ears; they're just tenacious.

Somalis are people-oriented and affectionate, but are not lap cats. They don't like to be cuddled and when picked up usually are all wiggles until you relent and put them down. When you're relaxing on the couch, they prefer to be near rather than on you. They do, however, want to be involved in every aspect of your life. Open a drawer and your Somali will be there to peer in, and stick a curious paw inside, too. Somalis are the best home entertainment you can buy, and they are more like people than cats— small, hairy, hyperactive people. Very energetic and high spirited, Somalis cavort like kittens until well into old age.

CONFORMATION

Like the Abyssinian, the Somali is a ticked or agouti breed (see the Abyssinian profile, page 62). Somalis have few genetic defects but, like their shorthaired relative the Aby, they are prone to plaque, tartar buildup, and gingivitis. Untreated, gingivitis can lead to the dental disease periodontitis that can lead to tooth, tissue, and bone loss, which can undermine a Somali's overall health. Renal amyloidosis, a hereditary disease that can lead to kidney failure, have been found in some Somali lines. Erythrocyte pyruvate kinase deficiency (PK Deficiency) is an inherited hemolytic anemia that occurs in Abyssinian, Somali, and some other shorthair cats. The deficiency of this regulatory enzyme causes an instability of red blood cells that leads to anemia. A genetic test is available at the Veterinary Genetics Laboratory at the University of California, Davis. This tool helps breeders screen out affected or carrier cats. Responsible breeders screen for PK deficiency; before you buy, ask if the breeder screens for PK deficiency and provides a written health guarantee.

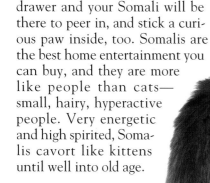

This ruddy Somali has a magnificent tail brush.

HISTORY

The Sphynx is not the first instance of hairlessness in domestic cats. This natural, spontaneous mutation has been seen in various locations around the world for more than a century, and probably much longer. *The Book of the Cat* by Frances Simpson, published in 1903, mentioned a pair of gray and white hairless cats, Dick and Nellie, belonging to an Albuquerque, New Mexico cat lover named F. J. Shinick. Called the "Mexican Hairless," these cats looked similar to today's Sphynx, and supposedly were obtained from Indians around Albuquerque. According to Mr. Shinick's letter, "The old Jesuit Fathers tell me they are the last of the Aztec breed known only in New Mexico." It's unknown if that was true, but Dick and Nellie died without producing offspring.

In 1950, a pair of Siamese cats in Paris, France, produced a litter that included three hairless kittens. The results were repeated in subsequent matings of the same pair, but breeding the parents to other Siamese cats produced no new hairless kittens.

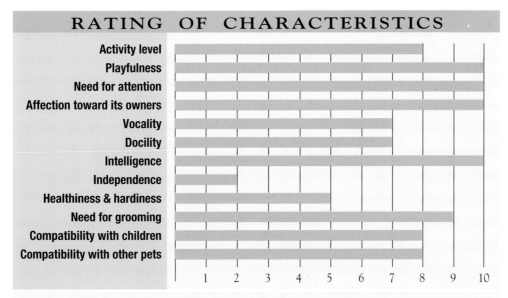

Harlequin Sphynx.

RATING OF CHARACTERISTICS

Characteristic	Rating (1–10)
Activity level	10
Playfulness	10
Need for attention	10
Affection toward its owners	10
Vocality	7
Docility	7
Intelligence	10
Independence	2
Healthiness & hardiness	5
Need for grooming	9
Compatibility with children	8
Compatibility with other pets	8

1—breed exhibits the least amount of this characteristic, 10—breed exhibits the most of this characteristic

✳ **Championship status in all associations**

Other hairless specimens turned up in Morocco, Australia, North Carolina, and, in 1966, in Roncesvalles, Toronto, Ontario, Canada, where a pair of domestic shorthairs produced a litter that included a hairless kitten named Prune. A breeder obtained the parents and began a breeding program; the breed was named the Canadian Hairless. Prune was mated with his mother, which produced one hairless kitten. In 1970, CFA granted provisional status to the breed. This line had a number of difficulties; the gene pool was limited, and some kittens died from

Exposure to sun intensifies Sphynx colors.

undiagnosed health problems. In 1971, CFA withdrew the recognition due to the breed's health problems.

The last of Prune's line was sent to Holland to Dr. Hugo Hernandez in the 1970s. In 1978 and 1980, two hairless female kittens believed to be related to Prune were found in Toronto. They were sent to Holland to be bred with Prune's last surviving male descendent. One female conceived, but she lost the litter. None of Prune's descendants went on to become the Sphynx breed we know today.

In 1975, Minnesota farm owners Milt and Ethelyn Pearson discovered a hairless kitten had been born to their normal-coated farm cat, Jezabelle. This kitten, named Epidermis, was joined the next year by another hairless kitten named Dermis. Both were sold to Oregon breeder Kim Mueske, who used the kittens to develop the Sphynx breed. Georgiana Gattenby of Brainerd, Minnesota, also worked with kittens from the Pearson line, using Cornish Rex as an outcross.

At almost the same time (1978), Siamese breeder Shirley Smith of Toronto, Ontario, Canada, found three hairless kittens on the streets of her neighborhood, which she named Bambi, Punkie, and Paloma. The descendants of Bambi, Punkie, and Paloma in Canada, along with the descendants of Epidermis and Dermis in Oregon, became the foundation of today's Sphynx. The breed has made considerable strides since its inception due to a group of dedicated breeders.

While most fanciers have welcomed the Sphynx as unique and exotic, some members of the cat fancy wish that the Sphynx would put on some clothes. Like other breeds that have diverged from the basic design, the Sphynx has drawn some negative attention. In addition, the gene that governs hairlessness can be considered a genetic disorder, since the cat is more susceptible to both heat and cold. On the other hand, fanciers argue that we humans are more or less hairless compared with our closest relatives, and with a dap of sunscreen we manage to get by just fine.

Association acceptance followed the breed's creation quite rapidly for such an unusual breed. TICA accepted the breed for championship in 1986. In 1992, CCA recognized the Sphynx for championship. In 1994, ACFA followed suit. In 1998, CFA recognized the new and improved Sphynx lines for registration and in 2002 accepted the breed for championship. The breed is now recognized by all North American cat associations, as well as Fédération Internationale Féline (FIFe) and the Governing Council of the Cat Fancy (GCCF) in Europe.

PERSONALITY

According to the old French breed standard, the Sphynx is "part monkey, part dog, part child, and part cat." The breed does seem to possess some personality traits of each, despite what geneticists might say about such a combination. To say Sphynxes are lively is an understatement; they perform monkey-like aerialist feats from the top of doorways and bookshelves.

Wrinkles are a desirable trait in the show Sphynx.

Very devoted and loyal, they follow their humans around, wagging their tails doggy fashion, kneading with their padded toes, and purring with delight at the joy of being near their beloved humans. They demand your unconditional attention and are as mischievous (and lovable) as children. And despite all that and their alien appearance, they are still entirely cats, with all the mystery and charm that has fascinated humankind for thousands of years. While the Sphynx may not be for everyone, its unique appearance and charming temperament has won it an active, enthusiastic following.

CONFORMATION

The Sphynx only appears hairless—its skin, or parts of it, is covered with a fine, almost imperceptible ves-

GENERAL	The most distinctive feature of this cat is its appearance of hairlessness. The Sphynx is of medium size and body conformation with surprising weight for its size. The body feels warm and soft to the touch, with a skin texture akin to either a soft peach or a smooth nectarine. The Sphynx is sweet-tempered, lively, and amenable to handling.
BODY	Body is medium length, hard, and muscular with broad rounded chest and full round abdomen. The rump is well-rounded and muscular. Back line rises just behind the shoulder blades to accommodate longer back legs when standing. Boning is medium. Neck is medium in length, rounded, well-muscled, with a slight arch. Allowance to be made for heavy musculature in adult males.
HEAD	Modified wedge, slightly longer than it is wide, with prominent cheekbones, a distinctive whisker break, and whisker pads giving a squared appearance to the muzzle. The skull is slightly rounded with a flat plane in front of the ears. The nose is straight, and there is a slight to moderate palpable stop at the bridge of the nose. Prominent, rounded cheekbones which define the eye and form a curve above the whisker break.
EARS	Large to very large. Broad at the base, open and upright. When viewed from the front, the outer base of the ear should begin at the level of the eye, neither low set nor on top of the head. The interior of the ears is naturally without furnishing.
EYES	Large, lemon shaped, with wide-open center while coming to a definite point on each side. Placement should be at a slight upward angle, aligning with the outer base of the ear. Eyes to be set wide apart with the distance between the eyes being a minimum of one eye width. As no points are assigned to eye color, all eye colors are accepted and should be harmonious with coat/skin color.
LEGS AND PAWS	Legs are medium in proportion to the body. They are sturdy and well-muscled with rear legs being slightly longer than the front. Paws are oval with well-knuckled toes; five in front and four behind. The paw pads are thick, giving the appearance of walking on cushions.
TAIL	Slender, flexible, and long while maintaining proportion to body length. Whip-like, tapering to a fine point.
COAT	Appearance of this cat is one of hairlessness. Short, fine hair may be present on the feet, outer edges of the ears, the tail, and the scrotum. The bridge of the nose should be normally coated. The remainder of the body can range from completely hairless to a covering of soft

268

COAT (continued)	peach-like fuzz whose length does not interfere with the appearance of hairlessness. This coat/skin texture creates a feeling of resistance when stroking the cat. Wrinkled skin is desirable, particularly around the muzzle, between the ears, and around the shoulders. There are usually no whiskers, but if whiskers are present they are short and sparse.
COLOR	All colors and patterns accepted. Color and pattern are difficult to distinguish and should not affect the judging of the cat. White lockets, buttons, or belly spots are allowed.
DISQUALIFY	Kinked or abnormal tail. Structural abnormalities. Aggressive behavior endangering the judge.
ALLOWABLE OUTCROSSES	American Shorthair, Domestic Shorthair/Domestic Sphynx outcross. Sphynx born on or after December 31, 2015 may have only Sphynx parents.

tigial layer of down that gives the skin the texture of chamois. Heterozygous Sphynxes (those that possess only one copy of the hairless gene) usually exhibit more hair than homozygous Sphynxes (those possessing two copies). Wrinkles are a desirable trait in the show Sphynx. It isn't really more wrinkled than any other cat, though; you can see the wrinkles because of the lack of fur. The lack of coat makes the Sphynx feel like warm suede to the touch.

Sphynx refrain from shedding all over your couch but can still make you sneeze; even furless cats can cause a reaction in people with allergies. This is because it's not cat hair that causes the allergic reaction in humans, but rather an allergenic protein called Fel d1 secreted in the saliva and the sebaceous glands. This protein is spread onto the skin during grooming. Sphynx groom themselves just as much as any

other breed, and produce as much of this protein. In fact, without all that hair to absorb the secretions, Sphynx can actually cause more severe allergic reactions in some people. It's important to spend a good amount of time in the presence of a Sphynx before buying if you're allergic to cats, even if your allergies are mild.

Not having fur doesn't mean the Sphynx doesn't need grooming. In fact, they need daily attention. Sphynx must be regularly bathed to remove collections of oily sebaceous secretions on the skin. These secretions are normal; it's just that Sphynx don't have hair to absorb them. They must be bathed regularly to remove those oils. Oily cats may leave grease stains on the furniture or develop blocked pores, lesions, or skin infections. Because of the size and lack of hair in the ears, owners must clean the ears regularly to avoid wax buildup.

HISTORY

The Thai is long, lithe, and as graceful as a small panther.

Named for the country in which the Siamese originated, the Thai is the official breed name in TICA and in a number of the European registries. The Thai is the natural pointed cat you find in Thailand today, and it closely resembles the Siamese of the late nineteenth and early twentieth century, before selective breeding made the face longer, the coat shorter, and the conformation more svelte. The breed is known in Thailand as the Wichienmaat and elsewhere as the Old-Style Siamese. The Thai is decorated in the colorpoint pattern (sometimes called the pointed or Himalayan pattern), which includes a pale off-white body and dark-colored points (face, ears, legs, feet, and tail); and has short hair and large, deep blue eyes, and a semi-foreign, medium to large sized body. The Thai has a body and head type less extreme than the Siamese more commonly seen in the show hall. The body is moderate in type, not extreme or svelte.

RATING OF CHARACTERISTICS

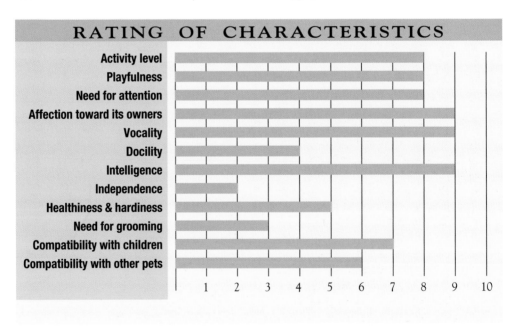

Characteristic	Rating
Activity level	8
Playfulness	8
Need for attention	8
Affection toward its owners	9
Vocality	9
Docility	4
Intelligence	9
Independence	2
Healthiness & hardiness	5
Need for grooming	3
Compatibility with children	7
Compatibility with other pets	6

✳ **Championship status in TICA; championship status in CFF and UFO under name of Old-Style Siamese**

In some associations, the Thai is synonymous with Old-Style Siamese; CFF accepts the Old-Style Siamese, and UFO accepts the Old-Style Siamese, as well as the Old-Style Balinese and the Old-Style Colorpoint. Other associations and fanciers refer to the breed by the term Applehead, which is more colloquial and informal.

No one knows for sure exactly when the pointed pattern cat of Siam originated. The Wichienmaat was described and depicted in *The Cat-Book Poems*, a manuscript that was written in the city of Ayutthaya, Siam, some time between 1350 C.E. when the kingdom was founded, and 1767 C.E. when the city was destroyed by invaders from Burma. The illustrations in the manuscript clearly show slender cats with pale coats and dark points on the ears, faces, feet, and tails. Exactly when the document was written is unknown because the original, painstakingly handwritten and decorated with illustrations and gold leaf, was made of palm leaf or bark. When the document became too fragile, a fresh copy was made, and the new scribe would sometimes bring his own interpretation to the work. This makes it difficult to date. But whether it was written more than 650 years ago or only close to 300, it's still very old; likely the oldest manuscript about cats in existence. A beautifully made copy of *The Cat-Book Poems* that was specially commissioned by King Rama V of Siam is kept secured and preserved in Bangkok's National Library.

According to historical accounts, these living works of art were treasured for hundreds of generations and were the companions of royalty and religious leaders. Because the Siamese was so valued in its native land, the cats were rarely given to outsiders, so the rest of the world didn't become acquainted with the breed until the 1800s. Siamese cats were exhibited in 1871 in the first modern-style cat show at London's Crystal Palace, organized by Harrison Weir, known as "the father of the cat fancy." At the event, one journalist described the Siamese as "an unnatural, nightmare kind of cat." Others fell

The Thai's body and head type are less extreme than the svelte Siamese more often seen in cat shows.

in love with the exotic breed's unique color pattern, graceful body style, unique head shape, distinctly wedge-shaped muzzle, and charming personality. Another important feature is the breed's very short coat, first described in Europe by Harrison Weir in his 1889 book *Our Cats and All About Them*, Europe's first book on pedigreed cats.

In spite of early naysayers and the difficulty importing the cats, the Siamese quickly gained in popularity in Europe. The first Siamese standard, written in 1892 in Great Britain, described the Siamese as "a striking-looking cat of medium size, if weighty, not showing bulk, as this would detract from the admired svelte appearance . . . often distinguished by a kink in the tail." At that time, the admired lithe appearance was not nearly as svelte as the extreme type of show Siamese today. Kinked tails and crossed eyes were common then as well, although both are now considered faults in both the Thai and the extreme Siamese.

The Siamese was brought to the United States and quickly became established with the developing and enthusiastic American cat fancy. Siamese must have become used to posh dwellings from its years with royalty; the first Siamese imported to North America lived in the White House. In November 1878, David B. Sickels, a U.S. diplomat stationed at the consulate in Bangkok, sent a Siamese cat to first lady Lucy Hayes. In a letter that can be viewed in the Paper Trail archives of the Rutherford B. Hayes Presidential Center, Sickels wrote, "I have taken the liberty of forwarding you one of the finest specimens of Sia-

mese cats that I have been able to procure in this country . . . I am informed that this is the first attempt ever made to send a Siamese cat to America."

In the early 1900s, breeders set out to "improve" the breed, and over decades of selective breeding, the Siamese became more and more extreme. By the 1950s, many show Siamese had longer heads, bluer eyes, finer boning, and slimmer legs and bodies than the Siamese common at the turn of the century. Many people liked the changes in the Siamese, while others preferred the original moderate look of the breed. The two types began to diverge, with one group becoming more extreme in style, and the other remaining moderate in conformation. However, by the 1980s, moderate Siamese were no longer considered show cats, except in the household pet category; mainstream breeders were breeding for a much more svelte cat, and being rewarded for their efforts by show judges.

In the 1980s, the first breed clubs dedicated to the moderate style appeared in Europe and North America, such as the World Cat Federation in Germany, Prestwick-Beresford Old-Style Siamese Breed Preservation Society in North America, the Old-Style Siamese Club in England, and the Happy Household Pet Cat Club in North America. The Old-Style Siamese Club notes that Siamese outcrossed to non-oriental breeds in order to obtain a cobbier look are not Siamese, and are not recognized or registered as Siamese by the OSSC or by the Governing Council of the Cat Fancy (GCCF).

In 1990, the World Cat Federation in Europe created the name "Thai" to differentiate the Old-Style from the extreme Siamese, and granted the breed championship status. In 2001, breeders began importing pointed cats from Thailand to establish a healthy gene pool for the Thai breed and to preserve the genes of Southeast Asia's native cats while they are still distinct from extreme Western cats, which had acquired certain hereditary genetic diseases and conditions. In 2007, TICA granted preliminary new breed status to the Thai, and in 2009 accepted the Thai into the advanced new breed class, making it possible for breeders in North America and Europe to work together and show under a single breed standard. In 2010, the Thai was granted championship by TICA. The breed is also accepted for championship by CFF and UFO under name Old-Style Siamese.

According to fans, the Thai is the most wonderful, loving, entertaining cat in the known universe.

PERSONALITY

According to fans, the Thai is the most wonderful, loving, entertaining cats in the known universe. Thais are very intelligent, self-assured, playful, determined, curious, active, and have a highly developed sense of humor. They love their human companions with a passion; living with the Thai is a bit like living with active but loving children. They'll get into everything you own, paw through your purse, nose through every open drawer, and help you select the correct items from the refrigerator. They like to get a bird's eye view of the daily action, so don't be surprised to see your Thai at the top of your highest book shelf. However, their all-time favorite game is to follow you around and help you with every activity. If you open a drawer to put away socks, Thais will leap right in to help you arrange them.

Thais are great talkers. They aren't as loud and raspy as their extreme Siamese counterparts, but they're still plenty chatty. They'll greet you at the door when you come home and chat about their day, or complain about the vast amount of time you've been gone. They also communicate with attention-getting taps of their paws or by jumping on your shoulder and giving you head presses or kisses.

More than most breeds, Thais need their per diem of love and affection. If they are ignored or neglected, they become unhappy and depressed and may act out, using their high intelligence to make you aware of their dis-

273

GENERAL (TICA STANDARD)	The ideal cat of this breed is a medium to slightly large, pointed cat of foreign type, descended from and resembling the indigenous pointed cats of Thailand. It cannot be stated enough that the Thai should not be extreme in any way, but its appearance and personality should reflect its Thailand heritage. The Thai is not, and should not resemble, a native Western breed.
BODY	Moderately long, lithe, and graceful like a small panther. Well-toned, but neither tubular nor compact. High enough on legs for desired foreign type. Underbelly is mostly level and parallel to the ground and firm. However, a slight amount of loose skin on the underbelly below the flank is permissible. Boning medium, graceful, neither refined nor coarse. Musculature firm but lithe, not meaty or dense. When picked up, cat weighs about as much as, or slightly more than, one would predict visually.
HEAD	Modified wedge, medium width with rounded cheeks and tapering muzzle. Head is longer than wide, but not extreme or narrow. Cheekbones curve inward to where the muzzle begins. Muzzle is wedge shaped, but rounded on the end like a tapering garden spade. Forehead is flat and long. Nose nearly straight, but with a slight downhill slope starting just above the eyes and ending just below the eyes. In profile, nose may be straight or slightly convex.
EARS	Medium in size to slightly large, wide at the base, oval tips. Tip of ears point outward at an angle slightly closer to the top than side of the head (35 degrees from vertical). Allow for very light furnishings.
EYES	Medium to slightly large, a very full almond shape, not oriental. Set slightly more than an eye width apart. A line from inner corner through outer corner of eye meets outer base of ear. Eye color blue. Deep blue shades preferred. Brilliance and luminosity are more important than depth of color.
LEGS AND PAWS	Legs medium length, graceful in form, but not coarse. Feet oval shape; medium size in proportion to cat.
TAIL	As long as the torso, tapering gradually to the tip.
COAT	Silky; very little undercoat. Not a painted on coat, but definitely close-lying. Length very short to short.
COLOR	Body color preferably a very pale off-white. Evenness of the body color and contrast with the points are more important than extreme whiteness. Point color appropriate for color class, dense and even. Mask, ears, feet, and tail should match in color.

DISQUALIFY	Pronounced stop in profile. Pronounced convex forehead. Distinct ear tufts. Fluffy fur with dense undercoat ("teddy bear" coat). Cobby body. Obesity. White lockets and buttons; white toes and feet (including paw pads); patches of white in the points. Eye color other than blue. Disqualification: Visible tail fault. Crossed eyes. Visible protrusion of the cartilage at the end of the sternum (xiphoid process).
ALLOWABLE OUTCROSSES	Siamese

pleasure. Expect a tap-dance on your shoulder and a bellow in your ear to get attention.

Thais are also sensitive to your tone, and reprimands hurt their sensitive feelings. If you must spend much time away from home, a compatible cat companion will help keep your Thai from becoming lonely and bored. They are easy to care for and need little grooming; once a week is usually enough.

CONFORMATION

The Thai is a semi-foreign, medium to large cat with a moderate body and head type. The body is long, substantial and solid, and is neither cobby nor svelte in type, nor in any way extreme. The shape of the Thai's head is a modified wedge, medium in width with a tapering muzzle, longer than it is wide, but not extreme or narrow. The ears are medium in length, and almost as wide at the base as they are tall. The Thai's coat is silky, close-lying, with very little undercoat. The length is short to very short, but it doesn't have the "painted on" appearance of the Extreme Siamese.

The defining feature of the breed is its pattern. In CFF and UFO the Old-Style Siamese (as it's called in those

associations) comes in one pattern, colorpoint, also called point restricted, and four coat colors: seal, chocolate, blue, and lilac. TICA, however, in addition to the original four colors also allows red point, cream point, blue-cream point, lilac-cream point, and colors in lynx point, tortie-lynx point, and parti-color point.

The points of the body—ears, face mask, feet, and tail—are darker than the rest of the body due to a temperature-controlled enzyme that creates greater depth of color at the parts of the body farthest away from the heart. These areas are a few degrees cooler, and so the color is concentrated in those areas. There is a clear contrast between the light body color and the darker points, and all the color points must be the same shade. Body color generally darkens with age. In TICA, the only allowable outcross is the Siamese, used when genetic diversity is needed. No outcrosses are allowed in CFF and UFO.

According to Thai fanciers, the Thai is generally healthier and hardier than the Extreme Siamese. Responsible TICA breeders are working hard to make sure the Siamese used for outcrossing are free of genetic diseases.

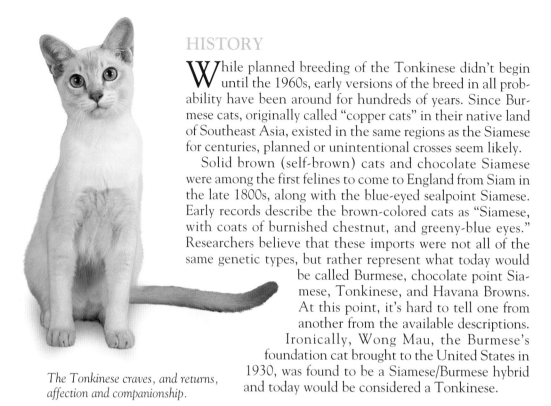

HISTORY

While planned breeding of the Tonkinese didn't begin until the 1960s, early versions of the breed in all probability have been around for hundreds of years. Since Burmese cats, originally called "copper cats" in their native land of Southeast Asia, existed in the same regions as the Siamese for centuries, planned or unintentional crosses seem likely.

Solid brown (self-brown) cats and chocolate Siamese were among the first felines to come to England from Siam in the late 1800s, along with the blue-eyed sealpoint Siamese. Early records describe the brown-colored cats as "Siamese, with coats of burnished chestnut, and greeny-blue eyes." Researchers believe that these imports were not all of the same genetic types, but rather represent what today would be called Burmese, chocolate point Siamese, Tonkinese, and Havana Browns. At this point, it's hard to tell one from another from the available descriptions. Ironically, Wong Mau, the Burmese's foundation cat brought to the United States in 1930, was found to be a Siamese/Burmese hybrid and today would be considered a Tonkinese.

The Tonkinese craves, and returns, affection and companionship.

RATING OF CHARACTERISTICS

Characteristic	Rating
Activity level	10
Playfulness	8
Need for attention	8
Affection toward its owners	8
Vocality	8
Docility	5
Intelligence	8
Independence	4
Healthiness & hardiness	5
Need for grooming	2
Compatibility with children	7
Compatibility with other pets	7

1—breed exhibits the least amount of this characteristic, 10—breed exhibits the most of this characteristic

✳ **Championship status in all associations**

These Siamese and solid-colored cats were exhibited in Europe during the late 1800s and the early 1900s.

Soon after, however, such cats fell from grace. In 1930, the Siamese Cat Club announced, "The club much regrets it is unable to encourage the breeding of any but blue-eyed Siamese." Solid-colored cats lacking blue eyes were accordingly banned from competition and disappeared from the cat fancy.

The Tonkinese got a fresh start as a recognized breed in the early 1960s, when Canadian breeder Margaret Conroy crossed a sable Burmese with a sealpoint Siamese. The product of the cross was a cat of intermediate temperament and type, which Conroy originally called the "Golden Siamese." When the Tonkinese began, both the Burmese and the Siamese had not yet been transformed by selective breeding into their current conformations. The Siamese had yet to attain its extremely sleek show style, and the Burmese was not yet as compact and cobby, nor the head shape as broad and rounded. Still, combining the two and achieving a uniform and consistent head and body type was challenging for Tonkinese breeders.

Aqua eye color is characteristic of the mink color pattern.

GENERAL	The ideal Tonkinese is intermediate in type, neither cobby nor svelte. The Tonkinese should give the overall impression of an alert, active cat with good muscular development. The cat should be surprisingly heavy. While the breed is considered medium in size, balance, and proportion are of greater importance.
BODY	Torso medium in length, demonstrating well-developed muscular strength without coarseness. The Tonkinese conformation strikes a midpoint between the extremes of long, svelte body types and cobby, compact body types. Balance and proportion are more important than size alone. The abdomen should be taut, well-muscled, and firm.
HEAD	The head is a modified slightly rounded wedge somewhat longer than it is wide, with high gently planed cheekbones. The muzzle is blunt, as long as it is wide. a slight whisker break, gently curved, follows lines of the wedge. Slight stop at eye level. In profile the tip of the chin lines with the tip of the nose in the same vertical plane. Gentle rise from the tip of the nose to the stop. Gentle contour with a slight rise from the nose stop to the forehead. Slight convex curve to the forehead.
EARS	Alert, medium in size. Oval tips, broad at the base. Ears set as much on the sides of the head as on the top. Hair on the ears very short and close-lying. Leather may show through.
EYES	Open almond shape. Slanted along the cheekbones toward the outer edge of the ear. Eyes are proportionate in size to the face.
LEGS AND PAWS	Fairly slim legs, proportionate in length and bone to the body. Hind legs slightly longer than front. Paws more oval than round. Trim. Toes: five in front and four behind.
TAIL	Proportionate in length to body. Tapering.
COAT	Medium short in length, close-lying, fine, soft and silky, with a lustrous sheen.
COLOR	Natural, champagne, blue, and platinum in solid, point, and mink patterns. Allowance to be made for lighter body color in young cats, and for less contrast in older cats. With the dilute colors in particular, development of full body color may take up to 16 months. Cats do darken with age. Point color: mask, ears, feet, and tail all densely marked, but merging gently into body color. Except in kittens, mask and ears should be connected by tracings. Nose leather color should correspond to the intensity of the point color. There will be more contrast between points and body color for the champagne and platinum than for the natural and blue.

DISQUALIFY	Yellow eyes in mink colors. White locket or button. Crossed eyes. Tail faults.
ALLOWABLE OUTCROSSES	None.

To distinguish the breed from the Siamese, the name was changed to "Tonkanese" in 1967. In 1971 breeders voted to change the name to "Tonkinese" after the Bay of Tonkin off southern China and North Vietnam. The name was attractive and had a nice exotic ring to it, even though the breed did not come from the Bay of Tonkin area. In collaboration with other notable breeders like Jane Barletta of New Jersey, Conroy wrote the first breed standard, which was presented to the Canadian Cat Association (CCA). The Tonkinese was the first breed to be developed in Canada.

In 1971, CCA became the first cat registry to grant championship status to the Tonkinese. CFF recognized the Tonkinese in 1974; TICA followed in 1979, the year they formed as an association.

The road to acceptance wasn't always smooth. Many new breeds can't achieve acceptance without a period of controversy, and the Tonk was no exception. Achieving acceptance and support from the cat fancy community was as challenging as achieving a good head type. In October 1979, the CFA passed a "five-year rule," requiring new breeds to remain in the newly established non-competition miscellaneous class for five years. Some Tonkinese breeders thought the rule was specifically designed to hold the Tonk back, since the Tonkinese

breed association planned to ask for provisional status in 1980. However, the setback only made Tonk breeders and fanciers more determined to promote the breed and achieve eventual acceptance. The CFA granted championship status in 1984. By 1990, all of the major associations had accepted the breed for championship.

PERSONALITY

The Tonkinese has a winsome personality, not surprising since the Burmese and Siamese are prized for their temperaments. Faithful followers say the Tonkinese has the best of both breeds. Its voice is milder in tone than the Siamese; however, it does believe in feline free speech and wants to share all of the day's adventures with you when you come home in the evening. The Tonkinese craves, and returns, affection and companionship. Unlike the rest of your busy family, it will always join you for dinner. It has an unflagging enthusiasm for life and life's pleasures, and loves interactive toys, such as human fingers and the tails of its cat companions. It makes every close encounter a game. While Tonkinese cats willingly adapt to humans and animals alike, they may annoy more sedate breeds and therefore might do better with members of their own breed or other active breeds.

Tonkinese are particularly popular among cat lovers who remember the Old-Style Siamese with affection and want a cat with a less extreme body style than currently exists in the show Siamese. If the Tonk of your dreams isn't immediately available, breeders usually maintain waiting lists, since demand is high.

CONFORMATION

The Burmese gene responsible for the sable color is a member of the albino series of gene alleles and causes solid black to appear dark brown by reducing the amount of pigment in each hair. The Siamese gene for point-restricted color is also part of this alleles series. Because the Siamese gene is only partially recessive to the Burmese gene, the Tonkinese can come in three patterns: solid, like the Burmese; pointed, like the Siamese; and mink, a combination of the two. Mink used to refer to the look and feel of the Tonkinese's soft silky coat, but now refers to the mink pattern unique to the Tonkinese. With this pattern, the shading from point color to body color is subtle and not as sharply defined as with the pointed pattern. The body displays a pale to medium shade of the darker point color. All three types are important in Tonkinese breeding programs. Breeding two mink Tonkinese cats together produces offspring with an average color ratio of 1:2:1, 25 percent solid, 50 percent mink, and 25 percent pointed Tonkinese; however, breeding a pointed Tonkinese to a solid Tonkinese will produce 100 percent mink Tonkinese.

If the Tonk of your dreams isn't immediately available, breeders usually maintain waiting lists.

HISTORY

No one is really sure how or where this ancient breed originated. Often recounted is the hypothesis that the Turkish Angora developed from the longhaired Pallas's cat (*Otocolobus manul*), a small Asian wildcat about the size of the domestic, but this is doubtful. The Pallas's cat has fundamental differences from the domestic feline and is unlikely to mate with domestics unless no other mates were available. Too, its differences would insure a number of generations of sterile males. It is far more likely that the Turkish Angora developed from the African wildcat, like all other domestic cats. The recessive mutation for long hair in felines probably occurred as a spontaneous mutation centuries ago and was perpetuated through interbreeding in confined, mountainous areas that would limit outcrossing, such as regions in Turkey. The French naturalist De Buffon, writing in the later part of the 1700s, wrote that cats with long fur came from Asia Minor, a pen-

Solid white Turkish Angora with bright amber eyes.

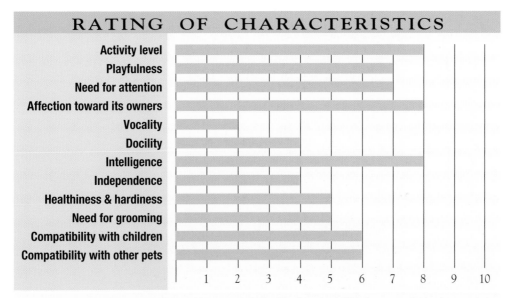

RATING OF CHARACTERISTICS

Characteristic	Rating
Activity level	7
Playfulness	7
Need for attention	8
Affection toward its owners	8
Vocality	2
Docility	4
Intelligence	8
Independence	4
Healthiness & hardiness	5
Need for grooming	5
Compatibility with children	6
Compatibility with other pets	6

1—breed exhibits the least amount of this characteristic, 10—breed exhibits the most of this characteristic

❋ Championship status in all associations

insula in southwestern Asia that forms the Asian part of Turkey.

However they developed, longhaired cats have been noted in Turkey and the surrounding neighborhoods for centuries. According to the legend, Mohammed (570–632 C.E.), founder of the Islamic faith, was so fond of cats that he once cut off his sleeve rather than disturb his beloved Angora Muezza, who was sleeping in his arms. Formerly called Ankara cats (the name of the Turkish capital was changed from Angora to Ankara in 1930), Ankara is also home to longhaired Angora rabbits and goats prized by the Turkish people for their long, fine hair.

Longhaired cats were imported to Britain and France from Turkey, Persia, Russia, and Afghanistan as early as the late 1500s. The Angora had definitely found its way to Europe by the early 1600s, and by the late 1700s Angoras were being imported into America.

In the early days of the cat fancy, Angoras were highly prized. As the story goes, one Angora owner turned down an offer of $5,000 for her favorite Angora at an 1890 cat show in London.

Gradually, however, the Persian became the preferred type of cat in the European cat fancy. The Angora was used extensively in Persian breeding programs to add length and silkiness to the Persian coat. Later, the Governing Council of the Cat Fancy decided that all longhaired breeds should be simply called "longhairs." Also confusing was the tendency of cat fanciers to call any longhair a Persian or Angora,

regardless of its bloodline. Persians, Angoras, and Russian Longhairs were bred together indiscriminately. Except in their native land, Angoras ceased to exist as a pure breed. They stopped appearing in the show halls and from registration records. By the 1900s, Angoras had virtually vanished.

In the early 1900s, the government of Turkey in conjunction with the Ankara Zoo began a meticulous breeding program to protect and preserve the pure white Angora cats with blue and amber eyes, a program that continues today. The zoo particularly prized the odd-eyed Angoras (cats with eyes of differing colors), because they are believed to be touched by Allah. Mohammed's Angora, Muezza, was believed to be an odd-eyed cat.

Because the Turkish people valued the cats so highly, obtaining Angoras was very difficult, but in 1962 Liesa F. Grant, wife of Army Colonel Walter Grant who was stationed in Turkey, was successful in exporting a pair of the zoo's Turkish Angoras to America, complete with certificates of ancestry. These imports revived interest in the breed, and soon other breeders began going through the difficult process of exporting Angoras, and developing the breed. A Turkish Angora breeder advertising "imported lines" usually means they have foundation stock from Turkey. The Grants were instrumental in achieving CFA recognition for the Angora.

White Turkish Angoras were accepted for CFA registration in 1968, and for provisional competition in 1970, the first U.S. registry to do so. In 1972, white Angoras were accepted for championship competition. It wasn't until 1978 that all the other Turkish Angora colors were accepted for championship competition like their all-white kin. While numbers are still small and breeders few, the breed still has a dedicated and growing fan-base of fanciers.

PERSONALITY

Angoras seem to invoke strong responses in their humans with their symmetry, intelligence, and devotion to their humans. Angoras bond with their owners completely; an Angora is not happy unless it is right in the middle of whatever you're doing. They enjoy a good conversation and can keep up their end of the discussion with the best of them. Angoras are good-natured, but determined. Once an Angora gets an idea into its head, you might as well just give in and spare yourself the lengthy argument.

Angoras have a great need to play and enjoy playing a good-natured joke on their favorite humans every now and then. They love practicing their pounce, on scraps of paper or unsuspecting human toes, whatever catches their fancy. When in movement, which is most of the time, Angoras seem to flow with the grace of dancers.

Odd-eyed Turkish Angora.

Highly intelligent, Angoras are problem solvers that like to be in control of their surroundings; they will only tolerate being held for a few minutes before jumping down to bat at sunbeams and chase feathers. They'll stay in the room, though, so you can watch their antics admiringly.

The Angora is known for its swimming prowess, and will even plunge in for an occasional swim. Not every Turkish Angora enjoys water, but some do, with varying degrees of enthusiasm.

CONFORMATION

While pure white Turkish Angoras have been the norm for many years, Angoras in other colors are becoming increasingly popular. As is true of any breed, the pure white, blue-eyed Angora can be born partially or totally deaf. This is not a defect of the Angora breed itself, but rather a defect in the dominant W gene that produces white coat color and blue eyes in felines. This gene has been linked to a form of degenerative, hereditary deafness that affects the organ of Corti in the cochlea of the ear. Odd-eyed Angoras will generally be deaf in only one ear, on the blue-eyed side. While hearing-impaired Angoras must be kept out of harm's way, they otherwise enjoy life just as much as their hearing siblings and adapt to their hearing loss with no problem.

GENERAL	A balanced, graceful cat with a fine, silky coat that shimmers with every movement, in contrast to the firm, long muscular body beneath it.
BODY	Medium size, however, overall balance, grace, and fineness of bone are more important than actual size. Males may be slightly larger than females. Body is long and slender, possessing greater depth than width, oval rather than round (not tubular). Shoulders the same width as hips. Rump slightly higher than shoulders. Finely boned with firm muscularity.
HEAD	Small to medium, in balance with the length of the body and extremities. Shape a medium long, smooth wedge. Allowance is to be made for jowls. Profile: two planes formed by a flat top head and the line of the nose meeting at an angle slightly above the eyes. No break. Muzzle a continuation of the smooth lines of the wedge with neither pronounced whisker pad nor pinch. Nose medium in length. Neck slim, graceful, and rather long. Chin firm, gently rounded. Tip in profile to form perpendicular line with nose.
EARS	Large, wide at base, pointed and tuffed. Set closely together, high on the head, vertical and erect.
EYES	Large, almond shaped, slanting slightly upward with open expression. Each eye color can include much variation within defined spectrum. Acceptable colors include blue, sky blue to sapphire; green, gooseberry to emerald; green-gold, gold or amber eye that carries greenish cast or ring; amber, gold to rich copper but no green cast or ring; odd eyed, with one blue eye and the other green, green-gold, or amber. Odd-eyed cats should have similar depth of color in both eyes.
LEGS AND PAWS	Legs long. Hind legs longer than front. Paws small, round, and dainty. Tufts between toes preferable.
TAIL	Long and tapering from a wide base to a narrow end, with a full brush.
COAT	Single coated. Length of body coat varies, but tail and ruff should be long, full, finely textured, and have a silk-like sheen. "Britches" should be apparent on the hind legs.
COLOR	Any color or pattern with the exception of those showing hybridization resulting in the colors chocolate, lavender, the Himalayan pattern, or these combinations with white.
DISQUALIFY	Cobby body type. Kinked or abnormal tail. Crossed eyes.
ALLOWABLE OUTCROSSES	None.

284

HISTORY

When the Ark arrived at Mount Ararat some 5,000 years ago, Noah must have been a bit busy keeping the animals from stampeding in their eagerness to touch dry land. In the hustle and bustle, Noah didn't notice when two white-and-red cats leapt into the water and swam ashore. When the flood waters receded, the cats set out for Lake Van, located about 75 miles (121 km) to the south of Mount Ararat, where they have lived ever since. At least, that's one charming legend about the appearance of the Turkish Van, an ancient breed that has inhabited the Lake Van region of Turkey for Heaven knows how long. Turkish Vans can also be found in the nearby areas of Armenia, Syria, Iran, Iraq, and areas of Russia.

Red van pattern Turkish Van.

RATING OF CHARACTERISTICS

Characteristic	Rating (1–10)
Activity level	9
Playfulness	8
Need for attention	8
Affection toward its owners	8
Vocality	7
Docility	4
Intelligence	8
Independence	5
Healthiness & hardiness	7
Need for grooming	5
Compatibility with children	7
Compatibility with other pets	7

1—breed exhibits the least amount of this characteristic, 10—breed exhibits the most of this characteristic

✳ **Championship status in AACE, ACFA, CFA, CFF, TICA, and UFO**

The history of this magnificently tailed swimming cat is at least as intriguing as the legends. Also called the Swimming Cat, the Van is known for its fascination with water. The likely explanation for the Van's interest in swimming lies in the extreme temperatures in its native region. No kind and gentle environment here; Lake Van, the largest lake in Turkey and one of the highest lakes in the world, knows extreme temperatures in both summer and winter. Since summer temperatures reach well above 100°F (37.8°C), the Van may have learned to swim to cool off. Or perhaps the breed was hunting herring, the only fish that can survive in the briny water of Lake Van.

Whatever the reason for the Van's tolerance of water, it probably explains the development of the cashmere-like, water-repellant coat. Most domestic cats hate getting wet, possibly because they must spend hours putting their fur back in order. The Turkish Van's cashmere-like coat is water resistant, allowing the cat to go dog-paddling and come out relatively dry.

No one knows for sure when the Turkish Van arrived in the Lake Van region or where they came from. Although a relative newcomer to North America, this Turkish breed has lived in the Van region for thousands of years. Native ornaments dating as far back as 5000 B.C.E. depict cats that look remarkably like the Turkish Van. If so, the Van could well be one of the oldest cat breeds still in existence.

Vans were reportedly first brought to Europe by soldiers returning from the Crusades some time between 1095

Eye color can be blue, amber (above), or odd eyed.

and 1272 C.E. Over the centuries, the Vans were transported throughout the Eastern continents by invaders, traders, and explorers. The Vans have been called by a variety of names: Eastern Cat, Turkish, Ringtail Cat, and Russian Longhair. Being cats, Vans probably didn't answer to any of them.

The modern and better-known history of the Van began in 1955 when British citizens Laura Lushington and Sonia Halliday were given two Van kittens while touring Turkey. Since the breed was not known in Britain at the time, they decided to work with the cats and try to get them recognized by the Governing Council of the Cat Fancy (GCCF).

English breeder Lydia Russell was also instrumental in acquainting the public to the Van breed and sparking interest from fanciers in Great Britain and Europe. Russell also assisted new breeders obtain Turkish Van breeding stock. At first, the going was slow. Obtaining Van cats meant numerous trips to Turkey, and the cats had to pass through lengthy quarantine periods to enter England. Nevertheless, Vans were found to breed true, and in 1969 the hard work paid off when the Turkish Van was given full pedigree status by The Governing Council of the Cat Fancy (GCCF). In addition to GCCF, the Turkish Van is accepted by the Fédération Internationale Féline (FIFe), Cat Aficionado Association (CAA) of China, and the Australia Cat Federation (ACF).

The first Van kittens arrived in America in the 1970s, but it was not until breeders Barbara and Jack Reark started working with the breed in 1983 that the Vans began to flourish in North America. In 1985, TICA granted the Turkish Van championship status. CFA accepted the breed for registration in 1988, and in May 1993 the Van achieved provisional status with CFA, and championship status in May 1994. Even though the breed is still rare, interest has slowly grown.

Until the 1980s, Turkish Vans were not officially recognized in Turkey although highly prized as pets by the Turkish people. Today the Vans are being preserved by the Turkish College of Agriculture in connection with the Ankara Zoo, the longtime breeder of the Angora. Vans are no longer permitted to be exported from Turkey, and most new breeding stock comes from Europe.

PERSONALITY

While you might be drawn to the Van for its fascination with water, you'll fall in love with the breed for its other qualities. Vans are energetic, agile, and intelligent. They are extremely healthy and "get along with people swimmingly," notes one Van owner. You may need a few months of working out to keep up with them, however; Vans are famous for their action-packed temperaments. They are talkative, demand attention from their human servants, and show great gusto at dinnertime. Breeders also say that Vans are known for their deep attachment to their preferred people, and sometimes that makes transferring a Van from one household to another difficult. They tend to pick out one or two people in the household, usually

GENERAL	The Turkish Van is a natural breed from the rugged, remote, and climatically varied region of the Middle East. The breed is known for its unique, distinctive pattern; the term "Van" has been adopted by a variety of breeds to describe white cats with colored head and tail markings. The Turkish Van is a solidly built, semi-longhaired cat with great breadth to the chest. The strength and power of the cat is evidenced in its substantial body and legs. This breed takes a full 3 to 5 years to reach full maturity and development.
BODY	Moderately long, sturdy, broad, muscular, and deep-chested. Mature males should exhibit marked muscular development in the neck and shoulders. The shoulders should be at least as broad as the head, and flow into the well-rounded ribcage and then into a muscular hip and pelvic area.
HEAD	Substantially broad wedge, with gentle contours and a medium length nose to harmonize with the large muscular body, ears are not to be included in the wedge. Prominent cheekbones. In profile, the nose has a slight dip below eye level marked by a change in the direction the hair lays. Allowances must be made for jowling in the males. Firm chin in a straight line with the nose and upper lip; rounded muzzle.
EARS	Moderately large, in proportion to the body, set fairly high and well apart; the inside edge of the ear is slightly angled to the outside with the outside edge fairly straight but not necessarily in line with the side of the face; wide at the base. Tips are slightly rounded. Insides should be well feathered.
EYES	Moderately large, a rounded aperture slightly drawn out at the corners, set at a slant, equidistant from the outside base of the ear to the tip of the nose. Eyes should be clear, alert, and expressive.
LEGS AND PAWS	Moderately long, muscular legs. They are set wide apart and taper to rounded moderately large feet. Legs and feet should be in proportion to the body. Toes, five in front, four behind.
TAIL	Long, but in proportion to the body, with a brush appearance. Tail hair length is keeping with the semi-long coat length.
COAT	Semi-long with a cashmere-like texture; soft to the roots with no trace of undercoat. Due to the extremes in climate of their native region, the breed carries two distinctive coat lengths and allowances must be made for the seasonal coat. The summer coat is short, conveying the appearance of a shorthair; the winter coat is substantially longer and thicker. There is feathering on the ears, legs, feet, and belly. Facial fur is short. A frontal neck ruff and full brush tail become more pronounced with age. The above description is that of an adult, allowances must be made for short coats and tail hair on kittens and young adults.

COLOR	Van pattern only on glistening chalk-white body with colored markings confined to the head and tail is preferred. One or more random markings, up to color on 15% of the entire body (excluding the head and tail color), are permissible. Random markings should not be of a size or number to detract from the van pattern, making a specimen appear bicolor. A symmetrical pattern of head markings, divided by white up to at least the level of the front edge of the ears, is desirable.
DISQUALIFY	Total absence of color in the area from eye level up to the back of the head or tail; definite nose break; genetic/skeletal defects, such as flattened ribcage, kinked or abnormal tail, incorrect number of toes, and crossed eyes. Color in excess of 15% of the entire body (excluding the head and tail color).
ALLOWABLE OUTCROSSES	None.

the ones who deal with them initially, and bond with them forever.

Cat water fountains are a big hit with the Van; sometimes they'll sit in front of the fountain and stare in fascination for hours at the trickling water. Vans will often join their owners in the shower. Many Turkish Van cats enjoy a dip in the pool, bathtub, sink, in a pinch even the toilet. Van owners quickly learn to keep the lid down, and must be careful about allowing unsupervised access to water. Turkish Van kittens can get into particular trouble with this fascination. Even Vans that don't enjoy swimming are still fascinated by water, and will dunk their toys in water dishes and play in dripping faucets. Some will even learn to turn on faucets; they are very intelligent cats.

CONFORMATION

The Turkish Van is often confused with the Turkish Angora, but put them side by side and it's easy to see that they're entirely different breeds. The Angora is smaller and more delicate than the Van and does not have the classic "Van pattern," a term borrowed from the Turkish Van that is used to describe any cat that has a mainly white body and colored head and tail markings. The color should not take up more than 20 percent of the entire body. The Van pattern is governed by the dominant white spotting factor piebald gene (S), which gives them patches of white along with spots of color. This gene is hard to control and therefore makes breeding Turkish Vans with the proper color pattern difficult.

Some Vans have a color patch between the shoulder blades called the "Mark of Allah." Just as the M on the tabby's forehead is said to be a gift from the Virgin Mary, this "thumbprint of God" is considered good luck in Muslim countries.

CHAPTER SEVEN
NEW OR EXPERIMENTAL BREEDS

*"I have studied many philosophers and many cats.
The wisdom of cats is infinitely superior."*
—Hippolyte Taine

INTRODUCTION

The last 100 years have seen an explosion in the number of recognized cat breeds. Prior to the 1800s cats were kept as mouse catchers and companions (not necessarily in that order), but little thought was given to breeding them for particular characteristics. In the middle 1800s cat lovers began taking an interest in showing their special companions and entering them for competition. The cat fancy as we know it today began in 1871 when the first modern-day type of cat show was held in London's Crystal Palace (see the discussion of cat shows in Chapter Eleven). At that show, 170 cats were exhibited, including British Shorthairs, Persians and Angoras, as well as Siamese. The show was such a success that exhibiting pedigreed cats suddenly became all the rage in the United Kingdom.

Since then, the art of cat breeding, and creating new breeds, has become something of an international pastime to fanciers of *Felis silvestris catus*. More than half of the breeds recognized by our cat associations have existed for less than fifty years, and we can count on more to come in the years ahead as fanciers identity and promote feline variations.

New cat breeds are either classified as spontaneous mutations (like the American Curl and Scottish Fold) or are created by hybridization of two or more previously known breeds (like the Himalayan and the Ocicat). The requirements for acceptance of a new breed are stringent and vary depending upon the association. To be accepted, a new breed—or new color of an existing breed—must first be recognized for registration, and then accepted into a non-championship class often called new breed or color (NBC) where the breed, or rather the breeders and fanciers championing the breed, must prove the breed's uniqueness and worth. The requirements for acceptance of a new breed, or a new color within a breed, vary from association to association; a number of steps are involved to get to that coveted championship status. However, even if all the conditions are met, the association's board has a final vote whether or not to accept the breed for advancement, and there's no guarantee the breed will be advanced. As you'll see in some of the following profiles, the road to acceptance can be long, hard, and fraught with difficulties and impediments.

For example, in CFA, in order for a new breed to be considered for registration status and acceptance as a miscellaneous breed, fanciers must submit an application signed by at least ten breeders who are working with the breed; a tentative standard including a list of acceptable colors; classification information, including what breeds are allowed in the pedigree; breed category (longhair or shorthair), length of time outcross breeds will be allowed, breed's classification (natural, established, hybrid, or mutation); and registration applications for at least fifty specimens of the new breed. A breed committee chair elected by the breeders is to be the breed's representative to the CFA board. In addition, not required but highly desirable (it's politic and well-advised for the breeders to show the board they're serious), for the breeders to form a CFA-affiliated breed club, and create and distribute a breed newsletter in which news and accomplishments can be published; the board and CFA central office should receive all copies. If accepted as a miscellaneous breed by the CFA executive board, the breed may be exhibited in the non-championship miscellaneous class.

When a breed is accepted for miscellaneous or provisional status, the cats can compete in the non-championship classes; they cannot earn awards in championship competition. However, it's important for the breed to be exhibited so judges can see, examine, and become familiar with the breed. Breeders can and should form a breed committee and elect a breed committee chair to be the representative to the CFA board, and copies of the breed newsletter should be distributed to CFA and CFA board, and provide status and activity of the CFA Breed Club.

The next step is the provisional breed class (called NBC in some associations); this class is for any registered cat or kitten of a breed that has been accepted for registration but not yet accepted for championship competition. In CFA and CFF this is called provisional; in AACE and ACFA, this class is called new breed or color (NBC). In CCA this is called the new breed category. In TICA, a breed progresses from preliminary new breed to advanced new breed, and then to championship. In UFO a new breed goes from provisional to new breed or color, and then to championship.

In CFA, for a breed to be granted provisional status, the breed must have met all the requirements for miscellaneous status, the application must include a list of at least twenty-five active breeders, at least one CFA breed club must have been formed, and fanciers must provide sufficient facts about the proposed breed to demonstrate its potential value to the cat fancy and show the proposed breed's differences between existing recognized breeds. This includes completed favorable judges' evaluations indicating that the breed standard is understandable and indicative of the cats of that breed being presented in the show ring. In addition, 100 specimens of the breed must be registered over a period of not less than five years, and fanciers must present a definitive breed standard, a list of acceptable colors, and a cutoff date for breeds allowed in the background ancestry. Also (again, not required but highly desirable), examples of the breed should be presented to the CFA board at one of the regular meetings, and the status and activity of the CFA breed club should be provided.

The final step is championship; attaining this ultimate achievement usually takes years and tests the commitment of the breeders involved, which is one of the intentions of the process. The breeders and fanciers must be completely committed to their breed and its advancement to make it this far; by the time they achieve championship, the breed and its followers will have proved themselves worthy of the status. However, attaining all the necessary requirements is not a guarantee of advancement, even if acceptance was granted at the previous two levels. In the words of CFA's championship show competition requirements, "The

Board of Directors, on its own motion, will accept any Provisional Breed for Championship competition when, in the opinion of the Board, such action is proper . . . CFA recognizes that quality and benefits to the fancy are more important than mere numbers."

In order to consider a breed for championship competition in CFA, once all the requirements for miscellaneous and provisional status have been satisfied, the board must be presented with an application that includes a list of at least twenty-five active breeders; a breed standard that has been agreed upon by the breeders; a list of acceptable colors for championship competition; and registration paperwork of 100 cats of the breed. In addition, proof must be submitted that at least twenty-five different cats have been shown in CFA shows throughout all the regions. Also needed are additional positive judges' evaluations indicating the breed standard is understandable and indicative of the cats being shown in the ring. The championship breed package must arrive at the CFA central office by August 1 for consideration at the CFA February board meeting. As you can see, getting a new breed recognized is not a simple process; it takes the concerted effort of many cat fanciers over a long period.

Following are profiles of some of the new or experimental breeds. All have achieved some association acceptance; some are currently seeking additional association acceptance, and others are working toward championship or acceptance in additional associations. The personality charts have not been included in these profiles because many of these breeds will require more time to settle into a uniform pattern of behavior.

HISTORY

The Burmilla cat breed originated in England in the early 1980s, by an accidental crossbreeding between a silver Chinchilla male named Jemari Sanquist and a platinum European Burmese female named Bambino Lilac Fabergé. (In North America, the silver Chinchilla is a color division of the Persian breed, with a pure white undercoat and black tipping on the hair ends, giving the coat a characteristic sparkling silver appearance.) English breeder Miranda Bickford-Smith née von Kirchberg of the Astahazy Cattery had purchased a pedigreed Chinchilla male as a pet for her husband. However, shortly before Sanquist was to be altered, he had one last fling with a pedigreed Burmese female, who had escaped from her heat-imposed isolation. Soon after, it was clear that Burmese Bambino would have a litter fathered by Chinchilla Sanquist.

Bambino gave birth on September 11, 1981 to four Chinchilla/Burmese hybrids, all shorthaired shaded silver females. Bickford-Smith named the kittens Galatea, Gemma, Gabriela, and Gisella, and in a few weeks so was impressed with their attractive foreign type and short dense coats that she called friend and prominent cat breeder Therese Clarke of Kartush Cattery to give her opinion of the cats. Clarke shared Bickford-Smith's excitement about the appearance and temperament of the hybrids, and

Burmilla kitten, 4 months old.

they teamed up to develop them as the foundation of a new breed.

Clarke was particularly impressed with the foreign type of Galatea and Gemma from that first litter, so she adopted Gemma to establish her foundation Burmilla lines while Bickford-Smith kept Galatea to serve as the foundation of their new breed. In addition, Bickford-Smith arranged another mating between Sanquist and another of her best Burmese queens. In March 1982, this mating resulted in a single male kitten, Jacynth, who joined Gemma at Clarke's Kartush Cattery.

✳ **Championship status in ACFA, CCA, and UFO in both longhair and shorthair lengths; CFA in the Miscellaneous Class, TICA in the Experimental Category (both hair lengths)**

A mating between the longhaired Chinchilla Persian and the shorthaired Burmese will always produce short-haired offspring, because one copy of the recessive gene for long hair must be inherited from each parent for long hair to appear in a kitten's physical appearance. Therefore, Gemma and Galatea were both shorthaired, but both also carried the recessive gene for long hair from their Chinchilla father, and the recessive solid or 'self' gene from their Burmese mother. Both also had appealing foreign body and head types, and Clarke and Bickford-Smith decided that their new breed should resemble Gemma and Galatea, yet be different enough not to be taken for any existing breed. They wrote the breed standard with these guidelines in mind, and then came up with a name for their new breed. With a bit of thought they came up with the Burmilla ("Burm" for the Burmese, and "illa" for the Chinchilla); they immediately rejected the "Chin-ese" as being most inappropriate, and the Burmilla had a nice ring to it.

Adventurous and bold as kittens, Burmillas grow into sweet-natured, people-oriented adults.

They backcrossed Gemma and Galatea to the Burmese and soon obtained the body type they wanted. However, in 1983 Miranda Bickford-Smith became interested in the different varieties that were being produced during the breed's development, while Clarke was focusing on the original shorthaired Burmilla blueprint. Therefore, they agreed to expand their efforts and would develop the breed in two different ways: Bickford-Smith would develop the Burmilla and its additional colors and hair lengths within the Governing Council of the Cat Fancy (GCCF), and Clarke would focus on the type of Burmilla seen in the foundation cats Gemma and Jacynth within the newly formed Cat Association of Britain (CA). In 1984, Bickford-Smith and Clarke formed the Burmilla Cat Club to attract new breeders and promote their new breeds. In 1994, the Burmilla was recognized by the Cat Association of Britain, and in 1995, the Burmilla was accepted for championship in the GCCF.

Although the original standard called for a shorthaired cat of foreign type, a longhaired version soon arose; since the Chinchilla Persian is a long-haired cat and long hair is inherited via a recessive gene, many Burmillas carry the recessive gene for long hair. Longhaired Burmillas were produced when two shorthaired Burmillas carrying the recessive longhair gene were bred together. When both parents inherit one copy of the longhair gene, statistically one in four of their kittens will inherit two copies of the longhair gene and exhibit long hair; the other three will have short hair but two will inherit one copy of the recessive long-hair gene. In Great Britain the long-haired version of the breed is called the Tiffanie; in 1991, the breed was recognized by the Governing Council of the Cat Fancy. In GCCF today the Burmilla is accepted as part of the Asian cat group, along with Bombay and Tiffanie.

In 1984, two Burmillas were imported into Denmark by Burmese breeder Birgit Nehammer of Thamakan Cattery. She began a Burmilla breeding program and started several new lines by crossbreeding her two imports with her own Burmese. The breed gained fans and acceptance in that country. Soon after, the Burmilla Breeders Association of Australia was formed, and the Burmilla breed was shown and bred in Australia and New Zealand, to wide acclaim. In 1994, the Burmilla was granted recognition as a shorthair breed by the Fédération Internationale Féline (FIFe).

In 1995, the breed crossed the Atlantic and was introduced to North America. The CFA-affiliated Burmilla Enthusiasts of America was formed to promote and advance the breed. Now recognized by five associations including the Canadian Cat Association, the breed is catching on with American cat fanciers. In ACFA, CCA, and UFO the Burmilla is accepted in both long and short hair lengths for championship.

PERSONALITY

The Burmilla's temperament gives you the best of both its parent breeds—the personality of the active, mischievous, demanding Burmese is tempered by the tranquil, easy-going, affectionate Chinchilla Persian. Fanciers rave about the Burmilla's unique and captivating personality.

Adventurous and bold as kittens, Burmillas grow into sweet-natured, people-oriented adults. Not as active as the Burmese, Burmillas are still are full of life and enjoy a good game of catnip mouse wrangling. Their favorite games, however, are those they share with their human companions. Whirling feathers, laser light toys, round mice to fetch again and again—these throw the Burmilla into an ecstasy of delight. A ball of scrap paper will serve just as well, provided you're there to share the fun.

Like the Burmese, they are also very curious and intelligent; whatever you have hidden in that closed room or closet is cause for a full investigation by the inquisitive Burmilla. This determined breed will figure out a way into that closed door or cupboard, particularly if they notice you'd rather they didn't. Anything left out in the open is fair game, too; don't expect keys, socks, glass cases, pens, or the contents of your purse to remain where you put them. Small movable items immediately become toys. Watch out: you may catch your Burmilla tapping out texts to their Burmilla buddies.

After a good romp, your loyal and loving Burmilla will want to cuddle into your lap or arms, or curl up beside you on the couch for some petting, purring, and catnapping. Not overly vocal, Burmillas do have a loud, deep-throated purr that they switch on the moment you slide your hand down their silky backs. In all, it's the Burmilla's intelligent, affectionate, enthralling personality that wins the breed enthusiasts and exhibitors.

CONFORMATION

The medium-sized breed has strikingly green eyes that are large and outlined with black, as if it were wearing eyeliner. Its ears, meanwhile, are medium to large, with a slightly rounded tip. But the Burmilla's most attractive feature is its soft, dense coat, which may be tipped or shaded in many combinations of colors. The Burmilla also has a thick undercoat that makes the coat plush, but also increases the amount of grooming necessary to keep the Burmilla looking neat.

The Burmilla is generally a healthy breed, although some lines are prone to certain diseases and conditions. Because of the crosses with Persians, one inherited health problem known to exist in some Burmilla lines is polycystic kidney disease (PKD), an incurable disease that causes renal failure. Fortunately, a PKD genetic test is available from the Veterinary Genetics Laboratory, UC Davis, which helps breeders screen out affected cats. PKD testing is recommended for British Shorthairs, Burmillas, Exotics, Himalayans, Persians, Persian hybrids, and Scottish Folds. Be sure to talk to your breeder about this and any other health concerns, and buy from a breeder who tests for PKD and provides a written health guarantee.

GENERAL—ACFA STANDARD	The Burmilla's appearance is that of an elegant cat of foreign type and medium size.
BODY	Medium length and size. Rounded chest of medium width. Back straight from shoulder to the rump.
HEAD	Gently rounded top of head with medium width between the ears; wide at eyebrow level and jaw hinge, tapering to a short, blunt wedge. Profile shows a gentle dip. Tip of nose and chin should be in line. Chin is firm with good depth.
EARS	Medium to large, broad at base with slightly rounded tips; set with slight forward tilt in profile. Viewed from front, outer line of ear continues that of face.
EYES	Large; placed well apart at slightly oblique setting; curved upper line angled toward nose with fuller curved lower line. Luminous and expressive, outlined with basic color. Color any shade of green; yellow tinge acceptable in kittens and cats under two years of age.
LEGS AND PAWS	Legs slender with strong bones. Feet neat and oval.
TAIL	Medium to long with medium thickness at base; tapering to a slightly rounded tip.
COAT— SHORTHAIR	Short with a silky texture; smooth lying with sufficient undercoat to give a slight lift.
COAT— LONGHAIR	Fine and silky coat medium long, except over the shoulders, without a woolly undercoat. Ear tufts, furnishings, and full tail plume preferable.
COLOR	Pattern is more important than color; color descriptions not taken into consideration in show ring. Patterns: Chinchilla/shaded, hairs evenly tipped with appropriate color; Chinchilla, tipping about $1/8$ of entire hair length; shaded, tipping about $1/3$ of complete hair length. Colors: blue, chocolate, lavender (lilac), silver, sable, champagne, platinum, blue-cream, blue cream sepia, cream, shell, cameo, sepia, blue sepia, blue cream sepia, sepia cameo, shell sepia cameo, cream sepia cameo, cream shell sepia cameo, and tortoiseshell.
DISQUALIFY	Incorrect eye color in adults. Cobby or oriental body. Coat too shaggy.
ALLOWABLE OUTCROSSES	Burmilla LH and SH, Burmese, Foreign Burmese, and Chinchilla Persian (used only once as foundation breeding of a new line and not to be repeated in that line).

The Munchkin's short legs are the result of a natural mutation.

HISTORY

The cat fancy's version of downsizing—the Munchkin—has cat fanciers on both sides hissing over whether the breed should be recognized. While most new breeds have to face periods of resistance before acceptance can occur, the battle over this breed has been particularly long and heated because it raises questions regarding where unique variety ends and abomination begins. This point has been previously raised within the cat fancy concerning breeds such as the Sphynx and the Manx, now widely accepted breeds. The word (or words to that effect) was even applied to the Siamese when it made its debut in London in 1871.

Short-legged cats have been documented as early as the 1930s in England. According to records, these short-legged cats survived for four generations before World War II took its toll on the cat population of Europe. One such cat was also reported in the Soviet Union in the 1950s and dubbed the "Stalingrad Kangaroo Cat" for its tendency to sit up on its haunches. But the breed as we know it today began in Louisiana, USA.

In 1983 music teacher Sandra Hochenedel of Rayville, Louisiana discovered two cats hiding under a pickup truck where they had been cornered by a bulldog. Hochenedel rescued the cats and took them home, later noticing three things—both were female, both were pregnant, and both had short, stubby legs on normal-sized bodies. She kept Blackberry, the black-haired kitty, and gave away Blueberry, the gray-haired cat. What happened to Blueberry is unknown; all of today's all registered Munchkins can be traced back to Blackberry and one of her sons. When Blackberry had her litter,

✳ **Championship status in AACE, TICA and UFO in both longhair and shorthair lengths**

Hochenedel discovered that Blackberry had given birth to both short and ordinary long-legged kittens. One of the kittens, a handsome male Hochenedel named Toulouse after French painter Toulouse-Lautrec who, due to a bone disease, had an adult-sized torso but child-sized legs. Hochenedel gave Toulouse to Kay LaFrance, a friend who lived in Monroe, Louisiana. Using Toulouse, LaFrance established her own colony of Munchkins on her Louisiana plantation. Since LaFrance's cats were allowed free access to the outdoors and were not altered, a semi-feral population of Munchkins developed around Monroe, where they competed very well with their long-legged friends for prey and mating opportunities.

Blackberry vanished after having only a few litters, but her genetic legacy continued. Since LaFrance allowed Blackberry's son, Toulouse, to wander around unaltered, in short order a good sized population of short-legged cats lived on LaFrance's property. Since cats in heat care little about their partners' leg length (or much of anything else), Toulouse and his short-legged offspring had no trouble competing for mates with their longer-legged rivals.

Hochenedel and LaFrance, seeing how well the cats were doing on their own, thought this might be the beginning of a new breed.

They named the breed after the little people of Munchkinland from the classic 1939 movie *The Wizard of Oz*, and contacted Dr. Solveig Pflueger, M.D.,

Ph.D., allbreed judge and TICA's genetics committee chair. Dr. Pflueger conducted a study to assess the inheritance and expression of the Munchkin's short legs. She found that an autosomal dominant gene (a dominant gene residing on a chromosome that's not a sex chromosome) caused the long bones of the legs to be shorter than usual, and that the mutation had apparently occurred spontaneously within the feline gene pool. Concerned that these cats would have spinal dysfunction, degenerative disc disease, or hip dysplasia like the short-legged Dachshund, Corgi, and Basset Hound dog breeds, the breeders had the spines of a number of Munchkins examined and X-rayed by David Biller, D.V.M, head of radiology at the College of Veterinary Medicine at Kansas State University. No problems were discovered, but at the time the breed was so new and bloodlines so limited that the studies were not considered definitive. Independently, breeders had their oldest Munchkins X-rayed and examined for signs of joint or bone problems. No problems were found, but opponents pointed out that absence of proof wasn't proof of absence, since the oldest Munchkin was only about thirteen years old at that time, and the others X-rayed were younger still.

Hochenedel and LaFrance wrote the first breed standard, and established a breeding program. Other breeders soon joined their cause and established their own Munchkin breeding programs. In 1991, the Munchkin was introduced to the public at the nationally televised INCATS TICA show at Madison Square Garden in New York City, to both acclaim and resistance. They tried to gain recognition for the Munchkin with TICA at that time, but were turned down on the basis that not enough was known about the breed.

In 1994, the Munchkin breeders tried again, and this time the breed was accepted into TICA's New Breed development program in September of that year. TICA's New Breed development program is overseen by TICA's genetics committee, which tracks the pedigrees and monitors the breeding statistics as a breed develops, including the outcrosses used to develop the breed. This program confirmed that the gene governing the short legs was dominant; any cat that possesses the gene will have the foreshortened legs, and can pass along the trait to its offspring.

As of May 1, 1995, the Munchkin was recognized for New Breed and Color (NBC) status in TICA. When the acceptance was announced, one of the long-time TICA members resigned her ten-year judging position, saying the breed was an affront to any breeder with ethics. Others shared her sentiments, feeling that the short legs would cause crippling back, hip, and leg problems in the future, although no evidence existed that the Munchkin is prone to such problems.

However, other judges and fanciers were more tolerant or open-minded, and many cat lovers were enthusiastic about the new breed. Negative attitudes toward Munchkins are more frequent within the cat fancy than from the general public, say breeders.

Ironically, the controversy surrounding the breed contributed to its growing popularity. Because of articles in *The Wall Street Journal*, *People*, and other publications, demand for the sports car of the cat fancy increased until breeders had trouble meeting the demand. Waiting lists were long, and the supply limited. The sports car of the cat fancy commanded sports car prices, too, and breeders were concerned that unscrupulous people would take advantage of the Munchkin's popularity and use unethical backyard breeding practices.

After years of development and controversy, the Munchkin achieved TICA championship status in May 2003. Today, the breed is accepted for championship in AACE, TICA, and UFO in both long and short hair, but as of yet have not been able to receive recognition in ACFA, CCA, CFF, and CFA. The Munchkin has been accepted by some associations in other countries as well, such as the Waratah National Cat Alliance in Australia, the United Feline Organization in the United Kingdom, and the Southern Africa Cat Council in South Africa.

Other associations have refused to accept the breed; the Fédération Internationale Féline (FIFe) added to their rules they won't recognize any breed "showing as a breed characteristic a dominant gene resulting in shortened limbs and legs and other physical defects, for example, the Munchkin." The Governing Council of the Cat Fancy (GCCF) released a statement in 1991 that it "will strongly discourage anyone from importing such a cat [as the Munchkin] and that there was

Classic (blotched) red tabby Munchkin. All colors and patterns are accepted, including the pointed pattern.

no intention of recognizing this or any other new breed which was based on abnormal structure or development."

To keep the breed healthy and to widen the still relatively small gene pool, outcrossing to long-legged domestic longhairs and shorthairs that are not members of recognized breeds will continue in the future. Because of this, the body and head conformation, as well as color, pattern, hair length, and coat type, may vary as new genes are introduced. Prices have come down, but the Munchkin is still a rare and popular breed. Waiting lists can be long, but Munchkins are not as expensive as they once were. If you are flexible about gender, color, and pattern, your wait will be shorter.

The Munchkin breed has so caught the interest of some fanciers that new Munchkin breeds are in the process of being developed, usually hybrids of the Munchkin and other pedigreed breeds. These include the Napoleon Cat, crosses between Munchkins and Persians, the Skookum, crosses between Munchkins and LaPerms, and the Minskin, crosses between Munchkins and Sphynxs, Devon Rexs, and Burmese. So far, such breeds have achieved little recognition in the cat fancy.

PERSONALITY

For their part, Munchkins, oblivious to the controversy surrounding them, go on being just what they are—cats—self-assured and outgoing. Shortchanged in the leg department doesn't mean short on intelligence or personality. Friendly and people-ori-

Calico Munchkin longhair. Both long and short hair lengths are accepted.

ented, Munchkins make devoted companions, and they get along well with other cats, dogs, and people. They love to wrestle and play with their long-legged feline friends, happily unaware that there's anything different about them. Nor do their feline companions treat them as members of the vertically challenged. It's only humans who look at them askance.

Fanciers assert Munchkins can do anything an ordinary cat can do, except leap to the top of the kitchen counter. Some fanciers consider this a feature, however, instead of a disadvantage. Despite the short legs, Munchkins run fast, bounding like ferrets and taking corners at full speed. To get a better view, they often sit up on their haunches rather like prairie dogs. They can climb trees, cat posts, and curtains as well as any cat. However, they can't jump as high because the shorter back legs don't provide as much leverage. Munchkins can jump onto most beds, chairs, and couches, but may take a scenic route onto a chair or other lower item before attempting your desk.

Munchkins are also known as magpies, often borrowing small, shiny objects and stashing them away for later play. Proficient hunters, Munchkins love a good game of catnip mouse, but when playtime is over, they want a warm lap to snuggle into and strokes from a loving hand, like any cat.

CONFORMATION

The Munchkin mutation is a form of short-limb dwarfism called pseudoachondroplasia, which results in short limbs but a body and head of normal size. Problems associated with the Munchkin mutation are lordosis (abnormal downward curvature of the spine) and pectus (flattened ribcage that can put pressure on lungs and heart). While these conditions exist in other breeds and in random-bred domestics as well, Munchkins seem to be prone to these disorders.

If only one parent possesses one copy of the dominant Munchkin gene (in other words, when a short-legged Munchkin is bred to a long-legged Munchkin or to an outcross), approximately 50 percent of the kittens will inherit the Munchkin gene and have short legs, and about 50 percent won't inherit the gene and therefore will have ordinary long legs. Put another way, if a Munchkin is born with long legs, it cannot possess the gene for short legs; a simple dominant gene always shows itself in the physical appearance of the cat.

When two short-legged Munchkins are bred together, something surprising occurs, because the gene that gives Munchkins their short legs is semilethal. Without this lethality, such a mating on average would produce kittens in a ratio of 1:2:1; 25 percent long-legged kittens, 50 percent short-legged heterozygous kittens (kittens that inherit one copy of the Munchkin gene), and 25 percent homozygous kittens (kittens that inherit two copies of the Munchkin gene). However, homozygous kittens die inside the womb, so breeders actually get an approximate ratio of 1:2:0; 25 percent long-legged kittens, 50 percent short-legged heterozygous kittens, and zero percent short-legged homozygous kittens. Such litters are smaller than usual because of this flaw. This has not been studied enough to be proven without doubt, but the small litter sizes and the fact that no Munchkin has ever been born with two copies of the Munchkin gene strongly suggests that this is the case. Therefore, domestic cat outcrosses and long-legged Munchkins will continue to be used in breeding programs.

One of the problems with breeding outcrosses and long-legged Munchkins is what to do with the long-legged offspring that are inevitably produced. Some breeders specialize in popular colors and patterns, such as the pointed pattern, to make it easier to find homes for long-legged cats.

GENERAL (TICA STANDARD)	Munchkins exhibit shortening and may have slight bowing of the long bones. The spine is unaffected. The short legs do not hamper mobility or survival ability.
BODY	Thick semi-foreign body, not compact. Back gently slopes upward from shoulders to tail. Well-rounded chest and firm hips. Angulated shoulder blades are acceptable. Boning medium, without undue bulk. Firmly developed muscular strength.
HEAD	Modified wedge with rounded contours, in proportion with body. High, defined cheekbones. Chin firm, but not overly prominent; aligns with nose. Muzzle moderate with gentle contours in proportion with head. Prominent whisker pads are acceptable. Nose medium in length; slight bump is acceptable; slight stop. Forehead is flat.
EARS	In proportion with head, broader at base, ending in slightly rounded tips; placed as much on top of head as on sides; not flaring; alert. Lynx tip furnishings are acceptable on longhair cats only.
EYES	Walnut shaped; spaced rather wide apart giving an open and alert expression, and at a slight angle toward base of ears. No relationship between coat and eye color.
LEGS AND PAWS	Legs short, set evenly apart when viewed from front or back. Upper and lower forelegs equal in length. Hind Legs thigh and lower leg approximately equal in length. Back legs slightly longer than front legs acceptable. Feet are round, compact in proportion with body. All four feet pointed directly straight forward, not inward or outward.
TAIL	Carried erect when in motion, tapering to a rounded tip. Not overly thick. Length of the body.
COAT— SHORTHAIR	Medium to short. Solid colors may have a less dense coat. Texture semi-plush, all-weather, resilient, with medium undercoat and lustrous appearance.
COAT— LONGHAIR	Semi-long. Texture flowing and silky, all-weather, with moderate and medium undercoat. Slight to moderate ruff permissible. Britches are shaggy; tail has full plume.
COLOR	All categories, divisions, and colors; white lockets or buttons permitted.
DISQUALIFY	Withhold awards: short cobby body, curly coat. Disqualify: Sway back. Excessive bowing. Appearance of being a recognized breed miniaturized.
ALLOWABLE OUTCROSSES	Domestic longhairs and shorthairs, not members of recognized breeds.

HISTORY

The Nebelung (NAY-bel-ung) breed began the way so many of our breeds began—a stray cat wandered out of the mist and developed into a unique new breed. This breed's saga began in the early 1980s, when a shorthaired black female feline and her black longhaired Angora-type suitor produced a litter of three. One of the shorthaired black females was given to the son of computer programmer Cora Cobb of Denver, Colorado, who named the kitten Elsa. In August 1984, Elsa produced a litter of her own, with the help of a shorthaired Russian Blue-type tomcat. Both Elsa and her blue-haired boyfriend must have possessed the recessive gene for long hair, because Elsa's litter of six included one beautiful longhaired solid blue male. Quite taken with the handsome blue fuzz ball, Cora Cobb adopted the kitten and named him Siegfried after the hero in her favorite Wagner opera, *The Ring of the Nibelung*.

As Siegfried grew, Cobb was taken by Siegfried's beauty and devoted personality—he was the most loving, devoted cat she'd ever known. When Elsa's next litter, fathered by the same Russian Blue-type tom, produced a lovely longhaired female kitten that possessed many of Siegfried's delightful characteristics, Cobb obtained her and named her Brunhilde, after the heroine in Wagner's opera. The blue female was beautiful and sweet, and her silky hair was longer and lighter than Siegfried's. Now that Cobb had a matching set of these loving and beautiful blue cats, she decided to see if she could

preserve their beauty and loving temperament by breeding brother to sister. If she could produce cats as extraordinary and beautiful as these two, Cobb thought, everyone would want one.

When Cobb moved to El Paso, Texas, in 1985, she took Siegfried and Brunhilde with her. In 1986, Brunhilde accepted her brother as mate, and about two months later she produced a litter of three blue longhairs. To Cobb's delight, all three inherited Siegfried's Russian Blue body type and Brunhilde's longer, glossy blue fur. Since Cobb was unfamiliar with the genetics of breeding cats, she didn't

The Nebelung's coat catches the light, giving the fur a luminous quality.

✴ **Championship status in AAFA, CFF, and TICA**

Affectionate and devoted, Nebelungs form close life-long bonds with their human companions.

know that blue, longhaired kittens were the only possible outcome of Siegfried's and Brunhilde's rendezvous. Both long hair and blue coloration are governed by recessive genes; to express those traits in their physical appearance each had to possess two copies of each gene. Since both Siegfried's and Brunhilde had solid blue coloration and long hair, all offspring would have both traits as well.

Cobb named the breed the Nebelung, a German word that loosely means "creatures of the mist," an appropriate name for a feline that magically vanishes into thin air when strangers come to visit. She decided to see what

it would take to establish her new breed of cat. On the advice of TICA's genetics chairperson, Dr. Solveig Pflueger, to whom Cobb turned for guidance in establishing her new breed, Cobb wrote the Nebelung's standard almost word for word from the Russian Blue's, except for the coat length and the general opening description. TICA accepted the Nebelung for registration in September 1987.

At first, Russian Blue breeders weren't at all excited about Cobb's longhaired newcomers, and Cobb had difficulty finding breeders who would provide stud service, or sell her good quality registered Russian Blue breeding stock. Finally, the owner of Supreme Grand Champion Vladimir of Castlecats agreed to offer her cat for stud with one of Brunhilde's daughters, who produced a litter in June 1988.

Since then, the number of Nebelungs has slowly grown and, despite setbacks, the breed has caught worldwide attention. The Nebelung has appeared twice on the front cover of a Japanese cat magazine, and Nebelungs were shown and sold at the 1989 TICA cat show in Paris, France.

As of May 1, 1997, the Nebelung was granted championship status in TICA, a major step forward that brought the breed national and international attention. Today, Nebelungs are recognized by ACFA, CFF, and TICA, as well as the international associations the World Cat Federation (WCF), and Livre Officiel des Origines Félines (LOOF). Breeders have catteries in many countries including the Netherlands, Belgium, France, Germany, Poland, Russia, the United Kingdom, Canada, as well as the United States. Numbers are still small and breeders limited, so it remains to be seen if the Nebelung will catch the fancy's attention again, or fade away into the mist.

PERSONALITY

The best thing about Nebelungs, say fanciers, is their personality. Affectionate, sweet, and loving, Nebelungs form close bonds of love and trust with their human companions and stay extremely devoted and loyal their entire lives. Nebelungs are playful, affectionate, and intelligent, and follow their favorite humans from room

to room to keep an eye on the action. Sit down, and your lap will quickly be filled by silky soft fur; Nebelungs enjoy sitting beside or in the laps of their chosen humans to receive their due of petting and pampering. They tend to bond with a select few humans and stay loving and dedicated throughout their lives.

This breed likes a steady routine, will learn yours quickly, and dislike disruptions to their habits; Nebelungs need time to adjust to household changes. They tend to adapt slowly to changes in their routines or the routines of their humans; if you go back to working full time after being at home for many months, Nebelungs may have trouble adjusting. It's important to make sure that your Nebelung gets plenty of love and attention during times of change. If you must leave a Nebelung alone for long hours, provide a compatible cat companion to keep your Nebelung company while you're away earning the cat food. Early socializing can help your Nebelung adapt more easily.

They are soft-spoken unless something is seriously wrong, such as empty food dishes or cat boxes that are not up to the Nebelung standard of cleanliness. This breed tends to be particular about their environment, and will make their feelings known about litter boxes that offend their sensitive noses or cuisine that doesn't meet their high standards.

Nebelungs are generally reserved around strangers, ranging from hiding-under-the-bed timid to warily eyeing intruders from a safe distance. Given the sometimes unpredictable behavior of some humans, this could be inter-

GENERAL (TICA STANDARD)	The goal of the Nebelung breeding program is to produce a blue cat with the same type as those imported from Russia in the nineteenth and early twentieth centuries and to combine this type with a thick shimmering coat of medium length.
BODY	Well-proportioned and athletic, semi-foreign in type. The overall body structure is long and graceful with medium boning. The cat should appear neither rangy and leggy, nor cobby and short. Musculature athletic, not bulky, and proportioned to carry body length and weight. Both males and females well-muscled. Proportion and general balance is more desired than mere size.
HEAD	Modified wedge in good proportion to body. More pointed than rounded, although longer hair may give a rounded look. Straight line from tip of nose to tip of chin. Muzzle medium length; puffy whisker pads. Forehead straight to level of upper edge of eye. Tip of nose has such a shallow concave curve that it appears virtually straight. No stop, break, or nose bump.
EARS	Large and pointed, set to continue the modified wedge.
EYES	Very slightly oval, medium size, and widely spaced. Color green with yellow/green mixture allowed. In kittens, changing from yellow to green; should show green halo around pupil by eight months. As vividly green as possible at maturity; could be two years or more. The more richness and depth of color the better.
LEGS AND PAWS	Legs long with medium boning. Feet medium-sized, well-rounded ovals with generous tufting between the toes. Appears to stand and walk on balls of feet.
TAIL	Tail hair must be longer than on body. Length is in balance with the length of the body; ideally, at least equal to the body length from rump to shoulder blades.
COAT	Medium-long over body with increasing length from shoulder area to tail. Males may display neck ruff; females to lesser extent. Fur is longer on tail. Feathering behind ears of lighter shade of blue is desirable. Texture soft two-layered coat, suitable for all weather, resistant to water. Outer coat fine and silky; semi-long over body, beginning at shoulders where coat is slightly shorter. Pantaloons on hind legs. Allowance for seasonal changes. Adult coats may take up to 2 years to fully develop.
COLOR	Coat color is blue, sound to the roots, with a soft lustrous sheen. Silver tipping desirable, but not mandatory. Lighter shades of blue desirable; silver tipping may not be evident. Undercoat layer is very soft down, lighter blue in contrast to guard hairs of outer coat. Emphasis is on soundness of color, not on individual hue.

DISQUALIFY	Any white spots or lockets; full penalty for eyes with no green. Rangy or cobby body. Underweight, poor condition. Weak chin.
ALLOWABLE OUTCROSSES	Russian Blue.

preted as a sign of this breed's extreme intelligence. To their chosen family, however, Nebelungs are affectionate and playful.

CONFORMATION

The Nebelung is a beautiful breed, with a semi-long, luminous blue coat tipped with silver, snapping green eyes, and a long, elegant body. The primary difference in conformation between the Nebelung and the Russian Blue is coat length; otherwise, the standards are almost identical. Whereas the Russian Blue's coat is short and dense, the Nebelung's fur is medium-long, silky, and possesses a dense undercoat. The bright blue color is contrasted with silver-tipped guard hairs, and therefore the coat catches the light, giving it a luminous, misty quality. Even with a dense undercoat that makes the coat stand away from the body, the fur resists matting and does well with a good once-a-week brushing.

Even with its dense undercoat, the Nebelung's fur only needs a thorough once-a-week combing.

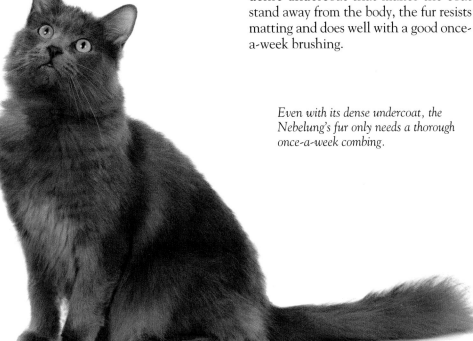

SAVANNAH

HISTORY

This hybrid breed was originally created by a mating between a domestic cat (*Felis silvestris catus*) and an African serval (*Leptailurus serval*). The exact details regarding the breed's beginnings are at times ambiguous and contradictory, however, we do know the first hybrid, a female named Savannah who would become the foundation cat of the Savannah breed, was born on April 7, 1986, the product of a tryst between a male African serval and a female Siamese-type domestic cat. Bengal breeder Judee Frank of Philipsburg, Pennsylvania obtained the male serval cub named Ernie from serval breeder Suzi Wood of New Jersey, ostensibly as a mate for Judee Frank's female serval.

Evidently, however, Judee Frank's actual plan was to breed the serval to a domestic cat and produce a hybrid. To that end, Frank raised the serval cub with the female kittens from a litter of barn cats, with the idea that Ernie and the kittens would grow up together, form family bonds, and eventually be willing and able to mate. This plan did in fact work, because when they were grown Ernie mated with one of the females, a sealpoint Siamese look-alike. The mother cat weighed about eight pounds while her serval beau weighed between thirty and thirty-five pounds (13.6 to 15.8 kilos). On April 7, 1986, the female domestic gave birth to an eight-ounce spotted female kitten, the first recorded serval/domestic hybrid. However, because of the stigma among cat fanciers concerning cross-breeding cat species, at the time and for some years afterward Judee Frank told everyone the resulting hybrid kitten was a happy accident.

The extraordinary first generation F1 (filial 1) kitten had characteristics of both her domestic cat mother and her serval father. From the serval side of her ancestry she inherited large ears, long legs, rangy body type, thick medium-length tail, spotted coat pattern, facial expressions, body language, and wariness of strangers. Like her domestic mother, she was a talker, athletic and active, and used the litter box properly. Reportedly, she was very affectionate but had an assertive temperament and disliked being held or restrained in any way.

According to Judee Frank, she had agreed to give Suzi Wood the first serval cub sired by Ernie as payment for him and his services. However, according to Suzi Wood, Judee Frank owed Wood the first kitten of any kind sired by Ernie and therefore Wood felt she was owed the hybrid kitten. Judee Frank denied Wood's claim, but Suzi Wood managed to gain custody of the kitten anyway.

Suzi Wood named the kitten Savannah, after the African savannahs that are the serval's native habitat. Wood made plans to breed Savannah back to domestic males when she grew up. She decided the breed should be called the Savannah as well.

As Savannah matured, she grew quite large, tipping the scales at fifteen pounds (6.8 kilos). Suzi Wood tried to interest a number of domestic males into courting the hybrid cat, but Savannah made strange growls,

✳ **Championship status in TICA; AACE and CCA in New Breed or Color class; UFO in the Provisional Class**

Savannahs need daily interaction and play-time with their human companions.

trills, and other odd nondomestic cat-like noises, particularly when she was in heat, which frightened her potential suitors. None of the domestic males wanted anything to do with her. After some thought, Wood decided a deaf cat wouldn't be alarmed by Savannah's freedom of speech. She obtained Prince Albert, a thirteen pound (5.9 kilo), pure white, blue-eyed, completely deaf Turkish Angora from breeder Lori Buchko of Hightstown, New Jersey.

Albert and Savannah quickly bonded and became lifelong companions and mates. On April 5th, 1989, Savannah produced one stillborn and two live second generation (F2) kittens: a solid white male and a spotted female. Around April 1990, Savannah had another litter of two, of which only

the one male survived. After Albert and Savannah produced these two litters, however, Savannah suddenly became unable to conceive. Only one F2 female kitten was born in those two litters, and Suzi Wood soon discovered that all the males were sterile, a phenomenon very common in hybrids and particularly so in the early generations. The Savannah breed could only be propagated via female lines, as the males were sterile for the first five generations. The one fertile female, named Kitty, was given to Lori Buchko in exchange for Prince Albert. Since all the male kittens were sterile and Savannah had stopped producing kittens, Suzi Wood's plans to develop the new breed came to sudden stop. In addition, Lori Buchko had retired from breeding and wasn't interested in using Kitty to create a new breed.

Suzi Wood wrote several articles for animal publications about Savannah. One of the articles came to the attention of Patrick Kelley of Los Angeles, California, who had been interested in exotic-looking domestic cats for many years and who had hopes of starting a new breed of large, spotted, feral-looking domestic cats. Excited about the description of Savannah, Patrick Kelley contacted Suzi Wood, and was disappointed to learn Savannah was no longer able to conceive and all the male hybrids were sterile. However, Wood told Kelley about Savannah's one remaining fertile offspring—Kitty, owned by Lori Buchko. Wood introduced Kelley to Buchko, who in 1989 sold her Kitty to Patrick Kelley, on the condition that he promised to make the Savannah into a bona fide breed.

Kelley was eager to do just that, but he found promising was easier than doing. He contacted Leslie Bowers, TICA's business manager and executive secretary, to find out what steps were required to establish a new breed, and get it recognized by the cat registry. The requirements were daunting, but that didn't dampen his enthusiasm. However, he realized he would need help, and lots of it, if he was to be successful. A single person could found a new breed, but it took many breeders and exhibitors, and many generations of cats, to get a hybrid breed recognized and accepted for show status.

Patrick Kelley contacted both Suzi Wood and Judee Frank, but neither was interested in taking the breed further. Kelley then approached Bengal breeders, who he thought would be as excited as he was about developing this new hybrid breed. Not only were they unexcited, most wanted nothing to do with Kelley or the new hybrid. Kelley persisted, however, and finally found one breeder, Joyce Sroufe of Ponca City, Oklahoma, who had Bengals, Egyptian Maus, Ocicats, servals, Asian leopard cats, and other small wild cats. She shared Patrick Kelley's enthusiasm for developing the Savannah into a new breed.

Their original idea was to use Egyptian Maus and Spotted Oriental Shorthairs as outcrosses, since both were spotted, and the Oriental's large ears could be an asset to the breed.

Joyce Sroufe and Patrick Kelley conferred on the Savannah's desirable characteristics, and together they created the first Savannah standard. In February 1996, Patrick Kelley presented the standard to TICA's Board of Directors. The Savannah was approved for registration status at that meeting. However, the breed hit a snag at this point, because the same day the Savannah was approved for registration, TICA put in place a moratorium on all new hybrid breeds. This meant Savannahs could be registered with TICA but they could not progress to advanced new breed or championship status.

Discouraged but undaunted, Joyce Sroufe and Patrick Kelley continued to promote and develop the breed. Patrick Kelley's second generation (F2) Savannah, Kitty, was bred back to a domestic male, producing the first litter of third generation (F3) Savannah cats. Kelley focused on setting up a presence for the breed and its breeders on the

Internet; Kelley's SavannahCat.com website became the foremost promoter of the breed on the Internet. Later he had success promoting the Savannah breed in print publications such as *Cat Fancy Magazine*, in web articles, and on certain television programs.

At the same time, Joyce Sroufe worked to produce new Savannah lines, refine the breeding process, and recruit new breeders. At the beginning, this took much trial and error to find cats that were compatible with servals and early generation hybrids. Some breeds were used because they resembled the desired Savannah look (short spotted coat, body conformation, head and ear type, etc.). However, size was important since servals are so much larger than the average domestic cat. To make mating possible, Maine Coons, Serengetis, Bengals, Bengal crosses, and other breeds known for their size and heft were used to produce first generation Savannahs. In addition, spotted Oriental Shorthairs, Egyptian Maus, Ocicats, and non-pedigreed domestic cats were used. Sroufe was the first breeder able to create more first generation (F1) serval/domestic cat hybrids, due to her expertise in breeding both exotic and domestic cats. Sroufe shared

Savannahs are outgoing, active, and very playful.

her knowledge with other breeders and mentored new fanciers who wanted to learn. Later, she was the first to breed down the necessary six generations to produce fertile males. Because of her contributions to the breed, some consider Joyce Sroufe the founder of the breed.

In 1997, Sroufe introduced the Savannah at the TICA Westchester Cat Show in White Plains, New York, which brought new breeders to the Savannah and a huge demand for pets from the public. Sroufe provided pet-quality kittens for cat-lovers (though never enough for the demand), and provided breeding females and eventually fertile males for other Savannah breeding programs. As the breed progressed, making its way through the requirements needed to progress to the next level of acceptance, the standard was reworded and refined, and the acceptable outcross breeds were narrowed down to Oriental Shorthairs, Egyptian Maus, and domestic shorthairs.

In 2001, TICA lifted their moratorium on new hybrid breeds and accepted the Savannah into TICA's New Breed program. Lorre Smith, the first TICA Savannah Breed Chair, was instrumental in convincing the board of directors to lift the moratorium, and in addition worked with Savannah breeders to refine the breed standard and facilitate the breed's advancement through TICA's required steps; with Smith's help the Savannah rose through the ranks more rapidly than it otherwise would have. In May 2004, the Savannah was accepted for provisional new breed status, and in May 2008, the Savannah was accepted as an advanced new breed. Finally, in May 2012, the Savannah achieved full championship status in TICA.

Lisa Jeffery of Ontario, Canada, was the first Savannah breeder to show Savannah cats in Canada. Jeffery helped write the breed standard, and was instrumental in getting the breed accepted by the Canadian Cat Association (CCA). CCA accepted the Savannah for registration in 2006, and in the New Breed category in 2007. Owning servals is illegal in Canada, but Canadian breeders have been able to import F1 and F2 Savannahs to develop their Savannah lines.

Now that the breed is a fully accepted TICA championship breed, the vast majority of matings are Savannah to Savannah. To be shown for championship in TICA, a Savannah must be what's called a Stud Book Traditional (SBT), which means a cat shows at least three generations of Savannah-to-Savannah breeding on its pedigree. Outcrosses are no longer permissible, but since TICA is a genetic registry that understands the potential need for some breeds to use outcrosses, it is acceptable to outcross to three breeds: Oriental Shorthair, Egyptian Mau, and Domestic Shorthair. However, whenever an outcross is used, whether Serval, Egyptian Mau, Domestic Shorthair, or even an earlier generation of Savannah, that line has to start over, and will require three more generations of breeding Savannah to Savannah before the fourth generation becomes showable as championship Savannahs. Today, outcrosses are not common, since it takes that line all the way back to the beginning. Those breeders who use outcrosses are usually breeding serval to domestic cat; this starts a brand new line and adds a fresh new bloodline to the breed, and since any outcross requires starting over, it doesn't take the breeder back any farther than an acceptable outcross would. Any responsible Savannah breeder starting over with a serval will outcross to a cat breed that complements the Savannah in type and pattern.

Savannahs remain a rare breed and quite expensive, although they have come down from their original prices. One reason is that all early filial males are sterile; it's not until generation F6 that a substantial number of the males are fertile. In addition, starting new lines using serval cats and domestics is challenging for several reasons. First, owning servals is illegal in some states, while other states require a permit from the USDA. Second, domestic cats have an approximate sixty-five-day gestation while servals gestate for about seventy-three days. Due to this difference in gestation, first generation (F1) Savannahs born to domestic cats are often born prematurely and survive only by human intervention with around-the-clock care and feeding. This makes starting new Savannah lines very challenging.

PERSONALITY

Savannahs are intelligent, active, affectionate, and very people-oriented; some fanciers say this breed is more dog-like in their devotion to their human companions than cat-like. They like to keep a close eye on all human activities, usually following their preferred people from room to room so as not to miss a single interesting event, such as cupboards opening or food being prepared, or any playing, petting, or pampering that might come their way. When you come through the door after even a relatively short time away, Savannahs welcome you home by loving leg rubs and bumping foreheads; these "forehead-presses" or "head-butts" (depending upon their degree of enthusiasm) show their delight over your return.

Loyal and loving, Savannahs form deep bonds with their human fami-

GENERAL (TICA STANDARD)	Overall impression of Savannah is a tall lean graceful cat with large, bold markings on tawny, gold, orange, silver, black, or black smoke background; replica of serval cat from which it originated but smaller in stature.
BODY	Torso long, lean, and well-muscled with full deep rib cage, prominent shoulder blades, slight but not extreme tuck-up and rounded rump. Hips and thighs full, long, and somewhat heavy in proportion to body. Medium boning with density and strength; musculature firm, well-developed, yet smooth.
HEAD	Face forms equilateral triangle; triangle is formed by brow line over the eyes, sides follow down jaw bone with rounded finish at muzzle; above triangle forehead and ears form rectangle from brow line to tops of ears. Muzzle is tapered with no break; whisker pads not pronounced. Head small in proportion to body. Chin tapers to follow triangle of head. Nose is slightly protruding. From front, nose wide across top with low set nostrils; from profile, slight downward turn at end, giving rounded appearance. Head set on long neck.
EARS	Remarkably large and high on head; wide with a deep base, very upright and have rounded tops. Outside base of ear starts no lower on head than height of eyes, but may be set higher. Inside base of ears set close at top of head; ideally, a vertical line can be drawn from inner corner of eye up to inner base of ear. Ear furnishings may be present; pronounced ocelli desirable.
EYES	Medium sized and set underneath a slightly hooded brow. Top of eye resembles a boomerang set at exact angle so corner of eye slopes down line of nose. Bottom half of eye has almond shape. Eyes moderately deep set, low on forehead, and at least one eye width apart. Tear stain markings present along and between eye and nose. All eye colors are allowed and are independent of coat color.
LEGS AND PAWS	Legs longer than average, well-muscled, without appearing heavy or overly delicate. Back legs are slightly longer than front legs. Feet oval; medium in size.
TAIL	Medium to thick in width. Medium in length, ending between hock and just above ground level when standing; preferred length just below hock. Tail tapers slightly to blunt end.
COAT	Short to medium length with good substance and slightly coarse feel. Coarser guard hairs cover softer undercoat; spots have notably softer texture than guard hairs. Coat is not inordinately dense and lies relatively flat against body.

COLOR	Spotted pattern only. Black, brown (black) spotted tabby, black silver spotted tabby, and black smoke. Bold, solid markings preferred. Spotted pattern made of bold, solid dark-brown to black spots, which can be round, oval, or elongated. In black, Savannah ghost spotting may occur. In all divisions, any visible pattern must be spotted.
PENALIZE	Rosettes. Spots that are any color other than dark brown to black. Any distinct locket on the neck, chest, abdomen, or any other area not provided for in standard. Vertically aligned spots or mackerel tabby type stripes. Whippy tails undesirable. Cobby body. Small ears.
DISQUALIFY	Extra toes.
ALLOWABLE OUTCROSSES	None.

lies, provided their human families give them the love and attention they need in return. Particularly when Savannahs are kittens, they need daily interaction with their favorite humans, lots of it, if they are to grow into the loving, devoted companions they can be. Savannahs are sociable and usually get along well with other household pets, provided the proper introductions are made in the beginning. Savannahs get along well with well-behaved children.

Savannahs are outgoing, active, and very playful cats, with a well-developed sense of feline curiosity. Many enjoy a rough and tumble game with flexible feathered wands, laser light toys, and feline "fishing poles." Larger Savannahs do well with small dog toys made of sturdy materials; some cat toys are too delicate for the rambunctious Savannah. Savannahs particularly enjoy toys in which their favorite humans take an active role. Most love to play games of fetch, and will retrieve a ball over and over for you to throw.

Many Savannahs also love to play in, or with, water; some enjoy a swim or a bath—as long as it's their idea, of course. Some will even join their owners in the shower. Given the choice, some Savannahs enjoy a tub filled with tepid water in which to splash and play over more usual cat games.

Some Savannahs love getting your attention by getting into trouble; tell your Savannah to stay off the top of the refrigerator, and there you'll see her, peering down at you with huge ears cocked forward, watching your reaction with a small self-satisfied cat smirk on her face. Combine that with avid curiosity, and you'll find your Savannah frequently opening doors, drawers, and cabinets with strong, agile paws. Savannahs particularly love heights, and they often can be found perched on the highest bookshelf or cat tree, taking in the sights from a Savannah's eye viewpoint.

Despite their exotic appearance, Savannahs don't differ much from other domestic cats in their care and behavior. Breeders recommend Savannahs as indoor-only pets, and suggest that Savannahs experience the great outdoors at the end of a lead or from inside a securely fastened run or outdoor enclosure. Savannahs are usually easy to train to walk on a lead using a harness or specially designed walking jacket, and breeders recommend leash training so they can get the extra exercise they need. Unlike dogs, however, Savannahs won't stay at heal, or even understand the point of doing so; like the cats they are, they believe they're graciously taking you out for a walk. Enclosures are particularly helpful, as long as they are covered completely and securely. Due to their long legs, Savannahs are excellent jumpers and like the serval often perform high leaps straight in the air. Some have been known to jump up to eight feet high (2.4 m) from a standing position.

When introduced young, they will adapt well to most living situations, and will peacefully share their territory with dogs, other cats, and well-behaved children. Breeders note that early socialization is particularly important for this breed, so it's wise to find a breeder who raises the kittens underfoot.

Your Savannah, like all domestic household pets, should always be neutered or spayed. Even though early generation Savannah males are sterile, neutering prevents behavior issues and unpleasant elimination habits, such as spraying. The Savannah is not for everyone, but for those who seek a unique pet and lifelong companion, the Savannah fits the bill.

CONFORMATION

The large, spotted hybrid is smaller in stature than the serval and domestic in temperament. The Savannah is lean and graceful, with an impression of wildness; Savannahs resemble servals in visual aspect and bearing. The most striking features are boldly spotted golden, silver, or black smoke coat, the three-quarter-length tail, and the tall, muscular build. The Savannah is one of the largest domestic cat breeds, so large that in 2011 Guinness World Records authenticated an F2 Savannah named Trouble, owned by Debby Maraspini of Savannah Island Cattery in Walnut Grove, California, as the world's tallest cat. In October 2011, Trouble measured nineteen inches tall (48.3 cm) from toe to shoulder blade.

Savannahs can range in size from eight pounds to occasionally over twenty pounds when mature. Males are usually larger than females. In TICA, only spotted pattern Savannahs are accepted for exhibition in the champion classes. Acceptable colors include brown spotted tabby, silver spotted tabby, and black smoke. Savannahs in nonstandard colors and patterns, such as solid black or tabby striping or marbling instead of spots, may be registered but not shown for championship.

Note: before considering purchasing a domestic cat with wildcat ancestors, be sure to check your state's laws regarding the owning of hybrids. It's also strongly recommended that you research your county and city laws, and your homeowner association rules if applicable, prior to buying hybrid animals. More information can be found online at www.hybridlaw.com.

HISTORY

The Snowshoe is a beautiful blue-eyed breed that combines the best qualities of the vocal, supple Siamese and the easy-going, sturdy American Shorthair. This shorthaired breed makes a terrific companion.

The breed got its start at the end of the 1960s when Siamese breeder Dorothy Hinds-Daugherty of Kensing Cattery in Philadelphia, Pennsylvania, produced a litter that included three Siamese kittens with pure white mittens. While most breeders would have been appalled to find the white spotting factor in their supposedly pure Siamese lines (see Chapter Four, page 39), instead Hinds-Daugherty was intrigued by the adorable kittens and their unique pattern. Instead of quietly giving away the mittened kittens, she decided to turn these mavericks into a breed. She set out to reproduce the look by breeding one of her sealpoint Siamese with a bicolor American Shorthair. The resulting offspring lacked the Siamese's pointed pattern because both parents must have the recessive gene for the pattern to express in offspring. By breeding the resulting kittens back to Siamese mates, however, Hinds-Daugherty achieved the desired result—a pointed pattern cat with a middle of the road body style and four white mittens. Continued crosses with American Shorthair bicolors added a white inverted V pattern on the nose and muzzle in some of the kittens, which Hinds-Daugherty thought was a charming variety.

She named the new breed "Snowshoe" since the kittens looked like they had just romped through glistening snow. She wrote a preliminary standard, exhibited her cats at local shows, and approached CFF about registering the Snowshoe. After quite a bit of persuading, CFF approved the Snowshoe for exhibition only.

After a few frustrating years Dorothy Hinds-Daugherty decided getting the Snowshoe accepted wasn't her destiny, and she closed her cattery and abandoned the breeding program. Fortunately for Snowshoe fans, breeder Vikki Olander Martes

Lynx point Snowshoe kitten.

* **Championship status in AACE, ACFA, CFF, TICA, and UFO**

(then Vikki Olander) of the Furr-Lo Cattery in Virginia had taken up the Snowshoe challenge, and she continued working with the breed. Olander wrote the first complete breed standard, recruited new breeders, and gave the breed a paw in gaining recognition; in 1974 the American Cat Association (ACA) and CFF accepted the Snowshoe as an experimental breed.

By 1977, however, Vikki Olander was the only Snowshoe breeder left in North America, as one by one the other breeders lost interest and dropped out due to the difficulty in breeding Snowshoes that came close to meeting the demanding standard. The white spotting factor is one of the most unpredictable genes with which to work, and breeders have had limited success in getting it under sufficient control to produce more uniform patterns. Fanciers who began breeding Snowshoes with high hopes have moved on to less challenging breeds, or have given up breeding altogether. For a time it seemed the Snowshoe was just a passing fad.

After three lonely years of struggle to keep the breed alive, Vikki Olander was ready to give up, too. Help arrived in the nick of time; breeders Jim Hoffman and Georgia Kuhnell contacted CFF for information about the Snowshoe, and CFF referred them to Olander, the only breeder still registered with them. Hoffman and Kuhnell brought badly needed enthusiasm and energy, and recruited other enthusi-

asts to breed the Snowshoe. Together they obtained CFF championship status in 1983. Olander closed her cattery in 1989, but by then a new group of dedicated breeders had joined the very exclusive Snowshoe club. By 1989, nearly thirty documented Snowshoe breeders were actively breeding and exhibiting their cats. In 1990, ACFA granted championship status, and in 1994 the Snowshoe was accepted as a championship breed by TICA. By 1994, AACE and UFO also accepted the Snowshoe for championship.

Today, all associations accept the Snowshoe except CCA and CFA. Breeders have been working toward CFA acceptance for many years, but never had enough breeders and registered, exhibited cats to meet CFA's stringent requirements. In addition, some North American breeders, rather than join the effort to gain association acceptance, have chosen to work with organizations and breed clubs outside the mainstream cat fancy. Snowshoes are often favored by people who like the Siamese pattern and personality but are not fond of the extremely svelte conformation of today's show Siamese. The Snowshoe has become is very popular with those who like the moderate head and body type of the Thai, also known as the Old-Style Siamese. A number of Snowshoe breeders also breed Old-Style Siamese and Old-Style Balinese.

The Snowshoe is still a rare breed, but has collected a small but dedicated group of breeders. Recently, breeders formed in The International Snowshoe Cat Association (TISCA) to promote the Snowshoe breed, and to encourage breeding toward TICA's Snowshoe standard, which is more forgiving than some of the other standards, which require a more exacting blueprint for the Snowshoe. In addition, the Snowshoe recently has been accepted for championship by the Fédération Internationale Féline (FIFe) in Luxembourg, Western Europe, and has been accepted for preliminary status in The Governing Council of the Cat Fancy (GCCF), in the United Kingdom. More GCCF-registered breeders are needed before the breed can progress to GCCF provisional status. The GCCF-affiliated Snowshoe Cat Society (SCS) was formed in 2005 to promote the breed in the United Kingdom; in January 2012 the SCS hosted the first United Kingdom cat show, in which seventeen Snowshoes were entered.

Snowshoe cats have loving, outgoing personalities.

PERSONALITY

Breeders brave enough to take on the Snowshoe challenge find that the breed pays back the effort in an abundance of love and devotion. Anyone looking for an aloof, standoffish cat need not apply for Snowshoe ownership—fanciers claim that Snowshoes don't realize that they're cats; instead, they consider themselves small, furry people. The Snowshoe has an outgoing personality, although some cats may be somewhat shy with strangers, most get along well with other cats. They are outgoing, loyal, and make ideal companions.

They love to perch beside you on the couch and touch you with a gentle paw until you get the message and give them some of the petting and pampering they're due. Very intelligent, Snowshoes can be taught a number of behaviors, such as fetch, but usually turn the tables and teach their owners a few tricks of their own, like getting out the treat sack on command.

Snowshoes are also known for their fascination with water, particularly if it's running. Turn on the faucet or flush the toilet and your Snowshoe will instantly materialize to stare with undivided fascination at the swirling water. They also enjoy running off with small personal items and dunking them into the sink or their water dish. If you're missing a sock, a pen, or other small item, first look in your Snowshoe's water dish; it's a favorite spot to deposit their finds. Some will even climb into the tub, as long as it's their idea. While not as loud or vocal as the Siamese, Snowshoes are never at a loss for words, but their voices are generally soft and melodic.

CONFORMATION

The ideal Snowshoe is a pointed cat, with the mask, tail, ears, and legs densely colored, clearly defined, and of the same shade. The mask covers the entire face, except in specified white areas, and connects to the ears by tracings. Two patterns are accepted, mitted and bicolor. Mitted Snowshoes have four even white boots extending to the bend of the ankle on the front feet and to just below the hock on the back feet; bicolor also has the white mittens and a white inverted "V" extending from the mouth to the whisker tufts above the eyes. One of the main reasons the Snowshoe hasn't attracted more breeders in the many years of its existence is that blending all the genetic elements together to create a perfect show Snowshoe is exceedingly difficult. Like snowflakes, every Snowshoe pattern is different.

Four traits in particular make it difficult. The first is the inverted "V" facial pattern that should extend from the mouth to the whisker tufts above the eyes. This pattern is governed by the white spotting factor; a gene symbolized as (S). This gene is incompletely dominant, and therefore if a cat inherits two copies of the white spotting factor gene, the cat will have larger areas of white than a cat that inherits only one copy. However, the effect is not consistent, and polygenes can affect the outcome of the white areas.

It's difficult to predict how this gene will express itself, or predict which kittens will inherit two copies of the gene. The second trait that gives breeders pause is the white boots for which the Snowshoe was named. This trait is governed by the white spotting factor as well. This trait is also difficult to control. Ideally, the boots should extend to the bend of the ankle in front, and to just below the hock joint on the back feet. Often, however, the white doesn't extend high enough or extends too high. Sometimes one foot or two will lack white altogether, and sometimes a Snowshoe will not possess any white at all. This can happen when the white is masked with a masking gene or genes; the white is still there, but because of the masking effect isn't expressed in the cat's physical appearance.

Achieving the perfect Siamese pattern and shading can be challenging, too. The most common colors are sealpoint and blue point, although some associations accept chocolate, lilac, red (flame), cream, cinnamon, and fawn. The lighter colors are less commonly used because they don't produce good contrast between the point color and the areas of white.

On top of everything, the Snowshoe standard calls for a body type that combines the heftiness of the American Shorthair with the length of the Siamese. Although the conformation is easier to perfect than the pattern, getting just the right head shape and ear set further complicates the already complicated. With this exacting standard, it's no wonder that creating the perfect Snowshoe is a tricky task.

GENERAL (TICA STANDARD)	The combination of short hair, modified wedge, semi-foreign build, and particolor points sets the Snowshoe apart from other breeds. The Snowshoe is a strikingly marked cat in a variety of unique patterns.
BODY	Moderately long but not extreme or oriental; not cobby or delicate. Proportionally well-balanced overall, well-built, powerful, agile; no extremes. Boning medium; musculature firm and muscular. Well-knit, powerful but not bulky, not delicate. Surprising heft in proportion to size when lifted.
HEAD	Broad modified wedge. Highset cheekbones with gentle contours. Overall shape is nearly as wide as long and resembles an equilateral triangle. Size in proportion to torso and legs. Chin firm. Muzzle proportional to head with a gentle break; neither extremely broad, square, nor pointed. Nose medium width, not too wide or too narrow, with a flat or slight nose bump.
EARS	Medium-broad at the base; continuation of the modified wedge, slightly rounded tips, in proportion to body.
EYES	Shape oval to medium oval or rounded oval with greater length than width. Slanted to the base of ears. Not protruding. Any shade of blue.
LEGS AND PAWS	Legs of good length—of a runner or jumper, medium boning, in proportion to torso. Feet in proportion to legs and torso. Oval tips.
TAIL	Medium at base, slightly and gradually tapering to the end; length in proportion to the torso.
COAT	Length short to medium-short. Texture smooth to the touch. Density permits coat to lie moderately close lying. Seasonal and geographical changes to be considered.
COLOR	Patterns mitted and bicolor; some white required on paws. Patches of color in white areas acceptable. Overall appearance predominates shape and detail of point and white areas. Definite contrast between point colors and white. Mitted: white is limited to paws, back legs, chest, and chin. Cat typically about one-quarter white. Bicolor: white facial pattern required. Various markings of white and pigment may occur. White areas generally occur on legs, thighs, chest, and chin. Cat typically between one-quarter to one-half white.
DISQUALIFY	No white on all four paws. Plush, wooly, or double undercoat. Long hair. Eye color other than blue. Bulky or cobby torso, frail or dainty torso, extreme torso length. Thin, whip-like tail.
ALLOWABLE OUTCROSSES	American Shorthair, Siamese.

YORK CHOCOLATE

HISTORY

In 1983 on a goat dairy farm owned by Janet Chiefari in Grafton, New York, a longhaired black and white barn cat named Blacky had a romantic rendezvous with a longhaired black tom cat named Smokey, which produced a litter of kittens that included one longhaired brown and white female kitten named Brownie. What the names of these cats lacked in originality, the kitten herself made up for with her attractive coloring and charming personality.

The next summer Brownie learned the facts of life from her handsome longhaired father, and produced a litter that included Minky, a longhaired black male kitten. In 1985 Brownie taught her now-grown son Minky about the feline facts of life, and they produced two kittens: Teddy Bear, a longhaired brown male, and Cocoa, a longhaired brown and white female.

By now, the farm had grown quite a crop of kitties with long lustrous coats. The farm's owner, Janet Chiefari, was not only taken by the cats' long, soft, richly colored coats and consistency of conformation, but also by their intelligence and sweet temperaments. As a goat farmer, Chiefari knew a lot about goats and goat breeding but little about cats and cat breeding; at the beginning she only knew that cats were adept at ridding her barns of rodents, and if left unaltered they multiplied quickly.

Chiefari started reading every book on cat genetics she could find. By 1989, Chiefari had converted her porch into a cattery, which she named Upon the Rock. She created a breeding program using Brownie, Minky, Teddy Bear, Cocoa, and all of their chocolate-brown offspring. Chiefari placed the ten kittens she chose not to use in the breeding program with responsible homes.

To Chiefari's surprise the cats bred true, producing solid and bicolor longhaired brown cats with smooth, nonmatting coats; Chiefari noted that their head shape, body type, and fur type were consistent from the beginning. Since long hair is governed by a recessive gene, and both parents had long hair, this meant each had two copies of the long hair gene. Therefore, the only possible outcome was longhaired kittens. In addition, Blacky and Smokey must have each possessed one copy of the dominant black gene (B) and one copy of the recessive brown allele (b) to produce Brownie; to express brown coloring, brown cats must inherit two copies of the b gene, one from each parent. After that point, whenever two brown cats were bred together, all the kittens were either brown or brown with white, depending upon the inheritance of the white spotting factor gene, which causes white mittens and patches of white (see Chapter Four).

By summer of 1989 Chiefari's cattery included twenty-seven longhaired solid brown or brown with white bicolor cats and kittens, and she was so enthusiastic about her new breed that she began to look for ways to promote them. In July 1989 Chiefari's veterinarian introduced her to Nancy Belser, a cat breeder and judge for the Cat Fanciers' Federation (CFF). Belser came out to the cattery and confirmed what Chiefari already believed—this

❋ **Championship status in AACE, CCA, and CFF; Experimental status in TICA**

breed was unlike any other in the cat fancy. Nancy Belser encouraged Chiefari to exhibit her cats in CFF. Chiefari's background didn't prepare her for the daunting task of starting a new cat breed, but she loved her cats and believed in them, so she jumped in with both feet. "Both feet, and total ignorance," she noted in a later interview. That September, Chiefari took Prince, a brown six-month-old male, to a CFF cat show and registered him in the household pet (HHP) kitten category. At that first show, Prince won four rosettes and took a first place trophy.

Excited by the warm response and quick acceptance she received at that first show, Chiefari started the process of bringing the York Chocolate into the cat fancy limelight by applying for new breed status with CFF and ACFA. The breed still didn't have a name, so after some thought Chiefari chose York Chocolate: "York" for her home state of New York and "Chocolate" for the breed's characteristic coloring. With help from CFF and ACFA, she wrote the first breed standard.

In March 1990, the York Chocolate was accepted as an experimental breed in both CFF and ACFA.

Around the same time, the first lavender kitten was born. When a cat inherits two copies of the recessive dilute color gene d, one from each parent, instead of the dense gene D, the color brown becomes a soft gray known

Inquisitive and curious, York Chocolates enjoy following their preferred persons from room to room.

York Chocolates are extremely friendly, even-tempered cats.

as lavender (see Chapter Four). Lavender and lavender bicolor were added to the standard.

It takes more than one breeder to gain acceptance in the associations, so Chiefari began to recruit other breeders, relatives, friends, and neighbors; just about everyone Chiefari knew got a pitch about the joys of owning and breeding York Chocolates. The number of York Chocolate breeders increased, and just two years later, 1992, the York Chocolate was granted championship status in CFF.

Canadian breeders Michèle and Frank Scott became involved with the breed, and together with other members of their newly formed York Chocolate Society were instrumental in gaining recognition with the Canadian Cat Association (CCA). In 1995, CCA granted championship status for the York Chocolate. However, CCA asked for minor wording changes in the standard, including that the York Chocolate Genetics Committee must give written approval for all domestic cats used as outcrosses in York Chocolate breeding programs. The main purpose of this rule was to prevent the sex-linked orange gene from becoming established in the breed, and was easily accepted by breeders.

Anna and Francesco Baldi from Verona, Italy were the first European breeders of the York Chocolate. They purchased several York Chocolates from Michèle and Frank Scott in Canada, and Emile Belisle and Pat Chew in the United States to establish their cattery. Although the Baldis are no longer breeding, they were instrumental in creating the International York Chocolate Federation (IYCF), an Italian-based organization of breeders and fanciers dedicated to preserving and promoting the York Chocolate. In 1997 IYCF members and other breeders and fanciers were successful in gaining the York Chocolate's acceptance with the World Cat Federation (WCF) based in Germany, and other international and European associations including the World Felinological Federation (WFF) in Moscow, Russia, the International Progressive Cat Breeders' Alliance in Upton, Kentucky, and the Feline Federation Europe (FFE) in Nuremberg, Germany. With the promotion and dedication of the associations, breeders, and fanciers, the breed is catching on in Europe, and this has helped breathe new life into the York Chocolate breed.

The York Chocolate is still quite rare. It is still being outcrossed with non-pedigreed cats that have the desired conformation and coat type. The goal is to preserve the York's sweet temperament, farm cat health, and vitality, sleek coat, and elegant body type. Breeders are limited, which prevents wider acceptance in the North American cat associations. However, its pleasing personality and chocolaty good looks have kept the breed going through ups and downs.

PERSONALITY

York Chocolates are an extremely friendly, even-tempered breed. They strike a nice balance between high energy and loving devotion. After a rousing session of fetch or catch-the-catnip-mouse, they want to snuggle into the lap of their preferred person for some purring and petting. Although not generally vocal, York Chocolates are enthusiastic purrers and make a characteristic "purrrt?" questioning sound when announcing their arrival, or alerting you to serious problems, such as empty food bowls.

Most Yorks enjoy being held and cuddled, on their own terms, of course, and are wonderful companions to the one special human person with whom they choose to bond. Although they are usually one-person cats and are intelligently cautious of strangers, they are friendly and affectionate to their extended family, including well-behaved children. Ordinarily, they get along well with other pets, as long as the proper introductions are made.

Intelligent and energetic, York Chocolates enjoy following their favorite humans from room to room to make sure all activities meet with cat approval. Yorks are also inquisitive and curious and insist on helping their preferred persons. Whether you're reading the paper, folding clothes, or working at your desk, Yorks want to keep on top of things—literally. Yorks also have a fascination with water and take every opportunity to leap into the sink or tub, sometimes even when you're trying to wash dishes or take a bath.

Because of this breed's barnyard background, Yorks are hardy and healthy and enjoy practicing their hunting skills whenever the chance presents itself, although breeders recommend York Chocolates as indoor-only cats. Therefore, Yorks are fond of toys that move, or in which you take an active role, and quickly become bored with playthings that just sit there.

CONFORMATION

York Chocolates are graceful cats with flowing lines, smooth glossy coats, and beautiful almond-shaped eyes that come in striking gold, green,

CONDITION (CFF STANDARD)	The ideal York Chocolate is a strikingly rich chocolate brown or lustrous lavender with a coat that has a glossy sheen and flows over body lines accentuating graceful, flexible body movement.
BODY	Size medium to large. Oblong, lengthy type with smooth flowing body lines. Neck is short to medium. Chest is full and rounded. Boning is sturdy; musculature firm. The rump slightly higher than shoulders. Males are larger, heavier boned, and more muscular than females.
HEAD	Medium size, in proportion to body, longer than wide when whiskers and facial hair are smoothed back. Head is modified wedge shape, beginning at nose and spreading to tips of ears. Muzzle is moderately rounded, neither short nor sharply pointed. In profile, skull is slightly rounded; nose has slight dip. Slight whisker break, gently curved, following lines of wedge. Chin is gently contoured; tip in an even plane with tip of upper lip.
EARS	Large, pointed, tufted, tilting forward, broad at base, set well apart continuing wedge line of the head. Ears are tufted inside, little hair is present on outside; leather may show through.
EYES	Medium in size, almond shaped, slanted slightly toward nose, conforming with wedge line of head. Eyes are at least one eye length apart. Color is striking gold, green, or hazel.
LEGS AND PAWS	Legs are medium to long in length and well-muscled. Hind legs are slightly longer than forelegs. Paws are large, round, and slightly tufted.
TAIL	Medium to long; length comparable to length of body; wide at base tapering to rounded end. Tail hair spreading out like a plume desirable in mature adults.
COAT	Medium long in length, smooth and glossy, following body lines. Texture is soft and silky to the roots, with no wooly undercoat. Hair is shorter on face, belly, and lower legs; longer on back, sides, and upper legs. Slight frontal ruff. Ears and toes tufted.
COLOR	Solid chocolate; solid lavender; bicolor chocolate and white; bicolor lavender and white. Chocolate brown color slow in developing. Kittens are significantly lighter than mature cats and may have some barring and tipping. Allowance made up to 12 months of age in judging color.
DISQUALIFY	Incorrect number of toes; tail kinks; eye color outside the standard; crossed eyes.
ALLOWABLE OUTCROSSES	Select domestic longhairs; no pedigreed breeds.

Tail hair should spread out like a plume in mature adults.

or hazel. Their bodies are oblong and lengthy with smooth flowing lines. Males are larger, heavier boned, and more muscular than females, and tip the scales at 14 to 16 pounds, while the females weigh in at ten to twelve pounds (4.5 to 5.4 kilos).

The rich chocolate color is slow to develop. Kittens (up to eight months of age) are lighter in color than mature adults and may have some barring and tipping on their coats.

8

CHAPTER EIGHT

THE AMERICAN DOMESTIC

"The phrase 'domestic cat' is an oxymoron."
—George Will

THE AMERICAN DOMESTIC

THE RANDOM-BRED CAT

Big or small, white or black, long- or shorthaired, the American domestic has always been Best of Breed in American homes and hearts. While the mixed-breed or random-bred domestic cat is not considered a breed as such by the cat associations, it has made a

Random-bred kittens may grow to be quiet or vocal, large or small, active or sedentary.

greater contribution to human culture than the purebreds have. Random-bred cats have been with us for thousands of years, while purebreds as such have been with us only since 1871 (if you judge the recognition of purebred cats to have started at Harrison Weir's cat show held in that year). Even cats whose origins go back hundreds of years, such as the

Siamese and the Angora, developed and bred haphazardly without much initial help from their human companions. In that sense, we owe all of our purebred cats to the random-bred domestic feline. Also, a number of our purebred breeds have been specifically bred with the American domestic or have arisen from the domestic gene pool. The American domestic deserves just as much love, quality care, and respect as the finest pedigreed grand champion.

Random-bred cats have advantages as companions as well, with their (often) healthier mix of genes and diverse personalities, colors, patterns, and conformations. The variation of American domestics is amazing. And as for sheer numbers, random-bred cats make up an estimated 95 percent of the cat population of North America.

Random-bred cats, however, do have disadvantages as well as advantages. Since the ancestry of random-bred kittens is generally not known and as a rule they don't breed true like most pedigreed breeds do, it's more difficult to predict what they will be like as adults. This is particularly true if the fathers are unknown since studies have found toms often pass on their temperaments to their offspring. Random-bred kittens may grow to be quiet or vocal, large or small, active or sedentery. While pedigreed cats do have their own unique personalities, they are more likely to follow the conformation and general disposition of their breed and therefore produce more predictable offspring.

Having a cat aboard ship was considered lucky, probably because of the cat's rodent-catching abilities.

HISTORY OF THE AMERICAN DOMESTIC

We don't know exactly when cats first arrived in America, but we can take a pretty good guess. Cats appear in American paintings and needlework samplers of the 1600s and 1700s, indicating that cats may have arrived with the Pilgrims. Cats probably voyaged on the European fishing boats that worked the coastal waters of America and came to shore when the boats put in to dry their catches.

It is thought that cats may have arrived even earlier; evidence suggests that cats may have sailed over with Columbus in 1492—bones of domesticated cats have been found at sites Columbus visited. Since these sites were abandoned before 1500 C.E., and since North America has no indigenous cat species from which the domestic could arise, likely these are remains of cats that came along for the ride. There's even some discussion about cats arriving with the Vikings in 1001 C.E., but no direct evidence exists to support (or disprove) this.

In any event, the settlers needed cats. In 1749 the importation of cats into America from Europe was approved to help deal with rat populations threatening the crops. The early pioneer cats established themselves as mousers and ratters in the fields and barns of the early settlers. No rosettes were awarded to these working cats; Best of Breed did not go to the feline with the finest conformation, color, or coat texture. The prize—life itself—went to the cat with the keenest brain, quickest paw, and strongest jaws, the cat that could best shape itself to survive the challenges of the New World. Life was tough in those days for human and cat alike. Over time, America's domestic cats multiplied and diversified and, with the expansion of the settlers, spread across the country.

Cats also established themselves in front of the hearths of the settlers, as paintings, samplers, and literary references of the times suggest. It's apparent that cats, even in the early days, were seen as companions as well as mousers. Cats did not entirely escape the paranoia of the religious zealots, particularly during the time of the infamous Salem witch trials, but for the most part cats were looked upon as allies.

When the European cat fancy began in 1871, America was not far behind. In 1895 the first large cat show was held in New York's Madison Square Garden, and the cat fancy was on its way into mainstream America. The American Cat Association, the first American registry, started in 1899

(see Chapter Five). From then on, cats gained popularity as companion animals rather than the perfect mouse traps.

By the late 1800s Americans discovered that cats have appeal in advertising and began using representations of cats to sell cigars, magazines, shoe polish, and other products. Black cats were often depicted because in early American folklore they were considered symbols of good luck. (Black cats as symbols of bad luck came from European folklore.)

Today, the focus has changed. Rather than using cats to induce people to buy products for themselves, the advertising is aimed at cat owners. Cat food and products are multi-billion dollar industries as ever more people come to appreciate cats for their clean and quiet ways.

Cats played an important role in colonial life.

OBTAINING A RANDOM-BRED CAT

Acquiring a domestic cat is certainly easier than getting a purebred, not to mention cheaper. Our nation's shelters are overflowing with beautiful, healthy cats and kittens that would love the chance to share your life. Visiting your local shelter or humane society is an excellent way of getting your dream cat, and most likely you will be saving it from that final walk down death row as well. If you have your heart set on a kitten rather than an adult cat, you might keep in mind that June is Adopt-a-Shelter Cat Month, and with the annual spring crop of kittens a variety of domestics will be available at your local shelter. Use the same criteria outlined in "Choosing a Kitten," Chapter Ten, to choose a domestic kitten or cat. You want a cat that's healthy, curious, and outgoing.

THE HOUSEHOLD PET CLASS

While preference and emphasis are given to pedigreed cats in the cat shows, the cat associations have household pet categories in which random-bred cats can compete. This is called the Household Pet class (HHP). HHPs eight months or older must be altered to be shown (proof of alteration is required), and in the CCA, CFA, and CFF they must not be declawed. TICA and ACFA allow declawed HHPs, and AACE and UFO neither promote nor

Longhaired domestic. Random-bred cats come in every hair length, size, body type, pattern, and color.

penalize declawing. As show rules can be modified, be sure to read the show rules and the bylaws of your chosen association for the guidelines governing HHPs; these are often available over the Internet. Many associations bestow titles on their HHPs. While different from the titles granted pedigreed cats, these titles indicate that the cat has won a particular number of shows, and has accumulated a certain number of

Shelters are overflowing with beautiful healthy cats that would love to share your home.

points, or other awards. In some associations, such as TICA, at the end of the year all of the accumulated points are added up, and additional national and regional titles are awarded to the HHPs with the most points.

The cats are usually judged on overall beauty, personality and demeanor, condition, balance, and proportion rather than on a specific breed standard; CCA and TICA are the only associations that have Standards of Perfection for HHPs. Judging HHPs is much more subjective than judging pedigreed breeds, and therefore flawless condition and appealing personalities are even more important. An outgoing, relaxed, people-oriented cat in prime condition will likely do well in this class.

As in the pedigreed divisions, meticulous grooming and excellent overall care are important if the cat is to earn awards. Of the 100 points possible in the TICA HHP standard (see page 340), beauty and coat are valued separately at up to 20 points for each, while balance and proportion are valued at up to 15 points for both. The eyes, ears, nose, mouth, and claws are valued at up to a total of 15 points for all. Personality is valued separately at up to 30 points. However, condition alone is valued at up to a full 50 points, 50 percent of the total possible points.

The HHP class is also used to show pet-quality purebreds that do not meet the standard closely enough to be shown among members of their own breeds. For example, straight-eared American Curls and Scottish Folds are shown in this category, as well as tailed Manx and "straight Wire" American Wirehairs who lack the wirehair gene and have ordinary coats. Non-pedigreed purebreds and cats that have only one pedigreed parent can be shown in this category. The category is also sometimes used to show cats not yet accepted as breeds. Fanciers do this to gain exposure for these new breeds and to allow the judges to handle and examine the cats.

Not all cat shows have an HHP division. Some cat clubs that sponsor the shows are more receptive to the HHP category than others. Contact the sponsoring association or the cat club holding the show to find out if the HHP category will be included and how it will be handled. The attitude of the cat club can affect your show experience. Cat clubs exist that cater specifically to household pets, such as the Happy Household Pet Cat Club (see Additional Information), an organization formed in 1968 whose primary focus is the HHP exhibitor and his or her cats. They accept all random-bred cats and pet-quality pedigreed cats, but it's not necessary to show a cat or even to own a cat to belong to the club.

Since the judging process is essentially the same for household pets as it is for pedigreed cats, the HHP class is a good place for cat lovers to break into the cat fancy. Many fanciers who have gone on to show prestigious pedigreed cats have started in the HHP class. Others never leave HHPs and continue to show their random-bred cats without ever moving on to pedigreed showing. While you'll never get rich showing in the HHP class (or in any other category, for that matter), the rewards can be just as great as for showing pedigreed cats. You may come home with winning ribbons, happy in the knowledge that others find your beloved kitty to be as beautiful and charming as you do. Even if your cat doesn't bring home a ribbon, you will have had a unique experience, developed a better understanding of the cat fancy, and enjoyed the time you spent with your feline companion and your fellow cat lovers.

All HHPs must be spayed or neutered to be shown.

HOUSEHOLD PET (HH) STANDARD
(TICA's Standard of Perfection for the Household Pet Cat)

Beauty . . . . 20 points
Personality . . . . 30 points
Condition . . . . 50 points
Coat . . . . 20 points
Eyes, Ears, Nose, Mouth, and Claws . . . . 15 points
Balance and Proportion . . . . 15 points

COLOR DIVISIONS All categories, all divisions, all colors.

HOUSEHOLD PET STANDARD
(TICA's Standard of Perfection for the Household Pet Cat)

GENERAL

The Household Pet comes in all colors and combinations of colors imaginable. Coat lengths may be short and sleek, full and fluffy, any combination of those, or somewhere in between. Tails may be long, short, kinky or non-existent. Eye color may be coordinated with coat color in almost any fashion according to the whims of Mother Nature. All coat and eye colors, and coat and tail lengths shall be acceptable.

The most important consideration for the Household Pet is its overall condition and well-being. The ideal Household Pet is scrupulously clean, well-fed, and altered. He seems to smile with good health and contentment.

BEAUTY

These points shall be assigned according to the taste of the individual judge. Many judges notice pleasing markings, colors and patterns. Overall grace and balance are often factors to be considered in the determination of beauty. In the Household Pet, beauty is very definitely in the eye of the beholder.

CONDITION

Coat must be absolutely clean and free of any trace of mats or parasites. The cat must be well groomed. Coat should have a pleasant appearance and feel. Eyes, ears, nose, mouth and claws must be clean. Eyes and nose must be free of any matter. Ears should be judged in a cursory way that doesn't disturb the cat, since a majority of rescue cats have had ear problems in the past, intense examination by the judge, tends to hurt or upset the cat. Claws must be clipped.

BALANCE AND PROPORTION

Cat should display overall proportion; thus, a small head on a large cat or vice versa would be somewhat disproportionate. Cat should also be of proper weight for its size. Overweight and underweight shall both be considered undesirable. Muscle tone should be sound. Some allowance may be made for older alters.

PERSONALITY	The Household Pet should be alert, friendly, and easy to handle. Allowance may be made for some nervousness due to unfamiliarity with shows. If a cat which must be removed from the cage by its handler is then fully amenable to being handled by the judge, no penalty shall be attached.
SEXUAL STATUS	All adult Household Pets (8 months and over) must be altered. Household Pets may not be registered without proof of altering.
DEFINITION OF LONGHAIR OR SHORTHAIR	Where there is a question as to the proper class of any entry, the length of fur on the tail shall be the determining factor. Hair of 1½ inches or more and fluffy shall be considered longhair (length may be slightly less in younger kittens). If there is still some question, notice should be paid to such details as long ear and toe tufts.
APPARENT PUREBRED HOUSEHOLD PETS	Household Pets of apparent purebred background shall be judged on exactly the same basis as all other Household Pets. They shall be neither penalized nor rewarded solely on the basis of their resemblance to one of the recognized breeds.
CONSIDERATIONS	Physical anomalies not allowed by most purebred standards shall be acceptable for the Household Pet. No penalties shall be attached for crossed eyes, kinked tails, extra toes or the like. As many Household Pets are redeemed strays, there shall be no penalties attached to such physical damage as torn or missing ears unless it appears that the problem is an on-going one indicating lack of care.
KITTENS	Kittens shall be judged as a single group, without regard to color class; i.e., longhair kittens judged as one group, shorthair kittens judged as one group. Kittens do not receive divisional awards.
WITHHOLD ALL AWARDS	No awards should be made to a cat that is obviously dirty or in poor condition. Temperament must be unchallenging; any sign of definite challenge shall disqualify. The cat may exhibit fear, seek to flee, or generally complain aloud but may not threaten to harm. A cat that bites shall be disqualified.

CHAPTER NINE

WHICH BREED IS RIGHT FOR YOU?

"I love cats because I enjoy my home; and little by little, they become its visible soul."—Jean Cocteau

CHOOSING A BREED

As a rule, it's easier to choose a cat breed compatible with your personality than it is to select an appropriate dog breed. Dogs, with their approximate 32,000 years of evolution, adaptation, domestication, and selective breeding, have a wider range of traits, sizes, needs, and temperaments from which to choose, while cats have a narrower range of behaviors, sizes, and personality traits. In addition, cats with their clean and self-sufficient ways usually adapt well to our lifestyles.

Still, as with most important decisions, buying a pedigreed cat or kitten requires careful consideration and planning. If your cat lives an average life span, you'll have it for almost as long as human children stay in the parental home, and perhaps longer if your cat is particularly long lived.

Do you love the look of the Persian? Think about all that grooming. Most longhaired breeds, and some double-coated shorthaired breeds, must be groomed regularly to keep the fur from developing mats and snarls, and the Persian is a particularly time-consuming breed in this regard. If you cannot devote daily time to your cat's grooming and don't have the time and energy to provide a thorough once-a-month grooming and bathing session, it's better to select a shorthaired breed that possesses similar traits to the longhaired breed you desire. For example, the Exotic Shorthair has the same body style and personality but has a short coat that's easier to care for. See the

The Persian and the Himalayan require a great deal of grooming.

LONGHAIRED AND SHORTHAIRED BREEDS

Breeds: Shorthaired	Breeds: Longhaired	Breeds: Longhaired & Shorthaired Varieties
Abyssinian	Balinese	American Bobtail
American Shorthair	Birman	American Curl
American Wirehair	Cymric	Exotic
Bengal	Himalayan	Japanese Bobtail
Bombay	Maine Coon	LaPerm
British Shorthair	Norwegian Forest Cat	Manx/Cymric
Burmese	Persian	Oriental
Chartreux	RagaMuffin	Pixiebob
Colorpoint Shorthair	Ragdoll	Scottish Fold
Cornish Rex	Nebelung	Selkirk Rex
Devon Rex	York Chocolate	Burmilla
Egyptian Mau	Siberian	Munchkin
European Burmese	Somali	
Exotic	Turkish Angora	
Havana Brown	Turkish Van	
Korat		
Manx		
Ocicat		
Russian Blue		
Savannah		
Siamese		
Singapura		
Snowshoe		
Sphynx		
Thai		
Tonkinese		

table above, listing the shorthaired breeds, the longhaired breeds, and the breeds that have both long- and short-hair varieties.

Do you love the stylish good looks of the Cornish Rex? This breed will drive you batty if you don't like cats active and always underfoot. Like the svelte, clean lines and pointed color pattern of the Siamese? This breed can be very annoying if you like peace and quiet at the end of the day. In other words, don't fall in love with the cat's appearance if you won't also love the cat's temperament. Cats are aesthetically appealing and may seem like furry works of art, but they must be respected as living beings with minds

Abyssinians, Cornish Rexes, and Bengals (among others) are high-energy cats that can get into mischief. If you like your home just so, a more sedate breed might be a better choice.

of their own if your experience with them is to be positive and rewarding for both of you.

Looking for a breed that will cause you no inconvenience whatsoever? There isn't one. While cats are clean, quiet, and more independent than dogs,

even the most self-sufficient and sedate will occasionally cough up a hairball, break a knickknack, or trip you up when you're hurrying for the phone. Kittens will in short order become cats, and in due time cats become old cats (if they live long enough) with special health needs and personality changes. All ages and breeds of cats need some grooming, and all need regular care— feeding, watering, cleaning litter boxes, grooming, vaccinations, veterinary appointments, quality time for petting and play, and so on. If this kind of responsibility will be difficult for you after the initial enthusiasm wears off, it would be better get a pet that requires less care.

GIVE IT SOME THOUGHT

Write down your reasons for getting a cat, and the traits that appeal to you. Perhaps you want a cat that's constantly in your lap, or maybe you'd prefer a cat that likes being near but doesn't get in your face. Maybe you like the kind of cat that keeps up a running conversation with you, or perhaps you'd prefer the "seen but not heard" type. By thinking about these factors ahead of time, you can spare yourself and your cat future difficulties.

- **Evaluate your budget.** Some breeds are more expensive than others. As a rule, if the breed is rare, it will command a higher price than a common one. Of course, that's not always true. The Persian, which is by far the most common breed, can command extremely high prices depending upon quality, bloodline, color and pattern, and even location. And even the least expensive breed, or a random-bred cat for that matter, costs a surprising amount of money when you consider the cost of food, cat litter, spaying and neutering, yearly health care including vaccinations, medical treatment for unexpected illness or disease, not to mention toys, bowls, bedding, and other necessary supplies.

- **Take a look at your lifestyle.** Do you have young children? Children and cats make ideal companions for one another, but choose a breed that's not high-strung or easily excitable. If your children are very young, you may want to hold off on buying a cat until they are a bit older and better able to understand that animals are not toys and must be treated for kindness and respect.

- **Evaluate your housing situation.** Pedigreed cats should be considered as indoor pets only. Actually, all cats, random-bred and pedigreed, should be kept indoors. Pet theft is a thriving business in North America today. Pedigreed animals are particularly targeted because they can be resold for a profit, but thieves steal random-bred cats and dogs as well. People called "batchers" make their living stealing pets from residential streets and selling them to medical research facilities, representing the animals as strays. Cats are also stolen for bait in the training of guard dogs and hunting hawks. When you consider these dangers, as well as the many other environmental hazards and diseases an outdoor cat faces, it makes sense to keep your cat inside. If provided

with ample entertainment, your cat won't miss the great outdoors.

- **Consider your schedule.** All cats require time, but some breeds require more than others. If your time is limited, choose a breed that is relatively self-reliant and has short, easy-to-care-for fur. Look for a breed with a high "independent" rating and don't choose a breed that has a high "needs attention" rating. If you have almost no spare time—for example, if you have a full-time job and many social obligations—a cat may not be appropriate for your lifestyle at all.

- **Consider the amount of time you are away from home.** Do you travel a great deal? Some breeds form very close bonds with their human companions and are distressed when left

Include your children in your cat's daily care and grooming. It's important to teach the next generation to be responsible pet owners.

behind. They don't understand why they've been abandoned by their beloved and trusted friends. The Oriental, for example, is very needy and doesn't do well if left alone for long periods. If you are gone for weeks or months out of every year, a less dependent breed would be a better choice.

Consider the following factors and their importance to you:

- Activity level
- Playfulness
- Need for attention
- Affection toward its owners
- Vocality
- Docility
- Intelligence
- Independence
- Healthiness and hardiness
- Need for grooming
- Compatibility with children
- Compatibility with other pets

Then go through the cat breed profiles and find all the breeds that come close to meeting your ideals. Use the chart on page 349 to help define what is important to you. Under the heading IDEAL RATING, write in the number of each characteristic that would most closely fit your ideal. For example, if you'd like to have an intelligent, playful, affectionate cat that needs little grooming, you'd put high numbers (probably 8, 9, or 10) under Playfulness, Intelligence, and Affection toward its owners and a low number (probably 2 or 3) under Need for grooming. Then fill in the rest of the categories according to your needs and desires.

Next, go through the breed profiles, and find the breeds that most closely match your ideal. It might be helpful to start with one or two traits that are particularly important to you. For example, if having a playful, affectionate cat is of primary importance, find the six breeds that rate highest in these areas.

Pedigreed cats adapt well to life indoors.

BREEDS BEING CONSIDERED	Choice A:						
	Choice B:						
	Choice C:						
	Choice D:						
	Choice E:						
	Choice F:						
	IDEAL RATING						
CHARACTERISTICS	Activity level						
	Playfulness						
	Need for attention						
	Affection toward its owners						
	Vocality						
	Docility						
	Intelligence						
	Independence						
	Healthiness & hardiness						
	Need for grooming						
	Compatibility with children						
	Compatibility with other pets						

Write the breed names in the spaces provided at the top of the chart. Then, under each breed name, write in the ratings of its characteristics as given in the breed profile in Chapter 6. By comparing ratings across the chart, you will be able to see which breeds come closest to matching your requirements in all of the other areas. You probably won't find a breed that matches your requirements exactly, but you should come up with several breeds that are very close.

When you've narrowed the playing field, talk to breeders of the breeds in which you are interested. It's important

349

to talk to people who have hands-on experience. Prepare a list of questions, and be sure to ask about personality, general care, health, grooming, and any other concerns you may have. Cat shows are good places to meet breeders and see specimens of the breeds themselves (see Chapter Five).

Most responsible breeders will make you aware of traits that may cause potential problems. Conscientious breeders want to provide good homes for their kittens. Making sure the potential owner clearly understands the breed will help prevent problems in the future that might result in the cat being given up or even abandoned. A surprising number of pedigreed cats wind up in shelters, usually because of behavior issues.

Don't be surprised if different breeders give you slightly different information. Cats can vary depending upon the bloodline, environment, and other factors. If a breeder gives you vastly different information from everything you've learned, however, you have to ask yourself why. That's why it's important to do your research ahead of time. If you are familiar with the general qualities and traits of the breed, its history, breed standard, and so on, it will be easier for you to judge the qualifications of the breeder.

COMPATIBLE BREEDS

You may want to get more than one cat. Getting two cats at once ensures that each has a playmate while you're away, and, in general, cats will better enjoy each other's company in adulthood if raised together as kittens.

Because a more active cat may annoy a less active one, however, it's a good idea to match your cat companions' activity levels, if you decide to get two kittens of different breeds. For

Not all breeds are compatible with each other.

example, the Persian would be a good companion for a Himalayan, Exotic, Birman, Ragdoll, or American Shorthair, because these breeds are similar in temperament. The Persian might not do as well with an Abyssinian, Cornish Rex, Ocicat, or Bengal. These breeds tend to overwhelm and dominate the serene and less active Persian. The following lists will give you an idea of which breeds are compatible—with you, and with their feline friends.

BREEDS GROUPED BY ACTIVITY LEVEL

Highly Active	Moderately Active	Sedentary
Abyssinian	American Curl	American Shorthair
American Bobtail	American Wirehair	Birman
Balinese	Bombay	British Shorthair
Bengal	Chartreux	Exotic Shorthair
Burmese	Cymric	Himalayan
Burmilla	Havana Brown	Nebelung
Colorpoint Shorthair	LaPerm	Persian
Cornish Rex	Maine Coon	RagaMuffin
Devon Rex	Manx	Ragdoll
Egyptian Mau	Munchkin	Scottish Fold
European Burmese	Norwegian Forest Cat	Selkirk Rex
Japanese Bobtail	Pixiebob	
Korat	Russian Blue	
Ocicat	Siberian	
Oriental	Snowshoe	
Savannah	York Chocolate	
Siamese		
Singapura		
Somali		
Sphynx		
Thai		
Tonkinese		
Turkish Angora		
Turkish Van		

CHAPTER TEN

CHOOSING A PUREBRED CAT

"*Some men are born to cats, others have cats thrust upon them.*"—Gilbert Millstein

FINDING A BREEDER

You can save yourself veterinary expense and heartache by being an informed consumer and finding a responsible, caring breeder from whom to purchase your purebred. Breeders are usually easy to find, unless the breed is rare or new. Finding a responsible, breeder is a little harder. While most breeders truly care about their cats and are committed to improving and preserving their breeds, other breeders are only interested in your money and care little about the quality, health, care, and socialization of their cats. Visit the websites of the associations (see Additional Information). The cat association websites are excellent places to begin, even before you visit a show. These websites provide a wealth of information: breed histories and standards, club and show information, bylaws and show rules, and lists of breeders. If you haven't decided upon a particular breed, the sites may help you narrow your search.

Check the listings of upcoming cat shows. Attending a cat show is a great way to become familiar with the breeds; you can meet and talk to reputable breeders and see their cats, as well as learn about the breeds and the cat fancy in general. Breeders who produce cats that meet the breed standard usually show cats; being able to say their kittens come from grand champion lines is a status for which breeders strive. You usually will not find breeders at cat shows who produce poor-quality cats. At such shows their cats are subject to scrutiny by experienced judges, exhibitors, and breeders who can quickly spot a bad apple. Politely ask questions of the breeders you'll meet there. Take your time. Don't make an impulsive decision that you may regret later.

You can also contact the cat associations; such organizations may provide lists of their members. These organizations usually have a written code of ethics their breeders agree to uphold. Before you decide to buy from a particular breeder, call or email the cat association, organization, or breed club to which the breeder belongs to check his or her credentials. Try to find a breeder with many years of experience. You want someone who knows the breed well and has experience in genetics and the particulars of breeding. Breeders with a poor understanding of genetics or little experience may make mistakes that affect quality or health of the kittens.

If you call breeders for information, call on weekdays, after 9:00 A.M. and before 9:00 P.M. On weekends breeders are often away at cat shows. If you're calling out of state keep the time zones in mind; 9:00 A.M. in New York is 6:00 A.M. in California. Prepare a list before calling. A responsible, caring breeder will be willing to answer your questions, if you are polite and respectful of his or her time. If the breeder lives far away, ask if photos are available. Breeders often have websites where they've posted photos of their cats and a variety of other information, often including content about their breed and its history, their cattery ethics, their breeding methods, and their principles and requirements regarding the placing of their kittens and cats. If they don't have a website, ask if material can be sent to you.

QUESTIONS YOU SHOULD ASK

First, ask how the kittens are raised. You want a kitten that has been raised underfoot in a loving home environment, rather than in an isolated cattery with little human contact. Also, ask if you can see both of the parents, either in person or in photos, or only the mother. By seeing the parents, you'll have a better idea of the adult appearance and temperament of the offspring.

Ask the breeder to provide names and phone numbers of people with whom he or she has previously placed cats. Ask these owners about their experiences with the breeder and the health and temperament of their cats. Of course, keep in mind that a breeder is likely to provide only the numbers of people who have had positive experiences.

Ask what vaccinations have been given, and whether a veterinarian has examined the kittens. Many breeders give vaccinations themselves. According to some breeders, certain breeds such as the Savannah may be harmed by the standard regimen of vaccinations, and this should be discussed with your breeder and veterinarian. If your breeder doesn't vaccinate, or advises you not to vaccinate, be sure to discuss the reasons why, and ask for information on studies or research to back up their claims before making a decision. In general, however, unless very good reasons exist not to do so, certain vaccinations should have been given. The diseases from which vaccines protect your cat are far more dangerous than vaccines themselves, although adverse

A responsible breeder's cattery will be clean and well-furnished with scratching posts, toys, cat beds, litter boxes, etc. The cats will be clean and seem happy.

reactions and side effects can and do affect a small percentage of cats.

Two types of vaccines exist: core and non-core. Core vaccines are recommended for all cats and kittens that are not vaccinated or that have an unknown vaccination history. The core diseases are highly contagious, have moderate to high mortality rates, and are widely distributed; in general, the vaccines give good protection from the diseases if boosters are given at appropriate intervals. In cats, suggested core vaccines are feline panleukopenia (feline distemper), feline viral rhinotracheitis, feline calicivirus, and rabies.

Non-core vaccines should be considered based on the cat's risk of exposure, underlying disease and medical conditions, lifestyle, geographic location, travel plans, and the disease and vaccine type being considered. For example, if the cat is indoor-only and will have no contact with infected cats, non-core vaccines probably won't be required. Vaccines considered non-core include feline leukemia (FeLV), feline infectious peritonitis (FIP), ringworm, and chlamydia.

According to the American Veterinary Medical Association (AVMA), kittens should be given vaccines for panleukopenia (feline distemper), rhinotracheitis (feline influenza), and calicivirus (feline herpes virus type I), and, at twelve weeks or older, the vaccine for rabies. The AVMA recommends a vaccine for chlamydia in areas and situations where the disease is a concern. The American Association of Feline Practitioners (AAFP) recommends against FeLV vaccinations

for cats that live indoors and have no possibility of exposure. FIP vaccinations should be given only to cats that have the possibility of exposure to the disease via contact with other cats. Vaccines for chlamydia (*Chlamydophila felis*) and ringworm (*dermatophytosis*) should be considered based on possible exposure and disease prevalence.

The first set of shots is generally given between eight and twelve weeks of age, and includes vaccinations for panleukpenia, rhinotracheitis, calicivirus, and rabies. Boosters for these diseases generally are given to adult cats at one to three year intervals. However, according to the AVMA and AAFP, cats at low risk of being exposed to disease need not be given yearly boosters for most diseases. The AAFP feline vaccination guidelines can be downloaded at *www.catvets.com*.

Since feline vaccine-associated sarcomas have come to light, particularly associated with feline leukemia virus and killed rabies virus vaccines, indoor cats may benefit from altering the frequency of these vaccines. Talk with your veterinarian about the right vaccination schedule for you and your cat. In addition, rabies vaccination requirements vary according to state and local laws; some areas require yearly rabies vaccinations even when the cat is kept entirely indoors. Check with your veterinarian or your local animal control.

In addition, ask if the cattery is free of feline infectious peritonitis (FIP), feline leukemia virus (FeLV), and feline immunodeficiency virus (FIV), also known as feline AIDS. No effective test or vaccine is currently available for FIP; however, tests and vaccines are available for FeLV and FIV. FIV and FeLV are deadly diseases and it's vital that testing be done on the parents and all cattery cats with which the kittens may have contact.

Ask for a copy of the vaccination record, particularly if the vaccinations are done by the breeder. When you get your kitten home, it's recommended that these tests be performed if the breeder didn't have them done. Ask if the breeder guarantees the kitten against contagious diseases contracted at the cattery and genetic disorders.

Finally, ask in what cat association(s) the breeder's cats are registered. This is important if you wish to show the cat, because each cat association has different show standards and rules regarding the breeds (see Chapter Eleven).

VISITING THE CATTERY

Whenever possible, choose a breeder whose cattery you can visit. Most breeders operate their catteries out of their homes. When visiting the cattery, let your eyes and nose be your guide: Does the place smell clean, or does it reek of urine and feces? Does the cattery look well cared for? Are the cats comfortable around people, or do they slink around and hide? Are toys, scratching posts, and other items in evidence, or do you get the impression the breeder views cats as a money-making venture?

Regardless of whether you're buying a pet-quality or show-quality kitten, ask the breeder for an explanation of the traits that determine the classifica-

tions. If the kitten is suitable for show, ask why. If he or she is truly familiar with the breed standard and is reputable, he or she should be able to give a rundown of a kitten's qualities and imperfections. Being familiar with the standard ahead of time is essential if you are buying a show-quality cat. You'll have a better understanding of the traits and flaws.

Typically, you'll have to wait before picking up a kitten. Responsible breeders do not release their kittens until they are at least twelve weeks old, and some hold onto their kittens for sixteen weeks or longer. Kittens taken away from their siblings and mothers too

Four-month old Birman kitten.

early can develop behavior problems, such as not learning to pull their punches when playing.

If the breeder has no cats or kittens for sale, he or she may recommend another breeder who does, because breeders often network with one another. Alternatively, you can ask the breeder to put you on a waiting list and inform you when kittens are available. Usually you must put down a deposit to be put on a waiting list, but, if possible, see the kitten personally before finalizing the deal. You can ask that such a clause be put in the contract.

QUESTIONS THE BREEDER MAY ASK

A responsible breeder will ask questions before selling a kitten. Try not to take offense if some of the ques-

tions seem personal. Caring breeders are attached to their cats and want to make sure their special kids go to loving, responsible homes. In fact, a breeder who seems eager to sell to just anybody could be a bad risk. If the breeder isn't concerned about finding good homes for the kittens, how much care do you think he or she put into breeding the kittens in the first place?

Expect the breeder to ask questions about your lifestyle. For example, he or she may ask whether you will be away from home a great deal, whether you have young children, what kind of housing you live in, and if you're willing to keep the cat indoors. If you rent, the breeder will likely want proof that the property owner will allow you to have a cat. The breeder may ask what you will feed the kitten, how you feel about declawing, and your views on spaying and neutering. The breeder may want to know what you would do if you couldn't keep the cat any longer, and about cats you've had in the past, and what happened to them. He or she may ask how much you know about the breed and about cats in general. Some breeders will ask for your veterinarian's name and phone number and will contact him or her.

PEDIGREED QUALITY

Quality can mean two things—it can refer to the health and condition of the cat, or it can refer to the show prospects. Keep in mind that "pedigreed" and "show quality" are not

Keep in mind that "pedigreed" and "show quality" are not the same thing.

the same thing. A cat can be pedigreed and not come close enough to the breed standard for competition.

When buying a kitten, you have two types from which to choose (sometimes three). Pet-quality cats are the most affordable. They are pedigreed and registerable, but in the breeder's expert opinion they will not be suitable for show competition because of cosmetic flaws of coat, conformation, or color. Show-quality cats are, in the breeder's educated opinion, outstanding examples of the breed and should do well in competition, and should have good potential for producing quality offspring. Show-quality cats are the most expensive, and sometimes breeders won't sell show-quality pedigreed cats to novice cat lovers. Some breeders also sell top show pedigreed cats; this means the breeder believes the cats can make finals consistently after they have achieved grand champion status and are good enough to compete for high regional or national awards. If you are interested in a show-quality cat, you may want to wait until the kitten is around six months old to buy it. For some breeds, a kitten's show prospects can't be judged with accuracy until that point.

Keep in mind that a breeder may genuinely believe that a particular kitten will be a show-quality cat and be mistaken. Kittens can change as they mature. On the other hand, you'll occasionally run into breeders who will sell their cats as show quality when they know perfectly well their cats aren't worthy of that classification. That's one of the reasons it's important to know the standard and gain as much information as possible about your chosen breed.

If you want a pedigreed cat as a companion only, pet quality is the way to go. A pet-quality purebred is just as healthy, special, and lovable as the finest grand champion, and will cost considerably less, too. If you decide you'd like to show your cat for the experience, you can always show a pet-quality purebred in the household pet category.

PRICE

Price varies greatly depending on breed, availability, area, color, gender, bloodlines, and show prospects. You can generally expect to pay hundreds of dollars even for pet quality pedigreed cats, depending on the rarity and popularity of the breed. Read the breed standard, talk to breeders, and take in a few cat shows before starting the selection process so you know what you're looking for and what the general price range is. If a breeder is selling his cats for much less or much more than the average, be wary. Ask yourself how the breeder produced the kittens so cheaply and where he or she cut corners. Medical care? Quality food? Cat litter? Breeding is expensive. Discounted pedigreed cats may have had inadequate care or may have health problems, genetic defects, or behavior problems. On the other hand, if he or she is selling for a great deal more than most other breeders, ask why. Be skeptical of claims that seem too good to be true. For example, "The cats are expensive because they're hypoallergenic and allergy sufferers can own

Whatever the breed, look for a kitten that's healthy, happy, and alert.

them," or "The cat is a special rare kind and you'll make tons of money breeding it." Any claims that don't pass the smell test are cause to choose another breeder.

If you find you can't afford the breed of your choice, talk to breeders about the possibility of buying an adult cat that has been retired from the show ring or from the breeding program. These cats, if show quality, would usually have to be spayed or neutered and be shown in the alter classes. Nevertheless, it's still an excellent way of getting a high-quality show cat. Although you'll miss the cute kitten stage, you'll miss the most mischievous and destructive stage of the cat's life as well.

CHOOSING A KITTEN

Whatever the breed, look for a kitten that's healthy, happy, and alert. A healthy kitten is curious and playful. Look for clean, soft, and glossy fur and avoid kittens with rough or dirty coats. Spread the hairs and examine the roots of the fur. If you see tiny black particles clinging to the hairs, this means the cat has fleas.

A healthy kitten's eyes are bright and clear and do not run. The face shouldn't have tear stains. The kitten should not sneeze or wheeze, and its nose shouldn't run. This could be a sign of respiratory problems or illness.

The ears should be clean and free of dark-colored wax, and the kitten shouldn't shake its head or scratch at its ears. That's an indication of infection or ear mites. Its anus should be free of fecal matter or evidence of diarrhea.

Gently pry open the kitten's mouth. A healthy kitten's gums and mouth are pink with no sign of inflammation. The teeth are clean and white.

A 12-week-old kitten should have its first set of immunization shots, and its fecal exam should show it to be free of parasites. Ask to see a copy of its veterinary records. A kitten's temperament is equally important. Cats are individuals; they behave according to their unique natures. In any given litter, you'll notice a range of behavior. However, one reason for buying a pedigreed cat is that it usually breeds true and conforms to the breed's temperament and body type. You can be sure the kitten will exhibit some or most of the breed's expected behaviors. Since you've chosen the breed for its personality as well as its look, observe the kittens as well as the parents for signs that they follow true to form. Tempt the kittens with a cat toy, and see how they react. Look for a kitten that seems curious, friendly, intelligent, and used to handling. Don't choose a kitten that cowers from your hand, runs away in terror, hisses, snarls, or struggles wildly. Avoid a kitten that appears passive or unresponsive as well. This could be a sign of health problems as well as temperament concerns. If all the kittens seem unaccustomed to human contact (provided they are more than six weeks old), find another breeder. Kittens with little early human contact are less likely to form strong, trusting bonds with their human companions.

THE SALES CONTRACT

Most breeders have conditions under which they sell their cats. Read the contract carefully. If you have questions or concerns about the conditions, ask the breeder for clarification. If you think the conditions are unreasonable or too restrictive, buy from another breeder. Once you sign the contract, you are legally and morally obliged to honor it.

Breeder contracts vary. Common issues addressed include declawing, breeding, spaying and neutering, and the cat's care, housing, diet, and medical treatment. Some contracts require you to keep the cat indoors and to give the breeder an opportunity to buy the cat back

Don't choose a kitten that cowers from your hand.

if you can no longer keep it. Many contracts prohibit the cat from being sold or given to pet shops, shelters, or research laboratories.

If the kitten is pet quality and not being sold for breeding purposes, the contract will usually require that you not breed the cat and that it be altered when old enough. It's also a common practice for the breeder to withhold the cat's papers until you provide proof of alteration. More often today, breeders have pet-quality kittens altered before giving them to their new owners. Given the pet overpopulation problem in this country, this is not unreasonable. Responsible cat owners refrain from breeding their pet-quality purebreds.

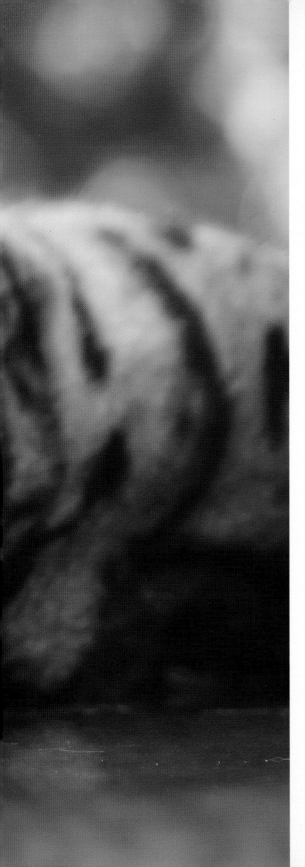

11

SHOWING YOUR CAT

"To err is human, to purr feline."—Robert Byrne

SHOWING YOUR CAT

BEFORE THE FIRST SHOW

Before you take your cat to its first show, you'll want to do some research. First of all, visit several shows so you can get a feel for the process. Visit the cat association websites for detailed show information, or contact them via email or phone (see the associations listed on page 374). In addition, cat magazines, such as *Cat Fancy*, print lists of upcoming shows.

Note which association will be sponsoring the show; your cat must be registered with the sponsoring association in order to be entered in the affiliated cat club's show. Your breeder will have provided a registration form for the association or associations with which he or she is affiliated, and a certificate of pedigree that lists the cat's ancestors for four or five generations. Fill out the registration form, and send it to the association, along with the registration fee. If the breeder has already registered the kitten, he or she will have given you a certificate of registration. In that case, you'll fill out the transfer of ownership section and mail the certificate (with the transfer fee) to the association. You'll receive a new certificate of registration listing your name and address.

Once you have the appropriate paperwork, your cat is eligible for entry into that association's shows. If you wish to show in a different association, you have to register your cat with that

association as well. The fees add up, so decide which association or associations are right for you.

Remember that associations differ, sometimes greatly, in their rules and requirements. What is acceptable in one association may be unacceptable in another. Knowing the rules ahead of time will save you frustration in the future.

WHICH ASSOCIATION?

One consideration is size and location. Some associations sponsor fewer shows than others. Others hold shows in particular areas (see Chapter Five). CFA and TICA are the two largest registries. The CFA sponsors hundreds of shows each year in most parts of the country, including Canada. TICA also sponsors numerous shows each year all across the United States and Canada. You'll be able to attend more shows closer to home if you register with one or both of these registries, unless you live in a region in which another association has an active club.

When you've chosen your association(s), read the show rules and bylaws, usually found posted on their website. This provides a wealth of information on how the association handles the show and outlines the rules you must follow. Since the breed standard can be different from association to association, also download a copy of

Don't encourage kittens to use their claws on tender human skin even in play; soon they'll be strong, full-grown show cats.

the standard for your particular breed. If your association doesn't have the standards or rules posted on their site, you can send for copies; often there's a small fee to cover mailing costs.

PREPARING YOUR CAT

Next, if your cat has never been shown, you'll want to prepare it for the commotion of the show hall. The cat's mental readiness is just as important as its grooming. Accustom it to being handled by strangers. A cat that scratches the judge won't make a good impression. Well before the show, have friends come over and pretend to judge the cat. If you can induce your breeder to give you a hand, so much the better. Have them hold up the cat, stretch it out, run a hand through its fur, and wave a feather in front of its nose. Get the cat used to being benched by keeping it in a small pen—inside the house, of course, and for short periods.

ENTERING THE SHOW

When you feel ready, and when you've found a show in which you'd like to enter your cat, download the entry forms and information about the show from the website, or call or email the entry clerk and ask for the information. Be sure to send the proper entry fee with your forms. The closing date for entering is usually a month or more before the show, so allow time for paperwork processing. Space is usually limited; enter as early as you can. Fill out the entry form correctly and completely and include the proper registration number, all the requested information, and the entry fee. Send all this to the show's entry clerk; usually this can be done via the Internet. Your breeder may be willing to guide you in the preparation of the paperwork for your first show. After all, the breeder's cattery will gain status if your cat becomes a champion. You may want to ask the entry clerk if he or she could bench you next to a friendly, experienced exhibitor so you have someone of whom you can ask questions. Exhibitors are usually happy to give you advice.

If you elect to have someone show your cat for you, name the person on

Your show cat's temperament and mental preparation is just as important as its meticulous grooming.

the form. Some exhibitors also put down a fellow exhibitor's name they know will be present so they can leave the show hall to buy snacks (or whatever) without missing the judging.

GROOMING

Preparations must begin well in advance if the cat is to make a good impression on the judges. In show terms, the "condition" of the cat means not only the health, but also the temperament and grooming.

Therefore, you'll want your cat to look its absolute best. Most exhibitors spend lots of time grooming, bathing, and preening their cats before the show. You'll want to do the same. About a week before the show, thoroughly comb your cat's fur, and then bathe the cat with a mild shampoo. Cat shampoos are available in most pet supply stores, although baby shampoo also works well. Meticulously clean the eyes, ears, and face with cotton balls and swabs. Many exhibitors end by powdering their cats with baby powder or other powder products specifically designed for their breed's coats. This adds body, absorbs oils, and enhances the show look. Be careful, though—colored chalk, tints, color rinses, and other "concealment media" can be cause for disqualification. A day or two before the show, clip your cat's claws. In all of the excitement, your cat may scratch you or the judge. Many associations disqualify cats whose nails aren't clipped.

Most exhibitors bring a grooming kit with them and groom their cats before entering the ring. For specific information on how to groom your breed, consult your breeder for tips. Many excellent grooming books are available as well.

ATTENDING THE SHOW

Before you leave for the show, pack up all the necessary equipment and supplies you'll need to make you and your cat comfortable. This includes grooming equipment, cage decorations, food and water dishes, litter, toys, cushions or cat beds, curtains or blankets, and any other supplies your cat might like. Don't forget to pack a lunch for yourself as well.

When you get to the cat show, you will check in at the door and learn where you and your cat will be benched. At this time you'll have the opportunity to get a show catalog (some associations include these in the entry fee, and others charge extra), which will help guide you through the show. Be sure to pick one up.

Find your assigned benching cage, and be sure to sanitize the benching cage with disinfectant before putting the cat inside. Set up the cage with the litter pan, water, food, toys, and a cushion for the cat to sit on. Put up any curtains or decorations that will make you and your cat feel at home. Cage decorations range from functional to elaborate. When you've settled in, give your cat a final grooming.

The cat's number will be called over the address system when it's time for the judging. Listen carefully; you'll hear something like this: "Cats 15 through 20 to ring two." It's easy to miss your number in all the commotion. Take the cat to the judging ring, and place

This beautiful Exotic and its happy owners pose with their winning trophy at the end of this presitgious cat show.

it in the numbered cage. Sit in the gallery chairs in front of the judging area. Don't try to talk to the judge while he or she is working. If you have questions, try to catch the judge later after the judging is over.

The judge removes each cat from the cage and examines the cat briefly. Judging styles vary; some judges keep a running monologue going; others judge silently. This is the hard part; even if you've done all you can to prepare, your cat may decide it doesn't care what the judge thinks and make a dash for the nearest exit.

After all the cats have been judged, the judge hangs ribbons on the cages of the cats who earned awards, and you

can remove your cat and take it back to its benching cage. When all the cats in a particular category are judged, the "finals" begin, where the cats judged the best examples of hair length, breed, or color (depending upon the show) are presented.

Even if your cat doesn't bring home a ribbon, remember that your cat is still your loyal companion and that the judges' opinions are just that—opinions. Try again. The next judge may have another view. Besides, your cat will always be Best of Breed in your household. In any event, you will have enjoyed a unique experience and developed a better understanding of the cat fancy.

GLOSSARY

AACE The American Association of Cat Enthusiasts.

ACA The American Cat Association.

ACFA The American Cat Fanciers' Association.

Agouti Hairs that are "ticked" with alternating bands of light and dark color, ending with a dark tip.

Allbreed Refers to a judge who is qualified to judge all of the cat breeds.

Alter A cat that has been spayed or neutered.

AOC Any other color.

AOV Any other variety; applies to any registered cat or kitten whose ancestry entitles it to championship or premiership competition but in some way does not conform to the accepted show standard.

Autosomal gene An autosome is a chromosome that is not a sex chromosome; genetic traits found on such autosomes are not sex linked.

Awn A secondary hair type coarser than the down hairs; these hairs form an insulating layer.

B.C.E. Before Common Era, the period coinciding with the Christian era B.C., preferred by some writers in consideration of readers who are not Christians.

Benching The area of the show hall where exhibitors display their cats.

Best in Show An award given to the cat judged to be the finest example for the entire cat show.

Best of Breed An award given to the cat judged to be the finest example of the breed in that show ring; a Best of Breed is chosen for each ring.

Bicolor A cat that is a combination of white and one other color.

Blaze A marking on the center of the forehead between the eyes; often runs down the nose as well.

Bloodline A group of cats related by ancestry or pedigree.

Blue A soft gray coat color.

Break An indentation of the nose at about eye level or between the eyes.

Breeches Longer hair on the back of the upper hind legs.

Brindle A scattering of the "wrong" colored hairs in another color.

Calico A cat with patches of black, red, and white.

Cameo A cat that possesses a red coat with white roots; also called shaded or smoke.

Cat show An event, usually held on the weekend, where cats are shown and judged.

Cat fancy The group of people, associations, clubs, and registries involved in the showing and breeding of cats.

Cattery A building, room, or area where cats are housed, bred, and raised.

CCA Canadian Cat Association.

C.E. Common Era, the period coinciding with the Christian era A.D., preferred by some writers in consideration of readers who are not Christians.

CFA Cat Fanciers' Association.

CFF Cat Fanciers' Federation.

Champion A cat that has achieved Championship status in an association.

Chinchilla A coat type where the white hairs are barely tipped with black.

Chocolate A rich medium-brown coat color.

Cinnamon A reddish brown color.

Closing date The date the entry clerk must have your entry in order for your cat to be eligible for competition in the show.

Cobby A broad, round body type, like that in the Persian and Exotic Shorthair.

Conformation The physical type of the cat, which includes coat length, color, bone structure, facial type, and many other factors.

Crossbreed The allowable mating of two pedigree varieties.

Dam female parent of a kitten or litter.

Declawed A cat that has had its claws surgically removed. Some associations don't allow declawed pedigreed or household pet cats to be shown.

Dilute A soft, pale version of a dominant color.

Dilute calico A cat with patches of blue, cream, and white.

Disqualification Elimination from cat show competition because of a serious fault.

Dome Rounded forehead of a cat.

Domestic A non-pedigreed cat.

Dominant In genetics dominance is a relationship between alleles of a gene, in which one allele masks the expression (phenotype) of another allele at the same locus. The dominant trait will always express itself in the physical appearance of the cat. See recessive.

Double coat A coat possessing a thick layer of awn and down hairs.

Down A secondary hair type that is soft and slightly wavy; much shorter than guard hairs.

Entire A cat that has not been spayed or neutered.

Exhibitor A fancier who has entered a cat into competition.

Fault A flaw in the color, coat, or conformation of a cat, causing a loss of awarded points.

Fawn A warm pink or buff color.

Felis silvestris catus The species of domestic cat.

Feral A domesticated animal that has reverted to the wild or that has been born in the wild.

Final The awarding of the rosettes to the top cats in each category.

Foreign A body type of Oriental appearance, as in the Siamese; also sometimes called Oriental.

Furnishings Refers to the hair inside the ears.

Genes Units of heredity that control growth, development, and function of organisms.

Genetics The study of heredity.

Genotype genetic composition, whether or not expressed in the physical appearance.

Ghost markings Faint tabby markings seen in some solid-colored cats; particularly noticeable in young cats.

Grand Champion A cat that has qualified for this title within a particular association.

Ground color The lighter color in between the darker color in the tabby patterns.

Guard hairs The longest of the three hair types; they form the coat's outer layer.

Harlequin A mostly white cat with patches of color usually on the extremities.

Himalayan pattern Pattern where the color is concentrated at the extremities of the body; also called the Siamese pattern.

Hock The ankle of the cat's hind leg.

Household Pet (HHP) A random-bred cat, or a purebred cat that is not registered or cannot compete with members of its breed. These cats compete in a special category called the Household Pet or HHP category.

Hybrid The offspring of two different breeds or species.

Jowls Cheek folds that are prominent in unneutered male cats.

Judging cage Individual cages in the show ring used to hold the cats awaiting judging.

Judging schedule Schedule that sets the order in which each judge will see the day's categories.

Kink A bend or bump in the tail; usually grounds for disqualification in show cats.

Laces White fur that extends from the paws up the back of the leg.

Lavender A pale pinkish gray shade; also called lilac.

Litter A family of kittens; can also mean matter used as toilet material for cats.

Locket A solid white spot.

Mask A darker area on the face, including the nose, whisker pads, chin, and around eyes.

Master clerk The person who compiles the information from the judging rings into one master catalog.

Mittens White areas restricted to the feet.

Mutation A change or "mistake" in a gene that results in a change in hereditary characteristics between two generations.

Muzzle Nose and jaw.

Necklace Darker markings encircling neck.

Nose leather Area of colored skin on nose, not covered by fur.

Odd eyes or odd eyed Term referring to a cat whose eyes are of two different colors; for example, one blue eye and one copper eye.

Oriental A long, slender body type, as in the Siamese.

Outcrossing The breeding of one registered breed to another, resulting in a registrable hybrid breed; also refers to the breeds allowable in the background of a registered hybrid breed.

Papers Usually refers to a cat's pedigree or certificate of registration.

Particolor Having either two or more colors (depending upon the association), or having any color or pattern with white.

Pattern The color distribution on a cat's coat that forms a particular pattern, such as the striped tabby pattern.

Paw pads The furless padded areas under the feet.

Pedigreed cat A cat whose heritage is documented and registered.

Phenotype The outward appearance of a cat.

Plane Surface.

Points The extremities of a cat's body, head, ears, tail, and feet; also can mean the points awarded in the show ring.

Polydactyl A cat that has extra toes; usually considered a show fault.

Polygenes Groups of genes that are small in effect individually and that act together to produce greater bodily characteristics.

Premier A cat fancy term referring to an altered, registered pedigreed cat.

Pricked Refers to ears held erect.

Queen A breeding female cat; a pregnant or nursing female cat.

Random-bred A cat that is not bred intentionally and whose ancestry is not known.

Recessive In genetics, a recessive gene is an allele for a characteristic that only is detectable in the physical appearance of the cat if the cat has two copies of the same allele. The characteristic is unable to express itself in the cat's physical appearance in the presence of the alternate dominant characteristic. (see *dominant*)

Recognition Official acceptance by one of the cat associations of a new breed or color.

Registration Initial recording of a cat's individual name and owner.

Ring clerk The person who keeps track of the entries being judged and records the judge's decisions.

Ring The area in which judging takes place.

Roman nose A nose that is slightly convex (curving outward).

Ruddy Reddish brick color used to describe Abyssinians and Somalis.

Sable Dark brown.

Scoring The system of keeping track of the number of points and awards each cat has attained; each association has its own system.

Seal Deep brown color; most often refers to Siamese and other pointed pattern cats.

Self-colored Solid colored.

Show cage The cages in the benching area where the entries are kept until it's time for them to be shown.

Sire Father of a kitten or litter; also means to father a kitten or litter.

Smoke A coat color that appears to be a solid color but that possesses white roots.

Standards The standards of perfection that outline the ideal conformation for each breed.

Status The award level for which a particular cat has qualified, such as Grand Champion.

Stop A change in the slope of the profile.

Stud A male cat used for breeding.

Stud book Records maintained by the cat registries that record cats' offspring.

Svelte Slender, firm, and trim.

TICA The International Cat Association.

Tipped A coat type that has colored ends to the hairs.

Tortie or Tortoiseshell Combination of black and orange or their dilutes.

Tubular Cylindrical; having the form of a tube.

Type The cat's conformation.

UFO United Feline Organization.

Undercoat The awn and down hairs.

Undercolor The color on the hair shaft closest to the skin.

Van pattern Bicolor in which the cat is mostly white with colored patches on the head and tail.

Wedge Used to describe a particular head type; a geometric shape with two principal planes meeting in a sharply acute angle.

Whippy Tail type seen in breeds, such as the Sphynx, Oriental, and Siamese.

Whisker break An indentation in the bone structure of the upper jaw; also called a whisker pinch.

Whole A cat that has not been spayed or neutered.

ADDITIONAL INFORMATION

AMERICAN AND CANADIAN CAT ASSOCIATIONS

American Association of Cat
   Enthusiasts (AACE)
P.O. Box 138
Sparrow Bush, NY 12780
Phone and Fax: (973) 334-5834
www.aaceinc.org

American Cat Association (ACA)
ACA Registrar: Ms Irene Gizzi
11482 Vanport Ave
Lake View Terrace, CA 91342-7140
Phone: (818) 896-6165
http://americancatassociation.com

American Cat Fanciers' Association
   (ACFA)
General Offices
P.O. Box 1949
Nixa, MO 65714-1949
Phone: (417) 725-1530
Fax: (417) 725-1533
www.acfacat.com

Canadian Cat Association (CCA)
5045 Orbitor Drive
Building 12, Suite 102
Mississauga, ON L4W 4Y4
Phone: (905) 232-3481

Fax: (289) 232-9481
www.cca-afc.com

The Cat Fanciers' Association, Inc.
   (CFA)
260 East Main Street
Alliance, OH 44601
Central Office Phone: (330) 680-4070
Central Office Fax: (330) 680-4633
www.cfa.org

Cat Fanciers' Federation (CFF)
P.O. Box 661
Gratis, OH 45330
(937) 787-9009
Fax: (937) 787-9009
www.cffinc.org
e-mail: CFFINC@live.com

The International Cat Association
   (TICA)
P.O. Box 2684
Harlingen, Texas 78551
Phone: (956) 428-8046
Fax: (956) 428-8047
www.tica.org

United Feline Organization National
   Office (UFO)
5603 16th Street W
Bradenton, FL 34207

Phone: (941) 753-8637
Fax: (941) 567-6853
www.unitedfelineorganization.net

INTERNATIONAL CAT ASSOCIATIONS

Australian Cat Federation, Inc. (ACF)
P.O. Box 331
Port Adelaide BC,
South Australia 5015
Phone: 08 8449 5880
www.acf.asn.au/
e-mail: acfinc@chariot.net.au

Coordinating Cat Council of Australia,
    Inc. (CCCA)
P.O. Box 347
Macedon, Victoria,
Australia 3440
Phone: 03 5426 1758
cccofa.asn.au/
e-mail: secretary@cccofa.asn.au

Livre Officiel des Origines Félines
    (LOOF)
1 rue du Pré St Gervais
93697 Pantin Cedex
France
Phone: 01 41 71 03 35
www.loof.asso.fr/actus/actus_loof-en.
    php
e-mail: administration@loof.asso.fr

Fédération Internationale Féline (FIFe)
B.P. 526
LU-2015 Luxembourg
Phone: +352 371569
Fax: +352 26374030
fifeweb.org/

Governing Council of the Cat Fancy
    (GCCF)
5 King's Castle Business Park
The Drove
Bridgwater, Somerset TA6 4AG
United Kingdom
Phone: +44 (0)1278 427575
www.gccfcats.org
e-mail: info@gccfcats.org

World Cat Congress (WCC)
Little Dene
Lenham Heath Road
Lenham Heath
Maidstone, Kent ME17 2BS
United Kingdom
www.worldcatcongress.org
e-mail: secretary@worldcatcongress.org

World Cat Federation (WCF)
Geisbergstr. 2
D-45139 Essen, Germany
Phone: +49-(0)-201-555 724
Fax: +49-(0)-201-552 747
www.wcf-online.de/WCF-EN/index.html
e-mail: wcf@wcf-online.de

OTHER ASSOCIATIONS, REGISTRIES, AND CLUBS

Exotic Cat Network
P.O. Box 707
Pearblossom, CA 93553
Phone: (818) 284-6432
www.savannahcat.com
e-mail: info@savannahcat.com

Happy Household Pet Cat Club
(HHPCC)
14508 Chester Avenue
Saratoga, CA 95070
Phone: (408) 872-0591
www.hhpcc.org
e-mail: questions@hhpcc.org

International Progressive Exotic
Breeders' Alliance, Feline Division
(IPEBA)
P.O. Box 311
Upton, KY 42784
Phone: (270) 531-3662
http://www.ipba.8k.com/
FelineDivision.html
e-mail: idba@idba.8k.com

The Old-Style Siamese Club
50 University Road
Colliers Wood
London SW19 2BX
United Kingdom
Phone: (0) 208-540 7132
www.oldstylesiamese.co.uk

Prestwick-Beresford Old-Style
Siamese Breed Preservation Society
(PREOSSIA)
http://home.comcast.net/~bevjoe3/
preossia/index.html
e-mail: bevjoe@pacific.net

Rare and Exotic Feline Registry (REFR)
P. O. Box 543
Walnut Cove, NC 27052
rareandexoticfelinereg.homestead.com
e-mail: rareandexoticfelineregistry@
yahoo.com

MISCELLANEOUS ORGANIZATIONS AND AGENCIES

Alley Cat Allies
7920 Norfolk Avenue, Suite 600
Bethesda, MD 20814-2525
Phone: (240) 482-1980
Fax: (240) 482-1990
www.alleycat.org
e-mail: info@alleycat.org

Alley Cat Rescue
3902 Rhode Island Avenue
Brentwood, MD 20722
Phone: (301) 277-5595
www.saveacat.org
e-mail: acr@saveacat.org

American Veterinary Medical
Association (AVMA)
1931 North Meacham Road, Suite 100
Schaumburg, IL 60173-4360
Phone: (800) 248-2862
Fax: (847) 925-1329
www.avma.org

Best Friends Animal Society
5001 Angel Canyon Road
Kanab, UT 84741-5000
Phone: (435) 644-2001
www.bestfriends.org
e-mail: info@bestfriends.org

Cornell Feline Health Center
College of Veterinary Medicine
Hungerford Hill Road
Cornell University
Ithaca, NY 14853
Phone: (607) 253-3414
Fax: (607) 253-3419
www.vet.cornell.edu/fhc

The Delta Society
875 124th Avenue NE, Suite 101
Bellevue, WA 98005
Phone: (425) 679-5500
Fax: (425) 679-5539
www.deltasociety.org
e-mail: info@petpartners.org

Fanciers Breeder Referral List (FBRL)
P.O. Box 254
North Chili, NY 14514
www.breedlist.com
e-mail: info@breedlist.com

Friends of Animals
National Headquarters
777 Post Road, Suite 205
Darien, CT 06820
Phone: (203) 656-1522
Fax: (203) 656-0267
www.friendsofanimals.org

Hybrid Law
www.hybridlaw.com

Veterinary Genetics Laboratory
University of California, Davis
P.O. Box 1102
Davis, CA 95617-1102
Phone: (530) 752-2211
Fax: (530) 752-3556
www.vgl.ucdavis.edu/services/index.
   php

Winn Feline Foundation
390 Amwell Road, Suite 403
Hillsborough, NJ 08844
Phone: (908) 359-1184
Fax: (908) 359-7619
www.winnfelinehealth.org
e-mail: winn@winnfelinehealth.org

BOOKS FOR ADDITIONAL
READING FROM BARRON'S
EDUCATIONAL SERIES, INC.,
HAUPPAUGE, NEW YORK

Behrend, Katrin
Apartment Cats, 1995

Behrend, K. and Wegler, M.
The Complete Book of Cat Care, 1991

Daly, Carol Himsel, D.V.M.
Caring for Your Sick Cat, 1994

Helgren, J. Anne
Communicating with Your Cat, 1999

Helgren, J. Anne
Himalayan Cats: A Complete Pet Owner's Manual, 2nd Edition, 2006

Collier, Marjorie McCann
Siamese Cats: A Complete Pet Owner's Manual, 1992

Davis, Karen
Somali Cats: A Complete Pet Owner's Manual, 1996

Davis, Karen
Exotic Shorthair Cats: A Complete Pet Owner's Manual, 1997

INDEX

Photo Credits:

Chanan Photography: pages 54, 158, 172, 173, 174, 187, 212, 214, 221, 277, 280, 307, 308, 311, 327, 328, 331, 335, 336.

Shutterstock.com <http://www.shutterstock.com>: Aivolie, page 346; Aksenova Natalya, page 253; Allyson Kitts, page 188; ANCH, page 108; Andrey_Kuzmin, page 334; AnnaIA, page 27; Anton Gvozdikov, pages 46, 49, 52, 57; ArjaKo's, page iv; artcasta, page 344; butterflydream , page 22; Catmando, page 5; Cheryl Kunde, pages 133, 17; chrisbrignell, page 11; cynoclub, page 350; DeborahDesiree, page 250; Degtyaryov Andrey, page 368; dien, pages 19, 167, 168, 201, 301; digitalienspb, page 337; Dmitriy Kalinin, page 232; Dmitry Kosterev, pages 16; 271; Dmitry Melnikov, page 361; Dmitry Zinovyev, page 34; Dorottya Mathe, page 165; Dr.Margorius, page 63; Dragos Iliescu, page 347; EcoPrint, page 9; Ekaterina Cherkashina, pages 21, 36, 92; Eric Isselee, pages viii, 18, 32, 36, 37, 39, 51, 71, 73, 86, 98, 102, 104, 106, 107, 118, 119, 120, 143, 157, 161, 162, 166, 192, 208, 234, 237, 238, 245, 246, 281, 283, 295, 357; Erik Lam, pages 89, 222, 317; Ermolaev Alexander, page 360; Evgeny Karandaev, page 33; Ewa Studio, page 139; fotomanX, page vi; HelleM, page 362; Hintau Aliaksei, page 128; Hintau Aliaksei, page 132; Ivonne Wierink, page 33; Jagodka, pages 123, 138, 147, 241, 242, 243; John Schwegel, page 24; John Wollwerth, page 323; Joop Snijder Photography, page 338; Jorg Hackemann, page 35; Jose Ignacio Soto, page 12; Joyce Vincent, pages 2, 41; Juice Team, page 42; Julia Remezova, pages 152, 199, 35; JuliaSha, page 30; Kirill Vorobyev, pages 32, 62, 91, 95, 261, 263, 266; Krissi Lundgren, pages 38, 58, 144, 255, 256, 258. 270; Lindasj22, pages 313, 315, 358; Linn Currie, pages vii, 72, 81, 101, 125, 127, 149, 155, 178, 179, 180, 183, 185, 193, 203, 204, 210, 225, 226, 260, 264, 267, 276, 285, 286, 294, 300, 304; Lucky Business, page 6; Marcel Jancovic, page 365; Marten_House, page 352; Mdmmikle, page 44; Nailia Schwarz, pages 230, 290; Nikolai Pozdeev, page 265; Paul Atkinson, page 78; Robynrg, page 17; Roxana Bashyrova, pages 34, 64; Sarah Fields, page 366; Sari Oneal, page 339; Scampi, page 216; Seiji, page vi; St. Nick, page 348; Stephen Mcsweeny, page 321; Susan Schmitz, page 196; Tamila Aspen (TAStudio), page 77; tankist276, page ii; Tatiana Makotra, page 218; Tom Pingel, page 332; Utekhina Anna, page 202; Utekhina Anna, page 228; Vasiliy Khimenko, page 249; Vasiliy Koval, pages 51, 130, 273; Veronika Trofer, page 364; Villiers Steyn, page 7; Viorel Sima, page i; vlad_star, page 76; Waldemar Dabrowski, page 142; Ysbrand Cosijn, page 342.

Printed in China
9 8 7 6 5 4 3 2 1

636
.8003
Hel
2013

Helgren, J.
Barron's encyclopedia of cat
breeds.
Aurora P.L. NOV13
33164005103424